'Sharp, rich and superbly ⸻ ⸻gler is sensitive to language, and she wields it brilliantly herself. Bons mot jostle with the kind of truth-skewering opinions that win reputations for restaurant critics... Ultimately, Vogler reveals why we eat what we do today – and it is fascinating.' *Sunday Times*

'Utterly delicious... I can't remember the last time I read a food book so interesting and so lively... The range of Vogler's reading is extraordinary... She has cooked up a banquet, and everything on the table is worth tasting at least once.' *Observer*

'This excellent history is full of fascinating facts about the food we eat... More tellingly, it pricks the pomposity of many of our social conventions surrounding eating.' *Daily Mail*

'A superbly researched romp through food, cooking and class in Britain... Full of history, *Scoff* is never heavy, thanks to Vogler's writing style and wit.' 'Best Food Books of 2020', *Independent*

'Vogler's book is a series of dazzling essays on subjects such as venison pasties, spices, Christmas pudding and Brussels sprouts. The learning and the range of references, from obscure Italian Renaissance texts to Bridget Jones, are astounding.' *Literary Review*

'With commendable appetite and immense attention to detail Pen Vogler skewers the enduring relationship between class and food in Britain. A brilliant romp of a book that gets to the very heart of who we think we are, one delicious dish at a time.' Jay Rayner

'Full of such fascinating, intelligent dissections of familiar foods and culinary practices... Superb.' 'Book of the Week' *The Times*

WITHDRAWN

'Pen Vogler provides a fascinating social history of British food through the centuries and throws in a selection of enticing recipes from the past for good measure.' 'History Books of the Year', *Daily Mail*

'So utterly fascinating that I read it in great greedy gulps, like a novel. Vogler is incredibly good company as she dismantles pretty much every assumption we make about how we, and other people, eat.' India Knight, *Sunday Times*

'Thoroughly enjoyable, lively and humorous.' 'The Best Books About Food', *Country & Town House*

'Essential... Astonishing to think that nobody has done this book before.' Rachel Johnson, *Air Mail*

'Pen Vogler is a smart, waspish guide to our national cuisine and what it tells us about ourselves. In short, sharp essays, she looks at, among other things, the class status of avocados and the revolutionary status of vegetarianism.' *The Herald*

'Excellent... A fun read... with some fabulous facts, tied together in an engaging and thought-provoking way.' *BBC History Magazine*

'Entertaining and thought provoking in equal measure – a thoroughly engaging read.' Sam Bilton

'An absolute gem.' Regula Ysewijn

———— ◆ ————

Also by Pen Vogler

Dinner with Mr Darcy
Dinner with Dickens

Scoff

A History of Food and Class in Britain

Pen Vogler

Atlantic Books
London

This paperback edition first published in Great Britain in 2021
by Atlantic Books.

First published in hardback in Great Britain in 2020 by Atlantic Books,
an imprint of Atlantic Books Ltd.

Copyright © Pen Vogler, 2020

The moral right of Pen Vogler to be identified as the author of this work has
been asserted by her in accordance with the Copyright, Designs and Patents
Act of 1988.

All rights reserved. No part of this publication may be reproduced, stored
in a retrieval system, or transmitted in any form or by any means, electronic,
mechanical, photocopying, recording, or otherwise, without the prior
permission of both the copyright owner and the above publisher of this book.

Every effort has been made to trace or contact all copyright-holders.
The publishers will be pleased to make good any omissions or rectify any
mistakes brought to their attention at the earliest opportunity.

10 9 8 7 6 5 4 3 2 1

A CIP catalogue record for this book is available from the British Library.

Paperback ISBN: 978-1-78649-649-2
E-book ISBN: 978-1-78649-648-5

Design and typesetting by Carrdesignstudio.com
All illustrations copyright © Dan Mogford, 2020

Printed and bound by CPI Group (UK) Ltd, Croydon CR0 4YY

Atlantic Books
An imprint of Atlantic Books Ltd
Ormond House
26–27 Boswell Street
London WC1N 3JZ

www.atlantic-books.co.uk

MIX
Paper from
responsible sources
FSC® C020471
FSC
www.fsc.org

For Simone, Miranda and Justin
With love

CONTENTS

CONTENTS

CONTENTS

Note: All recipes serve four unless indicated otherwise.

Introduction

Scoff¹ *verb* to jeer at

Scoff² *noun* food; a meal

The Chambers Dictionary

TWO YEARS AFTER the fall of the Berlin Wall, I was teaching English in a small town in what was then Czechoslovakia. The people of Liberec, twenty miles north of Prague, were blinking in the light of new problems and freedoms, such as the right to learn English and travel. None of my kind and respectful adult students had had the chance to discover Britain or any part of the West for themselves and they were courteously eager to learn everything my twenty-two-year-old self could impart. When I came to the lesson on British food in my TEFL book, I was a little apprehensive. Would all the book's talk of roast beef and fresh vegetables make it look as if I was crowing, I wondered, to people who'd been stuck behind the fried cheese and pickled cabbage curtain; and where I had seen no fresh fruit and vegetables in the whole of the winter months I had been there? I needn't have worried; they all already knew for a *fact* that British cooking was the laughing stock of Europe. No matter what I said about home cooking, local ingredients, international cuisines, I could see that they were having none of it. In spite of my inability to grasp the Czech language, I could tell a room full of scoffing students when I saw one.

Admittedly our international standing in the kitchen has, historically, never been good; no British chefs have given their names to the great dishes of cream, truffle and potato; the fame of British cakes tends to be domestic, unlike the Continental Torte families of Sacher, Linzer... It has been, right up to our current culinary obsessiveness, a centuries-old belief of our Continental friends – and many Brits themselves – that the British are insufficiently obsessed with food and that a bit more European-style passion would bring us more enjoyable meals, a more functional family life, better health and fewer laughable cafés and restaurants.

However, one classic British obsession has given us a huge stake in the business of food, and that is social class. In a country where even letters have a choice of first or second class in the postal system, how much more ideal is eating, with its innate social function and attendant rituals, as a way of firing up rivalry, envy and social unease and conveying the niceties of where we all sit on the social ladder.

How we serve food and how we eat it, our table manners, what we call our meals and what time we have them, all this has been a source of immense fascination to Brits for longer than our European friends have been taking sideswipes at grey mincemeat and lumpy custard. Everything we believe we choose to eat actually comes to us with years – often centuries – of value-laden social history. Our decisions about what we 'like' and how we regard food are influenced by our parents, their parents, our peers, but also by a long history and a wide network of social and political pressures. Foods have slid up and down the social scale, been invented or disappeared completely.

Most Brits could read a shopping basket as though it were a character sketch: Golden Shred or Oxford Marmalade; Typhoo or Earl Grey; Custard Creams or Florentines; Kingsmill or sourdough; stir-fry veg or Pot Noodle; battery or free-range; doughnuts or Chelsea buns. By the same token, how we behave at home isn't simply a matter of personal choice, but a series of clues about our background and upbringing. Whether you sit round the table as a family; how you push your peas onto your fork; whether you serve food, such as wild garlic or grouse, that hasn't come from a shop; all these are clues to who you are, as much as what socio-linguists would call the 'social markers' in your speech. A friend's mother once said that, when she was growing up, you were middle class if your father had heard of Saul Bellow and your mother knew what an avocado was. It's a distinction people still see; one journalist at the *Metro* newspaper described what A&E departments have started to call 'avocado hand' (an injury sustained by over-enthusiastic cutting of an unexpectedly soft fruit) as 'the most middle class injury ever'.[1] English novelists use food to tell us something about the status of their characters: Austen mocks vulgar Mrs Bennet for obsessing about her well-cooked partridges, whereas David Copperfield's obsession with batter pudding is pitiable not laughable, because he is hungry for food, for family and for security.

We take it for granted that more choice and refinement in food comes with money and social prestige, but it is determined by where – and when – you happen to be eating. Archaeologists believe they have pinpointed the emergence of what the sociologists call a 'differentiated cuisine' to Ancient Egypt, where a 'high and low cuisine' grew up alongside more sophisticated cultivation, food surpluses, wealth and power. There are no shortage of theories about why on earth early humans abandoned the fun and protein of a hunter-gatherer society for the back-breaking life of agriculture, but caste came early into the mix. Either a powerful, male elite organised matters so that they alone had access to the land and animals required for hunting, forcing the weaker members of the community to grow their own food; or – and the difference is subtle but significant – the men who chose or were chosen to hunt for food for the tribe gathered around themselves an aura of power. The association of hunting with aristocracy is ancient but not universal; the Indian caste system focuses on purity of food, with meat being less pure and therefore lower caste, so to move upwards meant becoming more vegetarian. Many parts of Africa still have a single cuisine, in which a whole community will eat porridge, meat soup, served with a relish made from okra, groundnuts, tomatoes or vegetable leaves; wealth simply enables you to have more food, rather than more choice. The anthropologist Jack Goody explains, 'What is different in Africa is the virtual absence of alternative or differentiated recipes, either for feasts or for class.'[2]

In our northern climate, the great differentiation was initially simply meat versus non-meat. The Norman overlords had the choice of several different types of meat (or fish on a fast day), but there was not much complexity at a feast; and perhaps because there was a limit to how much roast boar, venison, pheasant, hare, crane, heron, seal or porpoise one Lord of the Manor could put away, he came to demand more show and sophistication from his kitchens. This, of course, caused its own problems and the Tudor feast was marked by a series of distinctions: the higher up the table you were, the more variety you were permitted. It was a hard boundary to police, though. Ecclesiastical abstinence constantly tipped over into enjoyment and appetite, so in 1541 Archbishop Cranmer decreed the number of dishes which each rank in the clergy could eat from; unsurprisingly, after two or three months, 'by the disusing of certain wilful persons, it came again to the old excess', he reported glumly.[3]

The frequency with which medieval and Tudor kings and parliaments attempted to impose restrictions on diners seated towards the bottom of the table through 'sumptuary' laws is an indication of how toothless such laws were. In pushy, irreverent Britain, neighbours jostled to outshine one another and the fear of falling behind socially – as well as not getting enough pie – held more terrors than falling foul of petty decrees. This attitude contrasts with, say, medieval Germany where social conservatism made sumptuary laws far more effective.[4]

One plotline of this book mirrors Cranmer's story of attempted – and usually failed – control: one self-elected arbitrator or another decides that the members of a different (usually – but not always – less powerful) social class should stop eating what they want and how they want to, and start eating what is seemly, socially appropriate, good for them, or benefits society as a whole. Over the centuries the social clout of the arbiter changed; initially kings and archbishops attempted to use laws to keep those below them in their places. The emerging medical, ecclesiastical and educated class deliberately reversed the flow of traffic using the subtler instruments of education, argument and propaganda: in the dedication to his 1530 handbook of, among other things, table manners for aristocratic children, *De civilitate morum puerilium* (*On Civilized Behaviour in Children*), Erasmus is surprisingly boastful about his status: 'More true nobility is possessed by those who can inscribe on their shields all that they have achieved through the cultivation of the arts and sciences.'⁵ As this educated group grew and stratified further, its members increasingly looked below, rather than above, to assert what was appropriate, economic or healthy for the servants, workers or artisans who made up the next social class down. It was often a message that relied on its recipients being well educated enough to read it. When the eighteenth-century cookery writer Hannah Glasse famously addressed herself to servants and cooks, whom she called 'the lower sort' – in order to 'save the ladies a great deal of trouble' – she assumed that her 'lower sort' was able to read the cookbook she had written and expected 'ladies' to buy. Over the subsequent centuries, laws, taxes, education, arguments, advocacy and propaganda have been mustered as weapons in the food fight, increasingly unsuccessfully, unless the country is on a war footing. Every government skirmish involving taxes on sugar or hot pasties is fought back by complaints about 'lifestyle' taxes. Mostly, the food fight is waged between sections of the population, rather than through policy.

There is a food campaigning brigade in every generation that wants to educate, shame or cajole a different set of people out of their Turkey Twizzlers and burgers, takeaway fried chicken and TV dinners. In the twenty-first century, governments have preferred the social pressure of the village green to shame or nudge individuals into making the 'right' choices, rather than imposing top-down decisions. We saw this in the early days of the coronavirus pandemic of 2020, when there were sudden, unexpected shortages and stockpiling. Social media commentators shouted from the sidelines, attempting to shame individuals into suddenly exercising a collective restraint, a muscle that had turned flabby from lack of use.[6] Calm, of a kind, returned when the supermarkets decided to impose their own rationing, and some of the fears – of hunger and of unfairness – subsided.

We worry about social status on all sorts of levels. Are we popular at school or at work; do we fit in? Or rather, who do we fit in with? Our parents and their generation? Our peers? Or people whom we would like to call our peers, but who may be a bit more fashionable, or elegant, or cooler, or classier than we secretly know we are? One recurring theme in our food choices is how we reject food from previous generations because of our worry about its social status. While our geographical palate is now impressively wide, we have lost the taste for some interesting flavours, and the types of meat, fish, fruit and vegetables available to us have narrowed. We are happy to get a meaty fix from 'roast chicken' or 'smoky bacon' flavoured crisps, although the science increasingly warns us of the consequences of the fats and additives involved, but we shudder at the Roman appetite for parts of the real animals, cockscombs or sows' udders.

If we are going to kill an animal for food, why not eat everything? Lamprey pie was a commonplace on Tudor tables (and it was made for Elizabeth II's coronation feast), but where would we buy lampreys (now a pest in the American Great Lakes), except as frozen bait in fishing shops? Why, in an island with 36 million sheep, is it impossible to buy mutton from your local butcher or supermarket? And why has the Cornish pasty survived – thrived, in fact – whereas the venison pasties and pigeon pies of two centuries ago are hardly known?

The industrialization and supermarketing of food are often blamed for the changes in our diet (such as the disappearance of 'heritage' varieties of fruit and vegetables), and with good reason;

they have manipulated our tastes to fit with their supply chains and profit. But one purveyor of food, the French chef Auguste Escoffier, believed that it was the clamour for novelty from his wealthy diners, with their blasé palates or anxiety to impress their guests, that lay behind incessant change: 'I have ceased counting the nights spent in the attempt to discover new combinations, when, completely broken with the fatigue of a heavy day, my body ought to have been at rest.'[7]

Escoffier shared the fruits of his witching-hour laboratory in his monumental 1903 culinary textbook *Le Guide culinaire*, knowing that his haute cuisine for haute clientele would be seized upon and exploited by lesser chefs for less glamorous diners. (Unlike artists and writers, chefs had no legal copyright in their work, he complained.) This eternal cycle of innovation-copy-innovation is a neat summary of how the wealthiest social layer pay for novelty which then makes its way down the food chain. Soon, *pêche Melba*, created by Escoffier in honour of the Melbourne-born soprano Nellie Melba, found its way onto more modest tables, although without the original ice swan; by the 1950s it had become a dinner-party staple in suburban detached houses, until the occupants went on foreign holidays and discovered Black Forest gâteau. The peach melba, now made with shop-bought ice cream, tinned peaches and raspberry jam, continued its journey downwards to the glass dishes and doilies of the three-bed semis. By the time I encountered it in the 1970s, it was a pudding for children; no grander than a banana split.

The hours that we dine are hounded by the same social pressure. From the age of Samuel Pepys to today, our 'dinner' has been pushed back by about eight hours, as the upper classes ate later and later to distance themselves from the annoying middles; and the middles moved later and later to emulate them. Entire meals – luncheons and afternoon teas – evolved to plug the gap and offer a whole new area of social differentiation: how to serve tea (milk in first? milk in last?); how to distinguish your sandwich from something an agricultural worker eats; whether to eat 'luncheon meat'. Any British antennae will pick up something about your background if you have 'dinner' at midday or in the evening; or invite a guest to 'tea', meaning a mid-afternoon snack or an early-evening meal in its own right. Food is a marker – and sometimes a weapon – in the struggle of different socio-economic groups towards identity. Or, as the nineteenth-century French gastronome Jean-Anthelme Brillat-Savarin taught us, rather more pithily, you are what you eat.[8]

Only now, of course, it is more likely that you are what you don't eat, as any number of allergies and intolerances define those with the leisure and education to identify them. Now that the choice of foods on offer to us is staggering (in 2015 Tesco had a baffling 90,000 products in its range), we have to say something about our level of refinement not in terms of the breadth of our palate, but the opposite. 'Gluten-free' is, for sufferers of coeliac disease, an essential remedy; for others, it is more of a marker of sensitivity for which a food industry is only too ready to cater.

Sooner or later, when chewing over the ideas of food and social class, it is inevitable that we get tangled up in the twin values of good taste and tasting good. The General's caviar might not suit the hungry labourers in KFC. Many tastes – as anyone who watches a child encountering coffee, tea or Brussels sprouts for the first time – are learnt, rather than inherent. Cultural contexts quickly take effect; we enjoy the caffeinated lift of coffee, in spite of its bitterness; we learn to love the Christmassiness of sprouts; and get excited by the sensual slitheriness of a raw oyster. We might now be repulsed by the oily, rooty drink saloop, perplexed by the oysterish taste of salsify, or shudder at the rubberiness of tripe; but these are all tastes and textures our forebears have prized and which we could again, if the social conditions were right. By contrast, some wild plants which our ancestors used, not as calories but as 'physic', are valued by us as free food, because of the way our predominantly urban lives change our thoughts and feelings about the land and about what we have learnt to call foraging.

For younger people, drawing on a range of cultural influences in music, art, film and TV is a sign of social ease and sophistication; few people under fifty would only be interested in 'high' culture. The same is true of our shopping baskets. If there's a packet of sliced white nestling among the kale and almond milk, or PG Tips next to the pesto and quail's eggs, it suggests you are confident enough about your own tastes to pick and choose food from a wide range of different culinary cultures and world cuisines. A few younger people, from reasonably well-off families, have confidently told me that class is no longer 'a thing' as it was for their parents, because their generation happily switch between fast food and instant dinners one day, vegan or veggie another. It creeps into our vocabulary with terms such as 'builder's tea', more likely to be used by their clients than by builders, as a way of suggesting an admirably unpretentious and proletarian solidarity. Sociologists today see this as a part of 'cultural capital', which suggests that part of your middle-class identity is your broad and eclectic tastes.[9]

This idea of 'cultural capital' originated with the French Marxist sociologist Pierre Bourdieu. The son of a postal worker, who became one of France's foremost intellectuals from the 1960s onwards, his own experience fed into his assertion that cultural capital was the product of education, wealth and confident self-belief that your cultural choices are somehow 'higher'. He argued fiercely, though, that ideas of good taste are a product of our upbringing, surroundings and economic necessity. Loving 'binary oppositions', as all good French thinkers of the time did, he portrayed a working-class vs bourgeois preference for quantity over quality, belly over palate, matter over manners, substance over form. 'Good taste' for a working-class family meant conviviality, warmth, sharing. The plate for a portion of gâteau could be card torn from the cake box, rather than the clatter and fuss of cutlery and crockery. Eating out focused on being together at a counter, rather than the bourgeois restaurant where each table is 'a separate, appropriated territory'.[10]

Bourdieu undertook to explain why the poor and undernourished might choose hedonism over sobriety and nutrition. It is, he said, 'the only philosophy conceivable to those who "have no future" and, in any case, little to expect from the future'.[11] It is an issue which has perplexed and outraged food writers and social commentators for centuries. Hogarth, for example, explores the effects and hints at foreign culpability in his companion prints from 1751, *Gin Lane* and *Beer Street*. The 2019 Nobel Prize-winning economists Esther Duflo and Abhijit Banerjee called it 'Poor Economics', as they sought to occupy the precarious shoes of the poor in order to understand the choices that they made. They showed that immediate concerns such as overcoming boredom or seeking an instant lift with a cup of sugary tea might make more sense to someone in poverty than planning cheap and nutritious, but dull, meals. 'The poor often resist the wonderful plans we think up for them because they do not share our faith that those plans work.'[12] It was understood implicitly by sympathetic observers of London street life, in the early and middle nineteenth century, such as Charles Lamb or Henry Mayhew, but it took George Orwell to bang the drum to readers of *The Road to Wigan Pier* (1937):

> When you are unemployed, which is to say when you are underfed, harassed, bored and miserable, you don't *want* to eat dull wholesome food. You want something a little bit 'tasty'. There is always some cheaply pleasant thing to tempt you. Let's have three pennorth of chips! Run out and buy us a twopenny ice-cream! Put the kettle on and we'll all have a nice cup of tea! That is how your mind works... White bread-and-marg. and sugared tea don't nourish you to any extent, but they are *nicer* (at least most people think so) than brown bread-and-dripping and cold water.[13]

We are always looking for ways to lift our harassed, bored and miserable spirits and the food industry today is happy to make it as simple as possible. All the salt, sweet, carbs and fat of Orwell's chips and ice creams are there in a Pot Noodle and a Mars Bar, cheap as chips (or cheaper) and you don't even need to run out for them, or eat at a meal time, or share with anybody else (indeed, they are designed to be eaten solo).

Some of the most interesting writers about food are Charles Dickens, Charles Lamb and George Orwell; not cooks or professional foodies but writers fascinated by the way that food and drink are social magnets (and, sometimes, dividers) and whose passion for good food runs in tandem with their fervent commitment to the *right* for people to eat well.

There is a Hogarth, showing how badly the working classes choose to ingest their calories, and an Orwell, showing *why* they do, for every generation. Wars are one of the few situations which will induce the rich to accept a redistribution of wealth – via taxation – and nutrition – via rationing. Rationing in the Second World War brought up the level of nutrition for the bottom 50 per cent of society which suffered some degree of malnutrition, but brought down cholesterol and fat levels in the rest.[14]

While we commonly believe that those in poverty eat better now than in a hungry and murky past, there are too many exceptions and reversals to this rule for it to be a simple truth. The shocking reality is that the diet of those in poverty has worsened, acutely since 2008, and more generally in the last thirty or so years. There is a lot of irresistibly cheap food available in Britain; the lure of six sugary cakes or a deep pan pizza for a pound is leading to obesity, bad health, pasty skin, blood-sugar swings. Even cheap food hasn't solved the problem of reliance on food banks, food insecurity in children, and the kind of locally determined charity that the post-war Welfare State was supposed to eliminate.

This brings us to a significant underlying question: how much of what you eat is determined by income and how much by social class? The answer might have been relatively simple in the early modern period when income and social status mapped onto each other almost completely – but what is 'social class' now? Figuring out how many 'classes' there are is a rich seam for sociologists to mine. Three? Seven? A gradation? Several socio-economic groupings, some with new names such as the precariat and the technocracy? Not everybody agrees with what defines a class: income, wealth, education, social connections, cultural consumption?

We have learnt to be more cautious about making contemporaneous class pronouncements, aware that there isn't a direct overlap between the 'socio' and 'economic' bit of any attempt at a grouping, although we all seem to agree it has got something to do with avocado consumption. Generalizations are both friend and foe. The trilogy that we are all familiar with – working, middle and upper classes – is a legacy of the Victorian taxonomy: the first lived by manual labour, the second by non-manual labour, and the upper classes lived on their capital. It seems relatively easy to categorize a Victorian family as 'middle class' if the father gained his income from employment, rather than capital, the mother did not work, and they employed servants. Is using these terms for the pre-Victorian era anachronistic? And are they outdated in the twenty-first century? Even at the time, the boundaries were fuzzy and increasingly hotly contested, and words such as 'respectable' were deployed to patrol the grey areas between the status of, say, a tailor or a hosier or a glovemaker, and a property-owning shopkeeper. However, for all the problems of its sledgehammer subtlety, this familiar taxonomy is a useful background against which to spot changes in our food and our attitude to it. We all understand that for every trend there are outliers: the impoverished aristocrat eating roast grouse in an unheated country house dining room, or the millionaire entrepreneur who still loves the childhood taste of chip butties or Angel Delight. For the sake of your boredom threshold, and mine, I haven't attempted to caveat every example with an itemization of possible counterexamples from different ages, genders, geographical locations or ethnicities.

The infrastructure for the stories that follow is not contemporary or academic definitions of social class, but what people thought at the time, and the vocabulary they used to say it. How people wrote about privation is a good example. Commentators who used income as a measure were not only being analytical, as we'd expect, but their focus on words relating to income – 'poor' and 'poverty' – also indicated sympathy. Criticisms of the same income groups – usually for being overattached to bread or tea and not eating sufficient vegetables – tended to use a language of social status rather than income: 'the lower orders', 'the common people', 'the lower classes', 'the plebeian order'.

The voices of the poorest, the uneducated and the disenfranchised are, inevitably, missing from the earliest parts of these histories. We know very little about what the poor 'at the gate' thought about being given the lord's gravy-soaked trenchers, or whether they complained about the windiness of cabbage (although actions speak pretty loudly; the Peasants' Revolt of 1381 gives us a fair idea of what they thought about their lot on the whole). As social hierarchies became more complex over the centuries, and growing literacy led to a greater number of people leaving their own accounts, the input of voices becomes more complex and more contradictory. There are tensions between, say, a skilled factory worker whose focus is on providing his family with bread, meat and cheese, and the social campaigner who wonders, on his behalf, why he – or more likely his wife – doesn't provide the family with more porridge or soup. It's a tension we wrestle with today, between, for example, the mother (usually) of a family, who sees her role as keeping the family together and happy with food they like to eat, and the educators who want them to eat five portions of fruit and veg a day for the sake of their health.

Food isn't always just a way into social history; a symbol of socio-cultural values; a stand-in for love. When you are very hungry, it might just be food. Sometimes, as I've been writing this book, I've been hungry. I've skipped into the kitchen to see what these things I'm writing about *taste* like or, more accurately, whether I can figure out a recipe to make them taste good. Not always, is the answer. In the seven sections that follow, I have included recipes that do taste good and do adapt to the modern kitchen. Some are well loved and some semi-forgotten; all have made the cut both because I think they show something particularly notable about how our ideas of taste have been formed or have changed. The original recipes are gems of social history; they lure us into store cupboards and kitchens from the past, and invite us to look at the preoccupations of the recipe writers, cooks and eaters and consider where each sat in the social structure of the day. Every recipe has been modernized and tested by some willing cooks and I hope they offer a taste of past lives in a way that is also a pleasure for modern palates.

As my Czech students taught me, it is easy and entertaining to scoff at other people's food choices. Their image of British food was based on national identity. The Brits are surprisingly open-minded about other national cuisines, but within our own we have found it easy and entertaining to scoff at each other based on ideas of social class. One of the underlying questions in the stories that follow is whether our reputation for bad food was *because* of our class obsession. Have we put more time and energy into judging each other on what we eat and the way we eat it, or worrying about what people think of us, than trying to make sure everybody has the same access to good food? As the wonderful George Mikes said, from his perspective as a Hungarian-born adopted 'Brit': 'On the Continent people have good food; in England they have good table manners.'[15] One thorny question that kept scratching at me was this. If we have spent the last few centuries looking in the wrong direction, what has been happening in the space where we should have been looking? Have we allowed some really *bad food* – health-destroying, adulterated or overprocessed – into our lives, and into the lives of the poorest and most vulnerable, simply because we were concerned with the wrong issues?

This book looks at all the different ways that you can scoff *at* other people's *scoff* and, through stories of knives, gin, pasties, supper, avocados (and over fifty other ways of thinking about food), teases out why that matters.

PART ONE

◆

Tea and Confusion

Breakfast: or the Two Nations

To eat well in England you should have breakfast three times a day.

Somerset Maugham

ONE OF MY life pleasures is my food group. Five of us each bring a dish to make a dinner, usually constructed around a loose theme, such as a country or a season or, once and most memorably, something from our childhoods. Claire, a natural storyteller and gifted cook, charmed us with her stories from her childhood holidays in Donegal when her father would go scallop-dredging with a friend all night and they would welcome him and his catch home by knocking up yesterday's mash into farls. Even more charming was her re-creation of that breakfast of tangy, sweet scallops, set off by salty bacon and a moist pillow of potato bread.

This was breakfast? Without a slice of toast in sight. We ate it as a supper dish with a glass of something white and cold. But this is the point of the perfect breakfast food – at least for the leisured classes. It was never entirely necessary when dinner was a morning meal, held at 10, 11 or noon. But when dinner was held in the evening and supper became obsolete, rather than lose altogether the unbuttoned occasion and its cosy, savoury and uncomplicated dishes, it was simply shunted overnight into the next morning (see Supper, page 74). We think that the 'Full English Breakfast' is an enlightened coming together of the English country house and the labourers' cottage kitchen. In fact, the English country house learnt to do breakfast from the Celtic fringe.

The medieval Catholic Church forbad its monastic population from breaking their fast before the first Mass of the day. An early meal was something that marked out the corporeal worker from those dedicated to a higher, spiritual life; particularly since he or she had been working since sun-up or before and needed sustenance. The earliest courtly records are largely silent about breakfast, apart from an allocation or two of ale and bread for those who rose early. A physician in 1572 still thought that 10 or 11 a.m. was the best hour for meat 'if you can fast so long'.[1] Later dinners and the Reformation kicking of Catholic habits made an early meal of porridge, ale and bread more acceptable.

By the time the Essex poet Nicholas Breton sang the praises of summer in 1626 in *Fantasticks*, his hymn to the months of the year and hours of the day, dinner was around midday and breakfast had become universal. There was a pot of porridge over the fire at 3 in the morning when the milk maids were astir; the household servants would be digging in at 4 a.m.; the farm labourer put in a few hours of sweat and got breakfast at 8, along with the scholar, the shopkeeper, the ostler and, if he was lucky, the beggar.[2]

Some households decided to make breakfast a meat meal (or fish for fast days; herrings again). The housekeeping rules for the Tudor court at Eltham Palace, known as the Household Ordinances, offer us an engaging picture of the maids of Henry VIII's sixth wife, Katherine Parr, tucking into a daily breakfast of a hefty chine of beef.[3] The Restoration breakfast has no specific menu; Pepys breakfasts on the roast beef, chine of pork or collar of brawn from last night's supper eaten cold, or 'hashed' (refried)[4] or, once and slightly randomly, just radishes.[5] Tea and coffee, however, began to draw family and friends together over a table to form a sociable first meal. For Jane Austen's mother, staying with her cousins in Stoneleigh Abbey in Warwickshire, 'Chocolate, Coffee and Tea, Plumb Cake, Pound Cake, Hot Rolls, Cold Rolls, Bread and Butter, and dry toast for me' is a country house breakfast worth writing home about.[6] This was the era of the enriched dough and the toasting fork; Bath buns flavoured with caraway seeds, the brioche-like 'French bread' (see Bread, page 330) and Sally Lunns (still made in Bath to a secret recipe); and muffins, pulled apart around the middle and toasted. These displays of white flour, butter and the baker's art were the breakfast of the leisured classes around the fashionable centres of Bath, London and Brighton. The one time that well-shod Georgians indulged in a meaty but unsophisticated breakfast was while travelling. Jane Austen gives William Price an early breakfast of pork and mustard and Henry Crawford hard-boiled eggs before the two leave Mansfield Park for London.[7]

Labourers in the North usually got a better breakfast than their southern counterparts from the end of the eighteenth century. Food was cheaper than in the South and wages were higher as landowners increasingly competed with industry for labour. After an hour or two of work, men might have breakfast at about 8 a.m.: bacon with their bread, and perhaps coffee would be on offer as well as tea. Families in Cumbria, Lancashire and Yorkshire had higher standards of nutrition with milk and more oats. A labourer at Clitheroe in Lancashire calls his annual Easter Sunday breakfast of ham and eggs 'a good Cumberland breakfast', adding that he couldn't afford it 'above once in a year'.[8]

Wives and children, in the poorest households, lost out. In the West Country they often resorted to 'Tea Kettle Broth' – bread softened in hot milk and water.[9] Porridge wasn't a popular breakfast dish with more southerly workers. Charitable ladies, whose role was to visit the poor and sick with nutritious soup, imbibed the nineteenth-century self-help ethic and became reforming ladies who visited the needy to urge them to make nutritious porridge for their families for breakfast. Porridge and cheap saucepans are not happy partners, and many families rejected porridge burnt on the bottom of thin tin pans in favour of cheap bread.[10] The impetus is alive and well; the Tory peer Baroness Jenkin said in 2014 that one of the sources of food poverty was that the poor didn't know how to cook nutritious meals: 'I had a large bowl of porridge today. It cost 4p. A large bowl of sugary cereal will cost 25p.'[11]

Poor old porridge, its propensity to burn gives it a bad image in literature. Charlotte Brontë uses it as a weapon in the hands of the inhuman Mr Brocklehurst in *Jane Eyre* (1847), desperate to subdue the spirits of the wretched girls of Lowood school. 'Oh, madam,' he says to the head teacher, 'when you put bread and cheese, instead of burnt porridge, into these children's mouths, you may indeed feed their vile bodies, but you little think how you starve their immortal souls!'[12]

The North/South divide extended up the social hierarchy. Educated visitors to Scotland, Wales and the North wrote rapturously about the excellence of the breakfasts they found there. Even the hard-to-impress Dr Johnson acknowledged that the Scots 'must be confessed to excel us' in the matter. He found not only butter, but honey, conserves and marmalade (then uncommon on the English breakfast table) and concluded, 'If an epicure could remove by a wish in quest of sensual gratification, wherever he had supped, he would breakfast in Scotland.'[13] Tobias Smollett's Highland Breakfast in *The Expedition of Humphrey Clinker* (1771) was a marvel of local produce: honey, butter and cream, boiled eggs, goat's cheese, venison pasty. There was 'a bushel of oatmeal, made into thin cakes and bannocks' and, showing a particular delicacy of hospitality to the southern visitors, 'a small wheaten loaf in the middle, for the strangers' (see Bread, page 330). There is no hot tea and coffee, the job of warming the body being allocated, instead, to whisky, brandy and ale.[14]

The travel writer George Borrow is propelled around *Wild Wales* (1862) by a series of hearty breakfasts of Glamorgan sausages or mutton chops, but it is one at the White Lion Inn in Bala (still there) which inspires him to a pitch of excitement: 'What a breakfast! Pot of hare; ditto of trout; pot of prepared shrimps; dish of plain shrimps; tin of sardines, beautiful beef-steak; eggs, muffin; large loaf, and butter, not forgetting capital tea. There's a breakfast for you!'[15] It's a challenge to read it without rushing into the kitchen and rustling up eggs and toasted muffins as a stand-in for its savoury glories.

In Disraeli's *Sybil* (1845) the principal commercial inn of the novel's northern mill town serves up 'pies of spiced meat and trout fresh from the stream, hams that Westphalia never equalled, pyramids of bread of every form and flavour adapted to the surrounding fruits, some conserved with curious art, and some just gathered from the bed or from the tree'.[16] (Germany with its prized Black Forest and Westphalia hams was a thorn in the side of the competitive and proud ham-producers of Britain – particularly Yorkshire.) Inevitably, one of the inn's metropolitan guests complains (inaccurately) that you can never get coffee in *these places*.

In a book alternatively titled *The Two Nations* – that is the Rich and the Poor – this isn't just a breakfast; it is a *political* breakfast. Disraeli has already, humorously, established breakfast as a political meal, via two formidable aristocratic ladies who fret that men who socialize over breakfast are restless revolutionaries, dangerously chasing after ideas and gossip from the moment they are awake.[17] The other end of the breakfast spectrum is represented by a pale child, queuing for a loaf of bread, who says timidly that he is too dizzy to go home because he hasn't yet broken his fast.[18] The starving child is a standard Victorian literary device both realistic (they were not hard to find) and iconic: an unthreatening object of pity. Hungry men, by contrast, are sinister, like Dickens' Magwitch, or dangerous, like Sybil's machine breakers and rioters, or the hungry men and women behind the French Revolution.

Trollope, on the other hand, doesn't find these northern breakfasts appropriate for his southern county of Barsetshire (Salisbury, Winchester and Exeter), and certainly not for ecclesiastical life. In the rectory of Plumstead Episcopi he lays out disagreeably heavy forks and a formidably heavy basket, to contain a dozen types of bread, as well as dishes, napkins, boxes and containers for eggs, bacon, fish and kidneys, for the reader's disapproval, to show that clerical respectability has drowned out the proper considerations of religion and made the archdeacon forget that man does not live by bread alone.[19] His censure is close to that of the medieval Catholic Church; breakfast ballast was for manual workers, not men of the cloth. The sin is compounded by the choice of expensive but hefty and dull furnishings in the breakfast room.

It was a relatively new idea that you should devote an entire room to breakfast. The breakfast parlour began to appear in fashionable houses in the mid-eighteenth century. The first were elegant rooms with a round breakfast table; the breads, cakes, tea and coffee were laid out on a side table for two or three hours in the morning for family and guests to choose whatever hour and dish suited them best. They might rise at 8, spend a couple of hours writing letters, shopping or walking and eat at a modish 10 a.m. or so. In *Pride and Prejudice* (1813), Elizabeth Bennet has time to breakfast with her family at Longbourn, receive a letter brought by a servant and written that morning by her sister at Netherfield, walk three miles there and still find the fashionable Netherfield party assembled in the breakfast parlour. When ladies started to lunch (see The Sandwich, page 28) and then to share afternoon tea, breakfast became thought of as a masculine meal. Trollope's mid-century breakfast parlour with 'thick, dark, costly carpets', 'heavy curtains' and 'embossed but sombre papers'[20] was the pattern of the room which, with the meal, hit heights of impressiveness in the late Victorian country house and the sporting weekend.

The Victorian host and hostess had to deploy the finest, most fashionable French food for dinner (see The Dinner Party, page 66) but breakfast enabled them to make a different display of *British* food from their own lands. The great breakfasts from the North and from Scotland and Wales which had so delighted travellers were gathered in (and somewhat tamed) so that the sideboard of the perfect country house breakfast served as a map of power, ownership and Englishness. The home farm delivered whole hams or a Christmas round of spiced beef, as well as fried bacon and oozing sausages, eggs (poached, boiled, fried) from their hens, all kept hot in silver dishes with little spirit lamps underneath. In the shooting season there should be game pie or cold pheasant from the park or moorland. Kedgeree and devilled kidneys nodded to the Empire; smoked fish to our seas; marmalade to our history (vegetables were absent). Queen Victoria's love of Balmoral brought porridge in from the cold, so long as it was served with thick cream from a known herd of cows. Another Scottish inspiration, later in the century, when raising agents made this minor miracle possible, was to have scones alongside a range of breads and rolls. In the summer, your guests might finish by snipping onto their plate a small bunch of grapes, fetched from your hothouse, or spearing with a fork some strawberries or raspberries from your kitchen garden. In the winter, their existence would be testified to by home-made jams.

Mrs Beeton hadn't quite caught on to the social cachet of breakfast in her 1861 cookbook, and it wasn't until some better-connected breakfasters published cookbooks specifically devoted to the meal that her editors updated her *Book of Household Management*, to introduce new dishes to cooks and mistresses of the house who had never been offered kedgeree or devilled kidneys in a country house, or who didn't have a still room to make their own 'preserves'. This word was adopted from the idea of 'preserved fruit' to dignify shop-bought jam, earning itself a place in the non-U (see Doilies, Napkins and Tablecloths, page 243) lexicon of John Betjeman's poem 'How to Get On in Society' (see Etiquette, page 38). Marmalade came to replace jam for breakfast, but as it refused to change its name, its *consistency* provided the class-watchers with some subtle, but crucial, distinctions. Jilly Cooper's late twentieth-century upper classes have proper 'Oxford' marmalade on their toast as does her nouveau riche and aspirational character Samantha; 'she doesn't like it very much but she read somewhere that Golden Shred was common.'[21] Newspaper articles in the early twenty-first century noted that *runny* marmalade was the thing to serve as it showed that it had been home-made by somebody in the leisured classes and wasn't shop-bought.

Bacon and eggs made an early debut together thanks to seventeenth-century courtier and recipe magpie Sir Kenelm

Digby. As an afterthought to his recipe for Roman Pan Cotto he wrote, 'Two Poched Eggs with a few fine dry-fryed collops of pure Bacon, are not bad for break-fast.'[22] Who could disagree? But until eggs and chickens began to be farmed on entirely different systems in the US in the early twentieth century (see Roast Chicken, page 102), eggs were as much of a luxury as chicken and, in accounts of workers' breakfasts right up to the twentieth century, are conspicuous by their absence. Eggs would be found amid the chafing-dishes of the Victorian breakfast. (Gabriel Tschumi, Master Chef to Victoria, Edward VII and George VI, noted disapprovingly that, even after a five-course breakfast, servants would slip a couple of hard-boiled eggs into their pockets lest they felt a bit peckish before the morning tea break, which he took as proof of his belief that plentiful meals made servants greedy.) Bacon and eggs were, in some ways, first an attempt to imitate the country house idyll in a more modest urban home; and then, when the well-staffed idyll fell victim to the servant shortage after the First World War, an attempt to keep it alive. Food writers up to the Second World War complained about the monotony of bacon and eggs, while having to acknowledge that they had reached a status bordering on the iconic.[23]

The roster of staff responsible for the Great British Breakfast gave way to one housekeeper or maid and then, after the Second World War, shrank to one member of the family who kept the breakfast going with bacon and eggs, catering almost solely for the men of the house, according to Mass Observation* (and my own memory of my mother making B&E for my father and brother before work), while we girls had toast (or, thanks to the occasional diet, grapefruit). At weekends or holidays, bacon and eggs were supplemented with the limited number of characters familiar from every greasy spoon, bed and breakfast, and hotel today. Bacon, eggs and sausage. Toast and marmalade. Tea and coffee. Fried potatoes were a nod to the habit of country families to find a

---

* Mass Observation was a social research organization that collected details of everyday life from 1937 to the 1950s.

use for yesterday's cold potatoes. Fried tomato and mushroom edged their way onto the plate in the 1960s and 1970s, as did baked beans, if you were particularly unlucky, or black and white pudding for a nod to the meal's northern and demotic roots. Fried bread and hash browns were added for an extra-manly touch. The traditional restaurant Simpson's in the Strand called this plateful of death-threats to the heart 'The Ten Deadly Sins'. My friend James calls it 'The Godzilla'.

Just as the cooked breakfast ideal was taking off in middle-class households, it faced an existential threat from the Seventh Day Adventist W.K. Kellogg, who started his cereal business in America in 1906, convinced that a healthy diet would direct children away from deviancy (particularly masturbation that so horrified Victorians). His commercial genius was to recognize that, around the turn of the century, children of nearly all backgrounds, except the very poorest, were becoming a lucrative market. Most children have a sweet tooth and Kellogg's sweetened cereals, with free gifts inside the boxes and – later – cartoon characters on the packaging, appealed to them more than bacon, eggs, marmalade, or plain bread or porridge.

From the first, the marketers of breakfast cereals trod a careful line through the images that marked traditional class boundaries, with some surprising success. The patrician food writer for *The Times* Agnes Jekyll thought that our breakfasts were 'conserva-tive and often monotonous' and that we would do well to eat '*American Cereals*' (her italics) such as 'post-toasties, honey-grains, puffed wheat, or puffed rice'.[24] My mother who, like many of her generation, would not allow anything as vulgar as a milk bottle on the breakfast table, didn't demur at packets of cereal. A miniature box of Frosties or Coco Pops, chosen from a variety pack, was a huge holiday treat for us as children (the bigger box of plain cornflakes always going to an uncomplaining father). Like the quote (variously attributed to Aristotle and St Ignatius Loyola) that if you 'give me a child before he is seven he is mine for life', Kellogg's aimed to establish its brand loyalty early.

When Cereal Killer, a café in Tower Hamlets in London's East End, started selling cereals to hipsters, the owners discovered that they were falling foul of a century of cereal marketing which had turned cereals into the right of every child, irrespective of income. When a Channel 4 News interviewer asked the owners whether local kids could afford £3.20 for a bowl of cereal, it attracted the attention of Class War, a protest group whose name speaks for itself. Dispirited by the lack of press interest in their protests at luxury developments and estate agent chains, they arranged a 'Fuck Parade'; activists with pigs' heads and flaming torches daubed paint and threw cereal at the café, and were delighted when the coverage went global.

Old and social media coverage had a field day with the ironies: a group of highly educated protesters were terrifying people at a small business owned by two brothers from a deprived area of Belfast, who'd been too poor to go to university. Much was made of the problems of gentrification side by side with poverty; most of the area's schools run breakfast clubs to make sure all children have something to eat at the beginning of the school day. But, as one of the brothers put it in an open letter to Channel 4, they could simply have charged £3 for a coffee like many other local businesses and no reporter would have been at all interested. The same could be said for the Full English, available nearby for a fiver, or for £50 if you are choosy about your surroundings. But *breakfast cereal* belongs to children and is obviously another matter. As the Cereal Killer owners discovered to their cost, we are still Victorian enough to tolerate the image of the hungry adult, while we are roused by the image of the hungry child.

The Full English (or Scottish, Irish or Welsh) is probably the only British meal to have found favour with non-Brits and we, as a nation, are proud and protective of it. In spite of claims that the fry-up was slowly dying, killed off by its own high cholesterol, it is now more popular than ever before. The Full Victorian has been revived in high-end restaurants and hotels, serving omelettes and eggs benedict, smoked kippers, salmon and kedgeree to business people and tourists. And, if you are lucky, in a reversal of the end of the eighteenth century, some of the dishes get shunted over into supper.

To do breakfast justice at the weekend, we elide it with the midday meal to create the invented meal brunch, which is where some of the dishes of the Victorian and Edwardian country house breakfast, such as this kedgeree, really come into their own.

KEDGEREE

Colonel Arthur Robert Kenney-Herbert, who served with the Madras Cavalry in India and wrote recipes and household books under the name 'Wyvern', was a big fan of breakfast. His books, including *Culinary Jottings for Madras* (1878), saved many a memsahib from a fit of the vapours, as he explained how to get 'native' servants to cook fashionable French food and Anglo-Indian dishes such as 'kitchri'. Back home in England, he also published *Fifty Breakfasts*. This kedgeree recipe is inspired by both works.

MODERN RECIPE: THE COLONEL'S KEDGEREE

About 400g fish – smoked haddock fillets, or any white or oily
fish – or even seafood – you like (or need to use up)
2 bay leaves
240g basmati rice
Pinch of salt
4 eggs
50g butter
I large onion, diced
I dessertspoon turmeric
I dessertspoon curry powder or
mixed cumin and coriander – optional
Handful of chopped fresh herbs – flat leaf or curly parsley,
marjoram, coriander, chives – or mustard and cress

1. Cook the smoked fish by gently poaching it for 8–10 minutes in water with the bay leaves. Remove the fish with a slotted spoon, put it aside and cover it with foil to keep warm. Keep the cooking liquor.

2. Cook the rice with the retained cooking liquor and a pinch of salt (use less of it or add water, according to the instructions on your packet).
3. Get the eggs on to boil – about 10 minutes for hard-boiled; 6–7 minutes for soft-boiled – and then put them into cold water. Peel them under running water.
4. Melt the butter in a thick-bottomed pan and fry the onion until it is fully soft. Add the turmeric and other spices, if you are using, and fry for a couple of minutes.
5. Add the rice and stir well.
6. Pile into a dish, flake over the warm fish.
7. If hard-boiled, you can chop the eggs, in the Victorian way, or leave them as halves, in the twenty-first-century way.
8. Sprinkle with the herbs.

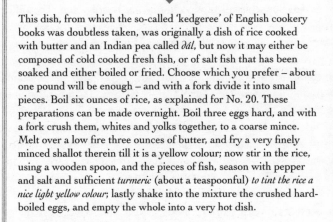

ORIGINAL RECIPE: KHITCHRI* (INDIAN)
From *Fifty Breakfasts* by Arthur Robert Kenney-Herbert (1894)

◆

This dish, from which the so-called 'kedgeree' of English cookery books was doubtless taken, was originally a dish of rice cooked with butter and an Indian pea called *dál*, but now it may either be composed of cold cooked fresh fish, or of salt fish that has been soaked and either boiled or fried. Choose which you prefer – about one pound will be enough – and with a fork divide it into small pieces. Boil six ounces of rice, as explained for No. 20. These preparations can be made overnight. Boil three eggs hard, and with a fork crush them, whites and yolks together, to a coarse mince. Melt over a low fire three ounces of butter, and fry a very finely minced shallot therein till it is a yellow colour; now stir in the rice, using a wooden spoon, and the pieces of fish, season with pepper and salt and sufficient *turmeric* (about a teaspoonful) *to tint the rice a nice light yellow colour*; lastly shake into the mixture the crushed hard-boiled eggs, and empty the whole into a very hot dish.

*Elsewhere in a recipe for 'kegeree (kitchri) of the English type' the Colonel omits the turmeric but includes garden herbs such as cress, parsley or marjoram.[25]

The Sandwich: the working lunch

Lunch is for wimps.

The fictional banker Gordon Gecko, *Wall Street* (1987)

IN MY FIRST office job in London in the early 1990s I was introduced to two types of working lunch. Our Chief Executive was over-fond of the boozy lunch to celebrate something – anything – the signing of a document would do. We learnt not to expect anything too rational from afternoon meetings. Words must have been said, as it was suddenly all sandwiches in the board room. The office assistant was despatched to Marks & Spencer or the sandwich shop, for cheese and pickle, prawn cocktail, egg mayonnaise and, a particular favourite – in the 1990s at least – sweet and spicy, unctuous coronation chicken. For one client lunch the accounts assistant, a tiny young woman from a Kenyan Asian background, was sent in his place, returning with a brown bag full of McDonald's hamburgers. The CE made a 'what shall we do?' face, but we cut them into quarters, and put them on plates for everybody to help themselves in the usual way. We all ate a token quarter each, perhaps to demonstrate something about our social unpretentiousness, but not so much that we were tainted by fast food.

At that time, the working lunch had become so much associated with the sandwich in Britain, that white, middle-class office queens like my CE forgot that for some people it could be something else: soup and a sausage roll, a cheese and onion pasty, or a plate full of meat, vegetables and starch, or a US-immigrant hybrid such as a slice of pizza, a taco or some tortured Nando's chicken. We thought we all at least agreed on what a 'sandwich' was, but it turned out that this was subject to interpretation, too. Though I suspect that Alpa, considering it beneath her dignity to run the errand, was also teaching us a lesson.

It is not coincidental that lunch and sandwiches, and, indeed, desks, were born at around the same time and have had analogous and, in some ways, aspirational careers. Both took off when the working day was beginning to be stretched out and atomized, moving towards the shape that we know it today.

There was no need for 'lunch' when dinner was around midday (the seventeenth century) or mid-afternoon (the eighteenth). Luncheon was born when dinner was pushed back to early evening – six o'clock or later. Fashionable society kept on dining later and later to put some clear blue hours between themselves and the mercantile and professional class below. The latter was eager to adopt the social cachet from the same hours; but men – it was usually men – with business to do also found it convenient to have a later dinner in order to fit more work into the day.

From the first, there was never a general agreement about what to call this meal. Although never formally defined, one would be hard-pressed to claim one's midday bread and cheese was 'luncheon'. Jane Austen – one of the earliest users of the word – had 'noonshine' in her letters to friends but also 'the nicest cold luncheon in the world' which greets the two eldest Miss Bennets at the end of a journey in *Pride and Prejudice*.[1] Her contemporary, Mrs Rundell, seems rather unsure of what to call it – or even what it might comprise: 'Where noonings or suppers are served... care should be taken to have such things in readiness as are proper for either'.[2] Maria Rundell's *A New System of Domestic Cookery* was initially compiled as a guide for her married daughters, and first published as a recipe book in 1806. She opens her book by stressing the importance of the lady of the house acquitting herself according to her rank in life: an unthreatening notion within the settled Georgian class structure of her time. Her book was welcomed by a middle-class readership, grateful for her common-sense advice on running a household without a huge income, and became a bestseller.

The words 'noonshine' and 'nooning' were related to 'nuntion' or 'nuncheon', found throughout rural areas up until the nineteenth century as terms for a piece of bread or a snack and some ale for manual workers. (See Picnics for further terms, page 383.)

In the preceding centuries, 'luncheon' (possibly from the French; possibly from the German) pops up in the record every now and then, suggesting a *lump* of bread or cheese or bacon. 'Lunch' (possibly from the Spanish) appears to imply a *slice* up until the time that Samuel Johnson sandwiched them together in his 1755 dictionary. He deduced that 'lunch' and 'luncheon' were both derived from 'clutch' or 'clunch', and meant 'as much food as one's hand can hold'. This very thing – the sandwich – then crops up a decade later: the cold beef between bread ordered by the Earl of Sandwich so he could stay at the gaming table. It's a great story slightly ruined by his biographer's more likely account that, as a Cabinet Minister, he was a workaholic who didn't want to leave his desk.[3]

The need for sandwiches and the need for lunch suggest a new kind of relationship between food and work. Food had always been brought to workers on the land by their wives or children, but the hunk of bread and cheese or bacon, eaten with your back to a hay rick, seems never to have gone by the name of 'sandwich'.[4] The new 'sandwich' had different requirements, such as the kind of knife needed to thinly slice a loaf of well-behaved bread, which would only be found in a well-equipped kitchen. It was (initially at least) made from beef, the meat of privilege; it would be made by a servant and brought into the library or study on a plate and a tray, perhaps with a glass of madeira or cup of tea, for somebody to eat in one hand while the other was occupied with the life of the intellect.

Sandwiches and desks hit it off immediately and established a long-standing partnership that survives to this day. The wealthy distinguished their work from that of the table-using craftsman by commissioning a more elaborate piece of furniture. The first were bureaus with a sloping lid which could be opened to provide a writing surface and knee-hole writing tables in the late 1600s. The 1750s and 1760s fledged not only lunch and sandwiches but new styles of pedestal and partner desks (the latter with drawers on both sides) still used today.[5] The country house library hosted the first elaborate mahogany versions; they escaped and slimmed down to be used in the homes and workplaces of writers, intellectuals and industrialists, and were increasingly stripped back until they occupied counting houses, offices and schools. The solo desk allowed one to eat in splendid isolation, separated from your *companions* – etymologically those who shared bread together (through Latin *com*, 'together with', and *panis*, 'bread'). The demand for literate and numerate workers in the growing mercantile and industrial economy brought in copyists, secretaries, bookkeepers and clerks who joined the lexicographers and politicians in this new desk-dining. Sam Weller's sociable and traditionalist publican father in Dickens' *Pickwick Papers* (1836) was baffled by this new and incongenial way of eating among the ranks of inky clerks in a counting house of a stockbroking company:

'Wot are they all a-eatin' ham sangwidges for?' inquired his father.
''Cos it's in their dooty, I suppose,' replied Sam, 'it's a part o' the system; they're alvays a-doin' it here, all day long!'[6]

Before desks and ham 'sangwidges' emerged to complicate the social landscape, most working people had a communal main meal – dinner – in the middle of the day. For the farm servants of the settled rural, pre-Enclosure world, it was usually made by the women of the farmer's household and eaten together around the kitchen table, or in the fields if they were busy or too far from home. Whole families who worked piecemeal, weaving on handlooms, sewing gloves, making lace, often in attic workshops, had to be up at first light to make the most of daylight, so might also have their midday dinner together (see Breakfast, page 16).

Those who had found work in mills in Manchester and Leeds, in the factories of the Midlands and the mines of Wales, Newcastle and the North Midlands had even more regimented working hours and less companionship. A child in the 1830s worked at a mill from 6 a.m. to 7.30 p.m., with forty minutes for dinner.[7]

It's a linguistic tick that survives to this day. Southerners and posh northerners have 'lunch' and 'dinner'. Northerners, particularly the working classes, still have 'dinner' between noon and 2 p.m. and 'tea' in the early evening (and perhaps 'supper' at night). For a long time, children had 'dinner'. In a Victorian house of a few servants the mistress might eat her 'luncheon' while the children and servants had their dinner. It might be the same food or, more likely, a rehashing of the employers' beef or mutton from the previous night or weekend, served with milk to drink and a solid pudding.[8]

It is a cause of endless hilarity and confusion for non-native English speakers and of some embarrassment for natives. The writer Helen Fielding, who grew up in Yorkshire, describes being invited to her tutor's house for dinner during her first week at Oxford. 'We duly turned up in the middle of the day to be greeted by kindly astonishment and a gracious attempt to explain how things worked in the sophisticated world we were about to enter.'[9] Nancy Mitford claimed that the word 'meal' was non-U (see Doilies, Napkins and Tablecloths, page 243) because it showed that you didn't know whether to say 'lunch' or 'dinner'. Jilly Cooper's joke is that the social climber, who starts with the familiar before quickly remembering the genteel, 'talks about "d'lunch", which sounds faintly West Indian'.[10]

If there was a North/South divide between dinner and lunch, there was a divide of a different sort between lunch and luncheon. The Almack's Club guide of 1829 was quite sure that 'lunch' was the preferred term[11] and many male characters, from Dickens to Bertie Wooster, always had a no-nonsense 'lunch'. But 'luncheon' belonged to women's lives for a century or so; it was what genteel ladies entertained one another with until the First World War catapulted them from housework or leisure into the workplace and war-work confiscated their domestic staff. The Second World War unmoored the 'eon' from 'luncheon' as women found themselves taking sandwiches to their new workplaces or joining the men for a hot, two-course lunch (or dinner). A graph showing the occurrences of the word 'luncheon' reveals a rapid rise from the 1890s, a peak in the 1920s and 1930s and a rapid decline in the war years.[12]

It took a long time for the governing classes to realize that, if adults needed sustenance in the middle of a long day, then children did too, and the money being spent on state education was being wasted if children were too hungry to learn. The Poor Law Act of 1834, making it illegal to provide charity outside of the workhouse, was ignored by a few charities, particularly in Manchester, Bradford and other industrial towns, which provided meals for schoolchildren on an ad hoc basis. It wasn't until the 1906 Provision of Meals (Education) Act that the supply of school meals by local councils was *permitted*; and it took much longer for them to be made widely available to children in need. Their northern origins and association with children made them widely known as 'school dinners'.

At my northern comprehensive many years ago, 'dinner ladies' served us hot, two-course 'school dinners' and we all knew where we were until some children brought in their own plastic boxes or bags of food, which were never referred to as dinner, but as 'sandwiches' or a 'packed lunch'. When I discussed it with a group of southern teenagers recently, they mostly had 'school lunches' but said that the people who served them were 'dinner ladies'; though at some smart London schools, even the 'dinner ladies' had become 'lunch ladies'.

Luncheon gave a new form to the day. Georgians paid their 'morning' calls up until the afternoon dinner time, when refreshment might be a slice of cake or a biscuit, some fruit and a glass of wine. Later dinners enabled ladies to entertain one another at lunch and then also pay calls in the afternoon before dinner, allowing men to continue to work; or play golf, or cricket or any of the new leisure pursuits such as the afternoon extra-marital affair. Early in the nineteenth century, suitable light lunch dishes recommended by William Kitchiner included a modest leg of goose on apple sauce, salt beef, or breast of veal with capers or the modish 'wow wow sauce' (piquant with vinegar, mustard and pickles). He admits that sandwiches are elegant and convenient for lunch (or supper) in his bestselling recipe book *Apicius Redivivus; or, The Cook's Oracle* (1817). Later in the century and up until the 1930s, ladies signified their status by serving food with French names (see French Food, page 166). *Consommé*, oyster *au gratin*, *poulet à l'estragon* (chicken stewed with wine and tarragon) for a favoured guest; or, for a more economical approach, *poulet de capilotade* (yesterday's chicken reheated with a sauce and served in a gratin dish).

Luncheon became the height of elegance for some, although in some fashionable circles it was chic to despise it. The society wit and botanist John Bellenden Ker classified it as a 'thing known only among the easy, listless classes of life'.[13] 'Lunch is for wimps', as a later fictional work zealot had it. Lord Macaulay, historian and politician, agreed with him, preferring a leisurely breakfast and a dinner to reward him for a full day's work. He resisted the blandishments of lunch until later in life, around 1853, when ill health compelled him to the 'detested necessity of breaking the labours of the day by luncheon'.[14]

Dinner, whether taken midday or in the evening, was the reward for work. 'Nobody hears of the labourer's or operative's *luncheon*,' Ker said scornfully and for a long time working men abjured the term.[15] In the 1960s, a house-decorator in Bristol, a bricklayer in Leeds and a motor mechanic in Sussex all talked to Mass Observation about eating their midday 'dinner' as they opened up what their wives described as a 'packed lunch'.[16] Marketers loved the words, though, hoping to imply some distinction to lowly tinned ham by rebranding it 'luncheon meat'. The 'ploughman's lunch' was a historically inauthentic invention of the Milk Marketing Board, anxious to persuade people to eat economy-boosting quantities of English cheese (which its own strictures had degraded into mass-produced and poor quality stuff; see Cheddar and Stilton, page 367).

While women of metropolitan households big enough for a servant or two were working out how to feed the children, the servants, their visitors and themselves in the middle of the day, their husbands were increasingly unlikely to join them. The French nobleman François de La Rochefoucauld noticed that the men and women of the English aristocracy in the 1780s led separate lives during the day (see Where We Sit, page 204), and this segregation began to be felt down the social hierarchy as city populations swelled and managers and clerks moved their families to the new Victorian and Edwardian suburbs – too far away for them to eat at home in the middle of the day.

For men, lunch places to suit different styles and pockets opened across the cities, taming the chaotic street economy of Henry Mayhew's London with its itinerant sellers of pea soup and hot eels, sheep's trotters, hot potatoes or ham sandwiches; people began to eat at predictable hours, between noon and 2 p.m., and with a predictable level of expenditure. At the cheaper end, a luncheon bar might sell a range of sandwiches, pies and pastries or specialize in sausages or pies, but not seats. Men stood to eat, keeping on coats and hats. An oyster shop might offer a wooden bench to perch on as you got to grips with its pickled salmon and soused mackerel or hard-boiled eggs;[17] there was a public house if you needed to quench an alcoholic thirst. A cookshop or 'ordinary' was something like today's workman's caff – soup 2^d, stew 3^d, beef and two veg 6^d [18] – and men in the City and the East End might go for the local delicacy at an eel pie and mash shop (a very few of which survive to this day). These lunches were usually the only meal most modestly remunerated workers would have away from home. For men wanting to talk shop over lunch there were cosy chop houses, spruced up with mirrors or stained glass which supplied benches, tables and meaty repasts (chops a speciality).

Taverns, known for their huge institutional dinners, also started serving turtle soup, steaks and roasts to businessmen in dining rooms of solid wooden furniture and dark velvet curtains. The sandwich was too useful a thing ever to be thought of as a shabby replacement for a 'proper' lunch; indeed, Mrs Leyel advised her readers, 'If a busy City millionaire can lunch on sandwiches and desires nothing better, why shouldn't sandwich lunches be popular in Mayfair?' A sandwich of creamed haddock, foie gras and lettuce, or a caviar toasted sandwich served with champagne, was far more likely to bolster the hostess's reputation than an indifferent, cooked, pretentious French menu.[19]

There is nothing like a war to make a government pay attention to the nutritional needs of the population. Just as the Second Boer War had alerted the nation to the poor physical state of working-class recruits, the First and Second World Wars helped bend the government's attention to provisioning the workforce; feeding them while they were at work was the answer. In the 1940s, state-run 'British Restaurants', canteens by a less socialist name, sold cheap, hot lunches (see Rationing, page 325). Factories employing more than 250 people working on munitions or other government work were required to provide a worker's canteen and by 1943 there were 10,462 factory canteens in the country.[20]

The subsidized canteen has long been a feature of industry. Today, in glassy, gleaming media and tech offices in London, staff perks include *free* lunches – and breakfast, dinners and snacks throughout the day; staff talk enthusiastically about the fresh fruit, hot breakfast, steaks, lobster, salads, vegan dishes, the occasional gourmet sandwich. However, there is no such thing as a free lunch – an old idea popularized by the free-market economist Milton Friedman – somebody, somewhere, pays for it with money. But these (mostly) young, very smart workers are also paying for it themselves in terms of their time and, possibly, health; local sandwich bars and cafés are paying for it in terms of lost income. At the other end of the scale, workers in the gig economy have to figure out how to provision themselves, without a structure to help them. An Uber driver recently told me he had a migraine because, now he was divorced and nobody cooked his meals, all he'd had for lunch – indeed, all he'd eaten all day – was a Wispa bar.

Most workers are in the middle; and for most of us that means a sandwich. Ever since Marks & Spencer shook the working world with its first pre-made salmon and tomato sandwiches in 1980, we have taken the boxed-up sandwich to our hearts – and to our desks. Sociologists call it 'desk-dining';[21] some joke about eating 'al desko'. The industry estimates that 4 billion sandwiches are sold a year and many more are made at home for packed lunches.

I can't say I'm a fan of the chilled wedge in its cardboard and film packaging hurried down in the middle of the working day. No matter how sunny its crayfish and rocket or hummus and red pepper filling, it always gets suffocated by the dead hand of chilled sliced bread.

But I appreciate that what I might be grumbling about is the context, because a lunchtime sandwich made with home-made bread, filled with good cheese and tangy chutney, eaten on a hillside? That is a picnic. Or a Reuben sandwich of salt beef, Gruyère and sauerkraut on warm rye bread; or a soft white roll filled with truffled Portabello mushroom, brought to you in a hotel with a glass of champagne? That is a feast.

Though, of course, it's a feast with a conundrum at its heart. How should I eat it? Deploying a knife and fork would have been ridiculous. Using the fingers, quite permissible in my own kitchen, felt a bit greasy for a fashionable London hotel. And that's why we have invented etiquette.

Etiquette: the civilizing or discriminating process?

We do not recommend the practice of eating cheese with a knife
and fork in one hand, and a spoon and wineglass in the other;
there is a kind of awkwardness in the action which no amount of
practice can entirely dispel.

Lewis Carroll, *Hints for Etiquette; or, Dining Out Made Easy* (Juvenilia)

WHILE CHATTING ABOUT this book to a journalist from a
working-class background, he told me that the subject
that caused the most friction between him and his middle-
class wife was the definition of etiquette. He had grown up to
experience it as a matrix of arbitrary signs designed to intimidate
and to form a barrier between him and an inaccessible group of
people. She saw it as an easy-to-pick-up system of good manners,
the purpose of which was to put people at ease and make sure
nobody behaved in a way that would annoy fellow diners.

Most people today agree with him; or say that they do.
Etiquette is laughably old-fashioned and hidebound, belonging
not to modern Britain but to seventeenth-century France when
visitors to Louis XIV's court were given a list of protocols on
their 'ticket' or *étiquette*. We all, broadly, subscribe to the same
rules. Whether we drink instant coffee from Styrofoam or artisan
coffee from reusable bamboo we know it would be shocking to
slurp from our neighbour's cup. We might quibble over elbows
on the table but nobody thinks it acceptable to blow their nose

on the tablecloth. Books of advice on how to dress, how to be influential, how to get ahead at work, how to date, to parent, to have a relationship, to conduct oneself over the internet (Netiquette) are displayed at the front of our bookshops. But etiquette books? They might be sold as retro amusements but they are outdated because, according to the German sociologist Norbert Elias, centuries of social pressure have effected what he terms 'the civilizing process'.[1] Or to put it another way, all those etiquette manuals have done the job.

Monks had been concerned with the morals and manners of young men since the twelfth century and, though they might have been from humble lineage themselves, could claim that they had learnt their understanding of good breeding from reading about the lives of David, Solomon and the Kings of Israel from the scriptures. Soon, their ranks were joined by professional servants such as John Russell, Usher and Marshal to Humphrey, Duke of Gloucester, in the mid-fifteenth century, who wrote poetic instructions to young men or 'Babees' on 'Demeanor', 'Curtasye' and 'Vertue', all words from the French, gathered under the term 'Nurture'. He was writing for the 'babees' or boys who were sent, from around the age of seven, to other households to learn how to behave through waiting on the lord at table, to be socialized, and educated in the arts and gentlemanly accomplishments such as hawking or hunting.[2]

The daddy of them all was Erasmus' *De civilitate morum puerilium* (1530). Erasmus was a scholar, not a member of nor a servant to the nobility, and the claims he made for his class were bold. His right to instruct these children of the aristocracy was based on a nobility of intellect and cultivation rather than genealogy. Although he dedicated his book to a prince, he made it clear that, since he was concerned with the whole morality of the individual of which manners are simply the outward show, boys of all classes would benefit.

Erasmus and Russell's instructions on table manners are rather distasteful to the modern reader. At uncomfortable length they tell their young male protégés not to copy the uncouth and fart, vomit, scratch, spit, pick their nose or blow it on the tablecloth, put a chewed bone back into a communal dish, or dip their meat directly into the communal salt. It is a relief to get to the details which have survived down the centuries; put your bread by your left hand and your knife by your right (the bread being used to convey food to the mouth, as a fork is today).

Norbert Elias argued that it took centuries to drum these lessons into children. Until the seventeenth century they were, however, generally addressed to male children and teenagers who, in any era, are more amused than disgusted by bodily impulses. In medieval and Tudor England, their corporeal lives were not private; they lived like puppies, sharing space, beds and food. They had to be taught that what to them was simply a fuzzy boundary between their own and their fellows' bodies and bodily functions needed to be sharply defined in a public space.

Although young women were sent away in similar circumstances – Anne Boleyn, for example, completed her education as a maid of honour in households in the Netherlands (now Belgium) and France – girls were not included in these books, in part because they didn't live the same rough-and-tumble existence as their brothers, but also because they ate less publicly and, initially, they mattered less. Yet young women did learn manners and charm in a less formal process; and as these characteristics became more potent than brute force in the court and noble households, women became more influential. And more demanding. Hannah Woolley, who published a number of successful books on household management in the Restoration and was one of the first women to make a living by her writing, complains bitterly that parents deprive their intelligent daughters of education while granting it to the 'barren Noddles of their Sons'.[3] Her view of education, though, is limited to manners and recipes.

Woolley's prescriptions are familiar. At table, sit up 'strait', keep your elbows off the table, don't be greedy, don't bawl aloud 'I hate Onions: Give me no Pepper'. The language is cheerfully corporeal: 'do not smack like a Pig'; accept food even if 'your Stomach nauseats' but quietly leave it on your plate 'without any palpable discovery of your disgust'. She tells a story of watching her hostess at one dinner 'sweat more in cutting up of a Fowl than the Cook-maid in roasting it; and when she had soundly beliquor'd her joints, hath suckt her knuckles, and to work with them again in the Dish'. This view of her hostess's nauseating behaviour doesn't stop her from confiding to the reader her physical repulsion: as if 'my belly hath been three quarters full, before I had swallowed one bit'.[4] While Hannah finds her friend's behaviour stomach-churning, her own degree of conversational intimacy would shock later generations, as there grew up a notion that it was unacceptable to bring to table either the unwanted thing (disease, corporeality, fights) or discussion of it.

Hannah Woolley's book wasn't visible a century later when Fanny Burney's socially naïve heroine Evelina wished for 'a book of the laws and customs a-la-mode, presented to all young people upon their first introduction into public company'.[5] Lord Chesterfield clearly believed the same, as his famous letters to his son include staccato instructions on the vile things *not* to do at table, and entertaining descriptions of how *not* to carve. He spends most of his consideration on table manners, inveighing against the drinking of health to one's fellows throughout the meal, once universal but beginning to be considered silly and vulgar. *Letters to His Son* (1774) was addressed to Lord Chesterfield's illegitimate son whose insecure birthright gave him a more tenuous position in society. It, like *Evelina*, emerged in the 1770s, an era when social change was slow but gathering pace so that the socially mobile began to reach for guidance; the first book to use the word 'etiquette' was *The True Gentleman's Etiquette*, published in 1776.[6]

Over the succeeding century, as advancing capitalism and urbanization offered money-making opportunities to more levels of society than ever before, those considered to be lower down the pecking order must have been aware of the contempt with which they and their manners were held by 'people of quality', who took it upon themselves to give them the necessary instructions. The books that Evelina had wished for began to pour off the presses. One of the earliest, *Hints on Etiquette*, a slip of a thing which might be tucked into a pocket or a reticule, was published in 1834 for the growing number of people in the country and 'mercantile districts' who, though perfectly respectable, did 'not know what is proper' for the society they aspired to. Its author, Charles William Day, who liked to write maxims under the Greek pen-name Agogos, doesn't spare the feelings of his potential readers.

Etiquette is the barrier which society draws around itself as a protection against offences the 'law' cannot touch – a shield against the intrusion of the impertinent, the improper, and the vulgar – a guard against those obtuse persons who, having neither talent nor delicacy, would be continually thrusting themselves into the society of men to whom their presence might (from the difference of feeling and habit) be offensive, and even insupportable.[7]

Etiquette guides, purporting to reflect society, were an ever-revolving business opportunity. Once they had made the secrets of social acceptance public, then Society would move on in the subtlest of ways (see Where We Sit, page 204). New etiquette guides were needed to instruct the reader in the terrible 'solecisms' and 'vulgarisms' which would betray *his* true class (though the readers were more likely to be female). Bertrand Russell was said to remark that the concept of 'the gentleman' was invented in England by the aristocracy to keep the middle classes in order. Although he might have added, 'and to make them some money'. An anonymous 'Member of the Aristocracy' promised the reader of *Manners and Tone of Good Society* (1879) 'a *direct* road to the obtaining [*sic*] a footing in society' by following the minutest detail of the etiquette of dinner-giving which he or she lays out in page after page. Etiquette guides enabled the reader to enter a fantasy world where they might be presented to the Queen or dine with a duchess. Who knows what hopes or anxieties the exhaustive instructions on invitations, introductions, rank, precedence, and where to place your bread roll, inspired in the breast of readers, many of whom, several rungs below 'Society', would never need them. Table mats, by the way, are *extremely vulgar*.

For some readers, however, bolstered by increasing wealth and influence, the manuals were key to what the sociologist Robert K. Merton called 'anticipatory socialization': changing your behaviour to mimic another tribe, or gang, or caste, as a preparation to joining them.[8] A proliferation of books, magazines and advice columns kept readers up to date with the latest minutiae and dire warnings of solecisms and vulgarisms. It's very vulgar for a lady and gentleman to enter the drawing room side by side. Ladies are not supposed to require a second glass of wine at dessert. Jellies, creams, blancmanges, iced puddings etc. are eaten with a fork, and *not* with a spoon.[9] Your dinner menu, if the food is not cooked by your French chef, should be written in French. If you could remember all this and dozens more such rules, they promised, you were through.

After the First World War, the rules changed completely. The social gatekeepers of the 1920s and 1930s presented it as a backlash against the ritual and decorum that had made their mothers' and grandmothers' lives such a trial. *Simplicity* and *informality* were the watchwords of Lady Troubridge's advice in *Etiquette and Entertaining* (1939). One way of striking the right note of simplicity, she advised her readers, was to tell the maid to say 'Dinner is ready, madam' instead of 'served'. 'It comes to the same thing, doesn't it, but we may as well be up-to-the-minute.'[10]

This emphasis on 'natural charm' and 'taste' rather than following the rules was an ostensibly more democratic form of being 'gentlemanly' or 'ladylike', but it also resonated with the archaic belief that only those of true 'breeding' could be 'well bred'. We find it still today, although the language has changed. Former royal butler Paul Burrell tells a story of a princely guest who, having made a soup of fruit, sugar and cream in his finger bowl, glanced at the Queen and realized he had erred. To save his feelings, she sipped from her own finger bowl. 'Now that's class,' he concluded.[11]

We haven't quite slipped the bonds of the etiquette guides, though. If you see an article or online piece about how to behave over afternoon tea in a hotel, or at a dinner party, the likelihood is that the source is *Debrett's*. Its guides promising to explain 'Correct Form' are still reached for when the stakes seem as high as they did to our Victorian predecessors: ultra-rich international families or business associates needing a social norm, or those members of the high-pressure but fluid society, such as the US meritocracy, who have started teaching etiquette to their children as yet one more competitive advantage.

Most people are happy with 'good manners', a phrase that doesn't have the fussy and fusty connotations of 'etiquette' but suggests adaptability and putting the ease of another person first. My mother used to tell me that good manners consisted not in *not spilling* the gravy boat, but in *not noticing* that the gravy boat had been spilt. Good management is just about good manners, a CEO once told me.

Etiquette alone is not now enough; *manners* are what count. But if, as Norbert Elias argues, our modern good manners are the result of centuries of pressure, then we must pay some credit to etiquette guides, with all their stuffiness, ludicrous minutiae and exploitation of social anxiety. And happily, that means that our journalist and his wife are *both* right.

Strangely, the part of our eating and drinking where we've decided that etiquette plays its biggest role in revealing something about the consumer is not the greasy sandwich or the slurpy spaghetti, but that clean, neat, easy to drink and most British of hot beverages, tea.

Tea: a now universal magic

When I worked on *Question Time*, I didn't invite my mother to the after-show dinner when we were in Manchester because my mum always had a cup of milky, sugary builder's tea with every meal. Wine? That's for posh folk. She died ten years ago and I'm still ashamed of myself...

Katie, by email

OF ALL THE memories and thoughts people have shared with me in the writing of this book, this is the one I find most poignant. It was sent to me by a successful television producer who gives her background as 'northern council estate, comprehensive school'.

There are still Two Nations, then. Those that drink wine at dinner and those that drink tea. The nation as a whole imputes a quasi-magical quality to tea at almost any other time of day and yet, as my colleague's email shows, we've chosen to find a great many things to distinguish the right tea from the wrong one: the milk, the sugar, the type of tea and, crucially, what meal you drink it with.

Although there are no records of tea's first importation to Britain from China, it is likely that it was originally a semi-medicinal gift from traders seeking aristocratic patronage in the early seventeenth century. It is tempting to assume the usual pattern of adoption by the court, when Charles II's Portuguese bride Catherine of Braganza brought her love of tea as part of her cultural dowry on their marriage in 1662. It was quickly adapted by court ladies, and then gentlemen, as a non-intoxicating alternative to the 'small ale' and wine which were standard, wholesome beverages, when water was not routinely safe (or classy) enough to drink.

It is remarkable, however, that some of the earliest references to tea are not from the court but from the merchant and middle classes, with advertisements for the miraculous health benefits of tea (first available at coffee houses) pre-dating Catherine's marriage. When Pepys looked for a break from his work at the Navy Office and 'did send for a cup of tee (a China drink) of which I never had drank before' on 25 September 1660, he was documenting a change of tea from a medical treatment for a few gouty grandees to the fuel of politics, business and academia of the burgeoning Oxford and London coffee-house scenes.[1] The coffee houses, sometimes known as 'penny universities' because of the breadth of conversation covered and their stimulating drinks, were responsible for spreading an interest in politics from the ruling power-base to the middle classes.[2]

A warm, convivial place with stimulating drinks inevitably seduced workers away from their occupations. Charles II tried to suppress the coffee houses because he worried that they were fomenting sedition. Rather than reveal his insecurity, he appealed to Londoners' sense of propriety when, in a proclamation on 23 December 1675, he banned these places of 'resort of idle and disaffected persons... as well for that many tradesmen and other, do herein misspend much of their time' instead of going about their professional duties.[3] He had misjudged how much coffee houses had already become part of national life, and the uproar meant the ban was quickly rescinded just a few weeks later. Charles also realized how much tax revenue from the importation of coffee and tea he would lose.

The king's conviction that stimulating drinks were not appropriate to the working classes was widely shared. Some thinkers were beginning to recognize that their time and labour were germane to the nation's prosperity; it naturally followed that it was unpatriotic of them to waste profitable work time on drinking tea. This idea forms the basis of Jonas Hanway's famously ridiculous *Essay on Tea* (1756), which denounces its supposed brain-addling, health-sapping effects (including scurvy, weak nerves and bad teeth), and the waste of time and money that was spent on it. To do justice to the philanthropic Hanway, he cared about the health and wealth of the working classes, even if his blame for their poor condition would have been more profitably directed at their starvation wages and inadequate provisions for the unemployed (he also, less controversially, allied its pernicious effects with those of gin).

His essay elicited tea's most ardent love-letter, from Samuel Johnson, who described himself as 'a hardened and shameless tea-drinker' who relied on it to stimulate his considerable intellectual powers and 'whose kettle scarcely has time to cool, who with Tea amuses the evening, with Tea solaces the midnights, and with Tea welcomes the morning'.[4] Johnson poured ridicule on all Hanway's arguments, except one. He believed that it was unsuitable for the 'lower classes of the people'; they didn't need it to stimulate intellectual endeavours and it 'supplies no strength to labour' or beneficial medical effects. Dr Johnson, along with Colley Cibber, Addison, Pope, Cowper, Coleridge and Sydney Smith, eulogized tea as a drink for the thinking classes, an integral part of the life of the coffee houses, just as the aristocracy were abandoning the open and egalitarian coffee houses in order to form their own members-only clubs.

Everybody worried about the exorbitant cost of tea, except the Exchequer for which it was a boon. The expense put those who claimed that tea was a necessary intellectual stimulant into a quandary. If they insisted that it should not be drunk by low-income labourers, was it inconsistent for them to complain that the hefty duty – sometimes as high as 160 per cent[5] – made it a luxury and not an essential? According to Dr Lettsom, a physician and philanthropist, 'many of the working classes, too desirous of vying with their superiors and imitating their luxuries, throw away their little earnings upon this fashionable herb'.[6]

From around 1725 the British East India Company, given a monopoly over tea by the government, promoted it heartily, helping tea, rather than coffee, to the status of Britain's national drink, particularly when wars with Spain and France cut off supplies of coffee from across the Mediterranean. Economists now consider that the East India Company was a heavily bureaucratic and expensive institution to run; and tea helped the government pay for it. The Company's monopoly drove up the price as it limited supplies to the markets at home and abroad. America threw the Boston Tea Party to show exactly what it thought of this (and, although beyond the scope of this book, this explains partly why it is so hard to get a decent cup of tea in North America).

Tea was expensive and yet the poor in Europe still drank it, to nobody's benefit. The seventeenth-century Danish doctor Simon Paulli argued that it had no advantages of health nor wakefulness, as 'Many Persons of Rank and Distinction have informed me', (the truth of the statement being borne out by the rank of the person speaking), and that the money wasted on bringing it from China, Tartary and Japan could be spent on 'relieving poor indigent Families at Home'.[7] This argument was enthusiastically taken up by John Wesley, founder of the Methodist movement, who in middle age burned with invective on tea's harmful effects on the health and wealth of the poor, but who quietly went back to drinking it in his more sensible later years. Jonas Hanway also argued that the money wasted on tea would be better spent on public works, envisaging a tea-less land of excellent roads, navigable waterways and elegant public gardens.

On the whole, Middle England didn't much care about these philanthropic objections to what was fast becoming an indispensable part of the warp and weft of social life, particularly as smugglers quickly cottoned on to the ease with which a light and portable product could find its way from Holland to Britain without bothering the Excise men. In 1777, in East Anglia, Parson Woodforde, who itemized his days and dinners so minutely and informatively in his diary written between 1758 and 1802, finds a supply of tea to fuel his busy social and clerical life. He isn't altogether happy about the procedure, but more because he jumps out of his skin when 'Andrews the Smuggler' knocks on his window in the dark, than from any moral scruples that he is cheating the government of its revenue.[8] Smuggling enabled tea to be drunk by everyone. François de La Rochefoucauld told his French readers:

> Throughout the whole of England the drinking of tea is general. You have it twice a day and, though the expense is considerable, the humblest peasant has his tea twice a day just like the rich man; the total consumption is immense.[9]

Prime Minister William Pitt the Younger took care of the expense in one action in 1784 after an enquiry, headed by the owner of Twinings tea merchants, unsurprisingly recommended slashing the duty on tea. After the Commutation Act reduced it from 119 per cent to 12.5 per cent, consumption rose from 5 million to 11 million pounds (2.3–5 million kilograms) in one year.[10]

Now that tea was relatively cheap, some philanthropists turned to questions of morality to show why they still believed the working classes should not be drinking the stuff. When a character in one of Colley Cibber's plays says he adores tea because it is an 'innocent pretence for bringing the wicked of both sexes together in a morning', the playwright is describing a class for whom morality was an optional accoutrement, and for whom the exorbitant cost of taxed tea – he was writing in the early eighteenth century – added to its kick.[11]

Without wealth and status to cushion them, tea drinking easily led to depravity with very real consequences for the poor, argued William Cobbett, as he set himself the task of showing the rural poor how to improve their dull and inadequate diet in *Cottage Economy* (1821); brewing beer to drink at home seemed to him to be a sensible way of keeping families nourished together. Tea had the opposite effect; it lured young men to the public houses to be corrupted; for tea-drinking girls the outlook was even worse:

'the gossip of the tea-table is no bad preparatory school for the brothel'.[12]

Not everybody followed Cobbett's skewed logic about tea leading people to the public houses. After the Commutation Act, Victorian philanthropists seized on tea as the means to salvation for the alcohol-ravaged lower classes. Temperance Meetings, designed to encourage the working classes to forego alcohol, were fuelled by tea; the Methodists were particularly keen on substituting tea for alcohol, quietly forgetting Wesley's youthful objections. Dickens, no fan of Temperance as he believed the working classes had as much right to a drink as any one, has a mocking scene in *The Pickwick Papers* when the publican Tony Weller gatecrashes the Brick Lane Branch of the United Grand Junction Ebenezer Temperance Association, and is horrified to see the amount of tea drinking going on; 'there's a young 'ooman on the next form but two, as has drunk nine breakfast cups and a half; and she's a-swellin' wisibly before my wery eyes,' he whispers, in horror, to his son Sam.

Tea became the prop and mainstay of the working-class diet; most of Mayhew's interviewees in *London Labour and the London Poor* (1851) describe how their day began with tea and bread in the morning, and then nothing until 'tea-time' when they got home, at which point they might have the same again. An 1863 census of the food of the labouring poor revealed their spendthrift habits; 99 per cent of adults had half an ounce (15g) of tea a week, suggesting the leaves were used and re-used until there was no brown life left in them.[13] The biggest threat to their health through tea was recognized – far more sensibly – as adulteration. Green tea was coloured with chemical dyes, often poisonous (Prussian blue, and sulphate or lime or gypsum). Black tea could not be degraded quite so dangerously and that is one reason why it was enthusiastically taken up when colonial tea plantations were established in British India, firstly in Assam and then in Ceylon (now Sri Lanka) and Darjeeling. A brainchild of the East India Company, these were intended to bypass the problems of supply from China, particularly when American 'Clippers' undercut the

Company by shipping tea faster than British ships. The initial seeds and plants were taken, illegally, from China by Robert Fortune, a Scottish botanist in Chinese disguise.[14] By the end of the century, black teas from colonial plantations in Assam, Darjeeling and Ceylon managed by 'skilled Englishmen' outstripped Chinese tea in sales. Black tea was no longer an exotic to be enjoyed by only a leisured class. It had become British.[15]

The steady supply of black tea from India, and an unquenchable British thirst, had established it as the drink for all classes by the First World War when it became part of the soldiers' rations. When the working classes were used as cannon fodder, no more was heard from the officer class and the liberal equivalent about tea being unsuitable for them. In the Second World War it was, along with sugar, meat, fat, bacon and cheese, a 'basic food', and everybody had 2oz (56g) of tea in their rations, enough for three weak cups a day. It was utilized by the government as an instrument of comfort and unity, served in air-raid shelters, factories and the Home Front and, being safer than either dirty water or alcohol as well as a great morale-booster, to every soldier and officer in the army. It was, as George Orwell said pointedly just after the war, 'one of the main stays of civilization in this country' (although he also admitted Eire, Australia and New Zealand into its magic circle).[16]

Once tea became a government-sanctioned equal opportunities drink, British society had to find other ways of delineating status. Going back to coffee, especially after dinner, appealed to bourgeois gourmands, who were already turning to Mediterranean food. To others, this was whether you took green China tea rather than black Indian. Most people's preference (around 90 per cent), however, was for black tea; and so the 'milk in first' ('mif') or 'milk in last' ('mil') controversy was whipped up. J.B. Priestley asked his *Saturday Review* column readers to send in examples of the 'subtle division between two classes', and then despised them for doing so, deriding their 'petty snobbery' against 'people who pour the milk in first' (or who said 'serviette' instead of 'napkin', knitted egg cosies, ate chocolates in the theatre and did not own a dressing gown).

Evelyn Waugh, writing to Nancy Mitford, seems to rather despise the people who have not imbibed rules of tea etiquette from birth:

> All nannies and many governesses, when pouring out tea, put the milk in first. (It is said by tea-fanciers to produce a richer mixture.) Sharp children notice that this is not normally done in the drawing-room. To some this revelation becomes symbolic. We have a friend you may remember, far from conventional in other ways, who makes it her touchstone. 'Rather MIF, darling,' she says in condemnation.[17]

It seems an arbitrary rather than historic choice; across the centuries tea warriors have insisted on one way or the other. And an odd choice. Cold milk, added to boiling tea, becomes slightly scalded, so why the twentieth-century mil classes chose the taste of scorched, takeaway tea in their own drawing rooms is beyond me.

The invention and near-universal adoption of the tea bag (96 per cent – according to tea.co.uk/tea-faqs) hasn't quite put paid to the mif or mil debate. My brother, a builder, complains that his millennial apprentices make tea by lining up a row of mugs, adding the tea bags, the sugar and the milk, and then the boiling water. But 'builder's tea' has become a more or less affectionate term for strong, tannic and unpretentious black tea; nowadays only manual workers tend to put sugar in it, although sugar was taken in tea from its earliest introduction in the 1600s (our seventeenth-century Danish friend Simon Paulli, having abjured all tea, then admitted he didn't mind a little *salt* in tea, but abhorred sugar in it. Which might be why the Danes became a coffee-drinking nation). Nobody bats an eyelid at the name English Breakfast Tea, as if tea grown in India or sometimes Kenya is the most naturally English thing in the world. It is an attempt to make 'ordinary' tea sound a cut above, although, given that it says nothing about the origin or quality, it's about as informative a name as 'French table wine' or 'cocktail'.

Your first cup of tea of the day – China, Indian, sugared, mif or mil, mug or cup – will reveal a lot about who you are and where you are drinking it. 'As one moves through the day the class indicators come thick and fast. The upper classes have coffee or China tea for breakfast, the lower classes Indian tea, which they drink very strong and very sweet,' says Jilly Cooper.[18] But, unlike other contested areas of food such as sugar, fat and meat, nobody now believes that the 165 million cups of tea drunk daily in Britain[19] shouldn't be equally available to anybody reaching for its wondrous properties of stimulation, warmth, community and solace.

There are dark forces at work, though. Fruit teas, herbal teas, decaffeinated teas, not to mention *coffee*, are all assailing our right and proper addiction to tea. According to *The Grocer* magazine, the socio-economic grouping ABC1s are more likely to dally with other sorts of beverages, while C2DEs are most faithful to traditional black tea.[20] However, if you add some diminutive sandwiches and a scone, and a full load of jam and cream, suddenly tea discovers its powers of refinement and aspiration. This is the world of afternoon tea.

Afternoon Tea: the Duchess of Bedford's sinking feeling

You can always trust the rich to turn greed into a fashion statement.

Nigel Slater, *Eating for England* (2007)

IT'S IMPOSSIBLE TO introduce the theme of this chapter without giving away my social background, or committing a solecism, depending on how you look at it. The phrase 'afternoon tea' is a vulgar tautology. The upper classes have tea, with a sandwich or cake, in the afternoon between lunch and dinner. The adjective 'afternoon' betrays me as a commoner, particularly a northern commoner, who expects a main meal in the early evening and calls it 'tea' (without the adjective); in which case the people who have tea in the afternoon call your meal 'high tea' to distinguish it from their default 4 o'clock tea. We can be kind to Henry James and attribute to his American ignorance his opening line of *The Portrait of a Lady* (1881): 'Under certain circumstances there are few hours in life more agreeable than the hour dedicated to the ceremony known as afternoon tea.'[1]

The times, as well as the content of the meal, are significant. Georgian ladies took their 'morning' calls any time up to their mid-afternoon dinner. In Fanny Burney's *Evelina* (1778), when Lord Orville asks her if she'll be at home 'tomorrow morning', she arranges to receive a guest at 'about three o'clock'.[2] After dinner, they took tea. Jonathan Swift, never a great flatterer of women (or anybody), describes the madam of his poem *Journal of a Modern*

Lady (1728) taking her 'evening tea' with a noisy clan of women who exemplify every vice he could fit into a stanza: pride, scandal, hypocrisy, scurrility, malice, vanity, impudence, affectation and ignorance. Quite a party to fit around a tea table.

Jane Austen's slight but meaningful references to tea and cake are after-dinner affairs. In *Mansfield Park*, humble Fanny is rescued from the unwanted attentions of the dashing (but dastardly) Henry Crawford by 'The solemn procession, headed by Baddeley, of tea-board, urn, and cake-bearers', because it gave her something to *do*.[3] Pouring tea and coffee was the job of the grown-up daughters of the house (or, in this case, as the daughters were indolent, the niece). Cake (probably a pound cake, a seed cake or a fruit cake), individual rout-cakes (made for a fashionable gathering or 'rout'), toasted muffins or toast were usually served, making after-dinner tea yet another occasion for a social visit which might also include cards or music. It offered a welcome change from the expense of a dinner party for the Georgian squeezed upper-middles; or, for those inclined to condescension, an opportunity to put lesser guests in their place. *Pride and Prejudice*'s entertainingly obsequious clergyman Mr Collins almost pops with excitement when Lady Catherine de Bourgh invites them, not just 'to drink tea and spend the evening at Rosings', but to *dine*.

Times were changing; dinner was being pushed back later by a metropolitan elite, always seeking to distance themselves from the class below or those living a less sophisticated, rural life. Jane enjoyed the comic potential of such a subtle class distinction. She wrote to her sister Cassandra, who was staying with wealthy relatives, that as they dined so early at home (around 3.30 p.m.), 'We drink tea at half-past six. I am afraid you will despise us.'[4]

Less than half a century later Queen Victoria and others in her circle were having dinner at 8 p.m., many hungry hours after luncheon. The doyen of tea historians, the American William Ukers, wrote in 1935 that we are indebted to Anna, Duchess of Bedford for filling this gap by inventing afternoon tea sometime in the 1840s when, he writes, 'she had tea and cakes served at five o'clock, because, to quote herself, she had "a sinking feeling"'.[5] It is a delightful line, much-quoted since, although his source remains obscure. The actress Fanny Kemble recalled being a guest along with the Duchess of Bedford, at Belvoir Castle in March 1842:

> My first introduction to 'afternoon tea' took place during this visit to Belvoir, when I received on several occasions private and rather mysterious invitations to the Duchess of Bedford's room, and found her with a 'small and select' circle of female guests of the castle, busily employed in brewing and drinking tea, with her grace's own private tea-kettle. I do not believe that now universally honoured and observed institution of 'five-o'clock tea' dates farther back in the annals of English civilization than this very private and, I think, rather shamefaced practice of it.[6]

What is interesting is how quickly the practice became, as Fanny Kemble said, 'universally honoured'. By the time Lewis Carroll wrote *Alice's Adventures in Wonderland* (1865), some twenty years later, its rituals and etiquette were sufficiently established to be ripe for subversion by the March Hare and the Hatter at a Mad Tea Party. It hadn't quite permeated down to Mrs Beeton's solidly middle-class *Book of Household Management* (1861); but in the 1880 edition, the writer acknowledged 'there is Tea and Tea' – high tea and 'the afternoon cosy, chatty affairs that late diners have instituted' which consists of 'little more than tea and bread-and-butter, and a few elegant trifles in the way of cake and fruit'. The domestic bible tactfully distinguished the two different kinds of tea not by social background but by the hours – the one in the 'house of the early diner' and the second for 'late diners'.[7]

Afternoon tea proved to be highly adaptable. It became a fixture of the townhouse, through the Victorian custom of being 'At Home' to your friends (pre-invited by a card announcing that you would be 'at home' on certain days) between about 3 or 4 p.m. and 6 and 7 p.m.; a perfect opportunity to fan the twin flames of the Victorian addictions to china tea services and arcane rules of etiquette. The country house tea represented, for a privileged few, the apotheosis of comfort; they could have toast and jam with nanny and the children in the nursery, wolf down sandwiches and crumpets in the billiard room after a day hunting or shooting, or settle down to a slice of sponge cake and gossip in the drawing room, before retiring to their rooms at around 7 p.m. to dress for dinner.

Long before Anna, Duchess of Bedford had her 5 o'clock munchies, workers, particularly at harvest time, would have had their 'beaver' or 'cheesing-time' at 4 o'clock, when the women would have sent them bread and cheese or seed cake into the fields for their mid-afternoon snack, enabling them to carry on working until evening. Their wives eventually started to have afternoon tea at the same time. In *Lark Rise to Candleford* (1945), Flora Thompson, remembering her late Victorian childhood in rural Oxfordshire, describes the younger mothers in her village pooling their resources of tea and sugar to have a sociable afternoon cup. Except for the largesse of fêtes and fairs, there was an uncrossable line dividing the sort of guests invited to either 'kitchen or dining-room tea'. When the socially ambitious schoolteacher Miss Shepherd tries to cross it, she is neatly but rather cruelly returned to her place:

> She had the satisfaction of ringing the front-door bell and drinking tea in the drawing-room; but it was a short-lived triumph. In a very few minutes she was out in the servants' hall, passing bread and butter to her charges and whispering to one of her monitors that 'Dear Mrs. Bracewell gave me my tea first, because, as she said, she knew I was anxious to get back to my children.'[8]

If the Mrs Bracewells of this world were unwilling to give the Miss Shepherds the social experience she longed for, the commercial world saw it as a great opportunity. Around the start of the twentieth century, entrepreneurs began to open tea shops for customers of all backgrounds; the Lyons Corner Houses were more aspirational than the ABCs (which grew from the Aerated Bread Company; see Bread and Butter, page 298) and catered for clerical workers. In Glasgow, Kate Cranston offered spaces for ladies to take tea together from the 1870s and opened her famous Willow Tea Rooms, designed by Charles Rennie Mackintosh in 1903. Tea rooms and department-store cafeterias provided the first safe and welcoming public spaces for women to dine without male guardianship; they were particularly useful for women from the suburbs or the country who did not have friends with drawing rooms in town to offer them what Agnes Jekyll called 'an hour of respite from their bewildering preoccupations' of a Christmas shopping trip.[9] Tea rooms have their place in the story of women's suffrage; taking afternoon tea with friends was not the political equivalent of chaining oneself to railings or throwing oneself in front of the king's horse, but it *was* a firm statement that women of all classes wanted choice, agency and emancipation and a place to meet one another outside the home.

The most successful tea rooms offered not just respite but grandeur; or the illusion of it, modelling their decor and service on the famous hotels which were beyond reach, although not beyond the aspiration, of their clientele. Theodore Dreiser, the American writer who was visiting London in 1913, noticed the glass chandeliers, the cream and gold decorations of the Lyons Corner House in Piccadilly and was loftily amused by 'the tall, thin, solemn English head-waiters in frock coats, leading the exceedingly bourgeois customers to their tables'.[10]

The grand hotels themselves have left the country house ideal of 5 o'clock tea far behind. Knowing that their clientele are generally tourists and visitors who are blissfully unaware that it is 'common' to call it 'afternoon tea', they have invented for themselves 'one of the finest British traditions', as the Ritz calls its 'afternoon tea', using a formula which suits their kitchens and their bottom line: the three-tiered cake stand of finger sandwiches, diminutive scones with Lilliputian jars of strawberry jam and doll's-house-sized, oversweet pâtisserie. It is an unvarying menu, but the extensive list of teas gives the illusion that the hotels are offering choice, in return for the £50 or so their customers pay. It is a long way from Constance Spry's 1950s insistence that it was not 'good taste to have too many small things';[11] instead one should offer one or two home-baked cakes – a fruit cake and a sponge cake – and toasted things – crumpets or teacakes, with anchovy toast striking a savoury note. Books and websites still offer etiquette lessons to those about to embark on afternoon tea in a hotel, with specific instructions on how to stir the tea (back and forth), break the scones (*not* with a knife) and eat the sandwiches (with, of all great surprises, the fingers!). Hotels did, however, keep the flame of afternoon tea alive throughout the 1970s and 1980s, when it had flickered out elsewhere to be replaced by the newly fashionable 'coffee morning'. Then when the coffee morning rapidly acquired an image of not very exciting, or chic, suburbia, afternoon tea was revived around the turn of the millennium, by our growing adoration of the National Trust and the village tea room, which allowed us to shed a decade or two of unromantic modern life for every mile we put between us and our urban or suburban homes.

In the last few decades, afternoon tea has, I think, reached its most perfect and uncomplicated expression in the cream tea found in Devon, Cornwall and other rural counties. Walk or drive until you find a cottage offering a 'cream tea', sit on a low sofa inside or at a table in the garden, and don't give a second thought to how to hold your cup or stir your tea, but enjoy what will probably be a well-made scone, clotted cream and good fruit jam with a dash of acidity. The only nod to place is geographical rather than social; somebody will bring up the difference between the Devon (cream first) vs the Cornish (jam first) rules. (See Cake, page 400, for a scone recipe.)

Whenever we sit down to eat, we will always find ways of showing our place. The lexicon can be confusing, though, because while the higher classes sat in low armchairs for *tea*, lower down the hierarchy people sat up at the table for high tea, as we'll see next.

High Tea: a bourgeois affair

It was a wonderful tea. There was a nice brown egg, lightly boiled,
for each of them, and then sardines on toast, and then buttered
toast, and then toast with honey, and then a sugar-topped cake.

C.S. Lewis, *The Lion, The Witch and the Wardrobe* (1950)

A CONFESSION HERE. My sister and I once sat next to two
leopardprint-clad, dyed-blonde-haired, Yorkshire-accented
ladies in Bettys Tea Rooms in Harrogate; they were having
afternoon tea with chips, and complaining to each other that Bettys
had gone 'right downmarket'. I thought it was hilarious. They were,
I now realize, exercising the eminently sensible northern habit of
making tea – as in 'high tea' – exactly what you wanted it to be.
To me, Dorothy Hartley's description of the massive Yorkshire tea
in *Food in England* (1954), served by the Craven Heifer Inn, reads
like an ode to happiness: 'ham, game pies, apple pies, parkin and
cheese, hot teacakes, jam and honey and black treacle, and tea'.[1]
There are no real rules about 'high tea', except it always has tea.
And usually ham.

Rather like the idea that the American accent is closer to that
of our Puritan forefathers than English, 'high tea' is probably
closer to the way we dined before 'the new style' of a succession of
courses came in in the early nineteenth century (see Small Plates,
page 223). There might be one or two courses, with a couple of
hot dishes served out and 'removed'; but essentially all the baked
hams or cold joints, the salmon, the salad, the numerous kinds
of pies, tarts and cakes are placed on the table at one time for

guests to help themselves and each other. High tea keeps to an early evening time of 5 or 6 o'clock; and everybody sits up at the table – the adjective 'high' (probably) distinguishes it from low drawing-room armchairs. Although high tea is associated with the North of England and Scotland, here not all teas are 'high'; it is likely that whatever is on the table – fish and chips, or shepherd's pie, or stir-fry – is your 'tea' (even without the drink); and that the meal you have had in the middle of the day is called 'dinner', just as it would have been for our medieval ancestors (see The Sandwich, page 28).

Predominantly a northern response to family needs and daylight hours, during the nineteenth century high tea was adopted throughout the Midlands and southern provincial England, as well as by the working classes in London and the South. When Dickens' wage-earning characters invite one another to dine, it is to tea; in *Bleak House* (1853), the law clerk Mr Snagsby and his wife invite the preacher for 6 p.m. and entertain him 'with dainty new bread, crusty twists, cool fresh butter, thin slices of ham, tongue, and German sausage, and delicate little rows of anchovies nestling in parsley, not to mention new-laid eggs, to be brought up warm in a napkin, and hot buttered toast'.[2] It doesn't yet need an adjective; it is simply known as 'tea'. It is a suitable meal to give someone of a nonconformist bent, too, given the enthusiasm the nonconformist churches had for tea as a replacement for alcohol (see Tea, page 45). It wasn't a switch that pleased every northerner; there would often be a jug of rum or, in Scotland, whisky for the men. In Mrs Gaskell's *Mary Barton* (1848), set in Manchester, Mary's mother sends her to buy bread, ham and eggs, her father adding 'sixpennyworth of rum, to warm the tea'.[3] Across the Pennines and into the next century, an anonymous-looking 'little brown jug' reassures the male tea-time guests in J.B. Priestley's play *When We Are Married* (1938).

Priestley's smug bourgeois couples are obvious candidates for high tea, given their solid, middle-class Yorkshire base; but it was also seen as the meal for working classes both rural and urban, as it could be eaten once the husband returned from his manual or agricultural work and the children from school. A pot of hot tea could transfigure the most familiar of cold rations – bread, oatcakes, cheese, ham – into a hot meal. Associated, as it was, with the North and the working classes, more patrician food writers could write (even in 1991) without irony, 'Lower down the social scale, tea meant high tea.'⁴

It was an attitude that irritated the Scottish folklorist F. Marian McNeill. In her hymn to *The Scots Kitchen* (1929), she wrote: 'People who normally dine late – that is, broadly speaking, those above a certain income level – are apt to look down on high tea as a bourgeois affair – as indeed it is.'⁵ But how foolish, McNeill thought, to turn your back on some of the best food the country produces because of a worry about status. As she pointed out: 'The fame of French cooking emanates not from her cosmopolitan hotels, but from the kitchens of the *bourgeoisie* – sensible folk who make an intelligent use of the natural products of their country.'⁶

She was right. 'High tea' was too good a thing for food-lovers – even aristocratic ones – to ignore completely. While practical British housekeepers had been dominating the cookbook market since the eighteenth century, the 1920s and 1930s produced a new kind of female food writer, such as Agnes Jekyll, Hilda Leyel or Alice B. Toklas, who incorporated recipes into essays about food and entertaining and who were often elegant and amusing and nearly always upper class.

But, beneath the sparkly suggestions for the perfect tea-time cake, their writings suggest that their class was feeling its way around new social realities. The servant structure had been all but destroyed by the First World War, necessitating a more modest mode of living. And, in the 1930s wealth and privilege sat uneasily against a background of depression and unemployment. How to acknowledge this and yet still be fashionable meant striking the right *tone*. Lady Troubridge, in *Etiquette and Entertaining*, decides that high tea could be made acceptable in one's own weekend cottage, so long as it was done the 'correct way' – a knowing embrace of 'farmhouse fashion' with not a genteelism in place; the butter in an earthenware crock, the jam in its own pot, the big brown teapot and *not* your best china.

Most people, however, do not read Lady Troubridge's *Etiquette and Entertaining*, and have no idea that their tea habits aren't shared by their neighbours from different social backgrounds. Jilly Cooper has Caroline Stow-Crat, her aristocratic archetype in *Class*, complaining that 'The worst thing about the lower classes... is that they never know when to leave. If she asks them round for a quick pre-dinner drink, they've always had their tea first and are all set to carry on drinking until midnight.'[7] Mike Leigh shows the reverse situation in his stinging class satire *Abigail's Party* (1977), when middle-class Sue brings a bottle of wine to what, she assumes, is her neighbours' dinner party, only to find they have all already had their *tea* and she has to rely on cubes of cheese and pineapple, crisps and peanuts to absorb the copious amount of gin she is served. (Spoiler alert; they don't...)

In the 1950s nearly three quarters of British families drank hot tea with their evening meal.[8] Those cups and mugs have been replaced by other kicks: alcohol, sweet fizzy drinks, fruit juice and bottled water. But sometimes only tea, with its powers to make a cold meal feel like a hot one, will do.

As you've probably gathered by now, I'm a bit of a fan of tea in every definition: drink, snack in the afternoon, main meal of the day. Loading a table in the garden or kitchen with bread, pies and cakes I've made over a leisurely couple of days is one of my favourite ways of feeding friends. You can deploy hot punch, cold fizz and the teapot with equal gusto. The words 'come for tea' are unlikely to provoke terror in any heart. Unlike the dinner party...

PARKIN FOR THE MANY

◆

Peter Brears tells the story of a doctor in Wensleydale, Yorkshire, at the end of the nineteenth century who recalls that at funerals '"the quality" had good old port and sponge cake and "the many" mulled ale and Yorkshire parkin'.[9] The use of oatmeal is typical of baking in the North of England, and explains in part why 'the many' northerners had better nutrition than their southern counterparts. For even better nutrition, serve with Wensleydale cheese. Parkin has become a Bonfire Night tradition in the North, and, like us all, gets better with age, so wrap it well in paper and keep in a tin for a week or two.

MODERN RECIPE

200g fine oatmeal
200g white or wholemeal flour
Pinch of salt
1 teaspoon mixed spice
1–2 teaspoons ground ginger
Grating of nutmeg
1 teaspoon bicarbonate of soda
100g golden syrup
100g black treacle
100g soft dark brown sugar
150g butter
1 egg
50ml cream or milk

1. Preheat the oven to Gas Mark 3/160°C and grease and line a 22cm square tin.
2. Combine all the dry ingredients except the sugar, making sure the bicarb and the spices are evenly distributed.
3. Melt together the syrups, the sugar and the butter until the butter is melted; don't allow it to boil.
4. Pour into a well in the dry ingredients. Mix well to combine.
5. Beat the egg into the milk, and then beat this liquid into the dry ingredients. You need a loose batter – add a little more milk if need be to give a thick pouring consistency.

6. Pour it into the tin and bake for 50–60 minutes until it feels firm and springs back to touch, especially in the centre. Cover it with baking paper if it is browning too quickly. Be careful not to overbake it as it will dry out.

7. Remove from the oven and, when it is still warm, turn out and cool on a wire rack.

ORIGINAL RECIPE: MRS MILLINGTON'S PARKIN, PRESTON

From *Good Things in England* by Florence White (1932)

Plain flour ½lb ◆ fine oatmeal ½lb ◆ black treacle ½lb ◆ brown sugar (demerara or raw) ¼lb ◆ butter and lard mixed ¼lb ◆ mixed spice 1 teaspoon ◆ powdered ginger 1 teaspoon ◆ nutmeg, just a grating ◆ bicarbonate of soda 1 teaspoon ◆ milk ½ teacupful

Time: bake in a moderate oven for about 1 hour

1. Rub the butter and lard into the flour.
2. Stir in oatmeal.
3. Add the other dry ingredients.
4. Then the syrup (slightly warmed).
5. Slightly warm the milk and dissolve the soda in it.
6. Stir it into the mixture.
7. A beaten egg may be added (the mixture must be quite light and fairly moist, so it is safer to use an egg than more milk).
8. Grease a large meat roasting or a Yorkshire pudding tin.
9. Pour in the mixture.
10. Bake as above.

The Dinner Party:
the middle classes' revenge

Dinners are given mostly in the middle classes by way of revenge.

Thackeray, 'Great and Little Dinners',
Punch (July–December 1849)

THE DINNER PARTY has got itself a bad name. In 2018, John Humphreys, on Radio 4's *Today* programme, echoed the UK's Justice Secretary in blaming the country's drug-driven knife crime problem on 'middle-class dinner parties'.[1] Or it is tainted by corruption; anti-competitive companies such as Google employ the friends of top politicians to make their case at Notting Hill dinner parties.[2] None of the people I asked in an (admittedly small and rather personal) survey said that they had dinner parties, although they cheerfully admitted that they had friends round for dinner. One friend distinguished between an obligation to go to 'dinner parties' with a carefully curated guest list of impressive people and 'dinner' or 'supper' with friends she really wanted to see.

Is this new? Of course not. Trimalchio's feast, one of the earliest recorded dinner parties in history, is a late first-century AD satire on the hideousness of the Roman dinner party. Trimalchio, the host, is an alcoholic braggart and former slave, a member of the lowest class of free men who is aiming to impress his guests with his displays of wealth, his execrable poetry and a succession of twelve courses of costly and ostentatiously disguised food, served by singing and dancing slaves.

It is surprising, after this endless catalogue of vulgarity and excess, that anybody ever dared host a dinner party again, and it seems that, in Britain anyway, nobody did until the nineteenth century. In the preceding two centuries people of the same social circle would 'give a dinner' or 'dine with' or have a 'dinner engagement' with one another perhaps a few nights a week. The guests might be staying for several weeks with their hosts, supplemented with a select party of friends and neighbours, who were very likely to know one another. Spending the evening with friends began with a 4 or 5 p.m. dinner, followed by tea and perhaps cake, and ending with a late-evening supper; with cards or music in between. It required staying power for the participants upstairs, and the servants downstairs even more so, but at least everybody knew what to expect.

For Mrs Bennet, the action of *Pride and Prejudice* leads up to what she calls a 'family dinner', which will bring about the long-anticipated engagement of her eldest daughter, Jane, to her wealthy suitor, Mr Bingley. Her guest list is an easy matter; in the settled social world of Georgian country life she dines with 'four and twenty families'. It became harder, and also more important, to define the company you *ought* to keep as the emerging mercantile class and industrialization moved people both geographically and socially towards an urban middle class or elite.

Britain is rarely credited with gastronomic innovation, but the formal, highly ritualized yet domestic dinner party emerged in Britain rather than anywhere on the Continent.[3] While Brillat-Savarin aphoristically championed the comforts of regional, bourgeois entertaining, 'To entertain a guest is to make yourself responsible for his happiness so long as he is beneath your roof',[4] the Brits were working out how to give a dinner (or go to a dinner) that either enabled them to rise in society, or keep out the people below who were trying to.

Whereas the eighteenth-century host and hostess gained their 'Honours of the Table' in serving guests and friends 'agreeable to their rank and situation in life',[5] the next century was all about attracting guests whose social standing would act as a gloss on your own. You did this, as Dickens points out with his awful Veneerings in *Our Mutual Friend* (1865), by getting yourself a reputation for giving 'excellent dinners – or new people wouldn't come'.[6] Everything about the Veneerings is 'bran new'; their status has arisen rapidly from their purchasing power and they set about to cement it with their dinner parties. Hard as this group of hopefuls tried to get it right, they were attacked for turning stylishness into ostentation and, worse, contaminating the whole dinner-party chain. Avoid anybody who gives 'what idiots call dinner-parties',[7] warned one anonymous Victorian doomsayer, before describing, at misogynistic and snobbish length, the 'dirty feast' given by those who aspire to the style of Belgravia but occupy 'cockney villas with romantic names',[8] where the unwitting and discerning (male) guest will leave feeling tainted by 'fourth or fifth-rate women'[9] and badly cooked, pretentious food. The sociologically minded barrister Thomas Walker warned those of his circle to ignore the style of the 'vulgar rich – the very last class worthy of imitation' and to settle for smaller, more relaxed dinner parties whose aim was 'real enjoyment' rather than 'vulgar luxury'.[10]

A full-blown Victorian dinner party required huge resources, in terms of kitchen facilities and servants: cooks and all the kitchen maids to help and wash up; footmen to impress; and a butler to orchestrate the cast and chorus, and serve the several wines. The move from dining *à la française* (see Small Plates, page 223) to *à la russe* was partly an arms race, an opportunity for hosts to parade a full regiment of servants before their guests. An aspirational Victorian tradesman might struggle to afford even one maid; and a couple might hire a less than skilled cook for the night and the local grocer to stand in as butler and also send out to the 'pastrycook' for pies or baked dishes and the dessert. It could never be relaxed and gracious entertainment when, as William Makepeace Thackeray pointed out, the smiling host is 'prey to secret terrors and anxieties' lest the 'butler' should commit some faux pas that shows him to be hired help; or the hostess is 'smiling through her agony' because she can't forget the kitchen, the cook and all the things that could be going wrong.[11] A host and hostess were only as good as their servants. The pseudonymous Launcelot Sturgeon, a rare defender of the cook, pointed out that the great men of London owed their 'estimation in society' to the excellence of their unknown and unheralded cook; unlike in France where a man gloried in the achievements of his family's chef.[12]

Whereas the Georgians 'give a dinner' for their peers, in William IV's London the phrase 'Dinner Party' began to come into use to suggest a very slight mix of social levels. The upwardly mobile Thomas Creevey, who became an MP from quite a modest background, was an early adopter of the term in the privacy of his own diary in around 1834. The story went that his friend Lord Sefton is amused to relay a message from the elderly and grand Lady Salisbury: 'As I find Creevey can't dine with us on Sunday, suppose we change our day to Wednesday.' The amusement comes because she calls him Creevey, as she would a social equal, and, as he writes delightedly, 'to have her dinner party put off for my convenience, is far beyond what any mortal could have predicted'.[13] As men of more insecure backgrounds found themselves with commercial heft and political power, it was understood that their political affiliation might be encouraged by some marks of attention, principally an invitation to dine. 'Invite them to dinner... remember their wives at assemblies and call their daughters, if possible, by their right names; and they will... change their principles or desert their party for you,' the political hostess Lady St Julian declares in Disraeli's Sybil.[14]

By 1895, Creevey's 'dinner party' is a term in common usage. Oscar Wilde's Algernon tells Jack, in The Importance of Being Earnest, 'It is very vulgar to talk about one's business. Only people like stock-brokers do that, and then merely at dinner parties.' And Lady Bracknell considers a firm of solicitors to have passed a barrage of social tests and become acceptable because one of them 'is occasionally to be seen at dinner parties'. The role of aunt and nephew in the play is to represent the mores and manners of 'Society', the group of wealthy and well-connected families who, listed in *Debrett's* and part of Britain's Landed Gentry, were safe material to give and receive invitations from. But, as Lady Bracknell suggests, the barriers of 'Society' were beginning to be porous. Respectable people such as doctors, lawyers and businessmen might seep through. Towards the end of the century, imported food brought down the cost of living[15] and dinner parties came within reach of tradesmen and managers. Social habits and manners became a particularly important way for the Lady Bracknells to define themselves as a class, and to instruct those lucky enough to be admitted. To business-friendly England, the result was a pleasingly booming market for etiquette manuals (see Etiquette, page 38).

The increasing lateness of the dinner hour and the disappearance of the hot supper meant that the extended evening of the previous century telescoped into a more intense focus on the one dinner. Supposed to bring people together, some felt that the structure of formal dinner parties of twenty people and more hindered genuine sociability. Guests were not introduced to one another, and might mingle in the drawing room for only half an hour before and after a long stint at table. Huge decorations obstructed conversation across the table; conversation with your neighbour was frequently interrupted by servants[16] and regulated by rules of small talk; discussion of the food was entirely off-limits. After her society dinner party in E.M. Forster's *A Room with a View* (1908), Mrs Vyse considers that her prospective daughter-in-law is 'purging off the... taint' of her bourgeois family as she is not always 'asking one how the pudding is made'.[17]

Punctuality for guests became important – almost an obsession: it showed that you were wealthy enough to carry a watch, and civilized enough to order your day and had left the prompts of sundown and cockcrow far behind. Arriving on time was a courtesy that demonstrated an understanding of the number of parts in the dinner-giving machine: the fire-laying, cutlery-polishing, table-laying, flower-arranging, dressing for dinner, cooking, serving, tea and coffee, washing up. Alongside the dinner the hostess also had to plan plainer meals for the nursery and the staff and, in a large house, differentiated meals for the upper staff (cook, butler, lady's maid, valet); there were hundreds of mechanisms which had to align in the clockwork of the day. This meant that punctuality for kitchen staff was also crucial. A dinner served late, or too long an interval between the courses, suggested a lack of care or expertise – or both – and provoked unease in guests and hosts alike.

It is hardly surprising that there was a twentieth-century backlash. The focus was on elegant, or informal, or stylish 'entertainment' as much, or even more than, the food itself and the influential tones of the Agnes Jekylls and Lady Troubridges of the 1920s and 1930s rang out to show that one needed paid help to entertain properly. The food, though, could be simple so long as it was good; even in the 1930s there were still experienced and excellent cooks, and having a cook who intuited your guests' needs was the highest form of hospitality. The delightful Mollie Moran, who started her career in the 1930s as a fourteen-year-old housemaid before becoming cook at Wallington Hall in Norfolk, describes catering for a shooting party of twenty, which included the British ambassador to Germany tasked with negotiating peace with Hitler. The menu, in her words:

> Fish? Not restorative enough. Pork? Too common... what that politician needed was a nice hearty bowl of Mollie's Irish stew... and sticky, sweet bread and butter pudding and a jug of fresh cream big enough to drown a German battleship.[18]

All this in an old kitchen with just an Aga and a kitchen boy for help. There was a lull in the war years when few had servants – nor much in the way of ingredients thanks to rationing, which made the full dinner party something of an overpromise. Mollie visited her employer during the war, now living in a worker's cottage as her stately home had been requisitioned, and looking ragged; a life of servants and cooks had ill-prepared her for the new reality of cooking and caring for her own family, let alone entertaining.

Judith Listowel, an aristocratic Hungarian journalist, welcomed post-war fiscal policies which almost bridged the chasm between rich and poor and, she thought, did away with the social exclusiveness and snobbery, 'the backbone of Society spelt with a capital "S"', because, she thought cheerily, people were simply too busy for bores. 'The social scene, in my childhood still darkened by a canopy of taboos, rules and rituals, is now light and roomy. Every woman has a chance to step on to it, and show what she can do as a modern hostess.' And to prove it she quoted her doctor whose cleaner was hosting a party for a family wedding, having learnt how to put on a buffet from carefully watching American films and TV advertising, and borrowing champagne glasses from the local police force.[19]

The term 'dinner party' began to re-emerge from the gloom of rationing, helped by Mediterranean holidaying and writers such as Elizabeth David who turned cooks' attention back to food – and with a vengeance. Dinner parties became focused on how to serve the kind of food professional chefs might produce in a restaurant; *The Good Food Guide Dinner Party Book* (1971) collected recipes from restaurateurs around the country for hostesses (or, the authors acknowledged, the occasional host) to recreate at home. The dinner party with the perfect food was fuelled by decades of television chefs and cooks; Fanny Cradock in evening dress serving up prawn cocktail and crêpes suzette; serial restaurateur Keith Floyd travelling the world to find fish stew, drink in hand. A series of mostly male restaurateurs on our televisions, from this day to the present, showed us how to cook food designed to impress, and became so famous they are known, like Jesus, by their first names: Heston, Jamie, Gordon, Nigel. Of their female counterparts, Delia's success is that she gives recipes for special occasions, having friends round and 'entertaining' but avoids giving instructions on how to host a 'dinner party'. Her carefully non-alienating recipes have made her a national treasure and the bestselling cookery writer and TV anti-chef from the 1970s to date.

At the turn of the millennium there was a battle for the soul of the dinner party. 'At least among the educated classes the private dinner party lives on. For that we should be grateful,' Roy Strong thought.[20] Nigella Lawson didn't see any reason to be grateful for the competitive dinner party with its attempt at restaurant-quality 'fancy, arranged food'. She thought that the kitchen supper was an unbearably twee term, but that the event itself was far more authentic than a 'dinner party'. Eating supper in the kitchen is what the right sort of people do; they are relaxed enough about their social status not to try to impress, and happy to serve food which, in Nigella's phrase, 'should reflect your personality not your aspirations'.[21]

The twenty-first century has not been kind to the dinner party, since *MasterChef* and *Come Dine with Me* turned it from a select gathering of the middle and upper classes in the privacy of their own homes, into a form of entertainment for the masses. It draws attention to the fact that sitting down together to eat is unusual, in a society when some families might only ever sit down and share a meal on Christmas Day (see Where We Sit, page 204). The habit of regular, informal meals with family and friends is enough to show that you have the time and space and inclination to do so. Television, which showed our doctor's cleaner *how* to entertain, has driven a middle-class flight from dinner-party territory, and a settling on the more exclusive *supper*. As Grayson Perry notes, 'The word supper, I think, implies a subtle rebuke to the aspirational classes who are gauche enough to hold dinner parties at home.'[22]

Supper: a subtle rebuke to the aspirational classes

There is no such thing as a 'country supper' in culinary or sociological terms. What there is, is 'supper', the meal that posh(ish) people eat at home most days in the evening... You can invite someone to 'supper' and know they will not expect tablecloths or candles or more than perhaps half a dozen guests... I know all this, of course, because I am reasonably posh myself – and if there really was such a thing as a 'country supper', I would expect to have been invited to one.

Hugh Fearnley-Whittingstall, *Guardian* (3 August 2012)

YOUR SUPPER, IF you have it, might be a mug of Ovaltine and a biscuit with the kids in the sitting room after homework or with evening telly; or a roast chicken from the Aga, some home-made bread with oozing, unpasteurized cheese and a bottle of Mersault, with friends at the kitchen table or around the fireside. It is simple enough etymologically, from the French *souper*, to sup. The word doesn't change much, though it becomes 'sups' if you are tweedy and a little old-fashioned, or 'kitchen supper' if you are graciously admitting somebody into your inner circle, often for reasons of politics or influence (see Where We Sit, page 204). The coinage which most delighted commentators when it emerged at the Leveson Inquiry into press ethics, in 2012, was from the News International CEO Rebekah Brooks. Trying to ameliorate an unsupportive article in *The Times*, she texted to David Cameron, then Leader of the Opposition, 'Let's discuss over country supper soon.' Of course, people were appalled by the implications of the man who was now Prime Minister being in hock to the press, etc., etc. But what every writer really wanted to get their hooks into was the term 'country supper', invented by this uppity journalist from a comprehensive in Warrington to schmooze a leading Eton-educated politician.

Early 'ordinances' for running the Duke of Clarence's household in 1469 show dinner at 10 a.m. and supper at 5 p.m.; moving to 9 a.m. and 4 p.m. in the winter to make the most of the daylight hours. Cardinal Wolsey, likewise, has the 'first dynner in eating dayes to begin at tenn of the clock or somewhat afore; and the first supper at foure of the clock on worke days'.[1] One suspects that, like the rest of the 1526 Eltham Ordinances from which this comes, it was partly wishful thinking, to try to bring some old-fashioned discipline to Henry VIII's court. Because dinner and supper were, by then, showing a marked tendency to slouch backwards in the day. Shakespeare is a helpful guide to chronometry; in *As You Like It* Orlando must attend the Duke at dinner, but promises Rosalind to be with her by 2 p.m. An early Shakespearean supper is 5 p.m., a late one is 9 p.m.; most usual might be 'About the sixth hour; when beasts most graze, birds best peck, and men sit down to that nourishment which is called supper'.[2] Christ's last Passover meal with his disciples becomes known in English (although not in the first English Bible) as the Last Supper: the meal before night, real or metaphorical, closes in.

Raucous or debauched late-night carousing happened at an even later 'rere-supper', frowned upon by people such as Wolsey who were trying to keep boisterous young gentlemen in order. The term becomes obsolete as suppers grew later, but the unbuttoned image does not. Late suppers were candlelit by necessity, always a lighter meal, fuelled by stronger drink but unweighted by heavy food, closer to bedtime and leading, for those with the luck or inclination, to sexy assignations. The lovers Antony and Cleopatra enjoy suppers together. Henry V and Falstaff are forever roistering at supper and drinking too much sack and, in Falstaff's case (Shakespeare carefully keeps the royal Henry out of this), cavorting with the prostitute Doll Tearsheet. Supper and entertainment of a more formal kind went together in public. Theseus, the well-ordered Duke of Athens in *A Midsummer Night's Dream*, calls for a masque, a dance, a play or some revels – anything to liven the three dull hours after supper and before bedtime.

Compared with the lionized British beefy dinner, supper was always a lighter and more sophisticated meal. The anonymous author of the satirical *Court and Kitchen of Elizabeth, Commonly called Joan Cromwel* (1664) took every opportunity to jeer about the lack of housekeeping refinement by the 'wife of the Late Usurper': 'Suppers likewise they had none' but boiled 'eight stone of beef' every morning.

This pattern of eating a great deal at dinner – by Restoration times about midday or 1 p.m. and getting later all the time – and being more moderate at supper was remarked on by the French visitor Henri Misson. 'Gluttons at Noon, and abstinent at Night', he said of the English in 1719.[3] Jane Austen nods to this idea at the supper party of Mr Woodhouse in *Emma* (1815), in whom she creates one of literature's most amusingly finickety characters. He offers a 'delicate fricassee of sweetbread' with asparagus for supper but decides that it is undercooked and sends it back to the kitchen, leaving his genteel but impoverished guest disappointed.[4]

It is a nice illustration, though, of what supper might consist of, and where it might be taken. Mr Woodhouse has a supper table that is drawn near the fire in the drawing room. The formality of the dining room is put aside and supper dishes were laid on small tables around the drawing room, adding to the informality and dispensing with the need for servants. The menu could be anything you fancied, or anything you had left from the day. Austen writes to her sister about a supper of tart and jelly which she had enjoyed with her friend Mrs Knight, in her dressing room. A few dishes might be sent up from the kitchen on a tray, rather than laid on a table, like the rather eccentric collection of widgeon, preserved ginger and black butter (a sort of apple jam) that the Austens gave to friends. Men, other than Mr Woodhouse, might have rather different ideas as to what constitutes the right kind of 'delicate little dish' for supper.

The Georgian politician and diarist Thomas Creevey marks up a host for his satisfying dinners and, in addition, a barrel of oysters and a hot pheasant 'wheeled into the drawing-room every night at ½ past ten'.[5] Where there were the pleasures of the town, the theatre or concert hall to occupy people, supper would be a smart meal taken to wring the last pleasure out of the day's entertainment, at a ball that might be at midnight or as late as 2 or 3 o'clock in the morning. A ball supper was a splendid thing to revive the guests after hours of dancing, flirting, cards and gossip. Set in a separate room, it refreshed and delighted the eye with crystal, coloured glass and silver glittering in candlelight. The food had to dazzle: whole salmon swimming in glistening aspic jelly, glazed raised pies, lobster salads, almond cheesecakes, fruit tarts, decorative baskets of dried fruits and nuts, coloured jellies and ices turned out into elegant shapes; cakes baked in fancy moulds and attractively iced, piped biscuits to be had with sweet wine; and, always, a towering mound of hothouse fruit. The only hot food would be a light soup. To fortify them for their cold night (or dawn) journey home, guests were served hot port and lemon, a concoction called negus. Late hours separated the idle rich from those who had to get up the following morning to work. The servants, of course, also had to tidy up and wash up before the morning.

Jane Austen never referred to herself as a working writer, but she might have welcomed supper as a meal which enabled her to get the business of the day done, as it did for the class of writers and intellectuals, or those who might work in the professions, such as law. Her contemporary, Lord Cockburn, a writer and judge, wrote a charming paean to the suppers he enjoyed in Edinburgh, even as he saw it going out of fashion around him:

'Early dinners,' says Lord Cockburn, 'begat suppers. But suppers are so delightful that they have survived long after dinners have become late... Almost all my set, which is perhaps the merriest, the most intellectual, and not the most severely abstemious in Edinburgh, are addicted to it... Supper is cheaper than dinner; shorter; less ceremonious; and more poetical... If there be any fun or heart or spirit in a man at all, it is then, if ever, that it will appear.'[6]

Cockburn's compatriot, the author of *The Cook and Housewife's Manual* (1826; see Carving, page 84), also held a warm regard for the 'light, shewy, exhilarating repast' which was supper.[7] The word is still a useful one for Scots and northerners who might have dinner in the middle of the day, but don't consider their evening meal to be 'tea', and the rest of the world has happily adopted the Burns Night Supper, rather than Dinner.

As Lord Cockburn noticed, the custom of supper was beginning to disappear. The early and mid-Georgian period was the golden age of supper. Even within the short lifetime of Jane Austen it was going out of fashion; her valetudinarian Mr Woodhouse in *Emma* 'loved to have the cloth laid, because it had been the fashion of his youth', although he hated to see any food upon it lest it made his guests unwell.[8] Thomas De Quincey, in an essay called 'Dinner, Real and Reputed', has a note of exasperation at what seemed to him to be an arbitrary change of name.[9] He complained that the meals taken in 1700 at 2 p.m. and 7 p.m. were called dinner and supper; whereas in the year he was writing, 1839, meals eaten at the same times were now called luncheon and dinner. He was right to a degree, but supper wasn't just undergoing a change of name at the beginning of the Victorian age, when he was writing; it was disappearing.

The time for dinner was moving later and later due to the exigencies of business and commerce and the ongoing requirement of every class to distinguish itself from whoever was below it by eating later (see The Dinner Party, page 66). It particularly suited Victorian morality to focus on the formality and etiquette of the dinner party, rather than give way to the informality of a late-night supper. Mrs Rundell, writing in the early 1800s for a reader who must always have an eye on economy, is already regretting the disappearance of supper, because it could be an elegant but *inexpensive* meal: 'An elegant supper may be served at a small expence by those who know how to make trifles that are in the house form the greatest part of the meal.'[10] Her later colleagues, Mrs Beeton, Alexis Soyer and a contributor to *Cassell's Dictionary of Cookery*, similarly dismissed the 'hot supper' as a thing of the past for a cosy, intimate gathering, although the calories might be supplied by a sandwich, the warmth by negus.[11]

Where it couldn't be so lightly dismissed was among the working and non-working poor for whom the rest of the day's meals were never so heavy or nutritious or filling as to render supper expendable. Hot, soothing mush before bed was the thing for exhausted workers. William Ellis recommends to his agricultural neighbours in mid-eighteenth-century Hertfordshire a posset made from hot milk, hot ale, sugar and bread; for families with a little more income it could be thickened with egg yolks or made richer with cream and nutmeg.[12] Or, Ellis suggests, they should have a 'wig', a small yeasted bun made with caraway seeds, which fitted into hungry corners of the day; Pepys has one with ale for a Lenten supper in the previous century. Dr William Kitchiner admired the ability of 'those patterns of industry, frugality, and temperance, the Scottish peasantry' to get by for supper (and breakfast) with a bowl of hot oatmeal porridge.[13]

The great meal of the agricultural working year, of course, was the Harvest Supper. Deliberately called 'supper' rather than dinner to show that it stood apart from the rest of the year's working meals, it pulled together a mixture of traditions; the name – supper – was borrowed from a wealthier class, and it was presided over by a 'Lord' and 'Lady': the foreman and his second in command. The food was provided by the farmer or landowner and there was no attempt to pretend it was anything but 'dinner': joints of roast beef and hams with vegetables, plum pudding and home-brewed beer. The riotousness and sense of celebration, with songs, merry-making and a lot of drinking, belonged to the supper and the time of day, by which time the wives and children might have been asked by the farmer's wife to come to the 'best parlour' for Harvest Cake, tea and lemonade.[14]

For the working poor, supper usually didn't vary much from other meals. Mayhew's Londoners might have just a sandwich but many would try to have something more interesting, certainly hotter: a meat pudding, or a 'trotter' for supper for the 'men and women, and most especially boys' who, having no cooking facilities of their own, have to buy their meals in the streets day after day.[15] George Orwell, describing the disgusting food that his landlords, the Brookers, gave him in *The Road to Wigan Pier*, is impatient with their attempts to gentrify it: 'For supper there was the pale flabby Lancashire cheese and biscuits. The Brookers never called these biscuits biscuits. They always referred to them reverently as "cream crackers".'[16]

Supper was important, too, for domestic servants who ate their main dinner early, while the family were engaged on the day's business. The servants cooked, served and washed up the family's dinner and had an exhausted meal of bread and cold meat or toasted cheese, perhaps while the family were eating their servant-free dessert or were entertaining one another in the drawing room. When the early twentieth century brought in early closing laws, supper returned to the private house. The restaurant critic Lieutenant Colonel Nathaniel Newnham-Davis regretted that these early closing laws killed the old-fashioned British supper of marrow bones and Welsh rarebits, buck rarebits and stewed tripe and onions in eating-houses. The same laws might also be said to have half-killed the servants or housewives who had to produce every supper at home.[17]

Agnes Jekyll at least thought about the servants when she suggested menus to be eaten after a play: 'a cold Soufflé of Lobster, prepared and served up just before the cook goes to bed'.[18] Presumably the dirty dishes would be awaiting the maid or the cook whenever she got up the next morning. Jekyll's trick was to write about food with all the freshness and modern sensibility of the 1920s which rejected the formality of the pre-war years, and yet assume that her readers had Edwardian levels of domestic comfort. This wasn't the case for everybody, as magazines for the middle or lower-middle classes of the time recognized, while still addressing themselves to aspirational matters of etiquette and entertaining. The weekly etiquette column in *Woman's Life* admitted in 1926 that 'Elaborate entertaining's always difficult for the servantless woman. That's why many people have given up asking people to dinner, and are having supper parties instead'.[19] The menu that the author suggests, despite its Frenchisms, was reasonably simple, providing one had a good grocer. *Poisson en Coquilles* turns out to be cold fish with pickle and mayonnaise in a scallop shell; *Gâteau de Marrons* is little more than chestnut purée.

The middle classes struggled with the formality of dinner parties in the servant-free and increasingly hard-working twentieth century, particularly women who were expected to produce the food, whether they also went out to work or not. Every generation seemed to discover the supper alternative for themselves. Dinner and supper took turns to ebb and flow. Just as supper emerged in the 1920s as a rejection of the formality of the pre-war years, so it did in the 1960s as increasing numbers of young, university-educated professionals felt that it was 'the old people who had dinner', as one Sussex teacher told Mass Observation: 'We used to be invited out to supper – anytime between 8 and 11 p.m.'[20]

The Establishment discovered the 'kitchen supper', a slightly twee term but a useful way of implying a big kitchen, a sizeable circle of family and friends and the sort of lifestyle in which the two frequently come together. Politicians discovered the art of bringing together disparate but useful people in the kitchen supper in the 1960s. The hostess Judith Listowel remarked on a Cabinet Minister who himself served superbly cooked food to his guests, who included 'a racing driver, a skating champion, a writer, a gaggle of MPs' in 'admittedly quite a kitchen, but nevertheless it is a kitchen'.[21] And 'kitchen cabinet' has come to mean the informal circle of supporters and advisors to the Prime Minister.

Dinner parties have again given way to supper, for those with wealth and kitchen space enough. 'Supper' implies not just the food, but the gathering of people round the table to eat it. An exhausted shift-worker or a group of twentysomethings with the munchies after an evening in the pub, eating late-night pizza in front of the telly, are seen to be 'snacking' rather than having 'supper'. A 2014–15 time use survey shows working-class people eat later at night (and less at breakfast), but their meals are more likely to be solitary.[22]

Supposedly informal, but in fact highly engineered, contemporary 'supper clubs' enable the rest of us to emulate an upper-class meal for a cost much smaller than having a mansion in Notting Hill and a house in the country. The supper club formula of fine food and entertainment is closer in form to medieval and Tudor suppers, with a film, a stage-set venue or jazz taking the place of minstrels or a masque. The Georgian heyday of the informal suppers of the ruling classes lives again in what Rebekah Brooks – but no one else – called the 'country supper'. For commentators, most of whom came from the supper-eating classes themselves, her coinage is the culinary equivalent of Eliza Doolittle saying 'not bloody likely'. Even the most innocuous of adjectives over the supper table, in English, can betray someone trying to pass herself off in a class she wasn't born into.

PART TWO

◆

Brit...ish

Carving: the whole hog

The *art of carving* is one of the most necessary accomplishments of a gentleman.

William Kitchiner, *The Cook's Oracle* (1822)

As I GREW up, like most people in my generation and before, my mother would cook the meat-and-two-veg Sunday lunch. She stuffed the chicken or the Christmas turkey, put rosemary and garlic under the skin of a joint of lamb, or rubbed olive oil into a rib of beef – she encountered the flesh and the bones with her hands; a doctor, she knew how bodies were put together. It was left to my father, though, who had never cooked a thing in his life, to work around the 3D trickery of meat, bones and joints and carve the thing. Fortunately for him, his clientele was hungry and non-judgemental and not, then, prone to quoting Mrs Beeton ironically: 'we can hardly imagine an object of greater envy than is presented by a respected portly paterfamilias carving, at the season devoted to good cheer and genial charity, his own fat turkey, and carving it well'.[1] We three daughters and a son didn't think there was anything odd about this division of labour, until we encountered feminism and it made us ask what now seems obvious. Why?

Carving is the action which most embodies the relationship between class and food because (ignoring, for now, Halloween pumpkins and ice sculptures) carving meant meat. Meat was the first and foremost indicator of social status on British tables since Norman times, or earlier (see French Food, page 166). Meat itself was also codified into a hierarchy. With some variations over time, it ran like this: venison, beef, mutton/lamb, chicken, pork, with other birds and different cuts and cures, particularly of pork, being slotted into the scheme. Kudos to he who provided this bounty. Yes, *he*. Because no matter how much a woman was involved in the rearing, buying or cooking, we shared the same story: here was meat on the table because of the status and potency of the male in the household. There was more than a whiff of biblical ordination about it; every churchgoer, even if illiterate, knew that God had made man master of 'the fish of the sea, and over the fowl of the air, and over the cattle, and over all the earth, and over every creeping thing that creepeth upon the earth'.[2] Wielding the carving knife gave him mastery, too, over how this luscious, rare protein might be allocated.

The carver's role encompassed social obligation, an assertion of potency, a means of distributing largesse, of showing favouritism. These were responsibilities that only those at the top of society were broad-shouldered and civilized enough to merit; carving became, simultaneously, the mark of a *man* and a *gentle*man.

The medieval lord would cut up a freshly killed deer at the end of the hunt, distributing different portions, umbles (guts), shoulder, flank, according to rank and right. His table would be laden with animal protein: large cuts of mutton and venison; whole birds; geese, mallard, crane, hare, cony; and fish – pike, tench, sturgeon, even porpoise – would be seethed or roasted and served whole. Swans and peacocks might be skinned and roasted; and then their skin and feathers put back on so that there was no question about what his guests were being served. Fifteenth-century Italian writers insisted that carving was only worthy of a well-dressed, good-looking gentleman of noble birth, and recommended 'Carving in the air' to impress diners: picking up a whole turkey and carving it in mid-air while slices of meat fell onto the plate below.[3]

Carving was done at table and here it was the duty, not of the top dog, but of the young pups who joined his family, often in their early or mid-teens. Every landed household had to be a finishing school for the gentlemanly arts of hunting, etiquette and the political nous needed to survive court intrigue. An early book of anonymously authored instructions, *The Boke of Kervynge* (1508), for those young men in 'service of a prynce or any other estate', explains how to serve, to butle, to be a pantler (in charge of the bread and the pantry). Each animal to be carved had a particular term associated with it, showing what a serious enterprise it was, particularly as it had to be accomplished without the aid of a fork – not introduced until the seventeenth century (see Forks, page 236). This list was picked up and repeated throughout books of cookery and etiquette for the next 200 years, long after peacock and crane had left the table and it was redundant:

Breke that dere
leach that brawne
rere that goose
lyft that swanne
sauce that capon
spoyle that henne
fruche that chekyn
unbrace that malarde
unlace that cony
dysmembre that heron
dysplaye that crane
dysfygure that pecocke[4]

This focus on carving as an *art* suggested that there was something natural about the idea that the crane or cony would only be found on the table of somebody with the leisure and education to practise it. Even if the purse of the working man could ever stretch to a capon or a duck, he wouldn't have the carving skills that a whole beast merited. The aristocratic obsession with the art of carving helped emphasize the idea that meat, particularly as whole birds or substantial joints, did not properly belong on the table of the poor.

Fish, too, had their own terms, which might sound rather Pythonesque to us: splatte that pyke, splaye that breme; sauce that tenche; traunche that sturgyon; undertraunche y purpos. The latter, a meaty mammalian fish, was a favourite way of dodging the restrictions on meat on fast days (see Almond Milk, page 306). Lest his lordship or majesty and guests got bored with the same old zoo, his cooks started to invent new ones. Richard II's cooks suggested sewing the front of a cockerel onto the back of a piglet, before roasting it on a spit and gilding it with gold and silver, to form a glittering cockatrice – a cock-a-pig – and they described how to make a family of hedgehogs from stuffed pigs' stomachs, stuck with pastry quills. Such fabrications might have been a poser for the carver, but sadly, if they came with their own carving terms, they have been lost to history.[5]

Across the Channel, French hosts began to direct their chefs' ingenuity not to creating new animals, but to hiding the corporeal evidence of the existing ones in fricassees and ragouts; the carving was done in the kitchen by the chef and it was seen as a more 'delicate' way of serving food. The English fashion was to serve meat in as identifiable a form as possible (see The Roast Beef of Old England, page 92). Carving was still seen as an essential mark of the gentleman, even in the great Whig houses which were bastions of French sophistication. The Whig Earl of Chesterfield, whose chef was the famous Vincent la Chapelle, author of *The Modern Cook* (1733), advised his illegitimate son on the fine art of becoming a gentleman of influence: 'We should use ourselves to carve adroitly and genteelly, without hacking half an hour across a bone, without bespattering the company with the sauce, and without overturning the glasses into your neighbour's pockets.'[6] You did not want to gain yourself a reputation as, in the words of Dr Kitchiner, a 'chop-house cormorant' who mangled the joint in order to give himself the daintiest morsel.[7]

Cookery books offered the culinary secrets from the male (often French) chefs in the kitchens of great houses, or pragmatic advice from a man (even one with no experience of running a household).

The housewife expected to be instructed in writing by a man, until the eighteenth century when middle-class female cooks and housekeepers began writing for the growing market of women of a similar background. Initially, there was no question that the female cook must wrestle with roasting whole animals and serve them up in prescribed ways. As Hannah Glasse wrote in 1747, 'Some love a Pig brought whole to Table.'[8] She probably means a suckling pig (a piglet), but spit-roasting anything in front of a fire presented its own challenges, particularly judging whether the meat is safely cooked through; it was known that uncooked pork was unwholesome. The best advice she can offer is that it is done 'when the Eyes drop out, and the Skin is grown very hard'.[9] Elizabeth Raffald's directions for serving boiled rabbits confront diners with their vulnerable little bodies, a memento mori for the table: 'pull out the jaw bones, stick them in their eyes, put a sprig of myrtle or barberries in their mouths, and serve them up'.[10] It is reminiscent of the whole boar's head: boiled, de-boned, roasted in its original shape, with a pippin in its open jaws to allow the heat to penetrate the whole. It was the job of the carver to neatly dispose of every part which might be considered a favourite by a guest. Mrs Rundell directs the cook who is roasting a hare, 'The ears must be nicely cleaned and singed. They are reckoned a dainty.'[11]

Women started to wield the knife in the dining room: nothing too taxing, just some of the lighter meats and the fish. Mr Knightley tells Jane Austen's matchmaking Emma, 'Invite him to dinner, Emma, and help him to the best of the fish and the chicken, but leave him to chuse his own wife.'[12] The lady who was to carve must have an elevated seat, a light sharp knife, and the dish in easy reach. The pragmatic Eliza Acton suggested that the cook removes the main bones, to make carving at table easier.[13] The host or the nearest gentleman to a lady would carve the stronger meats for her. Jane Austen was amused at a dinner to see that a gentleman, whom her sister Cassandra supposed was courting a lady of their acquaintance, was in fact sadly inattentive to her. She had to ask 'him to give her mutton twice without being attended to for some time'.[14]

Austen famously never shows us the action in the kitchen in her novels, maintaining the fiction that well-born women didn't descend to the level of pots and steam. Sir Walter Scott, by contrast, had no such middle-class squeamishness about the kitchen. His most celebrated literary cook came to be 'Margaret Dods', the fictional landlady of the Cleikum Inn in his novel *St Ronan's Well* (1823). When the Scottish writer Christian Isobel Johnstone came to publish her excellent cookbook *The Cook and Housewife's Manual* in 1829, she adopted Margaret, or Meg, Dods as her pseudonym. It allowed Meg Dods to take advantage of her fictional existence to move between kitchen and dining room, busily commenting on practicality and etiquette in both. Although she gives detailed instructions for carving the product of aristocratic sport, delicate game birds and mammals, perhaps for the first time in British eating, she demurs at the vision of the farmyard pig being elevated in the same way. 'We could wish that the practice of having this dish carved by the cook were universal; for, in this fastidious age, the sanguinary spectacle of an entire four-footed animal at table is anything but acceptable.'[15] The 'fastidious age' was being driven not by an innate civilizing of British attitudes to animals, but because of the change in European dining etiquette that spread from Paris from 1814. Jane Austen and Lord Chesterfield's world of dining *à la française*, in which whole dishes were placed on the table, was giving way to the gentility of dining *à la russe* (see Small Plates, page 223). As Meg Dods explains, 'We hope to see the day when all large troublesome dishes will be taken to the side-table, and carved by the *maitre d'hotel*, or whoever waits on the company, as is now the general practice of France, Germany, and Russia.'[16] One of the reasons for the great success of dining *à la russe* was that it reduced male performance anxiety over the dinner table and, in time, put an end to the idea that carving was the prerequisite of a gentleman.

Carving a whole beast is still done in the privacy of the domestic home. But for great public events, for practical as well as theatrical reasons, its arena is now outdoors. Crowds have always loved the drama and machismo of roasting a whole animal; roasted and carved in front of the masses, rather than to the select few in a dining room, it is a sign not of gentlemanliness but rugged individuality. During the Little Ice Age thought to have been between 1300 and 1870, on the few occasions that the ice was thick enough for a Frost Fair, entrepreneurs daringly roasted a whole ox on the frozen Thames.[17] Unlike in the well-appointed dining room, the cook and the carver in the public space are embodied in the same person and the pitfalls are not minor social embarrassments, but major opposition by snowstorms or, worse, melting the ice beneath.

Nothing demonstrated liberality more than the gift of a whole roast ox to the poor and it became a showy form of charity to celebrate a coronation or a jubilee. At the coronation of King George IV, a bill (in the collection of today's foremost food historian, Ivan Day), announces that a fat ox and four sheep will be roasted in the meadows outside Windsor to be 'distributed to the Poor and Industrious Classes'.[18] For the annual dinner of the Royal Agricultural Society at Exeter in 1850, Alexis Soyer roasted a whole ox by gas for a thousand guests; the leftovers made a dinner for 700 of the town's poor the following day.[19] Carving the whole beast was now done by the butcher; the job allocated by professional competence, rather than aristocratic entitlement.

Anne Walbank Buckland, one of the first female members of the Anthropological Institute, set out to assess late Victorian dining customs as part of a global framework, albeit one largely constructed by colonial ideas of civilization. She thought that roasting a whole ox was a 'barbarous mode of rejoicing', thankfully almost obsolete in 'these days of refinement' (she was writing in 1893). Better that people cooked their own joints in their own way 'instead of each slicing a half-cooked morsel from a burning carcase'.[20] She was nearly right, but ox roasts still exist for charity, such as in Houghton-le-Spring in County Durham, which in the twentieth century resurrected the practice from Bernard Gilpin (1517–83) who had an ox roast for his parishioners every Christmas (or Michaelmas), although with a somewhat updated idea of charitable giving, whereby the roast-ox sandwiches are sold and the money given to charity.

Cooking a pig in a fire pit was originally a Hawaiian technique which has been adopted by the American South as the ultimate in backyard barbecue hospitality. The methodology of cooking a whole animal in 'the fire pit' is intended to evoke a primordial human bond, a ritualistic sense of hospitality; but 'the pit-master' is a product, like our butcher at the ox roast, of the bourgeois economy of specialization and professionalism. The fire pit doesn't have British roots, but it is being adopted here, too. Like a barbecue, it unites people with food and fire, but it has a new kind of post-scandal prestige. If you give your guests great slices of fire-roasted pig, instead of barbecued burgers and sausages, you are promising them something noble and honest, proof against slime, horsemeat and other, euphemistically termed 'non-approved cuts' that scandalize consumers every time there's a news story about something grisly in their processed meat.

For every generation that seeks to shake off 'barbarous' or 'troublesome' ideas of serving whole animals, parts of the next generation reinstate it. We will, it seems, always be prone to the promise of social status that a whole roast animal or a substantial joint confers on the provider and the carver. It is difficult to imagine a contemporary version of Mrs Beeton's portly paterfamilias believing that flipping burgers or handing out sausages will earn him the same respect as carving a turkey. Processed and standardized meat is rather boringly egalitarian: the barbecuer can't offer anything better, only more, whereas the carver can find the best portion for the most favoured guest, the bountiful slices of roast meat and is larded with centuries-old notions of control, favour and munificence.

If you choose to roast a whole pig, the fat will melt into the meat, giving – all going well – beautiful, sweet and savoury meat which you can pull apart with two forks, or even eat with a spoon. However, in spite of the amount of pork, ham and bacon eaten in this country, the pig isn't the meat that we feel defines us. For that, we must look to roast beef.

The Roast Beef of Old England

On thousands of tables at Christmas-tide the roast beef of Old England smokes with appetising odour. From the lordly baron which always graces the Queen's table, and the goodly sirloin of aristocratic renown, to the humble but far from despicable aitch-bone, all is toothsome, wholesome, and highly esteemed alike by high and low, rich and poor.

Anne Walbank Buckland, *Our Viands* (1893)

AFTER A VEGETARIAN Christmas one year, I turned up at the home of my omnivorous cousins for Boxing Day. I must have looked wan and cadaverous in a nut-roasty sort of way because my aunt gave me a subversive look and said, confidentially, 'I'll make you a nice roast beef sandwich.' I've never forgotten the pleasure of that sandwich; how the teeth sank through the pillowy bread and met just the right amount of resistance from the mellow beef, the liveliness of the horseradish; the peculiar satisfaction of eating something so mightily and meatily politically incorrect. Eating beef locates you in a world of tradition, pride and defiant Englishness, which shares no common culture with nut-roast or spinach smoothies. It is the furthest you can go on the culinary spectrum to express English strength; beyond is iron girders. Even before roast beef's meteoric rise in the later seventeenth century, Shakespeare was appealing to the patriotic audience of *Henry V* by showing English soldiers as eaters of 'beef and iron and steel'.[1]

Before the eighteenth century, however, beef was an acolyte of the cult of venison and other game. Pepys harrumphed that a supposed venison pasty 'was palpable beef, which was not handsome' for the gentleman he aspired to be (see The Venison Pasty, page 260).[2] Beef was the thing for the likes of farmers and freeholders; the Yeomen Warders of the Tower of London were fed on pounds of it, first earning their name of 'Beef-eaters' under the Stuarts. Fynes Moryson, who travelled widely in the final decade of the 1600s, was struck by his own nation's obsession with deer parks, although he noticed that, being a 'prodigal' drain on the resources of some aristocrats, some were being turned over to cattle pasturage, to boost incomes with dairy and beef which, unlike venison, could be sold on the open market.[3]

Cows were prized for milk and cream; most adult male cattle were castrated to become oxen. Making money from beef had two hurdles: the animals were small and tough and, like all livestock, vulnerable to winter famine, when the only spare feed was sparse pasture and hay. Most beasts had to be slaughtered in the hope that stock levels could be maintained by breeding in the spring. The grain was needed to keep death from the human door. There were stories of husbandmen carrying emaciated cattle to their spring pastures. Grass nourished and fattened them throughout the year until the traditional slaughter day on 11 November, St Martin's Day.

Some Martinmas beef was cured to preserve it over the winter with sweet spices to complement and counteract the saltiness: cloves, mace, cinnamon and nutmeg plus the indefatigable black pepper and, if it was growing wild nearby, juniper. This was the basis for the eighteenth-century favourites beef *à la mode* or beef carbonadoed. In 1806, John Simpson, the cook to the Marquess of Buckingham, was calling it *Boeuf de Chasse* (hunting beef). The spices and the association with the traditional Boxing Day meet made it, as he said, 'more a Christmas dish than any other time of the year', at least for the hunting classes.[4] It was the spiced forerunner of what we know now as salt beef, imagining that it was bequeathed to us from New York delis. But if we are planting the Union Jack on the terrain, we must also acknowledge that its more disreputable relative, corned beef, is descended from the same family.

The problem of seasonality was cracked, broadly, by Charles, Second Viscount Townsend (1674–1738), who, noticing on his Continental travels that there were better strains of clover, grasses and turnips, developed these in rotation on his Norfolk farms and, for the first time on these islands, produced enough winter fodder for all his livestock, famously earning himself the name 'Turnip Townsend'.

Until the seventeenth century, when the principles of selective breeding began to be applied to cattle, animals were something between a quarter and a half of the current bull weight. One family on the Sussex weald, attempting to breed cattle in the sixteenth century, got their oxen to a mere 512lb (232kg).[5] By contrast, a modern-day Aberdeen Angus can weigh around 1,800lb (816kg). The average weight of cattle and sheep sold at Smithfield Market doubled between 1710 and 1795[6] and farmers and landowners began to take breeding seriously. There was a concerted push by landowners to make their acres more productive, grounded in arguments such as the one made by Edinburgh philosopher Adam Smith, that it was a patriotic duty to grow the economy. The Highland Clearances pushed people off the land in favour, principally, of sheep, but also cattle; breeds such as the Highland, Shorthorn, Belted Galloway and iconic Aberdeen Angus were beefed up throughout the eighteenth and nineteenth centuries and their meat became a matter of Scottish pride, as it still is. 'Scotch beef', farmed only in Scotland with high levels of animal welfare, was the first red meat to be granted the EU's status of Protected Geographical Indication (PGI).[7]

Pride in British beef grew in proportion to mistrust of all things French. French food within British society was a flag of the great Whig houses that prided themselves on grand entertaining and their French chefs. Joseph Addison, the political essayist who co-founded The Spectator, complained of being at a dinner where he was served something that looked like a roast porcupine (it was a larded turkey). He professed himself baffled by the hashes, dainties and delicacies he was offered and was disgusted to see that the 'noble Sirloin' was banished to a side table to make way for 'French kickshaws'.[8] However, his own Whiggish sympathies and his sardonic style (writing with the non de plume Isaac Bickerstaffe) suggest he had yeomanry belligerence in his sights as much as aristocratic Francophilia.

Henry Fielding, however, dives straight into culinary politics in *The Grub-Street Opera* (1731). The Whig Prime Minister Sir Robert Walpole is 'Robin' the butler (because he was 'robbing' the electorate). The honest English cook Susan, on being told not to waste good food on guests of no importance by her employer (a disguised Queen Caroline, George II's wife), breaks into song:

> When mighty Roast Beef was the Englishman's food
> It ennobled our hearts, and enriched our blood,
> Our soldiers were brave,
> Our courtiers were good
> Oh the Roast Beef of England
> And old England's Roast Beef!
>
> But since we have learnt from all-conquering France
> To eat their ragouts as well as to dance,
> Oh what a fine figure we make in romance!
> Oh the Roast Beef of England
> And old England's Roast Beef!
>
> Then, Britons, from all nice dainties refrain,
> Which effeminate Italy, France, and Spain,
> And mighty Roast Beef shall command on the main
> Oh the Roast Beef of England
> And old England's Roast Beef!

For the stolid classes of yeomen and artisans, superior in every way to the scrawny and devious French, what could be a more perfect image than the bull (and even its chief tormentor, the bulldogs used for bull-baiting) and the frog? Hogarth incorporated images of English beef and beer, against French vegetable soup – *soup maigre* – and frogs, in his propaganda pictures, such as *The Gate of Calais* and *The Invasion*. A century later, Thackeray, enjoying a sojourn in Paris and describing his many excellent restaurant meals, still saw it as his patriotic duty to celebrate the beef-eating Englishmen over the weedy French: 'Fancy a hundred thousand Englishmen, after a meal of stalwart beef ribs, encountering a hundred thousand Frenchmen, who have partaken of a trifling collation of soup, turnips, carrots, onions, and Gruyere cheese. Would it be manly to engage at such odds? I say, no.'[9]

Travellers to England had often commented on the amount of meat that was eaten there. Travellers to France, in return, commented often on the absolute misery of the French peasant – whose hunger was far worse than their English counterparts at the time and drove them to revolution. John Bull became the image of the honest, if sometimes queasily overweight and oafish, Brit in cartoons by Hogarth, Rowlandson and Gillray. For the masses, beef, and not revolution, was the thing to aspire to.

The French view of English beef wasn't vastly different. English travellers in France had earned themselves the name *les rosbifs* since the 1730s. Henri Misson, the French traveller in England in the early years of that century, noted that only the aristocrats with French chefs ate well; the 'middling Sort of People' had a dish of meat – likely to be roast beef – and a pudding. He was favourably struck by the disregard for social rank in the English cookshops, where there were spits bearing butcher's meat (beef, mutton, veal, pork and lamb) and a gentleman of wealth could go and dine handsomely on whatever meat he chose, a little mustard, a roll and a bottle of beer. 'A Frenchman of any Distinction would think it a great Scandal, in France, to be seen to eat in such a place; and indeed Custom will not allow it there; but in England they laugh at such Niceties.'[10]

Eliza Acton could still write, in 1845, 'The *Christmas beef* of England is too much celebrated to require any mention here', although in fact it was being edged out by the turkey for the middle-class Christmas.[11] English cooks never won prizes for their innovation, but it was grudgingly accepted that they could roast meat well. The kitchen fireplace with its range of spits, turned by half-naked boys in great Tudor houses, sometimes by dogs in little wheels in the eighteenth century, until clockwork jacks replaced both, was an ideal way to cook it. Britain's woods and mines gave fuel for fires to burn twenty-four hours a day; and the meat that rotated slowly in front of the fire – cooking, resting, cooking, resting – would turn out as soft as a cheek; it needed nothing more than mustard or horseradish and a good appetite. English cooks lost this edge when the range and then the oven began to take the place of the open fire in kitchens. If you eat beef roasted before a fire, you will realize that your oven-roasted meat has been half-baked, half stewed.

Beef was the pride of the 'middling-sort' and the envy of labourers' families, like the 30 per cent of families surveyed by Dr Edward Smith in 1863 who had never tasted 'butcher's meat'.[12] The Christmas roast beef might be counterfeited by a bullock's heart or half a cow's head.

Northern families fared best; it's no accident that Yorkshire pudding, roast beef's closest ally, comes from that county. It filled up the children and wife in a family while the man had the lion's share of the meat; but a Yorkshire adult, Smith found, ate 24oz (680g) of butcher's meat a week, compared with a mere 7oz (200g) in many southern counties. The families surveyed by Smith would, however, within the next decades have their diets transformed. The price of meat (and bread) halved from the 1870s to the early years of the twentieth century as cheap imported beef (and mutton) came to market in Britain in the refrigerated holds of steamships from Australia, Argentina and the US.[13]

The dinner-giving classes responded by turning the roast beef of old England into something complex, time-consuming and French, preferably with wine. Such is the Bœuf en Daube in Virginia Woolf's *To the Lighthouse* (1927) which takes Mrs Ramsay's cook three days to make to perfection.

But what really punctured British pride in beef as a national dish was the BSE crisis. It is hard to remain bullish on the international culinary stage when your national dish has been found to be so contaminated by a poorly regulated food chain that it could make you fatally ill. BSE, the horribly named 'mad cow disease', was first found in cattle in 1986 and, two years later, scientists discovered that it had been transmitted, with a long incubation period, to humans. The EU banned all exports of British beef between 1996 and 1999; France, as though remembering all those Hogarthian insults, continued the ban for a further three years. Millions of cows had been slaughtered and destroyed with, initially, inadequate compensation to farmers, which made them reluctant to report cases of the disease in their herds. Some 176 people in Britain have died from vCJD, the human form of BSE. Whatever anti-European feeling there might exist in Middle England, it's hard now to imagine English beef being used as an image of superiority.

Roast beef's long tradition of yeoman-class patriotism and anti-intellectualism doesn't sit well with a connected, educated and global world-view. Grain-fed beef has no part in an ecologically balanced future planet, with its spectacularly inefficient conversion of land to calories; twenty-eight times more than pork or chicken, and 160 times more than potatoes, wheat or rice.[14] Or in which thousands of hectares of Amazonian rainforest are being destroyed each year to give way to cattle pasturage, the land-grab of the Highland Clearances writ large. Deforestation, desertification and soil erosion increasingly look like the price of a roast beef sandwich.

The cultural change had already been afoot for decades, however. The Christmas beef was slowly being replaced in the hearts of Middle England by the turkey from the early 1800s, a transfer of affections greatly accelerated when Scrooge's gift to the Cratchit family put the turkey at the centre of the idealized Christmas dinner table. By the mid-twentieth century the Sunday joint had swapped places with poultry in terms of cost.[15] The Sunday joint is an occasional treat for families, but the individualistic steak allows diners out, particularly men, their beef fix while others might choose fish, white meat or veggie. In the decades since, the roast beef of old England has been replaced on our tables by the roast chicken.

SPICED BEEF FOR CHRISTMAS

◆

John Simpson calls his spiced beef *Boeuf de Chasse* as it was served for the traditional Boxing Day meet at Stowe House, the country seat of his employer. It's still a good bet for Boxing Day, whether you are in full hunting pink on horseback or just hunting for the aspirin, as it can be made well in advance and served cold with mustard, horseradish and lots of pickles, or hot with potatoes and greens.

MODERN RECIPE

Grass-fed, high-welfare beef joint – brisket, silverside, topside or flank

Curing salt per kilo of meat:

20g brown sugar
25g sea salt
5g saltpetre
(OR use curing salt as directed by the manufacturer)
10g black peppercorns
5g allspice berries
5g juniper berries

Optional (per kilo of meat):

2 teaspoons freshly grated nutmeg
About 12 blades mace (or 2 teaspoons ground)
1 teaspoon cloves (or the same quantity ground)

Brining time:

Two days per 2.5cm of meat, plus two days.

Plus stock vegetables:

2 small (or 1 large) onions
2–3 carrots, unpeeled and coarsely chopped
Bunch of thyme
A bay leaf

To spice:

1. Put the sugar, salt, saltpetre and whole spices in an electric blender and grind them (or just mix them if you are using ground spices).
2. Rub the beef all over with the curing mixture really thoroughly, getting it into every surface (including the fat) of the beef.
3. Put it in an airtight bag, or in a non-metallic bowl; make sure it is a snug fit and the bowl is well covered with cling film.
4. Keep it in the fridge and turn it every day so that it is well covered by the brine, which will begin to come out.

To cook:

1. Preheat the oven to Gas Mark 1/140°C.
2. Rinse the joint well to get rid of the excess salt and the gritty spices. Put it into a casserole dish, making sure it is a snug fit. Add approximately 280ml of water per kilo of beef, plus the stock vegetables. Cover it with a few layers of greaseproof paper (in the pot) and a tightly fitting lid. Put it in the oven for about 3 hours for a smaller joint (around 1kg) and up to 5 hours for a 2kg joint.
3. It is worth checking the salt level after an hour; if it's too salty, strain off the brine and add fresh water.
4. Let the joint cool in the pot, and skim off the fat as it cools.
5. You can eat it hot straight away or reheat it in the oven wrapped in foil. Serve it hot with mash, greens and mustard. Once cool, dry it and wrap it tightly in greaseproof paper.
6. Or, to have it cold, dry it, wrap it tightly in greaseproof paper and weight it for 24 hours, to help it get that characteristic salt-beef texture. Slice it thinly to add to a sandwich. Pickled vegetables and mustard of any kind are its best friends.

Well wrapped, it will keep for up to a fortnight in the fridge – depending on who's around to eat it.

ORIGINAL RECIPE: SPICED ROUND OF BEEF
(VERY HIGHLY FLAVOURED)

From *Modern Cookery for Private Families* by Eliza Acton (1845)

◆

Rub the beef well in every part with half a pound of coarse brown sugar, and let it remain two days; then reduce to powder, and mix thoroughly before they are applied to the meat, two ounces of saltpetre, three-quarters of a pound of common salt, a quarter of a pound of black pepper, three ounces of allspice, and four of bruised juniper berries. Rub these ingredients strongly and equally over the joint, and do so daily for three weeks, turning it at the same time. Just wash off the spice, and put the beef into a tin, or covered earthen pan as nearly of its size as possible, with a cup of water or gravy; cover the top thickly with chopped beef-suet, and lay a coarse thick crust over the pan; place the cover on it, and bake the meat from five to six hours in a moderate oven, which should not, however, be sufficiently fierce to harden the outside of the joint, which, if properly managed will be exceedingly tender. Let it cool in the pan; and clear off the suet before it is dished. It is to be served cold, and will remain good for a fortnight.

Beef, 20 to 25lbs, weight ◆ sugar, 3oz

2 days.

Saltpetre, 2oz ◆ common salt, ¾lb ◆ black pepper, 4oz ◆
allspice, 3oz ◆ juniper-berries, 4oz

21 days.

Baked 5 to 6 hours.

Roast Chicken:
murder most fowl

When I went in, I saw her in the back-kitchen which opened on to
the courtyard, in process of killing a chicken; by its desperate and
quite natural resistance, which Françoise, beside herself with rage
as she attempted to slit its throat beneath the ear, accompanied
with shrill cries of 'Filthy creature! Filthy creature!' it made the
saintly kindness and unction of our servant rather less prominent
than it would do, next day at dinner, when it made its appearance
in a skin gold-embroidered like a chasuble, and its precious juice
was poured out drop by drop as from a pyx.

Marcel Proust, *Remembrance of Things Past*, Volume I (1913)

O N A SAMPLE of three in our household (two of them feline),
roast chicken is the absolute favourite meal of all time.
They would happily eat it every day; however, since they
came into my life as kittens and I realized that their welfare and
happiness was entirely my responsibility, my attitude towards
eating animals has changed – if I am responsible for the animals on
my lap, should I not also be responsible for the ones on my plate?
I still love to give people roast chicken – my current passion is for
pot-roasting it with lemon, tarragon and vegetables, according to
a late Victorian recipe – but it is an infrequent treat; so when I do
I'll happily pay whatever it costs for a well-fed, organic chicken,
in the hope that it will have had as good a life and death as it is
possible for an animal destined for the pot to have.

My changing attitude is not all my own work. I am part of a larger social change, embracing veganism, vegetarianism and awareness of provenance. But it is also part of a longer historic change in which gourmandism, animal welfare and conviviality have had an uneasy triangular relationship, and humanity – in the shape of care about non-humans – only gets to elbow its way to the top in financially and socially secure societies.

The ancestor of our modern chicken, according to Darwin, was the Red Jungle Fowl, prized first by humans who loved to watch the fierce little birds fight to the death; images of cock-fights, such as those on an eighth-century BC Assyrian cylinder seal, pre-date any evidence that the scrawny birds ended up in the pot.[1] The hens that accompanied the males were eventually bred across the ancient world for their useful supplies, principally of eggs. Chicken meat came to be seen as something luxurious and – particularly the fat, castrated capons – somewhat effeminate. Pliny recalled the sumptuary laws that forbad serving more than a single, uncrammed pullet at a banquet and, as is usual with sumptuary laws, he describes how Roman bon viveurs got around them: instead of *cramming* (force-feeding) their hens, they fed them on grain soaked in milk.[2] The Romans also experimented with battery farming by caging the animals so closely they couldn't exercise.

Some believed chickens should be kept in darkness – sometimes blinded – so all they would do is eat and become fat. Some thought their fattening diet of barley and ale, or sweetened rice and milk, should be accompanied by a candle at night so that they thought it was eternal day. When they were fat, their diet was changed to gravel or powdered glass or brick to cleanse them.[3] Seventeenth-century housewives believed that cutting the legs off live chickens made them more tender; a practice reminiscent of the ammonia burns that modern factory birds get on their knees when, unable to support the weight of their overbred bodies, they collapse onto the excrement-covered floor, which will not be cleaned until the flock is slaughtered. Even sixteenth-century observers sometimes baulked at cramming capons and depriving them of all light, although mostly, it seems, out of enlightened self-interest. As the Elizabethan naturalist and physician Thomas Muffet noticed, it made their meat 'not natural' and their livers small, discoloured and unpalatable. He was very clear, however, who should be eating any sort of chicken. It is 'so pure and fine a meat' that it was worthy of only the finest of diners and 'no man I think is so foolish as to commend them to ploughmen and besomers [labouring women]'.[4]

Workers such as grooms, coachmen, drovers and stockmen relied on animals for their income. Aristocrats relied on them for their sport. Neither class was inclined to question their assumption that their rights over animals were absolute. A faint idea about welfare for the animals' sake began to glimmer in the Enlightenment, principally among an increasing intellectual middle class who, removed from the sharp end of working with and slaughtering animals, began – just began – to think more objectively about them (see Vegetables and Vegetarians, page 314).

When the first Act against cruelty to animals was passed in 1835, its aim was also to prevent 'the demoralization of the people'. One way of ensuring a moral proletariat was to ban the cruel sports they supported – cock-fighting, dog-fighting, bull-baiting and bear-baiting; the aristocratic pursuits of hunting, shooting and fishing survived to fight another day. Most of the early prosecutions for animal cruelty were against working men such as cab drivers and Smithfield butchers.[5] Goodness became an issue of education, wealth and background; to families who had to send their own children up chimneys and into factories to survive economically, consideration for animals was an unaffordable luxury. Kindness to chickens is now seen as a badge both of wealth and moral sophistication in places such as Silicon Valley, where a technocratic elite de-stress with their feathery companions. Heritage breeds such as the old-fashioned British Dorking are popular; their beautifully coloured eggs make the perfect dinner-party gift, showing, as they do, that behind them lie hundreds of thousands of dollars spent on the space for the birds to roam free, not to mention the hi-tech coops and the birds themselves.[6]

A roast chicken has long been associated with hospitality in the West, although it took a long time for the taste to fan out across the classes in Britain. In 1600, the Renaissance naturalist Ulisse Aldrovandi eulogized the chicken for the splendour of its meat, either boiled or roasted, 'our chief resource when friends or guests arrive suddenly and unexpectedly', as well as its eggs on fast days.[7] The French king Henri IV supposedly had a practical ambition for every peasant family to have a chicken in the pot on Sundays. White meat? A pot? The peasantry? How French that seemed to the spit-roast red-meat obsessed Brits, most of whom were entirely at home with Thomas Muffet's idea that the poor had no business eating something so fine. According to one Georgian bird-fancier, Britain had never been much of a chicken-eating nation, compared with the French or the Egyptians, who were credited with inventing artificial incubation. British farmers generally ignored it (except for the eggs) and it was a luxury – usually unattainable – for 'the lower or middling orders of the people'.[8] Even at the end of the nineteenth century, as the condition of the labourer was improving and he could afford more meat, chicken very rarely appears in the expenditure tables; he and his family aspired to beef, mutton or pork, and subsisted on the ubiquitous bacon or salted pork.[9]

The practice of battery hens was developed in the US in the early twentieth century by a businessman who realized you could separate chickens into meat providers and egg layers, and farm both more intensively. Big business had a product – intensively reared chickens – but no market. Maryn McKenna painstakingly reconstructs this moment in history to show how the chicken business assiduously created a market – predominantly for fried chicken and chicken nuggets – in the States.[10] Battery farming spread to Britain and the rest of the world so that chicken became cheaper than 'butcher's meat' for the first time in the 1960s. Now a worldwide intensive industry, its enthusiastic take-up by businesses in the developing world makes attempts to reclaim a cruelty-free life for chickens seem, to some, a first-world indulgence.

After centuries of being told that chicken was a luxury only for people whose rank entitled them to it, it is not surprising that having chicken on your plate is desirable for people who might be unsure of their own place in society. Meat of any kind, no matter how processed or cheaply farmed, is, in the words of a recent academic paper, 'a substitute for a perceived lack of socio-economic status'.[11]

Battery-farmed chicken, argued the chef Marco Pierre White, was a necessity: 'If they banned industrial farming, chicken would become a luxury item... If it wasn't for commercial farming there wouldn't be Sunday lunch for millions of families,' as though it was not possible for Sunday lunch to be comprised of anything else.[12] An academic study from the North of England in the 1980s showed *why* so many low-income families agreed with him, by attributing status directly to food. While all meat had equally high status, some was more equal than others. Chicken joined red meat on the 'high status' podium for wage-earning men; burgers, sausages, fish fingers came a distant second, though they were fine for kids and, by implication, families on the breadline. One husband in the study boasted that he had thrown his plate at the wall when the contents didn't match his view of his entitlement. As the half-joking 1982 comic classic *Real Men Don't Eat Quiche* says, real men know that 'all proper meals are centred around meat'.[13] Putting a roast dinner on the table on Sunday had become an obligation for the woman in a family of a low to intermediate income; if she didn't get the whole family to eat Sunday dinner together, she would feel guilty. The roast chicken manages to be what most of the women in the study called a 'proper dinner', yet without the troubling extra calories, fat and cost of red meat, which all provided other opportunities for her feelings of guilt to flourish.

However, some thinkers, writers and cooks continued to uphold ideas of animal welfare, even when it brought them into conflict with low-income families wanting a 'proper dinner', and those, like Marco Pierre White, speaking on their behalf. An increasing number of voices cried that the chicken in the pot, or on the roasting dish, should not be seen as a 'proper dinner' if the animal itself had led a wretched existence. The state of its life – and its death – also came to represent the status of whoever ate it, as well as whoever farmed it, argued Hugh Fearnley-Whittingstall in 2004. He witnessed the life of intensively raised broiler chickens, seeing their lack of space (less than an A4 sheet of paper per bird), de-beaking, overweight bodies crushing their own spindly legs and on and on with a catalogue of horrors. Eventually, he hoped, the chicken-eating public would pressurize the supermarkets into offering organic and truly free-range poultry as the norm, showing battery farming to be a moral aberration. Buyers of battery chickens had chosen to buy into 'ignorance, greed and cruelty'.[14] Accordingly, while providing and eating a well-raised organic chicken might well indicate something positive about your social status, choosing a battery chicken can only lower your moral status, which, in a properly ethical world, means your social status too.

His word 'choice' is interesting in the light of the Manchester wives and mothers surveyed in the 1980s who did not feel their choices were autonomous, but were held in a vice of social and familial restrictions. Many women, particularly single women, slipped out from under this social net to make their own dietary choices. The *Daily Mail* columnist and vegan Liz Jones puts it down not to fortune but to moral superiority, castigating the cooking-on-a-budget writer Jack Monroe for using chicken in her recipes and oppressing something lower down the food chain (it was free-range chicken, shot back Jack Monroe, and she noticed that Liz Jones's veganism didn't seem to stop her feeding prawns to her cats, or enjoying 'butter-soft' leather).

We will continue to battle over our roast chicken, perhaps until Winston Churchill's 1931 prediction comes true: 'We shall escape the absurdity of growing a whole chicken in order to eat the breast or wing, by growing these parts separately under a suitable medium.'[15] 'Clean meat', or 'cultured meat', could replace battery farming.

Although we might hate to think we are 500 years behind the French king Henri IV, we have allowed ourselves to come to believe that we have every right to a chicken in the pot – or the roasting dish – every week. It has not been hard for big business and marketing, together with our cookbooks, our families and our social desires, to turn this most delicious of dishes into something iconic. It isn't just a dish but, as the food writer Simon Hopkinson recognized in 1994 with the title of his bestselling book, *Roast Chicken and Other Stories*, it is a *story*.

Can we write a different story for roast chicken with a more ethical framework? Many people believe, as Churchill did in 1931, that science and business will do it, as they have with plant-based burgers. Is the Impossible Chicken possible? And if it is, will it simply be a different story, but with the same building blocks of social and moral differentiation between those at the top and those at the bottom of the wealth scale?

It isn't hard to see why people ascribe moral virtues or vices to chicken or any other animal in our food chain. Part of being human is to figure out what we are responsible for, and to construct for ourselves an ethical framework. And yet, if you look at it alongside the history of other foodstuffs, it emerges that we, in Britain, are rather prone to making moral judgements not just on our fellow eaters, but on the foods themselves. Which brings us to the story of the potato and why we love to mash it.

Mashed Potato:
disguising humble roots

I heard a bitter old Englishwoman say, 'To —— with your 'taty-pot;
they're only meat for pigs.' 'Sure, thin,' said a young Irishman –
he was a nice 'cute fellow – 'sure thin, ma'am, I should be afther
offering you a taste.'

Henry Mayhew, *London Labour and the London Poor*, Volume I (1851)

W
E HAVE, I think, that ridiculous foodstuff Smash to
thank for our rediscovery of the consolations of mashed
potato. We have learnt to love mash as a wholesome,
generous supporting act to so many meaty starring roles, or even
as an occasional solo turn which involves just a pile of mash and
a craving for hot, buttery comfort.

Industrialists had experimented with instant mashed potato
throughout the twentieth century, but it was Cadbury's launch of
Smash in the 1960s, and a wildly popular advertising campaign
in the 1970s (showing alien robots in hysterical laughter at
television pictures of a human peeling potatoes), that suddenly
gave what had become 'old-fashioned' mash the cachet of
authenticity. Pubs serving above-average food started putting it
on their menus, and calling it 'proper mash' lest any of their
clientele should think they were getting Smash. Jilly Cooper's
lower middle classes started to call it 'creamed potatoes', in the
belief that 'mash' was working class and therefore common.[1]
However, simple, unadorned mash had always been loved by

the nursery-food-loving upper-middles and aristocracy and was gaining status in the restaurant-going world.

Mash became seen by some chefs as the perfect canvas for other flavours; it started to show up at restaurants with grain mustard, garlic, parmesan. Next it got itself pimped up with smoked salt, or that wretched imposter 'truffle' oil (most of which is made with synthetic flavouring and has never been near a truffle) or even, in one unhappy marriage, pesto. It mixed with other roots such as celeriac and parsnip, the better to take flavours from further afield, such as chipotle or curry powder. But mostly it was made in restaurants with pounds of butter and cream to produce something entirely different from lumpy, proletarian mash, or smooth but equally proletarian Smash. Suddenly mashed potato had secrets! The eating-out classes were steered by chefs towards equipment such as potato ricers and techniques such as cooking the potatoes in milk, butter, cream, olive oil – anything rather than water. Nigella Lawson recommended her readers to recreate a starter she ate at Joachim Splichal's Patina in Los Angeles – a dish of mashed potatoes and truffles with warm Santa Barbara shrimp on top – by deploying a bag of frozen prawns and mashing and then whipping the potatoes to get the desired purée consistency.[2]

The potato, simply boiled and served with butter, in spite of occasionally being championed by more sensible cookery writers, has never been as interesting to British eaters as mash, who seem to want to make the potato (with added dairy) as un-potato-like as possible. The potato in its recognizable, knobbly form has had an uphill struggle to acceptability.

From their introduction to Europe by the Spanish conquistadors in around 1570, it took centuries of social engineering to coerce workers into growing and eating potatoes. The earliest recipes to include the 'potato root' were for sweet potatoes – rather more acceptable because, like many sweet, culinary discoveries, they were assumed to be an aphrodisiac. This is what Falstaff is hoping for before an erotic assignation in *The Merry Wives of Windsor*, crying, 'Let the sky rain potatoes'.[3] They belonged, according to *The Good Huswifes Handmaide for the Kitchen* (1594), in a 'tarte to provoke courage either in man or woman' together with those undeniable foods of Venus, the brains of three or four cock sparrows.[4]

For reasons nobody fully understood – perhaps because they were members of the poisonous nightshade family; perhaps because of the belief that ingesting them caused diseases like leprosy that made the human body as nobbly as themselves – they were held in deep suspicion by labourers and people with the poorest diets who might have most benefited from them. There were educated people across eighteenth-century Europe who, becoming aware that the tuber was an excellent fall-back for when the wheat harvest failed, wanted the poor to grow them, although they didn't fancy them much themselves. Denis Diderot, supposedly an Enlightenment thinker, remarked in his *Grande Encyclopédie* (1765) that 'The potato is correctly held responsible for flatulence; but what is flatulence to the vigorous digestions of peasants and workers?' (see Parmentier Potatoes, page 183). Thomas Malthus, John Evelyn, the learned members of the Royal Society, all saw the merit of the potato in helping to combat famine and urged it on their servants or the poor, but met with much resistance. A tenant's wife, advised by Jane Austen's mother to plant them in her own garden, countered, 'No, no; they are very well for you gentry, but they must be terribly *costly to rear*.'[5] Northerners were more pragmatic and better fed. William Ellis, who farmed in Hertfordshire in the mid-eighteenth century and recorded life for himself and his neighbours, was fascinated to hear that there were sacks of potatoes available in Manchester markets and that they were in 'common use by both poor and rich'. The poor boiled and mashed them; the richer sort might mingle them with a little wine and sugar and use them to stuff a hare.[6]

In Ireland, however, poor tenant farmers, desperate to feed their large families when their staple harvest of oats failed, took much more rapidly to the tuber, which awarded them maximum nutrition from the small parcels of land they rented. The majority of Irish landowners set their fields to raising cattle for beef, dairy and grain; much of it was exported to England, which was often where they lived themselves. In 1780, the Englishman Philip Luckombe, travelling in Ireland, saw that 'landlords first get all that is made of the land, and the tenants, for their labour, get poverty and potatoes'.[7] By that date, around 40 per cent of the Irish were dependent on the potato alone. It was extraordinarily successful in feeding the country and there was a population explosion from around half a million people in 1660 to 9 million in 1840. Thomas Malthus, for one, blamed the potato and he was probably right. Wheat on the same land might have supported around 5 million people.[8]

In England, then, the potato had also to battle for acceptance in the light of English prejudices against the Irish. The nineteenth-century Parliamentarian William Cobbett, self-appointed spokesperson and advisor to the English labourer, wrote that he would rather see England's poor hanged – and he with them – than see them live on potatoes. Instead, he gave workers instructions in baking, brewing and keeping livestock in *Cottage Economy*. He fretted that the diet of the agricultural poor, instead of its traditional reliance on wheat, was succumbing to the 'lazy root' of the Irish; a verbal association that lives on in today's 'couch potato'. Stretching the pun, he spurned it as 'the root, also, of slovenliness, filth, misery, and slavery'.[9] Up North, the physician Sir James Kay-Shuttleworth had the same worries. Addressing himself to *The Moral and Physical Condition of the Working Classes of Manchester* in 1832, he blamed Irish immigrant labour for teaching 'the labouring classes of this country a pernicious lesson', of demoralization, barbarism, ignorance, pauperism, most of which sins came down to relying on 'the general use of the potato as the chief article of food'.[10] Britons of all stripes, particularly in the South, proudly saw themselves as eaters of bread, not potatoes, and the tuber, in the eye of the Corn Laws storm, became, forgive me, a political hot potato. Richard

Cobden, Liberal statesman and co-founder of the Anti-Corn Laws League, which campaigned for cheaper bread for workers rather than higher income for landowners, silently invoked a backwards Ireland when he warned the House of Commons in 1842 that a 'potato-fed race' would never 'lead the way in arts, arms or commerce'.[11]

Monoculture is a frequent problem for peasant farmers with little education and much need. The Irish relied on the single, high-yield variety called the Lumper, which turned out to have no resistance to a new blight which came from the Americas in 1845. Within one season the sole foodcrop of approximately two fifths of the population had become black, slimy and rotten in the fields. Politicians and historians have raged about culpability for what became known as the Great Famine. Historians now agree that it killed, through starvation and related diseases, approximately a million people and saw up to another 2 million emigrate. Some English politicians of the time continued to blame Irish laziness and immorality for their misfortune, even while they continued to import food to feed the newly industrializing cities that were helping make England the richest country in the world. Ireland sent to England nearly three quarters of a million cows, pigs and sheep in 1846; Sligo sent nearly 800,000lb (nearly 362 metric tons) of butter to Liverpool in 1847. Even potatoes – Portaferry sent 20 tons (18 metric tons) to Liverpool in April 1847.[12] George Bernard Shaw called it not a famine but 'starvation. When a country is full of food, and exporting it, there can be no famine.'[13]

Political actions, such as closing the Irish ports to keep food in the country (which had helped ameliorate earlier famines), or organizing famine relief (the soup kitchens ran for only about six months in 1847), ran into conflict with beliefs that the immoral and shiftless poor had to learn to help themselves. Solutions, instead, ran along the lines of the Privy Council's, which proclaimed 24 March 1847 to be a day of prayer and fasting. Queen Victoria directed congregations to pray for the Almighty's tolerance of the 'manifold sins and provocations' which brought about 'extreme famine and sickness'.[14]

The potato, particularly in its whole state, had long been seen as crude and coarse and too reminiscent of the Irish poor for it to find favour in England. The English labourer should not bring himself as low as the Irish in their way of preparing them, Cobbett declared in *Cottage Economy*, 'that is to say, scratch them out of the earth with their paws, toss them into a pot without washing, and when boiled, turn them out upon a dirty board, and then sit round that board, peel the skin and dirt from one at a time and eat the inside'.[15] But he was fighting a rearguard action. His near-contemporary, Sir Frederick Eden, saw the potato as the key to self-sufficiency, one of the qualities that would lift the poor out of destitution. He argued that southern labourers would vastly improve their nutrition if, like their Cumbrian and Scottish counterparts, they planted 'a good patch of potatoes'.[16]

Cobbett's prejudice couldn't compete against the need for the middle classes to feed their families economically, even if it was only to enable them to afford the lavish entertainments that were an essential key to opening the door to society (see The Dinner Party, page 66).

In the eighteenth century, the potato's rare occurrence in cookbooks was usually hidden beneath a pie crust, until somebody hit upon the fact that it could, with butter and cream and a bit of elbow power, be transformed into something luxurious enough to put before guests. Hannah Glasse gets another cookbook first for her recipe in *The Art of Cookery Made Plain and Easy* (1747), and mash found its way into the family dinners of the 'middling sort', encouraged by women cookbook writers of good sense and an eye to economy. Eliza Acton gave three recipes for boiling potatoes in her 1845 classic cookbook *Modern Cookery* – the Irish way is with the peel on, which, unlike many of her compatriots, she did not disdain. Instead, with her usual good sense and spirit, she tells her readers that it is not the potato or its eaters that is immoral, but that domestic waste is an *abuse*;

'the "*waste*" of one part of the community cannot fail to increase the "*want*" of the remainder'.[17]

A bowl of formless mash didn't give quite the elegance required by the Victorian hostess, so Acton recommended pressing mash 'into a well buttered mould of handsome form' and browned in front of a Dutch oven.[18] While Dickens was despising 'our wise legislators' for responding to the famine with 'such rot' as a day of fasting, his family and circle ate potatoes in most meals, generally 'mashed and browned', according to his wife's book of menus (a cross between mashed and roast potatoes and utterly delicious).[19] The poor were less sure; a costermonger admitted to Mayhew that his donkey was 'fond of mashed potatoes' but, even for a donkey, they were second choice to the more expensive carrots.[20]

Bread still reigned supreme in the hearts of British consumers, though, and the First World War government worried about our consumption of expensive, imported wheat. Efforts by the Ministry of Food, established in December 1916, to get people to cut their bread consumption by a quarter lauded mashed potato as the saviour of the nation's diet of bread, pastry and puddings. The Ministry of Food gave demonstrations to bakers and sent potato loaves to local newspapers.[21]

It wasn't until the Second World War that the government felt capable of promoting the potato as an ingredient in its own right, nobbles, skin and all. It looms large in 'Dig For Victory' posters and the jovial Potato Pete (and not, of course, Potato Paddy), who gained something of a cult following; people sang little songs about 'him'. Growing and eating potatoes, instead of being seen as too close to poverty – particularly Irish poverty – for comfort, became patriotic. Potatoes were rationed for the first time in England in 1947. It was a deeply unpopular move. One MP described the unrationed potato as 'the last line of defence', particularly for the urban poor who could not grow this nutritious, filling and cheap crop for themselves.[22] Post-war rationing of potatoes sealed their place in the nation's heart, but, until we learnt to eat them new, it is their ability to be transformed into something else that doesn't look like potatoes – crisply chipped, comfortingly mashed, unctuously roasted – that has kept them there.

Although the potato has found its way into many folk dishes, its presence suggests that the recipe in question (or at least the potato-containing incarnation of it) is not particularly ancient. The Cornish pasty, with its regulation chunks of potato, is a good example of a dish where the past and present don't quite fit, as we shall see.

The Cornish Pasty:
trying to square the circle

It is said that the Devil has never crossed the Tamar into Cornwall, on account of the well-known habit of Cornishwomen of putting everything into a pasty, and that he was not sufficiently courageous to risk such a fate!

Cornish Recipes Ancient and Modern, compiled by Edith Martin (1929)

OR ME AND many people lucky enough to holiday in Cornwall, a hot Cornish pasty tastes of wave-bashed swimming, with peppery notes of almost-vertical coastal paths, a whiff of unreliable weather and the comforting warmth of happy days. There's usually an aftertaste of lying on the beach, comatose. The Cornish pasty has a lot of ballast.

For the county, the Cornish pasty is rather more culturally and economically significant. A much-loved and fiercely protected institution from, as Cornish pasty scholars say, 'time immemorial', it has its own association to protect its 'authenticity and distinctiveness', which has co-opted the might of the EU to protect the genuine article from imposters made in foreign parts; that is, anywhere beyond the River Tamar. Thanks to its Protected Geographical Indication (PGI), if you buy a Cornish pasty in Birmingham or Norwich, you can chomp happily in the knowledge that a) it will have been made in Cornwall; b) it will have a minimum of 12.5 per cent diced or minced beef; and c) real vegetables – a minimum of 25 per cent of potato, onion and swede. Only on the Celtic fringes, it seems, does the sweet, peppery tang of swede (mystifyingly called 'turnip' in Cornwall – reminiscent of their Scots' cousins 'neeps') have such a devoted following. And only a traitor or a foreigner would put carrot in a Cornish pasty. When, in 2008, the Department for Environment, Food and Rural Affairs (DEFRA) submitted its application for PGI on behalf of the Cornish Pasty Association, local MPs and MEPs nobly offered 'to eat any number of pasties in public!'[1] to support the campaign and emphasized its justification on the grounds of 'strong and well-established tradition'.[2] It assured the protection of jobs for something like 1,800–2,000 workers in the county (often described as 'Cornish people' but, like many workers in the food industry, likely to be seasonal or casual workers from beyond the immediate county) and the generation of millions of pounds for the Cornish economy; estimates vary between £65 million and £300 million.

The folk history of the pasty is as iconic as its crimped pastry edges and D-shape and much is made of its working-class, mining origins. It came into its own when tin and copper mining reached their zenith in the eighteenth and nineteenth centuries; it was robust enough to survive the journey down the pit and nourishing enough to keep a worker going all his sunless day. The thick pastry might have been held by our miner and then discarded, so he didn't ingest the dirt or arsenic on his fingers. Or it might not. The miner's initials might have been made in pastry down one end, so he could identify his half-eaten pasty. Or they might not. The trouble is, the historical record for Cornish pasties is rather patchy. There are black and white photographs of miners, posing for the camera, pasty in hand, but, as is commonly the case for folk or peasant food, there is little written evidence. The earliest recipes for pasties are for a landed or leisured class, whole joints of meat – usually venison – kept moist by pastry (see The Venison Pasty, page 260). The earliest pasty recipe in Cornwall, hailing from 1746, is in the County Records Office in Truro. Its whole joint of mutton, spices and claret is clearly not intended for the working man. It is quite a long way from the 'traditional' beef and root vegetable version we know.

> Take a Leg or Jigget of Mutton (the bones being taken out) is to be rubbed over with Cochineal, then spiced with Mace, Cloves & Allspice, of each an equal quantity, with Salt; a little Pepper. To which put in a pint of Clarret or Port in baking. The Crust as usual.[3]

There are many written recipes in cookbooks before the twentieth century for meat pasties, but very few containing potato. In the early 1900s, labourers were acknowledging that their food was better than their forefathers', and yet they still believed that potatoes didn't give them the strength that wheat or barley did.[4] The pasty was an ideal vehicle for both padding out and hiding the fact that you might be eating the despised but useful spud.

Pasties with meat, turnips or vegetables and bacon intended for the labouring classes start appearing in the record at around the end of the nineteenth century. A Devon man reported in the early 1900s, 'Pies and pasties are the great feature of the Cornish diet. The ordinary pasty of the Cornish labourer is clean, wholesome and nutritious.'[5] Sadly he doesn't tell us what was in it.

Connoisseurs today happily eat their way around the butchers and bakers of the peninsula to find the best. Ask a Cornish foodie who makes the finest pasties, and they might still root for home bakers – friends, siblings, parents – usually mums. As with any local food, made for workers from whatever is available, pasty fillings are traditionally a diverse affair. In the 1920s and 1930s, you could eat your aunty's sour sauce pasty made from sorrel, or your gran's windy pasty (filled with jam), and anybody with a shotgun could see his family fed with rabbity pasties. Edith Martin gathered recipes from her Women's Institute colleagues for date, mackerel, broccoli, rice, pork, eggy and chicken pasties from towns and villages around the county. The closest she comes to a 'Cornish pasty' is recommending turnip and potatoes with a bit of fat bacon or a lump of cream.

If a Cornish pasty makes the best use of local food, perhaps the most Cornish of pasty recipes was this one for a stargazy pasty, recorded by Edith Martin directly from the giver.

Mawther used to get a herring, clean 'en, and put same stuffin' as what yow do have in mabiers (chicken); sew 'en up with niddle and cotton, put 'en in some daugh made of suet and flour; pinch the daugh up in the middle and lave the heid sticking out one end, and tail t'other. They was some nice pasties, too, cooked in a fringle fire with crock and brandis and old furzy tobs.[6]

But neither the slightly tricky fish-heads-on stargazy pasty nor the genuinely ancient but indisputably posh venison pasty have gained such a foothold in our affections. The pasty owes some of its popularity to the English nostalgic obsession with meat and two veg; that lovely pastry crust gives even more tonnage and takes away the bother of having to sit around the table – no wonder teenagers love them.

McDonald's fast food owes some of its success to the idea that you can go into one of its 'restaurants' anywhere in the world and know exactly what you are getting. The Cornish pasty, subject to legal restrictions, now has something of the same status; it is reliable but homogeneous. DEFRA, the EU and the Cornish Pasty Association, while undoubtedly contributing much to the economy of Cornwall and the quality of what we eat, have also given us a contradiction. They have legislated about a traditional, regional, working-class food, but the very point of peasant food is that you make do; you use what you have to hand, in the season that you have it – it is diverse. If you can find a bit of protein or fat to feed your workers with, so much the better, but a legal requirement for a percentage of beef is neither 'traditional' nor 'authentic'. If we used the historical record to give us an 'authentic' recipe, we would be eating pasties filled with spiced mutton and claret, treading in the well-heeled footsteps of the beneficiary of that 1746 recipe.

If we acknowledge that the pasty is a working-class food, then we would allow in a ragbag of whatever the baker has to hand – fish, vegetables, jam, even carrots, which are anathema to the modern pasty-lover. If you go back a century, you would find a working-class prejudice against the potatoes which are now seen as an essential part of the Cornish pasty.

Does it matter? Whenever those arguments crop up about who has the right to make or sell a particular type of regional or peasant food, the story of the Cornish pasty shows that you can invent rules about ownership, but history will not necessarily back you up.

CORNISH HERBY PASTY

This good-natured recipe from Boscastle in Cornwall comes from a book published by the Cornwall Federation of Women's Institutes in 1929. The Herby Pasty is typical of traditional recipes from working communities, being eminently flexible about what could go in it, so it could be vegan, vegetarian or meaty.

MODERN RECIPE
MAKES 6

Pastry:

500g strong bread flour
250g lard or white shortening or butter
½ teaspoon salt
Ice-cold water

Filling:

500–600g of mixed greens from the garden or foraged.
The majority from spinach, beet, kale, chard, lettuce, spring cabbage, watercress, nettles. Smaller amounts of parsley, mustard and cress, borage, spring onion, wild garlic. The 'bits' mentioned in the original recipe might well be hairy bittercress.
2–3 shallots or small onion, finely chopped and fried
Approx. 100g chopped ham or cooked bacon or cheese
Salt and pepper
2 eggs, beaten

1. To make the pastry, mix the salt into the flour, chop the fat into small pieces, then rub it into the flour until the mixture resembles fine breadcrumbs. Sprinkle cold water over the surface, bring the mixture together. Knead it like bread, until the pastry becomes elastic – it will take anything from 5 to 10 minutes, or 3–4 minutes in a food mixer. Cover it with cling film and let it rest for about an hour.
2. Preheat the oven to Gas Mark 3/160°C.
3. Chop the toughest leaves and blanch in boiling water, then run cold water over them to cool. Using your hands, squeeze out the excess liquid and chop them. Finely chop the softer leaves and herbs. Gently fry the shallots until soft. Mix together the leaves, shallots and the

ham or bacon or cheese and a little salt and pepper. Bind with the eggs (leaving a little beaten egg for glazing the pastry, if you wish).

4. Roll out the pastry and cut five rounds 18–20cm across. Use the scraps to make a sixth round.

5. Lay the filling in the middle and fold the pastry over. Crimp it by brushing egg or milk on one surface and pinching the edges together. Then, starting at one end, fold the edge over and pinch between the finger and thumb, to get the traditional rope effect. Brush with milk or beaten egg.

6. Bake in the oven for 40–50 minutes.

ORIGINAL RECIPE: HERBY PASTY
From *Cornish Recipes, Ancient and Modern*,
compiled by Edith Martin (1929)

◆

Pastry

Any good pastry may be used but it should not be too flaky, nor too rich. A very useful pastry is:

1lb flour ◆ ½lb lard and suet ◆ ½ teaspoonful salt

Mix with water.

Well wash equal quantity of parsley, bits,* shallots (early), half quantity spinach, prepare some slices of bacon cut into small pieces and an egg well beaten. Pour boiling water over the parsley, bits, and spinach that have been cut into small portions, and let stand for half an hour, well squeeze all moisture out. Put on pastry with the shallots cut finely and the bacon, pinch up the edges of pastry allowing a small portion left open for the egg to be added, finish pinching and bake.

*Bits is a common herb believed to be only found in N. Cornwall. It is found in the hedges and on the cliffs. Gipsies pick it for medicinal purposes.

Peas: the fresh and the dried

A wealthy neighbor, without children, and fond of horticulture, generally triumphed. Mr. Jefferson, on one occasion had them first, and when his family reminded him that it was his right to invite the company, he replied, 'No, say nothing about it, it will be more agreeable to our friend to think that he never fails.'

Thomas Jefferson's grandson on the annual neighbourhood contest to serve the first peas of spring

WHO DOESN'T LOVE the story of Peter Mandelson, visiting a chippy in Hartlepool where he was campaigning to be an MP, pointing to some mushy peas and asking for some of that avocado mousse, as well, please. Rival politicians and journalists spread it like wild-fire, as the Labour politician's ignorance of working-class food was too good a story for anybody to worry that, in fact, more accurate sources pin it on a young American Labour Party campaigner who thought it was guacamole.

What are mushy peas anyway? As a child, I remember trying to mash the peas on my plate to magic up this half-forbidden guilty pleasure. There are a number of varieties of pea, and it helps to sieve through them. Mushy peas are now made from big, grainy, marrowfat peas, dried, soaked and boiled. Lots of current recipes talk about 'old English' or 'old-fashioned' pease pudding or soup, and call for yellow split peas which have had their coarse skins removed (probably mechanically) and give a smooth soup. But before the nineteenth century, pease pottage (thick soup) or pease pudding (even thicker soup, boiled in a cloth) would also have been made from dried *field* peas. Dried, these were hard as nails, enough to make a real princess black and blue all over, according to the Hans Christian Andersen fairy story. These were bought by street traders, soaked so they swelled up to double in size, and sold hot with salt, pepper and vinegar, as mushy peas are today. You might see them called grey, white or blue peas, relating to the colour of their flowers. Northerners complicate life further by having 'Carlin' peas, which might be the same as grey peas, or might be little dried dark brown peas, traditionally eaten on Carlin Sunday (Passion or 'Care', hence Carlin Sunday) – the Sunday before Palm Sunday. They are credited with keeping Tynesiders going in the Civil War, when Royalist Newcastle was besieged from the North.

All these peas dried well and had been used in Britain, since Roman times, for stomach-filling winter fuel. They frequently formed the basis of pottage, the thick soup made in the one cooking pot a family was likely to have; and into which went everything – roots, peas, bacon or pork bones – they might cobble together for dinner. It was genuine peasant food across Northern Europe (or, as Fernand Braudel has it, 'older than Europe itself'[1]), and never managed to shake off its humble reputation. Peas and pigs were common pot-fellows and pea and ham soup had a pragmatic origin: salted ham required a lengthy boil to become tender. Dried peas, which needed a lot of boiling, too, also formed the useful function of absorbing some of the salt from the meat. The (supposed) first ever chip shop, in Mossley, Lancashire (see Fish and Chips, page 377), started life as a pig-trotter-and-pea-soup hut; possibly the pea soup stayed on to become mushy peas, one of the only green (or greenish) vegetables the urban, industrialized poor would have had access to.

William Ellis gives a number of ways that the local farmer's wife would make this filling, old-English classic in the days when she had to feed the farm servants as well as the family. The most basic form had her boiling the pease directly in a pot with a pork bone, or a bit of bacon or pickled pork. They knew it as porridge (the later anglicization of 'pottage'). A thicker pottage made with milk and thickened with wheatmeal or flour was an indicator that you were a little better off; or perhaps something she kept for her family.

A little up Ellis's scale came 'pease-pudding', boiled within a greased cloth to form the traditional pudding shape, alongside the ham in a pot. It might be served as a 'solid green cannon-ball'[2] or broken into the porridge to form a soup. Ellis tells us that the 'Gentleman's' recipe for 'pease-soup' dispenses with the ham or bacon used by cottagers and farmers, as the recipe for higher ranks merited leg of beef and some herbs or spices. The beef is there just for the stock; it is 'boiled to rags' then taken out and given to the poor. A particularly delicate version would be made from 'green pease in their pods by scaling them, and then beating them in a mortar' and making the soup with other green things, 'parsley, marygolds, lettice, sorrel and mint'.[3]

This 'pease-soup' had left behind its labouring, pottage origins and become something more genteel; it became thinner (and greener) and took the merest edge off the appetite. Soup on a genteel table was part of a first course, not a sole course or meal in its own right. It was served first, then the soup plates were removed allowing diners to start on the other more substantial dishes that were on the table (see Small Plates, page 223). The young Jane Austen told her sister Cassandra that she was not ashamed to invite an unexpected guest to 'our elegant entertainment' of 'pease-soup, a spare rib and a pudding'.[4]

Green 'garden peas' were available only to those fortunate enough to have space to grow them in their gardens, or who sat at the top of a trading network. Fresh peas in the pod were sold on London streets from Chaucer's time: 'hot peascods' were offered with melted butter for the customer to dip into, perhaps removing the peas with their teeth and discarding the pod, perhaps eating the whole thing.[5] Mrs Beeton quotes Nicholas Fuller, the Elizabethan lawyer, as saying that peas were imported from Holland as 'fit dainties for ladies, they came so far and cost so dear'.[6] The, to my mind, rather delightful idea of serving fresh raw green peas as a dessert was begun at the court of Louis XIV, when he was given fresh peas on 18 January 1660, along with herbs and rosebuds, as a bribe by the head chef of the Countess of Soissons, who wanted a monopoly over the sale of liqueurs. The court became consumed by pea-fever; and some of the court ladies, having supped well with the king, 'risked indigestion' by scoffing peas in their own rooms before bed. 'C'est une mode, une fureur ['It's a fad, it's a craze],' the king's wife, Madame de Maintenon, confided to her diary.[7]

Perhaps it wasn't so crazy. Fresh peas continued to be served on genteel dinner tables with savoury, fatty duck or green goose (a goose slaughtered early in the year), the elegant equivalent to the ham-and-pea staple of the lower orders (see recipe for Duck and Green Peas in Forks, page 236).

Round, fresh peas are lively little things, impossible to put on a fork, but etiquette has long demanded a 'correct' way to eat peas. On no account may you scoop them up in the upturned curve of the fork; you must spear them on its tines. It is a method as far removed from the practical as possible, but the assistance of a knife is also frowned upon. Thackeray, in his Snob persona, describes discovering that a new friend 'ate peas with the assistance of a knife'. Naturally, the Snob had to cut Mr Marrowfat's acquaintance, sorrowfully, as he admitted he enjoyed his company and he had saved his life more than once, 'but, as an English gentleman, what was I to do?'[8] Peas are only for the not-really-hungry, at the other end of the scale from pease pudding.

Peas lose their freshness quickly (one wonders how fresh Nicholas Fuller's 'fit dainties for ladies' were). When the wonderfully named Clarence Birdseye discovered, in the 1920s, how to freeze them quickly and package them adequately, he created an industry which prevented crops from spoiling, and allowed more to be grown, frozen, packaged and shipped to millions whose ancestors might never have tasted them. Jane Grigson worries that the frozen pea 'caricatures the real thing, but so closely that it spoils it' and its ready availability means it has come to occupy the position of 'grey dried peas of earlier times'.[9] *Pisum sativum* (the Latin name meaning cultivated pea) is now the common-or-garden pea, a handmaid to every pub roast or child's meal. But frozen peas do not stand between us and malnutrition throughout the winter months. We should open our bag of frozen peas any month of the year, make green pea soup, give it to our kids with fish fingers and, perhaps, be thankful. And those lucky enough to be able to stand in the pea patch and pop open the pods, to eat their sweet little contents raw, shouldn't denigrate the closest that many people will get. But if we do, take a leaf from the ladies of Louis XIV's court, and serve fresh peas as a dessert.

Or remember the relish with which our 1920s forebears would have greeted a dinner of chops, mash, frozen peas and buckets and buckets of another new and life-changing invention, instant gravy.

The Gravy Wars

There is no such passion in human nature, as the passion for
gravy among commercial gentlemen.

Charles Dickens, *Martin Chuzzlewit* (1844)

THE ENGLISH CHANNEL is, as a gulf between us, as nothing,
compared with the chasm that separates a French sauce from
English gravy. A colleague told me that his in-laws have, at
sociable weekend meals, what they call 'gravy wars'. Her gravy is
an elegant, French *réduction* or *jus* designed, like Chanel N° 5, to
have the maximum impact with a few dabs on the plate. His is a
splash-it-all-over, expansive, flour-thickened gravy, served in a big
jug. Unwitting guests get caught in the cross-fire by choosing one
over the other; witting guests take both. It is the battle between the
English spit and the French stock-pot.

Alexandre Dumas naturally enters the fray on the side of our
French-style hostess in his *Grand Dictionnaire de Cuisine*, stripping
the argument back to essentials: 'French cuisine, the foremost of
all, owes its superior status to the excellence of French *bouillon*'.[1]
English cooks loved to emphasize their haute cuisine credentials by
imploring their readers to make *bouillon* as the French do. William
Verral was the chef and master of the White Hart Inn in Lewes,
Sussex. His chatty, confidential voice has come down to us in *A
Complete System of Cookery* (1759), along with a rather endearing
pride at being able to pass on to his English readers the wisdom
of his greatly admired French mentor, M. Clouet. Broth and gravy
should be 'the first thing in hand' as it is with the French.[2] We

should put 'garden things' (vegetables) into the pot with the meat (did we mention that this is what the French do?). We must not 'boil it to rags (as is the common practice) it makes the broth thick and grouty, and spoils the pleasing aspect of all your dinner'.[3] One can imagine William Verral pausing here as he's having to confront, head on, one of the major complaints that the British gravy-makers held against the French *jus*-makers: that of waste. Verral is keen to blame the celebrated English tendency to overcook everything: it 'hurts the meat that thousands of families would leap mast-high at'.[4]

However, he has to acknowledge the French reputation in England for outrageous extravagance in terms of boiling down meat for a tiny bit of *jus*. There was a story doing the rounds, apparently, that M. Clouet made 'the quintessence of a ham for sauce, and the gravy of twenty-two partridges for sauce for a brace'. He gets out of it by saying that it was 'beyond the credit of any sensible person; so shall leave that untouch'd'.[5] That eminently sensible person Maria Rundell did believe it, though, and fifty years later remonstrated against the lavishness of 'essence of ham' and 'that wasteful expenditure of large quantities of meat for gravy'.[6] The high Victorians Mrs Beeton and E.S. Dallas, the author of *Kettner's Book of the Table*, were boiling down Brillat-Savarin's story in *Physiologie du goût* (*The Physiology of Taste*; 1825) about the chef, Bertrand, steward to the Prince of Soubise, who ordered fifty hams for one smallish supper; one to be eaten, the others to be condensed into sauces. The urban, Francophile Dallas found it 'amusing';[7] Mrs Beeton slapped it down, reminding her thrifty British sisters 'there is no occasion, as many would have the world believe, to buy ever so many pounds of fresh meat, in order to furnish an ever so little quantity of gravy'.[8]

The French are renowned for their five 'mother sauces', refined through the fires of the nineteenth century by the founder of haute cuisine, Marie-Antoine Carême, and, a century later, by Auguste Escoffier. Escoffier refined Carême's original list of four to show that Béchamel, Velouté, Espagnole, Tomato and Hollandaise might form the basis of dozens of perfect accompaniments to meat, fish and vegetables. It is hardly surprising that French cooks in England used to complain about our single one:

> It is very remarkable, that in France, where there is but one religion, the sauces are infinitely varied, whilst in England, where the different sects are innumerable, there is, we may say, but one single sauce.

However, in Georgian times Louis Ude, the French author of *The French Cook* (1813), was not referring, as he might today, to gravy but...

> Melted butter, in English cooking, plays nearly the same part as the Lord Mayor's coach at civic ceremonies, calomel in modern medicine, or silver forks in fashionable novels. Melted butter with anchovies, melted butter and capers, melted butter and parsley, melted butter and eggs, melted butter for ever.[9]

Sauces were particularly beloved by the English upper classes, not only because they were so *French*, but because they were so tricky to negotiate. Chaucer's Prioress strains to counterfeit dainty manners, but doesn't quite pull it off; she doesn't dip her fingers in the sauce, 'too deep'. Chaucer leaves it up to the reader to know – or not know – that she shouldn't be doing it at all.[10] Being so splashy, sauces became beloved by the English, perhaps because it was another way of making etiquette – and forks – so important. It made eating with the hands impossible and let us shudder at gravy down a chin or a shirt front.

Although *Larousse Gastronomique* politely explains how to make gravy (forbearing a Gallic shrug and a *pourquoi?*), recipes for anything like 'gravy' in French – or Italian, Spanish or generally other – cookbooks are notable by their absence. The food historian Alan Davidson describes it as a peculiarly British incarnation of *jus* or *bouillon* or even *consommé*, adding, helpfully, that it is 'a term comprehensible to those who use it, but something of a mystery in the rest of the world'.[11] Americans are initiated in the cult of gravy, according to Harold McGee who sees it as the 'homely Anglo-American cousin of French sauces'.[12] Its most peculiar international marriage comes, though, perhaps in chicken tikka masala, which has some claim to being the most frequently served dish in British restaurants, and which unites Indian chicken tikka with the British appetite to have all their meat smothered in gravy.

So, gravy is something the British have proudly made up, all by ourselves, including, apparently, the word itself. *Chambers Dictionary* pontificates that a copyist gave us gravy by mistranscribing the 'n' in the Old French word for 'ingredient', *grané*.

An early 'gravie' is found in this recipe for 'A sauce for a rosted Stock Dooue [dove]', showing that by 1584 English cooks were using the word in a specific sense, which distinguished it from 'sauce':

> Take Onions and mince them not to small, and baste them in a little claret Wine, and when they be boyled almoste dry, put therto Vinagre, Sugar, pepper, and some of the grauie of the Stockdoue.[13]

Although there is some doubt as to how much 'gravy' could come from one stock dove, it is clear that gravy is what comes off the meat during roasting – it is the essence of meat – whereas a sauce is built up by skill from the stock-pot. The trouble is, the more the joint provides gravy, the dryer the meat becomes. Some seventeenth-century cooks would slash the joint as it was roasting, or squeeze it, to produce as much juice as possible; it's a culinary vicious circle because the gravy was now essential for lubricating a sadly desiccated piece of meat. Gravy became, perhaps, a little déclassé; something demanded by the sort of diner who has not been educated in the highest flights of French gastronomy to despise overdone meat. Indeed, to some French writers, the French predilection for smaller cuts of meat served in sauces – the ragout, or fricassee – was an indicator, not just of a better cuisine, but of a higher degree of civilization among the 'sauce nations' over 'the bleeding dish nations'.[14] There was something a little coarser, a little more animalistic about gravy that made it beloved of a less sophisticated class of people, as the landlady Mrs Todgers hints darkly to Martin Chuzzlewit about the 'passion' of her 'commercial gentlemen'.

But this passion provided a conundrum for the British cook. Mrs Todgers complained that trying to get the volume of gravy her lodgers required was adding twenty years to her age: 'It's nothing to say a joint won't yield – a whole animal wouldn't yield – the amount of gravy they expect each day at dinner.'[15]

Whereas their French cousins were condensing like mad, English cooks reached for all sorts of supplements to make the gravy go further; mushroom catsup, 'Harvey's sauce', caramel, salt, pickles, but, as happens so often in these cases (margarine, sugar-beet, potato-eating), a European scientist came to the rescue. Scientifically minded cooks of the nineteenth century became obsessed by splitting some kind of culinary atom to get at 'osmazome': a sort of umami-hit of protein. Mid-century the German chemist Baron von Liebig came up with a liquid Extract of Meat to benefit the meatless poor. As it was still priced beyond their reach, he carried on working, condensing and desiccating until he had it: the cheap, dried Oxo cube – each one costing a penny.

No longer would the Mrs Todgers of this world have the years taken off them. Passions for gravy could be satisfied by anybody with a penny for the Oxo cube and some boiling water. From its appearance on the market in 1908, Bisto (so-named because it 'Browns, Seasons and Thickens in One') promised to unite the country in one big, brown, gloopy puddle. Gravy, from being a tricksy, reluctant thing that the cook had to build up with stock bones and ham, or to coax from a roasting joint and bolster with whatever she could get her hands on, was now mixed in a jug and poured on Sunday roasts all over the country. It could be made with very little effort, like the *gravy train*, an expression which was first recorded in 1927.[16]

The Gravy Wars have not ended with an entente cordiale between English gravy and French *jus*, however. Having established that gravy is British, we can now allow the country to divide down lines of consistency, roughly equivalent to culinary class. Thick gravy is 'thought by some to be a bit common', says Nigel Slater, delicately. Thin, he declares, 'looks more elegant and simple on the plate. It has an integrity, a purity and a point to it which are lacking in the thick stuff.'[17]

I might be even more precise, and say that the best gravy is the one that comes, not just from the Bisto pot, or the meat joint, but from deep within the slowly simmered bones. The best gravy, in fact, is the savoury first cousin of another great British culinary love, jelly.

Jelly: slithering down
the social ladder

English cooks boast of calf's-foot jelly as their own peculiar invention, and the French freely accord this glory to the English kitchen.

Kettner's Book of the Table (E.S. Dallas; 1877)

JELLY IS THAT hilariously wobbly, synthetically coloured, chemically tasting stuff that is still a regular guest at children's parties. A packet of jelly is cheap, simple and entertaining enough to make; most children eat some of the squares of concentrated jelly before they make it into the hot water, which doesn't help already limited setting properties – a hot day can turn a wobble into a slither.

I didn't learn to love jelly until I started recreating eighteenth- and nineteenth-century jelly recipes with sharp, racy fruit juices or alcohol and realized the most fun you could have with jelly was by spending a day or two in making it. I pieced together a hen's nest with clear white wine jelly (elderflower for children), flummery eggs and lemon-rind straw; Smoking Bishop – port mulled with spices – became an alcoholic, Christmassy delight in an old-fashioned mould. I extracted the intense, red-berry hit from fruit that had dripped overnight through a muslin, like a particularly grisly crime scene. Half was mixed with voluptuously thick cream, and the layers were surrounded with pale, sugary ladies' fingers and red ribbon to make a beautiful Charlotte Russe. I painstakingly scooped out the flesh to make orange boat hulls for tart, quivering topaz jelly, an old-fashioned Christmas treat from Yorkshire.

Jelly has come down to us from a time when there wasn't such a strict division between savoury and sweet. The first 'gelees' were most likely to be meat or fish set in jelly, rather like brawn, and flavoured with wine and spices. You can see in the earliest recipes for a 'gelee of flessh' (in *The Forme of Cury*; c.1390), which calls for pigs' feet, snouts and ears, that the setting property of gelatine was already well known. The 'gele of fyssh' was the forerunner of jellied eels, which still cling on as a culinary anachronism, set with the collagen in the bones. Isinglass, derived from the swim bladder of fish, was a setting agent that made jellies possible for fast days; an ancient equivalent to the seaweed extracts such as carrageenan and agar, which make vegetarian jellies just about possible today – although their setting properties are much more precarious than gelatine. 'Blank Maunger', a white risotto of rice, chicken and almonds, which was the original 'sweetmeat', came from a different background but found its soulmate in jelly to become the creamy, tottering blancmange.

The first jellies were served with the first or second, predominantly savoury, course; one of the 'curious potages' that the medieval compilers of *The Forme of Cury* recommended 'for all maner of States bothe hye and lowe'. 'Gele' or 'gilly' lent itself to decoration more than most pottages; a feast to mark Henry V's 1413 coronation featured meat swans on a lake of jelly – 'gilly with swannys of braun [meat] ther in' – which was generously made not just for the king but also 'ffor other Estates'.[1] As the decorations became more elaborate, jellies found their way to the sweeter end of the meal, until the fashion for banqueting in Elizabethan and Stuart times gave them their best chance yet to shine.

Serving the dessert course at a separate banquet drew a clear line between savoury and sweet jellies, and between diners of the top rank and the rest. After the first two courses, the top-table guests peeled away from the household into a separate room or even a separate banqueting house to listen to music, to flirt and to eat preserved and fresh fruits, sweet oranges from Portugal, home-grown apricots and peaches, gingerbread, marchpane, moulded sugar sweetmeats and beautiful shimmering jellies, served in delicate glasses. Sir Hugh Plat's *Delights for Ladies* (1602) is a book of sweet recipes intended for banquets (as well as beauty preparations) and reminds us how much it allowed the hostess to display her (or her cook's) skills in making food resemble the most precious of materials. She might make a gleaming 'crystall gelly' from calves' feet – boiled, clarified with egg white and strained and strained again until it was clear – a remarkable achievement given not only the calves' feet but the added flavourings of nutmegs, cinnamon, cloves, ambergris, musk, Rhenish wine and lemon juice. Strawberries, mulberries or raspberries were stewed and strained to become a jewel-like fruit 'gelly' set with isinglass. The opal-like 'Leach' was a moon-white jelly of almonds and cream and flavoured with exotic rosewater.

Not everybody could aspire to a banquet, and the beauty of jellies was that their savoury origins allowed them to lend some glamour to more modest dishes. Hannah Woolley, writing in the Restoration, shared techniques for making spiced jellies, coloured with saffron, 'cutcheneel' (cochineal) and turnsole, to be eaten with soused meat, rather as we eat redcurrant or cranberry jelly with turkey today.[2]

In the age of Wedgwood and the ceramic revolution, jelly moulds made from stoneware or creamware meant that little jelly glasses gave way to elaborately moulded multi-coloured baskets of fruit or complex chequerboard patterns. Mrs Raffald gives instructions for making some of the fashionable designs of the day in her 1769 cookbook *The Experienced English Housekeeper*: playing cards, a sun and moon, a fish pond, a hen's nest, a green melon in flummery. The blancmange-like flummery could be made creamy with almond milk or cream and sometimes coloured with that rare (for then) flavouring, chocolate. Natural food colourings allowed the cook to design with white, yellow and green blancmanges.

Mrs Raffald's Solomon's Temple, with four smaller towers surrounding a taller obelisk, made from stiff flummery and chocolate, became famous. It set off a space race of competitiveness over the most towering buildings and temples, although always, owing to jelly's collapsible nature, on a Lilliputian scale. On the one hand this mirrored the change in perception of a sophisticated dinner table. As Meg Dods said, in 1829, 'At genteel tables, fat puddings, very rich cakes, and fat meat-pies have lost ground. Creams, jellies, and preserved and caramelled fruits or *compôtes*, take their place.'[3]

Jelly benefited twofold from the Industrial Revolution. Manufacturers experimented with moulds in deftly engineered and more effective materials: stoneware, creamware, copper, tin, culminating in the most useless mould of all in the 1960s – the plastic moulds to whose sides jelly seemed to be Sellotaped. And what should the rising industrialists do with their newfound wealth if not climb the social ladder, dinner by dinner, impressing their guests with jellies of newsworthy complexity. Chefs learnt to cheat the limits of jelly physics (that it collapses any higher than about 6 inches or 15cm) with internal supports which also had to be beautiful: spirals of white blancmange in the centre of translucent jelly towers; white stars or crosses to commemorate the Alexandra Cross or the Brunswick Star; a pyramid of clear jelly, shimmering over a macédoine of fruit, the weight of which just about held it together.

Jelly also had a career as a health food; calves' foot jelly had a reputation for being nutritious and easily digested and it was forever being taken by well-meaning ladies to the ailing poor, although, without the accompanying meat from the calves' feet, its calorie count was close to zero. Mrs Norris in *Mansfield Park* 'sponges' the 'supernumerary jellies' the day after a ball to take them home to 'nurse a sick maid', although the beauty of Jane Austen's portrayal of Mrs Norris is that the reader knows she has certainly filched this treat for herself.[4]

Its healthful reputation, although based on flimsy grounds, made it important enough to have commercial enemies. The influential German chemist Baron von Liebig (inventor of the Oxo cube – see The Gravy Wars, page 129) was eager to share with his fans, who included Mrs Beeton, 'the most convincing experiments' that proved that the newly commercially available gelatine had no nutritional value (compared, of course, with his beef extract): 'Ignorance and the love of gain exchanged the valuable constituents of flesh for gelatine which was only to be distinguished from common joiners' glue by its high price.'[5]

Commercial gelatine (advertised from the 1840s) did not, immediately, make the dinner-party classes abandon their jelly. The most dramatic still needed elegant moulds and skilful and patient cooks, but the commercialization of gelatine and growing medical awareness of adulteration in food meant that people started whispering about how it got its wobble. Once seen as jelly's strong point, calves' feet were still acceptable, but horses' feet, in a country that didn't eat horse, brought a shudder. As we've become more squeamish about eating every bit of an animal, with good reason given BSE and Foot and Mouth crises, manufacturers have attempted to hide the lowly origin of their product. Kraft, which makes the American Jell-O, glosses it thus: 'During the manufacturing of gelatine, chemical changes take place so that the final product, the composition, and identity of the original material is completely eliminated.'[6] Even in 1877 the clop of distant horses' hooves was enough to make the author of *Kettner's Book of the Table* say that it was one of the reasons 'that jelly has gone very much out of fashion'.[7] He also hints that the ubiquity of aspic was sending it the same way. This jelly, also made from calves' feet, and flavoured with sherry, Marsala or tarragon vinegar, was intended to add a gloss to hams, salmon, roast fowls, tongue, lobster salads and brawn (renamed 'galantine' for Victorian sensibilities), but became inescapably monotonous.[8] There it was at every dinner party and wedding feast; and there were the 'pensive jellies', as Dickens calls them in *Dombey and Son* (1848), resolving themselves into a 'lukewarm gummy soup', in the time it takes for the sordidly contracted marriage of Mr and Mrs Dombey to reveal itself to be a sham of gloss without substance.[9]

The Victorian love of elaborate, overcomplicated designs and competitively engineered wobbling towers kept jelly on dinner-party tables until the Edwardians rejected the fuss of Victorian food, and the First World War ended the idea that even middle-income families should aspire to employ a cook. In the end, it was probably the middle-class discovering that their children were human beings, with the right to have parties and other entertainments of their own, that did for jellies. Mrs Humphrey, in her *Manners for Women* (1897), implored, 'Hostess of the Lillyputs! Do have plenty of jelly, amber-clear and rosy red, sparkling like jewels, and saying many beautiful things to the minds of children that you and I used to hear, but have long ago forgotten.'[10] Rowntree's, Chivers, Hartley's all began making instant jellies and marketed them for children. From time to time would come an unsuccessful attempt to be invited back to the grown-up table at dinner parties. In 1978 Rowntree's ran a competition to find the best jelly recipes in Britain, eliciting 14,000 recipes of which the best were, apparently, a lurid collection of loaves to be served in slices on a bed of lettuce, such as jellied curry (any flavour jelly), jellied salad (dissolve a packet of lemon jelly in tomato soup... add cream cheese, salad dressing and a chopped green pepper), or all the ingredients of a fruit cake, with a packet of jelly (lemon, again) standing in for the butter and flour.[11]

The elegant jelly has fallen on hard times, but it looks to be getting a shot in the arm from two quarters. Vodka jellies have become popular with party-goers as the sugar and artificial fruit flavours help hide the taste of alcohol (so long as they are made with matching fruit-flavoured vodka). Thanks to some inspirational food historians (Ivan Day and Peter Brears) and jelly fanatics (Bompas & Parr) we are being reminded of just how spectacular, delicious and sophisticated jelly can be.

Gin-and-tonic, champagne or cocktail jellies with fresh fruit or flowers are a wonderful way to return the jelly to the adult dinner table. One of the more bizarre moves to make jelly 'grown-up' (to my mind), though, is to make what Delia Smith calls 'Christmas Pudding (Without the Pudding)'. I can't quite decide whether her Christmas pudding jelly is a light-hearted and light-in-calories alternative to a stodgy old tradition, or a parvenu attack on a time-honoured stalwart of the shires.

Christmas Pudding: charity and family

It does not represent a class or caste, but the bulk of the English nation. There is not a man, woman or child raised above what the French would call *prolétaires* that does not expect a taste of plum pudding of some sort or another on Christmas Day.

The Illustrated London News (Christmas, 1850)

IT'S THE FAMILY Christmas dinner table; the last sprout has been banished to the kitchen and the pudding chef is eyeing the table warily. Which will be most in demand? Christmas pudding, made to Eliza Acton's excellent 1845 recipe? Or that French upstart, the *bûche de Noël*? The first year after his death, the absence of my late, pudding-loving dad was keenly felt in the Traditionalists Camp and the chocolate log romped to the winning post. The plums – meaning the best bits, the dried fruit, rather than, technically plums or prunes – have become an object of revulsion to the young'uns in the family. After *centuries* of plum pudding worship by young and old, tastes have changed within a couple of generations; even those millennials who will allow a currant or two to pass their lips prefer to find them in a *panettone*. Why?

Unsurprisingly for so rich a dish, its origins are courtly. Before an anonymous British genius 'invented' the pudding, by boiling a stiff mixture within a greased and floured cloth, the mixture itself was the commonest food for all levels of society. Generally known as 'pottage', it could include anything: legumes and grain (see Peas, page 124) at one end of the scale, or grain enriched with wine, spices, meat, nuts and fruits at the other. A pottage of white breadcrumbs and sweet and savoury spices – mace, cloves, ginger, the ubiquitous pepper and, sometimes, expensive saffron – might be made with a white meat to form what was called a 'buknade'; or the pottage was served on its own to play a supporting role to the Christmas venison, perhaps lifted with a little sage and parsley from the winter herb garden, and dried sun-loving hyssop for one's health. Don't mistake the satisfying squidginess of the bread sauce on your Christmas table for demotic padding; its cloves, peppercorn and bay have an ancient and noble lineage. By the time of Elizabeth I, dried plums had joined the party, and 'plum' became a portmanteau term for dried fruit goodies; the Scots' soup cock-a-leekie, with its tradition of barley and prunes, is another direct descendant of plum pottage.

The Puritans didn't, technically, ban mince pies or Christmas pudding as is sometimes thought, but they did issue a public ordinance in December 1644 saying that, as Christmas Day happened to fall on a fast day, and as it had been ruined by people 'giving liberty to carnall and sensuall delights', the population were better off fasting. They specifically wanted to stop the poor having a knees-up, on the grounds that it was bad for them. The *Flying Eagle*, a Puritan news-sheet of 1652, abhorred how: 'The poore will pawn all to the Cloaths of their back to provide Christmas pies for their bellies, and the broath of Abominable things in their Vessels.'[1] The broath being, almost certainly, plum pottage. Unsurprisingly, it outlasted its Puritanical enemies and formed a welcome contribution to the party spirit of the Restoration.

The fruit and spice ingredients of Richard Briggs's 'Common Plum Porridge for Christmas' in *The English Art of Cookery* (1788) seem familiar enough to us, but the proportions would feed the village: 8 gallons (36 litres) of beef stock, 12lb (5.4kg) of currants, raisins and prunes, plus 4lb (1.8kg) of sugar, and cloves, nutmegs, lemons. Feeding the village was often its function. As a pudding, it was commonly served at harvest festival, when the farmer would thank his workers with a feast from his own purse. Flora Thompson shows, in *Lark Rise to Candleford*, that the tradition was alive and well at the end of the nineteenth century. 'And what a feast it was! Such a bustling in the farm-house kitchen for days beforehand; such boiling of hams and roasting of sirloins; such a stacking of plum puddings, made by the Christmas recipe.' Her world in rural Oxfordshire was circumscribed with rigid social boundaries, where even charitable giving was subject to a hierarchy, as she describes when, the following day, leftover food was taken to the bedridden, 'carefully graded in daintiness according to their social standing... A plum pudding was considered a delicate compliment to an equal of the farmer; slices of beef or ham went to the "better-most poor"; and a ham-bone with plenty of meat left upon it or part of a pudding or a can of soup to the commonalty.'[2]

Together with roast beef, it was a symbol of charitable benevolence, enabling celebrations to be shared throughout society. William IV gave a birthday party feast to 3,000 of his poor subjects in 1830. The American writer Washington Irving found it a compelling pattern; in *Bracebridge Hall* (1822) one of his scenes of idealized rural life is the wedding where the Squire ensured that 'all the peasantry of the neighbourhood were regaled with roast beef and plum-pudding, and oceans of ale'.[3] Dickens makes us laugh at the unexpectedly wealthy Pip in *Great Expectations* (1861), who is so taken up with the idea of charity he forgets the importance of celebration when he returns to his village home and 'formed a plan in outline for bestowing a dinner of roast-beef and plum-pudding, a pint of ale, and a gallon of condescension, upon everybody in the village'.[4]

Irving worried that the old British Christmas customs which had 'brought the peasant and the peer together, and blended all ranks in one warm generous flow of joy and kindness' were being discarded in the modern times of the early nineteenth century.[5]

Dickens translated his village society of 'peasant and peer' to the more contemporary urban relationship of employer and employee and his family in *A Christmas Carol* (1843). Here is the most famous plum pudding of all: 'a speckled cannon-ball, so hard and firm, blazing in half of half-a-quartern of brandy, and bedight with Christmas holly stuck into the top' and which everybody is too polite to say is rather 'a small pudding for a large family'.[6] It is not, however, yet a Christmas pudding. The name doesn't pop up until two years later at the head of the first 'Christmas Pudding' recipe in Eliza Acton's *Modern Cookery*. We know that Acton, a poet as well as a cookery writer with a deft turn of phrase and a knack for entertaining names for dishes, was a fan of Dickens because she named her recipe 'Ruth Pinch's Beef-steak Pudding' after one of his characters and she sent him a copy of her book. It seems likely that her excellent 'remarkably light, small, rich' recipe for 'The Author's Christmas Pudding' was a humorous homage to Dickens, 'the Author' in her recipe name. The wild success of *A Christmas Carol* had turned 'plum pudding' into 'Christmas pudding'. It was, as the *Illustrated London News* recognized in 1850, a 'national symbol', which was in the process of becoming anchored to a single day.

The problem comes with those '*prolétaires*', the servants, the indigent, orphans, the workhouse poor and those not in a large, loving family, such as the one that pudding-loving Queen Victoria and her husband presented to the world. The Victorians took to heart Washington Irving's symbols of 'Old Christmas', and put them firmly in the family home. The move from the bottomless pots of *pottage* to the shaped, individual *pudding* mirrored, not accidentally, the move away from Christmas as a communal celebration and towards a more controlled, less riotous, family-focused affair. *Plum* pudding stopped being a traditional charitable gift outside the home and became, instead, *Christmas* pudding, the focus of the family.

Except for the poorest, the Victorian Christmas dinner provided a rare focus of unity and shared experience in Britain and Ireland. The modern novelist Colm Tóibín enjoyed the idea that every Irish family in his town was eating the same dishes at the same time on Christmas Day, except 'The only difference between us and everybody else was that our Christmas pudding was better', being a recipe handed to his grandmother by the cook to the grand family who lived in the local castle.[7]

Could he say the same today after a few decades of individualism, competition, the free market and as much chocolate as you can eat? If you give people a *choice* at Christmas, what happens? The answer depends a lot on your age. Christmas pudding isn't just a taste; it is a lifetime of personal memories; it is centuries-worth of folk memories; it is almost unique in being a food and a cultural symbol of union across a nation. But if you are young, what is that besides the chocolate hit of a *bûche de Noël*?

Plum pudding had contracted a long-lasting and successful marriage to roast beef, which were the parents of much charitable giving. However, around the middle of the nineteenth century those bonds loosened, it changed its name (to 'Christmas pudding') and started a new and less charitable liaison with that foreign introduction, the roast turkey.

PART THREE

◆

Foreign Introductions

Turkey: its journey to greatness

A Christmas dinner, with the middle classes of this empire, would scarcely be a Christmas dinner without its turkey.

Isabella Beeton, *Mrs Beeton's Book of Household Management* (1861)

TRADITIONALISTS SUCH AS Irish chef and food writer Darina Allen worry that new turkey products have spoilt the annual treat of turkey at Christmas.[1] I'm not sure she need worry; of the 16 million turkeys slaughtered in the UK each year, 10 million of those are eaten at Christmas. And, although this means that 6 million become suspiciously round slices of white meat, 'turkey ham', turkey crown, the infamous Turkey Twizzlers and processed meat in the shape of toys for children, it doesn't change our image of the traditional Christmas turkey: a huge, gleaming, fabulous-looking bronzed beast. I love culinary traditions, although I'd rather we hadn't manacled ourselves to this particular one with its vapid, arid flesh. There are other ways. Pot-roasting it with herbs and vegetables keeps in moisture and adds flavour. I once tried to live the Dumas dream with a truffled turkey, although my single, sliced truffle was no match for the Himalayan bulk of a modern beast.

The turkey was domesticated by the Aztecs, and both wild and farmed turkeys were seized upon by the Spanish and brought back to Europe. Unlike the tomato and potato, which remained highly questionable for centuries, there was no disagreement about the wholesomeness of this import. The first to come to Britain were brought by the Puritan trader William Strickland, in 1524 or 1526, and his coat of arms, granted in 1550, proudly shows a 'turkey-cock in his pride proper'.

One of its earliest literary supporters was down-to-earth, although poetic, East Anglian farmer Thomas Tusser, whose *Five Hundred Points of Good Husbandry* (1573) is a homely and practical, month-by-month manual for living on the land, rendered in verse. By the time of its publication, the turkey had already earned its place on the Christmas table for farmers and yeomen as well as landowners, along with those Christmas favourites, brawn and 'shred pyes of the best' (mince pies made with meat such as tongue or offal). 'Turkey wel drest' comes last on a longish list of farmyard meats; the adjective might simply be a metrical necessity or it could imply that its awkward combination of slow-cooking breast and quick-cooking legs, albeit on a much smaller scale than modern birds, was already causing problems for the unwary cook.

Adopting it into the farm as Tusser does, and designating it, as Gervase Markham does in *The English Housewife* (1615), a 'lesser land fowl', unlike the prestigious peacock or swan (still eaten in the seventeenth century), clearly marked it for a wider market than the aristocracy. The turkey came at just the right time for Europe; a rapidly growing population was straining the limited increases in agricultural production and its bountiful flesh was a protein-rich godsend.

Nearly a century later, Robert May's bill of fare for Christmas Day also includes a turkey. French-trained chef to a series of English aristocrats at the Restoration, the tone of his *The Accomplisht Cook* (1660) is one of nostalgia for pre-Puritan luxury and fun. He reminisces about the wonderful feasts when frogs would hop out of a pie to make the ladies shriek; or you could conduct a pastry battle with real gunpowder; or pull an arrow from the side of a pastry stag, making claret gush forth like blood. May's turkey, roasted and stuffed with cloves, is merely the seventeenth of twenty meaty first-course dishes; along with other Christmas delicacies such as roast swan, a collar of brawn, venison (both roasted and in a pasty), two bran geese roasted, one larded, and minced pies (very like mince pies today but with chopped meat such as veal or tongue).

Robert May recommends fattening turkeys on barley, oats and malt, so it follows that they would be at their sleekest and fattest in the months after the harvest. It is no accident that Christmas was celebrated at a time when animals – both wild and domesticated – were in their best condition from summer and autumn grazing. Farmyard quadrupeds and fowl were slaughtered in December so they didn't compete for fodder with grain-eating humans (see The Roast Beef of Old England, page 92).

Earlier recipes for turkey reflect the wide varieties of culinary uses they were put to, suggesting that they were eaten at various times of the year, such as in a late seventeenth-century 'flesh sallet' made with fresh summer tarragon, chives, spearmint, parsley and chopped lettuce.[2] Sir Kenelm Digby, Renaissance man, courtier, diplomat, philosopher and snapper-up of aristocratic culinary trifles, shares a few secrets for preserving turkey meat; his 'souced' turkeys are kept in flavoured vinegar for a month, or you could 'powder' (that is, salt) a turkey, or pickle it with 'the Italian Marinating', which has mace and nutmeg added to the salt.[3] Hannah Glasse follows his recommendation for soucing turkeys so that it imitates the luxurious sturgeon – the fish from which caviar comes; elsewhere she suggests taking the bones out and stuffing it, which she thinks is more 'genteel', although easier for the carver than the cook (see Carving, page 84). Her famous recipe for Yorkshire Christmas Pie, in which the boned meat of a pigeon, partridge, fowl, goose and turkey sit within one another 'so as it will look only like a whole turkey', buttressed around the sides with jointed hare, woodcock and wild fowls, is probably the origin of the myth that the 'turducken' (a turkey stuffed with a duck stuffed with a hen, made specially for modern Christmases) hails from medieval times.[4] Don't get me wrong; it is a myth, but it's not necessarily a mistake. I've stuffed a partridge in a pheasant in a chicken, with layers of differently coloured forcemeat in between. It was messy, meaty and delicious; and attempting to bone the little blighters was an excellent way to pass the time, when the butcher declined the challenge.

As female cooks such as Hannah Glasse, and their middle-class employers, became more influential in the Georgian domestic world, turkey began to become privileged over other fowl. Mary Crawford in *Mansfield Park* archly tells Edmund Bertram, 'A large income is the best recipe for happiness I ever heard of. It certainly may secure all the myrtle and turkey part of it.'[5] Her worldly ambition makes it clear to the reader (and to her love rival, Fanny) that, in spite of their interest in one another, Mary and Edmund are materially unsuited, given his unworldly plans to join the Church. It also makes it clear that turkeys were still out of reach of most pockets; but every mention of food by Jane Austen's characters undermines their pretensions at grandeur, and there is a hint here that turkey is a social climber's view of what is desirable. By the end of the nineteenth century, the nostalgic Anne Walbank Buckland laments that, at the tables of the rich, the turkey is 'usurping' the place of the 'time-honoured sirloin' at Christmas; she also complains that it has 'superseded also the stately peacock', which puts her a few centuries behind the times. The adjective-less, usurping turkey is clearly neither noble nor stately.[6]

By the early nineteenth century, the turkey had come to be the very image of bourgeois food, such as the wonderfully entitled dish the 'Alderman' or 'Alderman in Chains' (described in Francis Grose's 1811 *Dictionary of the Vulgar Tongue*), which is a roasted turkey garlanded with sausages, recalling a city councillor or mayor and his gold chain. It became firmly anchored to Christmas with Dickens' enormously successful story *A Christmas Carol*, in which he showed the impoverished but domestically admirable Cratchit family enthusing over the family's Christmas goose, eked out with stuffing, and roasting in a public oven (because the family could not afford their own). Whereas country landlords might have ensured their tenants and workers had some kind of fowl or meat for Christmas, the urban poor, having no comparable benefactors, paid into goose clubs to guarantee their Christmas meat. The reformed Scrooge, taking the part of the pre-industrial, rural landlord, shows his largesse by buying the Cratchits the far more luxurious (and meatier) turkey, thus promoting them to the middle classes (which he backs up by giving Bob Cratchit a pay rise over a bowl of Smoking Bishop – a rather exclusive mulled port). Jane Welsh Carlyle, wife of Dickens' friend, the historian Thomas Carlyle, and herself a brilliant correspondent, reported that visions of Scrooge 'had so worked on Carlyle's nervous organization that he has been seized with a perfect convulsion of hospitality' and she was obliged to learn how to stuff a turkey for the unprecedented *two* dinner parties they threw on successive days.[7] It was a sign of how quickly the turkey was taking over the Christmas dinner table.

Like chicken, turkeys have been bred on an industrial scale since the 1950s to be bigger and more aesthetically pleasing. It is supposed that we are squeamish about seeing pitmarks where the feathers were on the Norfolk Black, which, though its flesh was judged the most flavourful, lost out to the plumper, smoother Cambridge Bronze. This in turn lost out, particularly in America, to the broad-breasted white turkey, so large that they cannot breed naturally and farmers rely on artificial insemination.

Geese do not take to intensive farming in the same way and so the nineteenth-century hierarchy between Christmas turkey and goose has reversed. To some North Country women such as Dorothy Hartley in the 1950s, when intensive turkey farming was beginning to take off on the now-disused airfields of Norfolk, turkey was a soft, southern replacement for a 'fine meaty goose for Christmas'.[8] By the turn of the twentieth century, goose was certainly seen, in Jilly Cooper's words, as 'more chic'.[9]

There is something comically embarrassing about the munificence of the turkey, and *cold turkey* does not have attractive connotations. Early signs of the struggle with what to do with the wretched leftovers include Gervase Markham's recommendations in 1615 for baking it in a 'good white crust, somewhat thick' as it is 'to come to the table more than once (yet not many days)'.[10]

The nineteenth century abounded with recipes for pulled turkey breast, hached turkey, devilled turkey legs (good for a bachelor party) and turkey in Béchamel sauce. Dickens' thank-you letter to his publisher, written eight days after Christmas, has an underlying note of desperation: 'The last remnant of that blessed bird made its appearance at breakfast yesterday – I repeat it, yesterday – the other portions having furnished forty seven grills, one boil, and a cold lunch or two.'[11]

There is a wonderful image of everything suburban, traditional and inevitable about the turkey in *Bridget Jones's Diary* (1996), when Bridget runs the gauntlet of her parents and their interfering friends at Una Alconbury's annual New Year's Day turkey curry buffet, and she is introduced to Mark Darcy. We love this kind of embarrassed, awkward forcing together of two very different people; and we love doing it in the kitchen too. Which is why bringing together the turkey with all the spices of the East seems such a comically English thing to do. Spices, however, were part of our culinary tradition long before the turkey; a history that has made them shorthand for 'long ago and far away', a technique that Keats uses with such knockout effect in *The Eve of St Agnes*.

Old Spice

And still she slept an azure-lidded sleep,
In blanched linen, smooth, and lavender'd,
While he forth from the closet brought a heap
Of candied apple, quince, and plum, and gourd;
With jellies soother than the creamy curd,
And lucent syrops, tinct with cinnamon;
Manna and dates, in argosy transferr'd
From Fez; and spiced dainties, every one,
From silken Samarcand to cedar'd Lebanon.

John Keats, *The Eve of St Agnes* (1819)

WHAT DUSTY HORRORS are there in the average British spice rack or cupboard? My cupboard must contain fifty or so of those little pots; I dare not look at the 'best before' dates. It is a geological record – of a horizontal sort – of my culinary enthusiasms over the years. Right at the back, laid down in some long-ago epoch, is the evidence of my medieval culinary adventures: long pepper, cubebs, galangal. A middle stratum is pitted with juniper berries I bought to marinate venison; that asafoetida marks my enthusiasm for dal; those allspice berries (once called Jamaica pepper) from the last Burns Night haggis I made. There was a time when I could hardly fill the pots of coriander, cumin and turmeric fast enough, before I'd use them up in my attempts to become Empress of Indian food. Black pepper lives in a huge grinder next to the oven, where it can be called upon easily. The layers closer to the front betray my love of cake. It is flecked with caraway – the punchy, slightly aniseed taste of nineteenth-century baking, the seeds suggesting life, rebirth, fertility, sexiness. And here too is ginger, nutmeg, cinnamon, cloves (try them ground in gingerbread).

Now more generally associated with baking in Britain, these last four spices were, famously, in medieval times, the taste of exotic, charismatic wealth. What made these desiccated twigs, seeds, bark, roots and gums so prized, apart from their flavour, was their aridity and hence their portability and longevity. Before spices were brought back from the Holy Land by the Crusaders, even the highest of houses would be eating salted meat and bread by the end of a long winter. Spices brought not only variety and interest to a seasonally limited cuisine but gave the developing European courts the chance to imitate the luxury of their more sophisticated Eastern and Arabic counterparts. In the late fourteenth century, Richard II's chefs created the first 'fusion food', so he could dine like a sultan on 'Egurdouce', a tagine of kid with raisins, pepper, ginger and cinnamon,[1] or a 'Tartlete' of white meat with dates, pine-nuts or almonds, raisins, sugar and spices, reminiscent of the modern Moroccan *pastilla*.[2] Sugar was originally treated as a spice and used in tiny amounts in savoury dishes.

The spice trade across the Indian Ocean was in the hands of Middle Eastern traders who guarded it jealously and – if necessary – violently. Pepper from the Malabar coast, cinnamon from Ceylon, cloves, mace and nutmeg from the Moluccas made their dangerous, lengthy way westward, changing hands in Alexandria, Istanbul and Venice and increasing in mark-up many times. Marco Polo recorded that, at the end of the thirteenth century, most of the spices went to the wealthy Yuan dynasty in China, ruled by Kublai Khan; the Arab traders were not sufficiently interested in the distant, undeveloped European market to try to exploit it directly. Europeans, however, growing in navigational competence and sea power, *were* interested in the source of such wealth. The Portuguese maritime explorer Vasco da Gama discovered a new route to the Indian Ocean around the Cape of Good Hope in

1497. He was followed with increasing violence by the Dutch East India Company in the seventeenth century. Their ships were under constant attack and eventual domination by the British. The British East India Company subjugated local rulers and took over plantations, markets and established monopolies in the Indonesian archipelago – called the Spice Islands – and India.

It was an enormously lucrative trade. Pepys describes his awe at walking through the wealth of a captured Dutch East India Company ship: 'Pepper scattered through every chink, you trod upon it; and in cloves and nutmegs, I walked above the knees; whole rooms full';[3] he enriched himself through an illegal purchase of the booty (which should have been first reported to the Crown), but managed to wriggle out of trouble, while his friend and partner in crime (or business) Captain Cocke wasn't so lucky. Pepys played a Twelfth Night joke on him by slipping a clove – the symbol for a knave – into the captain's slice of Twelfth Cake.

This kind of highly spiced and richly fruited Twelfth Cake was beginning to be seen as a medieval relic in the France of Pepys's time, when François Pierre de la Varenne burst onto the French culinary scene with *Le Cuisinier françois* (1651), his manifesto for fresh food which was allowed to taste of itself, perhaps lightly accompanied by herbs. Now that supplies were assured through European trade, and pepper, cloves and nutmeg were being used in a greater range of kitchens, French chefs started cultivating fresh acquaintances with parsley, chives, sage and *fines herbes*. It was a fashion that suited the growing British gentry class who were only too happy to put the Tudor and Stuart tastes in food and beliefs in rigid social hierarchies behind them. Matthew Bramble in Tobias Smollett's *The Expedition of Humphry Clinker* is an early localvore, proud that 'my table is, on a great measure, furnished from my own ground', including mutton, veal, poultry, dairy and 'sallads, roots, and pot-herbs and… all the different fruits which England may call her own'.[4] Equally proud gentry were aided by pragmatic women housekeepers and cookbook writers who were more interested in locally sourced food. In Keats's poem *The Eve of St Agnes* (1819), his medieval hero seduces the heroine with exotic, foreign spices. Spices for the Georgians were not only from far away but were increasingly seen as belonging to another time entirely, from 'ages long ago', as Keats reminds us in his wistful last verse.[5]

In Varenne's *Le Pâtissier françois* (1653), an apple torte might allow a little powdered cinnamon, but he laid down the rules that made French pâtisserie so different from the gingerbreads, fruit cakes and spiced biscuits that Britain's aggressive colonial trading made into regional specialities. When spice ships unloaded at Liverpool, Bristol and other western ports, merchants and grocers took their wares into towns, and pedlars took them on foot to even remote villages and farmsteads. Many of our traditional spiced biscuits and cakes come from the West of our island: Cumbria has Grasmere gingerbread; Lancashire has exported its Eccles cakes, variously spiced with cinnamon, nutmeg, allspice and cloves, but kept closer to its homeland the similar Chorley cakes, or Goosnargh cakes, lightly flavoured with coriander and caraway. Welsh cakes often have a pinch of mixed spice (although some leave it out), while that richly fruited and spiced Scottish treat Ecclefechan tart is from the eponymous birthplace of Thomas Carlyle, and the port of Edinburgh, according to Meg Dods, was the locus of the Scottish black bun. (See Cake, page 400.) Savoury dishes such as the peppery Cornish pasty, or the pork pie with its usual touch of mace, have also been bequeathed to us from the worker's kitchen, rather than the aristocrat's table. Whatever the gentry were serving on their dinner tables, spice was in British blood, through trade and notions of imperial entitlement; however, the increase in supply and speed of transit meant that prices were falling, and the British East India Company turned its obsessive attentions onto tea, opium and cloth.

Medieval tastes are still with us. The sweet, sour and spiced sauces of medieval food have been democratized in ketchups, catsups, brown sauces, Worcester sauce and Cumberland sauce. Black pepper (which produces white pepper, with its outer husk removed) formed 70 per cent of the spice trade in the seventeenth and eighteenth centuries, and is still a dominant flavour – although we would no more use it to hide the taste of rotting meat than our forebears did (once a commonplace schoolchild lesson). Farmhouse kitchens and bakeries have transformed the taste of the medieval banquet – cinnamon, nutmeg, ginger, sugar and sometimes cloves and mace – into buns, cakes and biscuits made with techniques not dreamt of in the medieval kitchen and within reach of even the lowliest of us peasants.

Baking, with its palate of sweet spices, has a homely domestic image, but we still tend to think of savoury spices as exotic. As we learn to cook Indian, Chinese, Thai or Indonesian food, we are rediscovering tastes of the medieval kitchen which had disappeared for centuries: the now commonplace ginger root, its cousin galangal, or long pepper, which gave mouth-heat to a pre-chilli Europe. A passion for the spices of the world is now fed by many different cuisines, but for two or three centuries we only had one love: curry.

Curry: an Anglo-Indian relationship

Now, to cook British food is as bizarre as being conversational in Anglo-Saxon... There is one small ray of good news: there is still food that is cooked in the Great British tradition of strong flavours, slow cooking, using tasty, cheaper cuts of meat and the old spices. Unselfconscious and flourishing and cooked by British people in Indian restaurants. What could be more British than a curry?

A.A. Gill, *Table Talk* (2007)

FOR MANY OF US, our first experience of restaurants is when, with the freedom and curiosity but moderate resources of living or studying away from home – as well as possibly late-night, post-pub hunger – we go for a curry. Like the old idea that having the Catholic Mass in Latin would enable you to worship anywhere in the world, nipping into any Indian restaurant anywhere in Britain presents us with the same familiar, mouth-watering litany of dopiaza, jalfrezi, dansak, tikka masala, mughlai, korma, tandoori, passanda and, of course, the vindaloo on which at least one young man will be likely to test his mettle. Just reciting this list makes me long for a poppadum and a Cobra. Recently, there have been some attempts by restaurateurs and diners to find dishes which reflect some of the regional specifics of the huge subcontinent of India, but for the last 300 years or so – more than twice as long as we have been eating, say, fish and chips – the generic 'curry' is what we have been eating.

Although we think of curry as an Indian import, in fact its most salient feature – the chilli – was another introduction from the New World via Europe. Before that, the first known English mention of 'carriel' – from a Dutch traveller to the East and West Indies – was of a fish seethed in broth and served with rice, which to him tasted 'sour' but pleasant.[1] For the earliest days of the East India Company, the 1600s, what was eaten in India stayed in India, until retiring nabobs (a corruption of the princely title *nawab*) brought back their acquired wealth and tastes to eighteenth-century London. Many returned with their own cooks and servants who found the spices they needed to cook at home in chemist shops and provision merchants and the scarce curry houses. The Mistress of Haymarket's Norris Street Coffee House declared in the *Public Advertiser* of 6 December 1773 that she sold 'true Indian curey paste'. (It's a contradiction that passed for truth in Britain for a couple of centuries; even after Madhur Jaffrey sat us down and explained that true curries were made from spices, not paste or powder, we still reach for the Sharwood's paste or the Patak's powder.) In keeping with many taverns of the day and most Indian restaurants of our time, she also offered a delivery service of 'dressed curey and rice, also India pilaws' to any part of town. In 1810 an Indian cook and servant, Sake Dean Mahomed, attempted to open the first Indian restaurant – the Hindoostane Coffee House – with cane furniture and hookahs. He seemed not to have had enough custom, as he filed for bankruptcy two years later. Early Indian catering experiments were in coffee houses, very specifically masculine places for the discussion of business or politics; ladies might go (accompanied) to a tavern, or a pastrycooks, but never to such a masculine preserve.

The English version of a curry, the 'devil', made with mustard, cayenne and curry powder, was also seen as food for riotous masculine occasions such as men-only tavern dinners. Dr Kitchiner proudly announced that he had written his cookbook 'with a spit in one hand, and a pen in the other' at a time when untried recipes were common currency.[2] It isn't hard to imagine his testers – whom he described as his 'committee of taste' – enjoying his 'deviled biscuit', an anchovy paste fired up with cayenne pepper or curry powder, as the 'ne plus ultra of high spiced relishes'. Without the inhibiting presence of women he describes 'the votaries of Bacchus' vying with each other in seeing who could eat the hottest food and drink the most.[3] Plus ça change. Thackeray, who wrote a rather sweet 'Poem to Curry', singing its praises as 'A dish for Emperors to feed upon', deploys it as a comic weapon in the battle of the sexes in *Vanity Fair* (1848). To please her greedy and indolent son Jos Sedley, the returning 'Collector of Boggley Wollah', his mother makes him a curry. Her guest, Becky Sharpe, wanting to impress this wealthy potential husband, eats it. The joke is on her, as she gasps for water to quell the unaccustomed heat from the cayenne; and doubly so when Jos and his father dupe her into eating the cool-sounding chilli to calm the fire in her mouth.

Hannah Glasse's 1747 recipe for 'Currey the India way', famous for being the first curry recipe in English, set the tone for the Anglo-Indian dish of lightly spiced onion and chicken (or rabbit) stew; hers was flavoured with peppercorns (meaning white pepper) and coriander seeds. Every cookbook thereafter had to have a curry recipe, although few of the writers had ever been to India. There was a marked Scottish taste for curry; when Mrs Hudson serves Sherlock Holmes curried chicken at around 8 a.m. he declares, 'Her cuisine is a trifle limited, but she has as good an idea of breakfast as a Scotch-woman.'[4] The most famous Scottish cookery writer of the nineteenth century, 'Mistress Margaret Dods', was happy to make her own curry powder and apply it liberally to cod, haddock, meat leftovers, even vegetables, as well as the usual fowls (1827). When she came to edit Mrs Rundell's popular cookery book *A New System of Domestic Cookery*, Emma Roberts, who *had* spent time in India, gave the 1840 edition its own chapter on 'Oriental Cookery', explaining that the recipes had been 'brought to perfection' thanks to the knowledge of officers from the Indian cavalry corps. A curry would be served to please and honour guests who had returned from their Indian adventures, or simply to give some exotic variety within the menu of a middle-class dinner party. Catherine Dickens would have been drawing partly on her Scottish heritage rather than any Indian connection when she served lobster, seafood or mutton curries, though I wouldn't blame any nation for her ghastly sounding rabbit curry smothered in white sauce.

The rule of the East India Company in India was enforced by private armies who were catered for by local, usually Muslim, cooks. Their curries, pilaus, relishes, dals, khichari, kormas and Indian omelettes served in the officers' mess gave many soldiers and visiting merchants a lifelong passion for Indian cookery. One such, Sandford Arnot, returning to England to teach Indian languages at the London Oriental Institution, translated a treatise of Indian cookery from Persian, Bengali and Hindustani in 1831. He directed the book rather pointedly to his countrywomen who, he says 'in these degenerate days', had considered it beneath their dignity to learn anything about 'the heat and smoke of the Bábarchí khánah, or even discussed its delicate processes with the swarthy operator'. Consequently, they had no idea, when they returned to Britain, how to cater for their husbands who would miss authentic dishes such as 'Fried Fowl of Muhammed Shah', painstakingly prepared with almonds, aniseed, cardamoms, cloves, cinnamon, raw ginger, lime and dry coriander, or the 'chatnee' of mango, flavoured with nigella seed and spearmint and kept in the sun for fifteen days.[5]

After the Indian Rebellion in 1857, when the East India Company became the government-controlled Raj, curry began to lose caste. The traders and military of the Company were supplemented by a host of ambitious middle-class colonial servants. Many brought their fiancées and wives: young women of little domestic experience who were quite bewildered as to how to conjure English dishes with French names from the produce available in the markets, or direct operations in dark or outdoor kitchens, or contend with the unknown and unpredictable actions of Indian cooks and servants. One thing that the Brits of the new Raj were sure about was that they were bringing 'civilization' to the subcontinent and that British standards of behaviour – dress, etiquette and Anglo-French menus – were essential.

Their best friend was the orderly and avuncular Colonel Arthur Robert Kenney-Herbert, writing as 'Wyvern', who told the ladies of Madras to make friends with their cooks to enable them to produce excellent, simple (by the standards of the day) and *English* food with a French, not Indian, accent, without resorting to Messrs Crosse & Blackwell. By 1878, when his *Culinary Jottings for Madras* was published, the time when an old India hand proudly served a dinner of eight or nine 'molten curries and florid oriental compositions', plus fresh chutneys, at a dinner was long gone and not lamented.[6] In the 1870s curry had no place on a formal menu, although it might still be found at the private breakfast or lunch table, often in the form of kedgeree; or at the masculine preserve of mess and club dinners. With the advance of the 'civilizing' process in India, Colonel 'Wyvern' was serene about the inevitable loss of 'caste' and quality of curry. His suggested remedy is surprising to twenty-first-century readers, concerned with some kind of geographical or ethnic authenticity. It involves having the right 'curry powder' (more convenient and more genteel than pulverizing each spice afresh with a grindstone, in the Indian manner), and the recipe for the one he offers was passed to him, not by a local cook, but by a departing memsahib, who recommended that everything is scrupulously weighed, to discourage pilfering. It makes over 20lb (9kg) of powder, which he is convinced that, if bottled, improves with keeping. To be fair, he does suggest ringing the changes with additional spices such as cloves, mace, cinnamon, nutmeg, cardamoms and allspice, and fresh ingredients such as fennel, lemongrass, bay leaves and green coriander. Colonel 'Wyvern' is, in his military and Victorian way, concerned with good food: the use of 'parsley except the curled English variety, should be considered absolutely penal'.[7] Worcester sauce should be avoided 'with the same studious care as a bottle of chloroform from a lady suffering from acute neuralgia'.[8] He embraced 'Our Curries' as a small but significant part of the Raj menu.

By contrast, the Anglo-Indian Flora Annie Steel, a couple of decades later, feels she can nowhere let slip her grip on civilization or femininity; she tells the Raj ingénue to treat her servants like children (administer castor oil if they get something wrong as it must be due to a puny childishness) and to serve almost entirely British and European food; in her chapter on fish there is but one, brief 'fish curry' recipe next to one for 'Dublin Lawyer', a weird horror of tinned lobster and sherry. She distances herself from the few 'Native Dishes' that are included only by request by stating most are 'inordinately greasy and sweet', although 'sweet' is an odd description for dishes where 'Curry powder' is the ingredient common to most.[9]

Poor Flora Annie Steel would have been horrified to discover that she was guilty of the very lapse that the Raj dreaded – being woefully behind the times of 'home'. In England, a more influential lady, fascinated by her Indian servants, and luxuriating in the title of Empress of India, which Disraeli enabled her to take in 1876, had the newly fashionable curry on the menu at Osborne House, the royal home on the Isle of Wight.

This new enthusiasm for the exotic offerings of the Empire, such as Wembley's British Empire Exhibition of 1924–5, paved the way for Indian restaurants that catered for the status-wary middle classes. The first was Veeraswamy, established by Edward Palmer in 1926, an Anglo-Indian importer of spices. Still on Regent Street today, it plays up a somewhat fictional Raj-era heritage, and boasts of its princely, opulent interiors, sophisticated food and prices to match. The Anglo-Indian food it served gradually cascaded down into the cafés that were being cautiously opened up around post-war Britain, often by Sylheti immigrants (from an area in modern-day Bangladesh). Most were seamen, looking for opportunities on dry land, rather than cooks, and it seemed easier to copy the Anglo-Indian menus from other establishments than to learn to cook the dishes they knew from their own villages.[10] Many took over defunct cafés in run-down areas, and added 'curry' to the end of a menu of comfort food for the working classes (hence chips with curry sauce), until they were certain that an all-curry menu would still bring in the crowds.[11] They learnt to produce cheap food quickly, and if authenticity was a casualty, it wasn't one that the average customer, bundling in from the pub at closing time, minded very much. One restaurateur explained that encouraging men into a display of masculinity by eating the hottest curry was a lucrative game; hot curries could be made – by anyone if Chef was away – with cheaper chilli powder rather than expensive spices and led to lots more lager sales.[12]

The relationship between Indian cook and British employer or customer has not always been a happy one. Customers assume a relationship to the curry – and those who cook it and serve it – that they would not to, say, a steak or a pizza. It is not surprising that second-generation Asians are abandoning their parents' restaurants for more prestigious and lucrative careers in law and medicine, while immigration policies are not enabling their replacements. Customers are trickling away, too, as they find they can heat a supermarket 'curry' in the microwave, add a jar of tandoori sauce to some meat or vegetables, or reach for authenticity with precise methods and ingredients and the right combination of fresh or dried, ground or whole, roasted or fried spices.

Unlike many culinary introductions into British life – tea, or the turkey, or even the tomato – the percolation of curry into British life has not been simply 'top down'. The post-war curry-house owners and cooks had no truck with the kind of social anxieties which beset the colonial classes in Britain. They opened premises where they could afford to, and local populations of people – factory workers, clerical workers searching for cheap and tasty food – were the first to pile in. Eventually every high street had an 'Indian restaurant' and the middle classes were only too happy to follow.

Whereas Indian food has been absorbed throughout all layers of social influence in Britain, the story of French food in this country appears only to be a consideration for a narrow, elite band. Its influence, however, turns out to be far more profound, for better and for worse.

French Food: male chefs and female cooks

> So much is the blind Folly of this Age, that they would rather be
> impos'd on by a *French* Booby, than give Encouragement to a good
> *English* Cook!

Hannah Glasse, *The Art of Cookery Made Plain and Easy* (1747)

SHARING *STEAK FRITES* with my Australian partner recently, he told me that to an outsider the Anglo-French rivalry over food was bemusing as they both seem so similar. We were in a Modern European restaurant; the frites were crispy, skinny and salty; the steak, ordered black and blue, truly sanguinary. Had we been in an English pub, the same raw material would have been served as 'steak and chips'; thicker chips, browner meat, the whole faintly redolent of cooking fat, and just as pleasing to the thousands of Brits who order it every day.

These non-identical twins hide a whole raft of love and admiration as well as hate and resentment that have characterized our relationship with French food for over a thousand years. Before the Norman invasion, archaeological records, recipes for medication, administrative records, ecclesiastical treatises on manners and morals, and etymology, rather than recipe books, give us a sense of the basic Anglo-Saxon diet of 'herbs' such as cabbage, spinach and cress; root crops of turnip, radish, onions and spindly forms of carrots and parsnips; plus whatever could be caught from the sea, river or land for the pot. Bread was honoured and our word for 'lord' comes from the Anglo-Saxon for 'loaf guardian' (see Bread, page 330).

The first record we have of contrasting Anglo-Saxon and Norman ways of dining after 1066 – or at least an embroidered version – is the Bayeux Tapestry. Before Harold, then Earl of Wessex, makes his voyage to see William in France, he and his nobles are stitched into an upper hall, raising bowls and impressive drinking horns to their lips, with some bread on the table to mop up the alcohol, but little else. The Normans, landing at Hastings, are shown feasting, not just decorously, but with a spiritual intensity akin to the Last Supper. William's half-brother Odo (who might have commissioned the tapestry) is in a Christ-like position, facing the viewer; there is more than a whiff of the Bible in the loaves and fishes beneath him, sewn onto the table; shapes of steaks and small birds are worked onto a spit being tended to by servants. There is much dispute about whether this is how the victors have embellished the truth, fuelled by the Anglo-Norman William of Malmesbury who, fifty years later, hinted that the Anglo-Saxons were hungover on the day of the Battle of Hastings, having spent the previous night drinking and singing.[1] The rowdy booze-up in Anglo-Saxon culture isn't wholly French propaganda; in the Anglo-Saxon poem *Beowulf* (written between the eighth and eleventh centuries), the warriors spend the night before Beowulf's battle with the monster Grendel drinking in the mead-hall.

The Normans set the tone for their culinary occupation as soon as they landed; one scene shows them helping themselves to livestock, in defiance of an axe-wielding local. Some memories are long; the great champion of English food, Dorothy Hartley, was still fuming – in the 1950s – that the new Normans kept the best food for themselves, demanding for their tables the Anglo-Saxon farmers' best breeding stock, or young animals which she calls 'froth', after the farmer and poet Thomas Tusser.[2] 'Today the Saxon English, as a whole, dislike veal; it is the foreigners who demand it,' she huffs, before pointing out that they forcibly enclosed land to keep the wild beasts for themselves and that 'these clashes made more hatred than the war between soldiers'.[3] The two languages gradually merged to become Middle English, keeping a lowly Old English vocabulary for the animals that the Anglo-Saxons tended and which have turned into our swine, cow, sheep, hen, deer – distinct from the Old French for the meat that the Normans consumed, which have become pork, beef, mutton, poultry and venison.

It is foolish to try to collapse the next 600 years into one phrase, but French and English food trod broadly parallel paths until the mid-seventeenth century when Oliver Cromwell brought war, hunger and official strictures against celebratory dinners and gave his aristocratic enemies yet more reasons to hanker after French food. *The Court and Kitchen of Elizabeth, Commonly Called Joan Cromwel*, a strange book purporting to be by Cromwell's wife (but probably written by the publisher, Randal Taylor), fulminated about the couple's parsimony, modest appetites and lack of interest in 'our French quelque-chose'. He contradicts himself, rather magnificently, by proceeding to give, among the 'ordinary and vulgar' recipes for eels (common in the Cambridgeshire Fens where the Cromwells lived) and mutton, directions for making 'mutton the French way'.

Charles II, meanwhile, returning triumphantly from France in 1660, brought a new taste for French ways which themselves had very recently been refreshed and liberated from the Tudor thraldom to spices by Varenne (see Old Spice, page 154). Court life began to sparkle with the new 'Champaign'.[4] Nothing was too fine, too exotic, or too French. Pepys, always alert to the latest fashion, and needing to make up after a row about her hairstyle, takes his wife, Elizabeth, to dine in Covent Garden at a new kind of place, a restaurant or French house, where the proprietor 'in a moment almost had the table covered, and clean glasses, and all in the French manner... and to our great liking'.[5]

Thus began another 400 years of the Anglo-French food fight, exemplified in Britain by the tension between Frenchified male chefs and resolutely English female cooks.

Like their French counterparts, Restoration chefs saw themselves as part of a noble, masculine project to restore and
reinvigorate the aristocratic European culinary tradition in Britain.
Robert May's 1660 autobiographical preface to *The Accomplisht
Cook* stresses his French training and the loftiness of his English
employers' tastes. It is echoed in part by William Rabisha whose
book *The Whole Body of Cookery Dissected*, published just one
year later, also vaunts his wide experience at home and abroad
cooking for the nobility, 'embassadors' and for the royal court
in exile. Rabisha is also making a claim for the chef himself who
is placing the art and science of cookery in a public sphere of
learning and knowledge which anticipates the Enlightenment. He
reassures his fellow chefs that they need not fear that he is sharing
his knowledge as he is already on a level so vastly superior to
'every Kitchen wench' who might also try to profit by it.[6]

Kitchen wenches notwithstanding, Rabisha bargained without
Britain's post-Restoration fluidity of social structure which
enabled entrepreneurs to quietly subvert his assumptions of
superiority. Hannah Woolley, the first Englishwoman to publish
a cookbook, was not the first woman to make a living for herself
by her culinary knowledge and practical experience as a cook
to the gentry. What was so innovative about her various books,
published in the 1660s, is that they not only addressed themselves
to a whole new audience – women – but to women of all ranks
or, as she delicately put it, 'all other of the Female Sex who do
delight in, or be desirous of good Accomplishments'.[7] She wrote
for gentlewomen who wanted to make preserves, creams and
medicines, for professional cooks in service and for the housewife.
Eliza Smith, too, believed that we had 'to our Disgrace so fondly
admired the French Tongue, French Modes, and also French
Messes' and offered her readers natural and wholesome receipts
that suited the products of our own country. She emphasized
that they actually worked and were suitable for both frugal and
sumptuous tables, unlike the cookbook writers who boasted of
their noble and princely patrons and produced impracticable,

whimsical, unpalatable, unwholesome receipts.[8] By contrast, across the Channel, François Massialot addressed himself to fellow professionals catering for 'the Houses of Persons of great Quality', believing that they had no need to specifically cater for 'the meaner sort of Country-People... because the Management of them may be easily perform'd'.[9] The first book for the bourgeoisie wasn't published until *La Cuisinière bourgeoise* in 1746, written by a cook known simply by the single name Menon.

Woolley and Smith paved the way for the most famous cookbook of the eighteenth century. Published in 1747, *The Art of Cookery Made Plain and Easy* by Hannah Glasse scoffed lustily at the extravagance and expense of French food, French chefs and the gentlemen who believed they must have both. She saw, rightly, that the jargon they used – 'the high, polite Stile' that talked of 'lardons' instead of 'pieces of bacon' – made their books inaccessible to the cooks, housekeepers and housewives who did 99 per cent of the cooking in the country. However, in spite of her professed scorn, like Eliza Smith and Randal Taylor before her, she cannot shake off the allure of 'The French way of dressing partridges' (with truffles), or 'kickshaws' (the anglicization of *quelque chose*).

In spite of its enormous success, Samuel Johnson complained that the recipes were not sufficiently modernized or simplified, and boasted that he could do better as: 'Women can spin very well; but they cannot make a good book of Cookery.'[10] Nobody called upon him to produce this superior cookbook because, in fact, modernization and simplification were, to a large extent, why female cooks in the eighteenth century not only dominated the market for cookbooks, but between them laid down the contemporary domestic palate. If there is a nostalgia in current times for fresh, locally grown, British food, then it is for the food of the eighteenth-century rural yeoman and gentry class, which would almost invariably have been cooked by a female housekeeper, cook or staff.

The eighteenth-century diarist Parson Woodforde had his niece Nancy to oversee a head- and under-maid; between them they would have produced this convivial dinner for his usual dining companions:

> A Couple of Chickens boiled and a Tongue, a Leg of Mutton boiled and Capers and Batter Pudding for the first Course, Second, a couple of Ducks roasted and green Peas, some Artichokes, Tarts and Blancmange. After dinner, Almonds and Raisins, Oranges and Strawberries, Mountain and Port Wines. Peas and Strawberries the first gathered this year by me.[11]

In France, the aristocracy kept away from their châteaux and parks for fear of missing out on court intrigue and preferment, until the Revolution and the Napoleonic Wars made the former a less dangerous place to be than the latter.[12] In contrast, the English upper classes were happy to spend whole seasons in their stately homes, particularly when it coincided with the season for blood sports. Their French-trained chefs would accompany them, to cook delicate white soup from pale veal or chicken and almonds, and prepare the warming, spiced port drink negus for ball suppers and show the local gentry what a French-trained chef on £60 per annum could do. English female cooks might earn only £10 a year but they could also produce something a hostess would be proud of. In *Pride and Prejudice* Mrs Bennett gives herself a congratulatory review for the dinner she eventually gets to serve Bingley and Darcy:

> The venison was roasted to a turn – and everybody said they never saw so fat a haunch. The soup was fifty times better than what we had at the Lucas's last week; and even Mr Darcy acknowledged that the partridges were remarkably well done; and I suppose he has two or three French cooks at least.[13]

French food was beginning to filter down into other classes via cookbooks, such as Hannah Glasse's or, later, those written by French chefs working in England, in which case they might anglicize their methods and foods. French chefs, such as Mr Darcy's, cooking from their own recipes or their own books, enabled the most privileged to eat French food which compared with the quality of their French counterparts.

It was in London, though, that the nationality of your master cook and the style of dishes on your table most powerfully denoted your political allegiance. The Whig Lord Chesterfield, whose letters to his son give such a wonderfully amusing portrayal of the demands of high-society life (see Carving, page 84), employed the prestigious French chef Vincent la Chapelle, author of *The Modern Cook*. It gave him great pulling power for his dinner parties in a circle where social cachet also meant political clout. *The Modern Cook* contains pull-out pages showing table layouts with bills of fare to match. One, for 100 covers, lists a first course of 175 dishes, the second of 166 (some of which were 'standing dishes' and some 'removes' which were replaced by fresh), plus sixty-six sallets, oranges and lemons and thirty sauces. There is also a third course in which boars' heads, woodcocks and plovers are joined by sweet cakes including the unusual 'small loaves of Pistaches and Chocolate'.

The palate, jaded with larks, tortoises, hares, calves' ears, is enlivened with costly stimulants such as truffles, cockscombs and crayfish. Although it is written in English it is deliberately international: a familiar dish such as a rump of mutton is served with parmesan; young rabbits are done 'the Italian way'; a 'Surloin' of beef is done 'en Balon'; hams are 'en Crepine'. It turns the dining table into a political manifesto, announcing liberality, cosmopolitanism and power. It was rich for satire; from Dublin, Jonathan Swift scorned the pretentiousness of French food and the employer who cared about it enough to be in thrall to their cook. In his satirical *Directions to Servants* he directs the cook, 'If a Lump of Soot falls into the Soup, and you cannot conveniently get it out, stir it well, and it will give the Soup a high French taste.'[14]

At the beginning of the nineteenth century, there was a tiny number of families who could afford French-trained chefs –

perhaps 400 – and their styles of dining didn't penetrate very far down society.[15] Mid-century, Mrs Beeton was clearly writing for Household Managers who didn't have the resources – or the understanding of the language – to fully imitate an aristocratic class with whom they would never come into contact. She gave helpful English translations of French terms: 'Fanchonnettes, or Custard Tartlets'. She explains 'Béchamel' as 'French White Sauce' and 'Pâte Brisée' as 'French Crust, for Raised Pies'.[16] By the end of the century London 'society' numbered around 4,000 families[17] and every city had its own jealously fought-over hierarchies. Aspirants came into contact with French dishes through restaurants and dinner parties. Good cooking was French cooking; a blazing star that attracted all the talent, the attention and the money, while British restaurant-goers drowned in badly made Brown Windsor Soup, boiled beef and carrots or sank with the weight of spotted dick.

By the 1930s, it seemed natural to patrician cookery writers such as Mrs Leyel and Agnes Jekyll to recommend dishes *à la Maréchale* or *à la marseillaise*.[18] The idea that having a French chef in an aristocratic house promoted one's social capital is delightfully pastiched by P.G. Wodehouse in Anatole, chef to Bertie's favourite Aunt Dahlia and 'God's gift to the gastric juices'.[19] Revered, overpaid and zealously guarded from various social malefactors who try to poach him, Anatole is in the great tradition of Vincent la Chapelle. His food makes Aunt Dahlia's house such a draw, only in this case not to the political elite of the day, but to Bertie Wooster or, as his aunt calls him, 'my gay young tapeworm',[20] and the various young bloods, eligible young women and incandescent paterfamilias who drive the plot.

After the privations of the Second World War, we turned to a different sort of French and European food to learn, again, how to cook and eat. Patience Gray in *Plats du Jour* (1957) and Elizabeth David in her books on French, Italian and Mediterranean food taught a hungry, bored generation of the middle classes that they should learn, not just the recipes, but the love of food of peasant and bourgeois Europe.

It took a few decades for cooks to start to explore some of the English equivalents. Pies, roasts, game, sausages were all celebrated on the menus of the gastropub, in Fergus Henderson's nose-to-tail eating and Hugh Fearnley-Whittingstall's celebration of ingredients from the land. We became proud of our Dingley Dell pork, Highland venison, Cornish cheese. The need to reconnect our urban lives to a rural ideal proved a stronger force than the aspiration to imitate a handful of aristocratic families. The long shadow of the French menu has shortened; only the Queen still requires hers to be written in French, according to her former chef, the very British Darren McGrady.[21]

Even if we banned the use of French terms from the contemporary British menu, its influence resides in almost every word and every dish, as the story of the stew shows.

Stews: a hotch-potch of names

George found half a tin of potted salmon, and he emptied that into the pot. He said that was the advantage of Irish stew: you got rid of such a lot of things.

Jerome K. Jerome, *Three Men in a Boat* (1889)

IT IS WINTER and our food pages and kitchens are full of comforting stews; beef stew with rib-sticking dumpling, homely and greasy Irish stew, or vegetable hot-pot with some kind of grainy legume… A stew works magic on the most unpromising cut of meat. Sometime after the BSE crisis subsided, I found ox-cheeks in Waitrose for a few pence each; almost too tough to cut with a kitchen knife, they become as soft as a marshmallow after a few slow hours in the oven. A good stew can also rise to the occasion; 'a piece of Stag's Flesh', as a 1723 recipe has it, isn't too good to benefit from a little white wine, lemon and capers as well as the bacon fat it needs for the journey.

A stew is always *comforting*; a stew is never elegant or grand and nowadays that is part of its appeal. It is infinitely adaptable to cuts of meat or fish; to vegetables and pulses; it can be cooked on the stove or in the oven; and the deeply savoury smell, and the warmth of a low, slow oven, bring comfort and joy. That long braise has been an essential way of cooking meat for as long as we've had fire and pots, particularly in the pre-fork days when we had to wrestle our food off the plate with a knife and spoon. But a stew has taken a long road before it has become at ease with itself, socially speaking, and all sorts of terms had to be co-opted from other languages until we found a place for 'stew' in our visions of cosy winter life.

If hierarchies, as some social scientists say, are stressful for those at the bottom, one of the comforts of a stew must surely be its egalitarian nature; everybody gets something of what's in the pot. It's quite a different meaning to the whole animal apportioned according to the status of those around, whether in the field after the hunt or in the kitchen before it was sent to the communal but strictly hierarchical table. A recipe for chickens in sauce from *A Noble Boke off Cookry* (probably from the 1460s or 1470s) reminds the cook to chop the birds for 'comons' but 'for a lord take hole chekins', which is part homage to status and part practical advice, as the commoner would be less likely to have his own, sharp knife. These days it is done at the point of purchase. A T-bone steak demonstrates something about the diner's sense of self-worth; meat-eaters whose wallets don't stretch to that are likely to end up with meat mush which might not look anything like an animal and be told to be grateful, like the despised Pip in *Great Expectations* 'regaled with the scaly tips of the drumsticks of the fowls, and with those obscure corners of pork of which the pig, when living, had had the least reason to be vain'.[1]

The seventeenth-century cook, inclined to both scale and grandeur, boiled fowls and joints of meat whole, lifted them out to be carved, and served the broth separately on a 'sippet' or 'sop' of bread, from whence comes the word 'soup'. English cooks took the basic idea of the Spanish stew, an *olla podrida* or *oglio*, and made it the epitome of rather tasteless gluttony. Gervase Markham's 1615 recipe plunders the stockyard, the skies, the deer park, the kitchen garden and the spice box, instructing the cook to start with 'gobbets' of beef, mutton, pork, venison (red and fallow), veal, kid, lamb, and then add potato roots, turnips and skirrets (a root like a white carrot). After a period of simmering, a fat pig and a crammed pullet go in the pot, followed by spinach, endive, succory (chicory), marigold leaves and flowers, lettuce, violet leaves, strawberry leaves, bugloss and scallions. Let it boil for a while, then in goes a partridge, a chicken in pieces, with quails, rails, blackbirds, larks, sparrows and other small birds. Seasoning came in the form of sugar, cloves, mace, cinnamon, ginger and nutmeg; and it was served on chargers, covered with prunes, raisins, currants and almonds. Did he seriously expect someone to make it, or was he hoping the grandiosity of the recipe would somehow reflect on his own status? Being the untitled, third son of a 'Sir Robert Markham' seems not to have been a rewarding life, judging by his voluminous publishing attempts.

The unknown author of *The Compleat Cook* (1655) is quite clear that the dish is ridiculous and is 'utterly against those confused Olios, into which men put almost all kinds of meats and Roots'.[2] 'Men' in this case might have specifically meant males rather than 'people'. It was a dish for a lordly purse, a masculine appetite, a huge kitchen and the strong arm of the well-paid male cook. It was, literally, a hodge-podge, from which the word derives; but as the word becomes more anglicized the dish comes down to earth. By the time Sir Kenelm Digby was promising to share the secrets of his friends' aristocratic kitchens in 1669, 'The Queen's Hotchpot' turns out to be a rather sensible recipe for stewed mutton.[3] The 'hot-pot' was in the race.

If one's stew was principally grain or vegetables then it was a 'pottage' (*podrida* shares the same root), like the 'mess of potage' Pepys has on his first visit to a restaurant, which he calls a French house or an 'ordinary' (see French Food, page 166). Pepys is pleased with his elegant restaurant dinner, which turns out to be three kinds of stew. The second course is a couple of 'pigeons *a l'esteuvé*', an early 'stew' via the French *étuve* meaning oven.[4] He then has a 'piece of *boeuf-a-la-mode*, all exceeding well-seasoned, and to our great liking'.[5] The French innovation was to add the seasoning to the meat, rather than serve a roast meat, English style, to which you added your own salt and mustard. The boeuf-a-la-mode is a kind of pot-roasted beef, popular for centuries (see The Roast Beef of Old England, page 92); there is an advert for an 'à la mode beef house' from 1885 in the British Library's collection.

Although the ingredients could be expensive – beef, wine or brandy and some vegetables – the idea of the à la mode beef house was to specialize at scale, bringing the price to affordable levels for the growing army of city workers. Even Dickens' impoverished, autobiographical David Copperfield could afford a plate as a treat every now and then.

In the domestic sphere, however, the enormous pots of mixed meats did not survive the feminization of food culture in the eighteenth century, when female cooks began to rule through their cookbooks and exert a stronger influence on the dinner table in smaller households. The fricassee – essentially just meaning a dish where the meat is fried – was elegant and easy to produce in smaller quantities, making it appropriate for a genteel eighteenth-century household.[6]

Although it suggests to us a creamy dish of white meat or mushrooms, in fact fricassee recipes included tripe, tongue, ox-palates, lamb and artichokes. Hannah Glasse, in 1747, used the terms 'to fricassee', 'to ragoo' and 'to stew' more or less interchangeably. Vegetables, oysters or chopped meat went into a 'stew-pan', with butter, herbs and gravy, to produce 'pretty little Dishes, fit for a Supper'.[7]

A ragout had a specific role in a grand dinner; the word is first found in French in 1642 and was initially anglicized as ragoo. Its parent word *ragoûter* meant to revive the appetite, suggesting that it had already been sated by too much luxurious food. The reader of *Pride and Prejudice* discovers all there is to know about the self-indulgent Mr Hurst, when he sat next to Elizabeth at dinner and 'who, when he found her prefer a plain dish to a ragout, had nothing to say to her'.[8] Jane Austen's contemporary readers would understand that the ragout had become symbolic in Britain for everything that was ostentatious and morally corrupt about French food and the pretentious saps who preferred it. It is a (slightly) more refined version of Henry Fielding's influential contempt for the ragouts of 'all-conquering France' and admiration for the roast beef of old England (see The Roast Beef of Old England, page 92).

The French, however, such as Massialot, saw the ragout as a gift of Divine Providence; it was the result of reason and intellect, drawing on the best ingredients and seasoning available across the world, which could 'remedy Nauseousness and Satiety'. 'This Book contains all the most exquisite a-la-mode Ragoo's that are now in Use,' he boasted.[9] It was no less than a symbol of civilization. Although anti-ragout feeling was aired publicly in England, in the privacy of their own homes it seemed many Brits succumbed to its charms. Hannah Glasse happily gave a recipe for mutton with a 'ragoo of turnips'. Privately, Jane Austen was pleased to order both some ragout veal and haricot mutton when she found herself in charge of the housekeeping as a young woman.[10] Interestingly, the word 'Harrico' or 'haricot', although from the Old French *halicoter* (to chop into small pieces), and also applied to something we might call a 'stew', never suffered the same pejoration in Britain.

Cooks had known how *to stew*, as a verb, for some centuries before it found its way into recipe books as a noun. Launcelot Sturgeon is an early user of the noun in one of his playful essays from the 1820s, which treated culinary matters in the same lofty manner that his contemporaries wrote about science and politics. (His tone offended the *Literary Gazette*, which prided itself on being 'A Weekly Journal of Literature, Science and the Fine Arts'. The reviewer blamed 'general education' for producing the pseudonymous Sturgeon, from a fishmonger background, who learnt his opinions from 'low ordinaries and cheap restaurateurs' and showed a complete ignorance of 'everything transacted at the table of a man of fashion'.[11]) His Swiftian advice to women cooks to 'NEVER TAKE SNUFF – unless when you are mixing a stew or stirring the soup' suggests the stew is something a little infra-dig, a world away from the cheffy, French ragouts or haricots.[12] Stews were for thrifty cooks, looking to conquer tough cuts of meat by cooking them long and slow, or secreting leftovers, or padding out a little protein with potatoes. This didn't mean that stews were always meltingly tender. English cooks were criticized for boiling their meat 'at a gallop', which made it unappetizingly hard;[13] Eliza Acton was sympathetic to the technical difficulties posed by the smoke and blaze of a coal fire, compared with the quieter heat from ash and embers of the French wooden fire.[14] Nor did it mean that all the elements of a stew were selected by the average British cook to complement each other. Poor suffering Little Nell in Dickens' *The Old Curiosity Shop* (1840) is obliged to eat a stew of tripe, cowheel, steak, bacon, peas, cauliflower, new potatoes and sparrow-grass (asparagus); it's the culinary version of the motley company from a travelling fair she finds herself in at the Jolly Sandboys Inn. Stew was further degraded, in some eyes, by dishes such as 'lobscouse', an eighteenth-century nautical version (although the word is probably borrowed from Scandinavia) thickened with ship's biscuits and adopted by the poor around Liverpool, from which the word 'Scouser' comes.

Joining the vogue for celebrity chefs to offer recipes for the working classes in the mid-Victorian period, Charles Elmé Francatelli recommended that cheap cuts of meat such as a knuckle of veal be stewed with 1lb (450g) of bacon, 2lb (900g) of rice, six onions, three carrots and peppercorns. For three hours. Quite where he thought a mill-worker with several children would find the time, fuel or ingredients he doesn't say. He uses the word as a noun in Irish stew, good for 'inferior parts of any kind of meat', but that particular country adjective never endeared any kind of food to the Victorians; and Irish stew suggested a smear of immigrant labouring-class habits for most of the century. Much rot has been written about whether a 'true Irish stew' might contain anything other than mutton or lamb and potatoes, as though it was a God-given recipe rather than a dish of comfort and convenience (see The Cornish Pasty, page 117). I can't help thinking that Jerome K. Jerome nails it:

> George said it was absurd to have only four potatoes in an Irish stew, so we washed half-a-dozen or so more, and put them in without peeling. We also put in a cabbage and about half a peck of peas.

George stirred it all up, and then he said that there seemed to be a lot of room to spare, so we overhauled both the hampers, and picked out all the odds and ends and the remnants, and added them to the stew. There were half a pork pie and a bit of cold boiled bacon left, and we put them in. Then George found half a tin of potted salmon, and he emptied that into the pot.

He said that was the advantage of Irish stew: you got rid of such a lot of things. I fished out a couple of eggs that had got cracked, and put those in. George said they would thicken the gravy.

I forget the other ingredients, but I know nothing was wasted; and I remember that, towards the end, Montmorency, who had evinced great interest in the proceedings throughout, strolled away with an earnest and thoughtful air, reappearing, a few minutes afterwards, with a dead water-rat in his mouth, which he evidently wished to present as his contribution to the dinner; whether in a sarcastic spirit, or with a genuine desire to assist, I cannot say.[15]

Until the mid-twentieth century, when the vogue for French terms for food evaporated up to all but the most rarified of restaurants and occasions, food writers had a sophisticated menu of terms: the daube, the casserole, cassoulets, the braise, the ragout, the fricassee.

Agnes Jekyll recommends a '*Potage à la Écossaise*' (supposedly a broth but dense with a lamb cutlet per person, root vegetables and the winter luxury of 'tiny new potatoes'), kept warm in a hay box, as the 'comforting' part of a motoring excursion in winter. Charity is part of such a generous dish, so in her column in *The Times* she reminds her readers to distribute the surplus of their feast 'on the nearest road-menders or country children', although she doesn't explain how a *potage* can be shared out.[16]

The post-war period of egalitarianism, the Welfare State and the supposed obsolescence of the class war (the claim made by Harold Macmillan) again made English cooks uncertain whether to reach for the homely English or pretentious French term for this dish. Jane Grigson shuddered at what the English term conjured up: 'the watery, stringy mixture served up in British institutions'.[17] The smell of stew is definitely not the aroma of the French peasant cassoulet or daube; it lurks in dingy passageways. Bertie Wooster, a great devotee of his aunt's French chef (see French Food, page 166), says sniffily about an antique shop that it is dark and smelly: 'I don't know why it is, but the proprietors of these establishments always seem to be cooking some sort of stew in the back room.'[18]

In *French Country Cooking* (1951), Elizabeth David rescued us by borrowing from the lexicon of the peasant and bourgeois kitchen, not the French-trained professional chef. She told her readers that an earthenware *casserole* was an essential part of the *batterie de cuisine*.[19] The cassoulets, choux farçis, daubes and civets that made their way onto middle-class dinner tables could not possibly possess the genuine charm of French country cooking, if they were cooked in an ordinary saucepan. She was backed up in the casserole's native land by the Swiss-born chef Joseph Favre, who suggested that the gleaming copper casserole be displayed on the wall so that it would impress upon visitors the wealth and civilized lifestyle of its owners.[20]

There is now some attempt to distinguish a casserole (which goes in the oven) from a stew (which blips on top of the stove) but the historical distinction was by no means so sure and we must let words change meaning in the kitchen as well as everywhere else. When the Victorians served a 'casserole' they offered baked rice, moulded in the form of the *casserole* itself and filled with a savoury mixture of meat.[21] The technical distinction between stew and casserole is lost in my kitchen and, I expect, many others. If you invite your friends round for a casserole, you are following in the footsteps of the *olla podrida*, the fricassee, the ragout or the daube. If comfort is what you are after, it's the stew for you.

It's the same story with the potato: mash for comfort, chips for ballast, and anything with a French name to impress. The story of *Pommes Parmentier*, though, shows that it is more of a culinary colloquialism than an expression of haute cuisine.

Parmentier Potatoes: food for the republic

W
HEN I FIRST encountered Parmentier potatoes I was delighted with them; little fried cubes with other delicious things. But I thought it an affectation to give fried potatoes the name of a human; on the whole, in Britain, we are happy to commemorate place names in our food, but other people have no business on our plates.

It is not, however, affectation, but affection. The dish is a tribute to the man who drove the *pomme de terre* to acceptability and single-handedly improved nutrition among the poor of France and, by adoption, the world. Antoine-Augustin Parmentier was a French pharmacist, captured by the Prussians in the Seven Years' War (1756–63). He spent three years in a Prussian prison eating potatoes without any detriment to his health. It does not seem remarkable to us, but in 1748 the French Parliament had declared that potatoes caused leprosy and forbad their cultivation.

The end of the eighteenth century saw poor harvests throughout Northern Europe; after a particularly bad yield in 1770, a prize was offered for the best essay on 'foodstuffs capable of reducing the calamities of famine'.[1] (*Zut alors!* Can you imagine the British government taking such a principled interest in our food as to offer a prize for its improvement?)

Parmentier, who had been campaigning on behalf of the potato since his conversion, triumphed with his passionate (although inaccurate) essay on the nutritious quality of potato starch. It won him a grant from Louis XV to write and research and the opportunity to stage some, now-famous, publicity stunts. Seeing that the potato, unlike almost any other culinary introduction from abroad, did not follow the usual course of early adoption by an elite, followed by a trickle down the social scale, his genius was to employ the 'nudge' effect, long before behavioural economists believed they invented it. He devised a series of campaigns, each aimed at changing the behaviour of different classes of people. He nudged the court by persuading Louis XVI to wear potato flowers in his lapel and his queen, Marie-Antoinette, to wear them in her hat. He won over the intelligentsia by staging potato-based banquets for influential guests such as Benjamin Franklin and the chemist Antoine Lavoisier. He planted potatoes in his 50 acres of sandy soil outside Paris, granted him by the king, to show that they would grow even in poor soil and piqued the curiosity of the locals by having guards posted around the plot. At harvest time, the story goes, the guard was removed and the peasants crept in to help themselves to what was obviously a highly valuable foodstuff. (In fact, potatoes prefer a sandy loam – well drained and friable enough for them to push out their roots, but nutritious.)

All of which helped, yet, like the potato in England in the Second World War, it was probably the manipulation of patriotism that finally made the French accept the potato in all its own, nobbly glory. Citizen Parmentier, having managed to survive the French Revolution, worked with the post-Revolutionary 'Commission on Subsistence and Provisions'. They wanted to persuade the people that, as the enemies of the Republic wanted France to starve, good use of land was a responsibility the citizens of the Republic bore, in return for their political freedom. Parmentier had already shown that potatoes could grow on sandy soil, and so the heaths, parks, rabbit warrens and hunting grounds of the nobility were ideal for growing tubers. *La Cuisinière républicaine* (*The Republican Cook*; 1794) was devoted almost entirely to the potato (and, incidentally, probably the first published cookbook in France written by a woman: Madame Mérigot, widow of a bookseller, whose son published her book).

To this day, the name 'Parmentier' in a dish shows that it is based on potatoes. *Pommes Parmentier* are cubed and fried in oil or butter (or a combination of fried and roasted), with parsley or other herbs, with perhaps a sweet and salty note from onion or bacon, if you have it. *Vive la Revolution! Vive Parmentier!*

We think of the humble spud as a truly British dish, but that other favourite staple, pasta, we attribute to the Italians; however, this is odd because pasta has been on our tables for several hundred years longer than the potato.

Macaroni: and other Olde English pastas

Everything you see I owe to spaghetti.

Attributed to Sophia Loren by everybody but herself

MACARONI CHEESE WAS a godsend to the mother and cook for a family of six; a huge dish of it would emerge bubbling from the oven, crispy breadcrumbs on top and a squishy half tomato in the middle to remind us all that we were middle class. Nowadays we would have a 'crisp green salad' alongside; in those days we were all happy to have uniform plates of the oozy, cheesy stuff and I envy my childhood digestion in encompassing it so readily. I can't remember who got the tomato (probably Mum). At university everybody ate spaghetti Bolognese, so to show true contrition at our middle-class command of the best of Italy's produce (as we thought) we learnt to call it spag bol. I once made lasagne for a university dinner party on the Baby Belling mini-oven on my corridor. Meat sauce, cheese sauce, dried pasta... Made from scratch, it took *hours*. Today we would call it *Grandmère* or *Nonna* cooking and it still has enough élan to be a dinner party dish.

Macaroni cheese hovers (if something so solid can do something so airy) between home-grown cheese on toast and fancy soufflé, in our regard. It is, however, closer to the home-grown than most of us realize. Contemporary Italian and English versions of it are probably descendants of the Roman. The first *English* recipe for it appears around 1390; 'macrows' or 'maccherone' were pasta pieces, boiled and served with butter and cheese. 'Losyns', so called, as is lasagne, because of their 'lozenge' shape, were dried, then cooked in meat broth and baked with grated cheese. On Lenten or fast days it could be closer to a sweetmeat, served with almond milk, saffron, sugar and coriander seed comfits (seeds covered in sugar). Hares were stewed and served with 'papdele', which were the same lozenge shape rather than the long, Italian pappardelle we know today.[1]

The compiler of A Noble Boke off Cookry tells the fifteenth-century cook how to make a paste of flour and water, flavoured with sugar, saffron and salt, and make the shape of 'lossengis', the breadth of your hand; which could be fried in oil.

Lozenges and papdele disappear from the pages of cookbooks for a while, but macaroni found its way onto the dining tables of people of quality and the 'middling sort'. It was not considered to be food for the poor, although the inventor, entrepreneur and amateur cook Sir Hugh Plat tried to change that with his pasta-extruding machine in 1596. He recommended pasta (supplied by himself) as the perfect food to victual the Navy on their increasingly lengthy and hungry voyages. In Continental Europe he might have been given a prize for coming up with a solution for hunger (see Parmentier Potatoes, page 183), but in Britain his pasta-extruding machine never quite took off.

Macaroni, far from being developed as a convenient way to feed the hungry in Britain, became a late eighteenth-century term of mildly xenophobic and homophobic abuse for young men who returned from their Grand Tour of Italy with an enthusiasm for its cuisine. 'Maccaronies' chose to wear foppish clothes and wigs of big, macaroni-like curls, topped off with a hat; hence the American disdain for Yankee Doodle who 'stuck a feather in his hat and called it macaroni'. The antithesis of the pro-British Beefsteak Club of blood-sport-loving Tories, 'Maccaronies' were effeminate and upper class (and probably gay),[2] making the term difficult to use in a culinary sense. The chef William Verral in A Complete

System of Cookery gets around it in the mid-1700s by borrowing a French word and directing his readers to bake 'macaroons' with cream or expensive parmesan (explaining that they are 'a foreign paste' like vermicelli, not sweet biscuits which was then, as now, a more usual definition of macaroon).[3] Vermicelli became, for a while, the preferred expression for the rich but homely dishes found on the tables of the country gentry and merchants' households in towns and cities. Hannah Glasse told cooks to make vermicelli themselves because 'this far exceeds what comes from abroad being fresher' and we would approve of her recipe for fine, gently sun-dried or fresh pasta, needing only a 'quick boil'. It took the place of the more usual bread and butter in puddings, baked with eggs or bone marrow and those eighteenth-century favourites, lemon, nutmeg and rosewater.[4] Elizabeth Raffald saw it as a savoury ingredient in ox-cheek soup or a rich 'Vermicelli' soup of veal, mutton, ham and vegetables, an ancestor of the homely chicken noodle soup.[5]

In Naples, meanwhile, entrepreneurs were figuring out how to mechanize the process. An Italian explained to Britons in 1806 how mechanical presses were being used in Naples to furnish 'the lower class of people' with macaroni, which they ate directly from the street-seller's pot or took away in their hats.[6] After (British-made) kneaders, extruders and cutters were installed in Naples factories in 1882,[7] its democratization, like that other Neapolitan protégé, ice cream, was unstoppable and manufacturers were praised for bringing food to the masses. Pasta became a universal food throughout Italy and, to a lesser extent, in the rest of Europe. During the First World War when durum wheat could no longer come from the principal growing region in the Ukraine – partly because of the collapse of Russian agriculture after the Revolution and partly because of supply lines – the USA started to grow its own durum wheat and feed successive waves of Italian immigrants the food they had become used to.

In 1957, one Italian writer lauded the world of pasta for being 'essentially a working-class place'.[8] Perhaps it is the same verifiable place as the spaghetti harvest outside Lugano, which the BBC solemnly showed in a documentary on April Fool's Day in the same year. This story of pasta, beginning in Naples, and feeding the poor of Italy, is the usual one, though it shows considerable historical amnesia. The biographers of pasta, Silvano Serventi and Françoise Sabban, point out that, in Italy, it extended to the lower classes of the population only once it had become industrialized in Naples. The Neapolitan style of dried pasta – cheap, long-lasting and convenient – overtook other forms. 'This triumph marks the unusual adoption of a working-class model of consumption by all the classes of a larger population.'[9]

Every generation in Britain believes that it has discovered 'real' pasta for the first time; and yet each version is simply a refinement of a generation before. Every few years we yo-yo between an image of pasta as the food of the peasantry and something exclusive. In the last century, Heinz tinned spaghetti in tomato sauce in the 1920s was followed by Elizabeth David's recipes for the *Spaghetti alle Vongole* and *Lasagne Verdi al Forno*[10] we choose in Italian restaurants, or even, very occasionally, the *Pappardelle con la Lepre* (with Hare Sauce) whose aristocratic English origins have been forgotten. We thought we loved the dried pasta from Italian delicatessens in the 1970s, until we discovered the revelation of fresh pasta (I still remember my first experience of eating fresh pasta, aged fourteen, in Italy. I was speechless. *This* soft, melting, mouth-caressing, ambrosia was tagliatelle?). When this became readily available in vacuum-packs in the supermarket, the crucial ingredient became, not pasta itself, but a sauce which couldn't be picked up from the chiller cabinet – knowledge – and we were assured by chefs and food writers that you had to have 'the perfect pasta for the perfect sauce', as the Italians apparently did.

In just a few short days in Britain in 2020, the image of pasta ricocheted back to one of a basic resource that stood between the people and hunger, making it a thoroughly British staple for the first time. At the beginning of the Covid-19 pandemic, shoppers, stockpiling for the lockdown ahead, emptied supermarket shelves of all kinds of pasta (except, sometimes, a packet or two of unloved wholewheat spaghetti). Fear of hunger returned pasta to its place of food for the people, a reminder that, although science and technology have eliminated famines from mass populations in Europe, the fear of them is deeply held in our communal DNA. Our reaction to the spectre of food shortages shows that, in Britain, pasta is as much a native food as it was in the 1300s; though now for the masses and not the elite.

MACARONI

◆

The original medieval recipe is a simple, comforting mac 'n' cheese, for a cosy night in, in front of the minstrels.

MODERN RECIPE
SERVES 4–6

For the pasta shapes:

300g flour (Type 00, or plain or semolina flour)
¼ teaspoon salt
100–150ml water

Plus:

50g butter
200g hard cheese, grated

Any flour will work. Type 00 and fine, plain flour makes a silky, noodle-like pasta. Harder flours such as durum wheat will make it more like Italian spaghetti.

1. Sift the flour and salt into a bowl. Make a well, pour in 100ml of water and mix together, adding a little more water until you have a stiff, dry dough. Knead it for about 8–10 minutes; wrap in cling film and let it rest in a fridge or cool place for 30 minutes.
2. Roll it out on a floured work surface to about 1–2mm. Cut into shapes or long strips. Leave them on a board or big plate for 30–60 minutes to dry. Boil in plenty of boiling water for 2–3 minutes.
3. Add some butter and grated hard cheese such as cheddar.

That's it!

ORIGINAL RECIPE: MACROWS
From *The Forme of Cury*, 1390s

◆

Take and make a thynne foyle of dowh, and kerve it on peces, and cast hem on boillyng water & seethe it wele, take chese and grate it and butter cast bynethen and above as losyns, and serve forth.

Ice Cream: the big business flavour theft

I cannot see a curious flavour on a menu, the curiouser and
curiouser the better, without wanting just a melon-ball scoop.
Myrtle berry and pear. Pumpkin and amaretto. Banana, cardamom
and ginger.

Laura Freeman, *The Reading Cure* (2018)

'VE YET TO meet that blessed person who sailed through childhood
with a mother who delighted both themselves and their friends
by serving all the correct, shop-bought party food. My favourite
story of culinary humiliation – because it seems so familiar and
yet even more dreadful than most – comes from my friend Isabel
whose mother served, to her judgemental little party guests,
ice cream which was not simply *home-made* (when, *obviously*,
acceptable chocolate, strawberry or vanilla ice cream came from
a plastic tub) but was also (collective shudder) *home-made brown
bread ice cream*.

Brown bread ice cream wasn't always a freak-show; at the
pinnacle of England's ice-cream-making expertise it was one of
many anglicized flavours which turned familiar and available
ingredients into splendidly exotic treats for the rich.

Sweltering, summer Naples was the unlikely birthplace of the
first European ice cream, where the first professionals discovered
that the temperature of valuable ice, when mixed with bay salt,
dropped sufficiently to freeze one of the Persian-inspired drinks

known as 'sherbets'. The secrets of these rare, expensive *sorbetti*, which they might flavour with strawberry, sour cherry, candied fruit, were closely guarded. One Neapolitan chef to the Spanish Viceroy, Antonio Latini, did share recipes in his book *Lo scalco alla moderna* (*The Modern Steward*; 1692–4), including one for a milk *sorbet* – perhaps the first published ice-cream recipe. Latini was clearly of an unusually expansive and generous cast of character, according to the story that he made sure the servants got to try some of the *sorbetti* the Viceroy and his guests were enjoying at a banquet.[1]

In England, by contrast, ice cream was strictly for ambassadorial circles. Lady Anne Fanshawe must have brought back her recipe for 'icy cream' from Spain or Portugal where she lived with her ambassador husband, Sir Richard Fanshawe. Her manuscript recipe from 1601 has the distinction of being the earliest extant European recipe but the demerit of missing out the bay salt so it was unlikely to have worked. A 'cream ice' of some sort was served exclusively to Charles II at the Garter Feast of 1671. Ice itself had a regal bearing; the first ice houses, with ice taken from frozen lakes or ponds or compacted snow, were built for James I in Greenwich in 1619 and they can still be found in the grounds of stately homes where they now chill their National Trust visitors, rather than the game, fish and wines for which they were intended.

In Britain, ice-cream-making came to be part of the dabbling in (or overseeing) of confectionery that ladies used for social prestige. The earliest published recipe for ice cream in 1718 had royal benediction if its author, Mary Eales, was the confectioner to Queen Anne as she claimed. Her instructions of how 'to ice' her creams of fruit, barley, eryngo (a plant also known as sea holly), chocolate, sack or almonds don't say anything about churning the mixture, so the result would be a formidably solid block for the diner.[2]

A few decades later, Hannah Glasse, pitying the 'Ladies who reside chiefly in the country, where they have no opportunity of procuring things from a Confectioner', offers them her own serviceable recipe for ice cream. The most famous London confectioners, Italian and French men, mastered the freezing and churning technique that stopped ice crystals forming and kept the texture smooth. They opened shops such as The Pot and Pineapple, where from around 1765 Domenico Negri sold 'All sorts of Ice, Fruits and Creams in the best Italian manner'.[3] Besides its pleasing alliteration, the exotic and expensive 'pineapple' and the Mayfair address left no doubt about the status of the customers it attracted, and by the time his business partner James Gunter took over and changed the name to Gunter's Tea Shop, it was an established port of call on the fashionable circuit. The location on Berkeley Square allowed ladies to keep their propriety intact by remaining in their carriages and eating ices brought to them from attendant gentlemen or waiters. The juvenile Jane Austen found such niceties hilarious. In *The Beautifull Cassandra*, written when Jane was twelve or thirteen, her anti-heroine visits a pastry shop, 'devoured six ices, refused to pay for them, knocked down the Pastry-Cook and walked away'. The older Jane, however, was happy to embrace the gentility of the ice-cream lifestyle. Staying with her wealthy brother, she reminded the real Cassandra, her sister, that they needed to attend to the homely orange wine, 'But in the meantime for Elegance & Ease & Luxury... I shall eat Ice & drink French wine, & be above Vulgar Economy.'[4]

Georgian ice cream was quite something. The flavours developed by confectioners such as the 'ingenious foreigner' Mr Borella, author of *The Court and Country Confectioner* (1770), were sophisticated and clean, reflecting tastes for desserts and drinks. Commercial and household confectioners began to experiment with bergamot (later used to flavour Earl Grey tea), jasmine, green and black tea, coffee and liqueurs and rum punches, as well as a wide range of fruit, including elderflower and nuts, such as 'burnt filbert' (hazelnut). Confectioners used pewter moulds to make ice creams in the shape of fruit, vegetables and flowers, painted with vegetable dyes, indigo or saffron. The famous salty-sweet parmesan ice cream shaped like a wedge of cheese was coloured with a burnt sugar skin.[5]

In 1822, Messrs Gunter informed 'the nobility', through *The Times*, that they could once again 'supply their Cream and Fruit Ices', having received a cargo of ice from the Greenland Sea.[6] Fifty years later, imports from the Arctic were routine; and the 'ice' was the high point of the middle-class urban dinner party, the more coloured and complex the better.

The doyenne of ices, at the late Victorian height of ice mania, was Mrs A.B. Marshall, who enjoyed offering delightful jokey recipes such as an apple ice cream, coloured green, textured with pistachio and formed in a cucumber mould; or the famous Nesselrode Pudding which accommodated every luxury available: cream, chestnut, brandy, Crème de Noyaux (almond-flavoured cream liqueur), coffee and dried fruit. It might be frozen within a sphere to resemble Christmas pudding, or frozen with a piece of pipe or bottle in the centre which, when removed, gave space for an iced macédoine of fruits. Hers is the ultimate in recipes for our old friend, brown bread ice cream; the crumbs are mixed with Crème de Noyaux or Maraschino, cream and white rum; the half-frozen ice is packed into moulds in the shapes of walnuts or strawberries and the frozen delicacy is served in paper cups. Aspirational hostesses could buy the moulds from Mrs Marshall's shop in Mortimer Street in central London, or attend her cookery school to learn how to use her patented ice-cream-maker, or even, eventually, liquid gas.[7]

In the footsteps of Antonio Latini, it was the Neapolitans who started to bring these exclusive treats to the, initially sceptical, masses in the nineteenth century. 'Ices in the streets! Aye and there'll be jellies next, and then mock turtle, and then the real ticket, sir... Penny glasses of champagne, I shouldn't wonder,' one street trader expostulated to Henry Mayhew in the 1840s.[8] However, the growing Italian population, initially in London and then Bedford and other more northerly cities, gave a ready market for the early Italian 'Hokey-pokey' ice-cream sellers. Their name might have come from the cry 'O' che poco' ('Oh, how little'), 'Ecco un poco' ('Here is a little'), or be a pejorative reference to their Catholicism and its 'hocus-pocus', a corruption of *Hoc est corpus meum* ('This is my body').

Cheap, sweet and hard as a brick, rumours abounded that their product was made from turnips. Although that was unlikely, the expression *Hoc est corpus meum* was a macabre fact. Health inspectors found bacteria, fleas, straw, human and animal hair (along with coal dust) in the 'penny licks'; ices were sold in glasses which were given back to the vendor and washed in a pail of increasingly filthy water. One appalled food writer shuddered at the appeal of the 'hokey-pokey' ice cream to slum-dwellers, calling it 'the delight of the street Arab, and the horror of the microbe and bacillus hunter'.[9] In the 1900s the adoption of wafers and cones as containers at least solved the problem of the shared ice-cream glass.

Ice-cream sellers lost caste along with their product; the dynastic confectioners of the eighteenth and nineteenth centuries became, in the twentieth, 'Ice Creamers', Nancy Mitford's pejorative reference to Italian immigrants.[10] When the musician Ralph Kirkpatrick described Stravinsky as 'looking from a distance for all the world like a soda clerk in an ice cream parlour', it was designed to take him down a peg or two.[11] Before the First World War, these American-style ice-cream parlours began to offer sodas, sundaes and splits, the first in upmarket Selfridges in 1909. Their offering was a simplified palette which, with the addition of flavourings and toppings, looked sophisticated – the antithesis of the previous century's complex, home-made shapes and flavours – but it helped usher in a more hygienic version of lower-cost ice cream to the high street. Wall's continued the trend when it started to mass-produce ice cream with US equipment in 1922 and sent its sellers out on tricycles pulling ice-cream boxes with the injunction to 'stop me and buy one'.

By the 1930s a 'twopenny ice cream' was one of the cheap, tasty treats which tempted the indigent away from sensible and nutritious food in Orwell's Wigan.[12] Over the twentieth century, ice cream became either a children's treat or an impulse purchase on a hot day. Episodes such as Glasgow's 'ice-cream wars', in which rival gangs sold drugs and stolen goods from their vans during the 1980s, tarnished its reputation as a street food.

We eat ice cream at the cinema, by the seaside or, increasingly, on the sofa; we are happy to buy it from markets, vans, stalls and shops. However, for many years, our lust for the hit of cold and follow-up of sweetness and taste brought a disappointing homogeneity. The ice cream of big business was a story of mass production and limited choice, cleverly disguised. The apparent luxury of variety offered by US firms such as Ben and Jerry's or Haagen-Dazs disguises a limited range of four flavours: vanilla, chocolate, strawberry and caramel, which are pimped up with bits of biscuit, nuts, freeze-dried fruit or sweet fruit purées (except for the occasional coffee or peanut outlier).

Artisan ice-cream-makers have rescued the stuff from industrialized luxury, and brought back the sort of ambition and experimentation that their Georgian predecessors would recognize. You might find the most sophisticated flavours in out-of-the-way vans and stalls: honey, rosemary and orange zest, or ricotta sour cherry; or the frankly weird, fresh from somebody's idea of a laboratory: 'apple turkey stuffing' (vegan) or black sesame halva. I once came down from a mountain in the Lake District after a day's walk in the sun to find an ice-cream van in a remote car park at the end of a lake. I would have been happy with a Magnum – easier to choose at least than from the flavours of hedgerows, orchards and kitchens it was offering. Plum, blackcurrant, almond, pistachio. I ended up with a cassis sorbet and remember its cold, reinvigorating intensity to this day.

BROWN BREAD ICE CREAM

The Irish food writer Darina Allen recalls this being known as 'poor man's praline ice cream'.[13] Mrs Marshall, queen of ice cream, made sure that the Victorians didn't think so, by including cream and liqueurs in her recipe.

MODERN RECIPE

For the ice cream:
6 free range egg yolks
60g soft brown sugar
1 vanilla pod or ½ teaspoon vanilla extract (not essence)
300ml milk
300ml single cream
300ml whipping or double cream
2 tablespoons (or more – to taste) of Amaretto or Crème de Noyaux or dark rum

For the breadcrumbs:
200g brown bread
100g soft brown sugar
40g butter

You'll need an ice-cream container and a freezer-proof bowl, or a plastic bowl with a lid.

1. For the ice cream, first make the custard. Whisk the egg yolks and sugar together in a small heatproof bowl until thick and pale. Add the vanilla extract, or slit the vanilla pod lengthways and scrape the seeds into the sugar mixture. Put the milk and single cream into a thick-based saucepan (add the vanilla pod if you used one) and very gently warm until just below boiling (you'll see some bubbles around the edge of the pan). Removing the pod, pour the milk in a steady stream over your egg mixture, beating well. Return the mixture to the pan, and stir over a low heat until the mixture is thick enough to leave a mark in the surface for a few seconds. Allow it to cool, beating all the time (you can speed this up by putting the pan in a sink of cold water). Whip the whipping or double cream, adding the alcohol towards the end, and fold it into your custard.

2. Put it in the freezer and, every 30–40 minutes, stir it enthusiastically with a fork – bringing in any frozen parts from the wall of the bowl.
3. Meanwhile, make the crumbs. Heat the oven to Gas Mark 4/180°C. Tear the bread into a blender goblet, add the sugar and whizz until you have fine breadcrumbs. (Or grate the bread and mix the sugar in with the crumbs afterwards.) Spread them over the base of a couple of thick-bottomed roasting tins or baking trays, and dot with the butter. Put into the oven and, when the butter has melted, make sure all the crumbs are well coated in butter and sugar. Continue to stir every few minutes until the breadcrumbs are nicely caramelized – about 15 minutes. Remove from the oven and let them cool.
4. After a couple of hours, when your ice cream is nearly frozen but just about soft enough to be churned with your trusty fork, take it out of the freezer and stir in the breadcrumbs. Put it into your container, cover it and return it to the freezer.
5. The breadcrumbs should be super crispy but they will get a little softer in the ice cream, so you could keep a few in an airtight container to sprinkle on top.

ORIGINAL RECIPE: BROWN BREAD ICE (CRÈME DE PAIN BIS)

From *The Book of Ices* by Mrs A.B. Marshall (1885)

◆

Make a pint of brown bread crumbs and mix them with 8 tablespoonfuls of noyeau or maraschino syrup, a few drops of vanilla essence, and 1 pint of cream or unsweetened custard, and freeze dry. Serve in a pile or mould. This is a good entremet or dessert ice, and is much liked for garden and evening parties. It can also be served as a supper ice.

Gingerbread: feast and famine

An I had but one penny in the world, thou shouldst have it to buy gingerbread.

William Shakespeare, *Love's Labour's Lost*

IN MY MOTHER'S copy of *The Continental Cookbook*, published in the early 1960s, there is a recipe for a gingerbread house. It must have been made for my eldest sister's birthday as a huge treat one year, for in my father's neat handwriting was written '17 ½ hours'. I used to gaze at it longingly but hopelessly, for no busy parent was going to spend that time making a cake for the third child of four. The home-made gingerbread house birthday or Christmas treat is for the child whose parents have the biggest luxury of all. Time.

In periods when a cook's time was relatively cheap, but exotic ingredients were costly, gingerbread was an extraordinarily iconic treat. Its earliest incarnations were strange concoctions of breadcrumbs, honey and various spices – not always including ginger. Chaucer's Sir Thopas in *The Canterbury Tales*, written in the late fourteenth century, is treated by his followers with royally spiced wine, together with 'gyngebreed' either made from or served with liquorice, cumin and sugar (the text isn't entirely clear).[1] A century later, the ingredients alone aren't enough to impress, and artistry was demanded to colour it red with red sanders (sandalwood) and decorate it with box leaves, pinned with cloves, perhaps so it resembled ornamental studwork.[2] A later, less sticky version was pressed into detailed wooden moulds, dried and covered with the thinnest layer of gilt. Gilding the gingerbread indeed. The moulds were usually in tribute to visiting dignitaries, but Pepys records 'taffies' – gingerbread figures of Welshmen, sometimes riding a goat – which were produced to mock the Welsh.

Away from court, gingerbread was enjoyed by agricultural workers at their annual fairs, from which the ginger biscuits got their name of fairings. It is also a treat long associated with children. Jane Austen slips a telling detail into *Emma* in which the local children dawdle around the baker's bow window, eyeing the gingerbread; a village street scene suggesting both plenty and a level of want which is unusual in her fiction, but which she delicately explores with the shabby genteel Bates family. In *David Copperfield* (1850), Dickens' semi-autobiographical novel, he enumerates various cakes, as if remembering a childish sweet tooth absent in most of his fiction; gingerbread is a treat for the child-like character of Mr Dick, who cannot be trusted with money so his benefactress opens an account for him at the cake shop (to the maximum of a penny a day). By this time, gingerbread also meant cake as well as biscuit. Eliza Acton's namesake recipe for Acton gingerbread is one of the first and best, skilfully made with lots of ginger, fresh lemons and a trace of cloves which hints at the early use of cloves as decoration.

Saints' days also gave a route for local delicacies to become part of parish celebrations, such as the Grasmere Rush Bearing which used Grasmere gingerbread (and a penny) as an encouragement for local children to take part in bringing rushes to St Oswald's church, around the feast day of 5 August. The makers of Grasmere gingerbread have cleverly caught the imagination of the many tourists visiting Wordsworth's village; the secret recipe devised by local cook Sarah Nelson in the 1850s is still, supposedly, locked in a bank vault. It's true that of all the Grasmere gingerbread recipes I've tried, none comes close to its apparent defiance of culinary science to be simultaneously cake and biscuit, dense and light, crumbly and moist, exotic and wholesome.

Hansel and Gretel, published by the Brothers Grimm in 1812, popularized the decorated gingerbread house, transfiguring the traditional festive treat into a Christmas extravagance in Scandinavia, Germany, the USA and, increasingly, in Britain. *Hansel and Gretel* uses the long-standing association of gingerbread with children to explore two contrasting folk preoccupations. One is the idea of the *Land of Cockaigne*, an adult medieval fantasy land of freely available food, drink, sex and leisure, easily adjusted to a childish palate of beautifully decorated sweetmeats. The other side of the coin is the threat of starvation. Hansel and Gretel are ejected from their home into the forest because there is a famine in the land and their parents have run out of food. At times, particularly in the fourteenth century, the population of Europe was reduced by something between 10 and 25 per cent as peasants starved to death. Localized famines throughout Europe were as common as harvest failure and war, until more efficient transport and markets allowed a better spread of resources by the end of the eighteenth century. The spectres of starvation, family breakdown and desertion, and the abuse to society of hoarding, even cannibalism, stalk the folklore of European peasantry.[3] While the rest of the land is starving, the witch has hoarded bread and cake (not forgetting the windows of spun sugar); and in case that doesn't adequately convey her offence against the common good, she also has the unnatural desire for the flesh of the children, for which she is punished by death.

In the West, famine is too long gone out of our folk memory for us even to be grateful. Yet we believe we have time famine. Gingerbread is still a treat; but for us to take notice of it at Christmas, it has to speak not just of the ingredients which almost anybody can afford now, but also of hours of loving, painstaking decoration with icing-sugar snow and icicles, colourful fruit sweets, windows of spun sugar. One day I will make one. When I have time.

PART FOUR

◆

Rooms, Plates and Cutlery

Where We Sit: and why we care

R. ATATOUILLE

The table was a large one, but the three were all crowded together at one corner of it. 'No room! No room!' they cried out when they saw Alice coming. 'There's *plenty* of room!' said Alice indignantly, and she sat down in a large arm-chair at one end of the table.

Lewis Carroll, *Alice's Adventures in Wonderland* (1865)

IF YOU HAVE a number of people round for dinner – unless they are family or very old friends – there is generally a moment of loitering around the backs of chairs as people work out where to sit. Depending on how much the host inclines to social engineering, couples might be separated, and men placed next to women to get an interesting social mix. I recently found myself about to seat a group of old friends and their grown-up kids, stopping myself just in time from trying to direct two transgender offspring into a boy-girl-boy-girl pattern, and instead resorting to 'north-south-north-south' to break up the families. Perhaps I'm just a dinosaur and nobody cares any more about *place à table* (often but incorrectly called *placement*, says *Debrett's*[1]). But just look up 'seating at wedding' on Mumsnet to see how emotionally significant where we sit at a table can be. There are plenty of woeful tales from women who, having been seated at an insulting distance from the 'top table' or their partners, have felt angry and belittled.

Would it be possible to please everybody? Arthur's Round Table, in legends from the twelfth century, is famous for giving all the knights around it equal status. The other side of the coin, of course, is that it also kept out women and other lower beings.

In the days when tables were created from trestles, turning the medieval Great Hall into a dining hall, the idea of a specially made round table, with a cloth wide enough to cover it (imagine the size of the loom – and the expense!), was a near-magical impossibility (see Doilies, Napkins and Tablecloths, page 243).

The community of the medieval hall was ruled by an assertion of will by the head of the household who enforced a long chain of command and codes of conduct. In the thirteenth century, the widowed Countess of Lincoln was given a crash course in how to behave like an Alpha Male by Robert Grosseteste, the Bishop of Lincoln, who told her where to place her grooms, freemen and guests and that she should make herself highly visible in the middle of the high table. Dining separately was a threat to the order and security of the communal table; the Bishop told her to forbid dinners out of the hall in secret or private rooms.[2]

In *Sir Gawain and the Green Knight*, written around a century later, the lines that describe Gawain being clothed and fed in his own chamber upon reaching a strange castle at Christmas time have a wonderful sense of transgressive luxury; it was quite usual for rooms to serve as both bedroom and a place to work, eat and converse, but the poet suggests that dinner in the private chamber also has an erotic charge. Gawain later takes a seat at the table on the dais with the lord and lady of the castle, where he is honoured by being served first, before each man was served as his status deserved.[3] The dais held one 'high table', raised above the others, which might be ranged at right angles to it – as they still are in the dining halls of Oxbridge colleges and public schools. Jilly Cooper said that the upper classes, on being served, start to eat immediately; a habit formed by the long refectory tables of their boarding schools and universities.[4]

The ornate salt-cellar, made from gold, silver or pewter and perhaps fashioned as a ship, shell or sea creature in homage to the origins of its costly contents, took on an iconic role in the centre of the high table where it was used by the lord and his favoured guests; those on lower tables had rougher containers – or none at all. It was occasionally used as a shorthand for social position, and the specific term 'above' or 'below the salt' was greatly popularized by *Brewer's Dictionary of Phrase and Fable* (1870).

It is hard to gauge exactly how much the women of the medieval household were part of these meals. Pictures of the time often show a male-only group ranged around a table laid for dinner. A few show them being joined by one or two high-born ladies; the ladies-in-waiting might be served in an adjoining room or would watch from a balcony. Women were not expected to play a vocal role in public unless, like the Countess of Lincoln, they found themselves unexpectedly the head of a household, until they married again. Women were kept out of their way for their own sake, lest their delicacy was offended by coarse manners (see Etiquette, page 38).

The presence of the lord and lady amid their retainers was a duty, but clearly it was an onerous one and by 1400 was becoming less common. An oft-quoted passage in *Piers Plowman*, written around 1370, laments the desolation of the hall, abandoned by the lord and lady. The rich wanted to eat together in a private parlour, not in the hall with the poor:

> Elenge* is the halle, ech day in the wike,
> Ther the lord ne the lady liketh noght to sitte.
> Now hath ech riche† a rule–to eten by hymselve
> In a pryvee parlour for povere mennes sake,
> Or in a chambre with a chymenee, and leve the chief halle
> That was maad for meles, men to eten inne,
> And al to spare to spille that spende shal another.‡ 5

As 'civilitie' was drummed into young men, the civilizing effect of women began to be seen as a social and educational good for their male peers. It became more common for women and men

---

* Desolate/sad.

† Wealthy person.

‡ 'spare the expense that another shall spend'.

of rank to eat together privately, but to the exclusion of men of lower ranks. Sugar, increasingly available as the Spanish cultivated and traded it, made these meals sweeter and more feminine. Sweet confections were served separately, rather than with other savoury dishes of the meal, giving rise to the 'banquet', the sweet course at the end of dinner. Fresh wafers and spiced biscuits, glittering jellies and soft creams, candied and fresh fruit in pyramids, were laid out in a separate room for the most select guests; some estates had a banqueting house in the garden, away from the servants and main household. The banquet gained a new degree of privacy to the inner sanctum of mixed-sex diners, and a reputation for raciness.

Charles II's Restoration in 1660 brought with it a new appetite for social eating and a new merchant class who could afford not only to dine, but to set aside one room simply for eating, recorded by Dr Johnson's *Dictionary of the English Language* for the first time as the 'dining-room' and also known as the 'dining-parlour' (in *Pride and Prejudice*). Its bespoke dining table and chairs were, for the first time, always in the centre of the room, ready for the next meal; a sideboard displayed silver cutlery and silverware. Gentlemen and ladies met before dinner in the drawing room or breakfast parlour (another innovation to distinguish the genteel household) until dinner was announced. Now the hostess invited the lady of the highest rank to lead a progression of guests, strung out in order of rank, to make their way to the dining parlour. The host then did the same with the gentlemen present. Everybody knew their grade, determined by social hierarchy – peerage, baronetage, gentry, professions, age and marital status – but 'Among persons of real distinction, this marshalling of the company is unnecessary, every woman and every man present knows his rank and precedence,' said the Reverend John Trusler, unhelpfully, in 1788, in one of the many publications on society that poured out of his own publishing business, before remarking that nothing marked someone out as ill-bred as much as putting himself in a higher than merited position.[6] And if you weren't a 'person of distinction' who had learnt this at your distinguished mother's knee, there were new publications to tell you who ranked higher: naval or army officers, land or wealth, married over single. Lydia, the youngest Bennet daughter in *Pride and Prejudice*, insists that her marriage has raised her status, rather than accept that her elopement has lowered it. The decorous members of the family, in various states of 'disgust', 'distress' and 'shock', watch 'Lydia, with anxious parade, walk up to her mother's right hand, and hear her say to her eldest sister, "Ah! Jane, I take your place now, and you must go lower, because I am a married woman."'[7]

In Jane Austen's lifetime, 'custom' decided that ladies could be better served if they were placed next to a gentleman, rather than gathered at one end of the table with their hostess. This delightfully named 'promiscuous seating' ushered in a whole new set of social anxieties as ladies had to seat themselves, or linger in the right spot hoping that the right gentleman would come and pull out her chair for her and then seat himself beside her. *Pride and Prejudice*, again:

> When they repaired to the dining-room, Elizabeth eagerly watched to see whether Bingley would take the place, which, in all their former parties, had belonged to him, by her sister. Her prudent mother, occupied by the same ideas, forbore to invite him to sit by herself. On entering the room, he seemed to hesitate; but Jane happened to look round, and happened to smile: it was decided. He placed himself by her.[8]

This morphed into the habit of gentlemen and ladies being paired off and entering the dining room as if it were Noah's Ark, two by two. It seemed almost to be a custom designed to show up houses mean enough to have narrow doorways and town staircases, which couples had to negotiate as best they might. Henry Cockburn was a lord, a lawyer and judge, a contributor to the *Edinburgh Review* and a leading member of Edinburgh society during the first half of the nineteenth century, but even with these advantages he remembered it as the 'alarming proceeding as that of each gentleman approaching a lady, and the two hooking together'.[9] The hostess of a smaller or urban house had to instruct her servants to bring up food so that they wouldn't coincide with guests entering the dining room; and architects had to work out how to keep the servants' stairs and passages as far apart from guests as possible. In the biggest houses the 'upper servants' had their own dining rooms so they ate apart from the rest of the domestic staff.

Seating became yet one more fraught element in the society dinner. Launcelot Sturgeon advised fellow gourmets on 'the most important point of good generalship – the selection of the ground on which the battle is to be fought'; one element of choosing your seat wisely was not to sit next to the hostess who might oblige you to carve for the whole table.[10] Married couples were separated by seating plans, in order to encourage open and sparkling conversation (a habit which survives today in the wedding dinner scenario which so upsets our Mumsnet readers); but convention allowed a newly engaged couple to sit together, so that the fragile fiancée might be guided through the demands of dinner by her new protector. In his travel memoir about his visit to London, Norfolk and Suffolk in 1784, François de La Rochefoucauld noticed that, while the beginning of the day was relaxed, at dinner time the tension ratcheted up as men and women came together. It struck him how much English women were sequestered at home, while their husbands spent their days in town, and there was a suggestion that the rituals of dinner were the result of a society where men and women were not able or encouraged to be at ease in each other's company. At the fashionable hour of 4 o'clock, guests had to present themselves in the drawing room, well-groomed and dressed for the evening. 'The standard of politeness is uncomfortably high – strangers go first into the dining-room and sit near the hostess and are served in seniority in accordance with a rigid etiquette. In fact for the first few days I was tempted to think that it was done for a joke.'[11]

One custom that remained constant from the Restoration to the twentieth century was that ladies withdrew after dinner to leave the gentlemen to enjoy whatever was fashionable for their time or their set; heavy drinking, politics, bawdy stories, peeing in the chamberpots kept in the sideboard for that purpose, cigarettes and cigars. There were variations – around the turn of the 1800s, it became acceptable for men to join the ladies in their own time, rather than wait for the host to give them all leave – but it remained constantly popular for centuries, perhaps because it was the first time all evening men and women could relax and enjoy, if they had a mind, the company of their own sex. Perhaps unsurprisingly, La Rochefoucauld thought that the time after dinner, when the ladies had withdrawn, was when English men were happiest.

Eating alone became, for some women, the way to avoid the stresses of mixed dining. Queen Elizabeth I famously came to hate eating in public, and presided over feasts without eating; her ladies-in-waiting would carry dishes into her private chamber where she chose what she wanted and they got the rest.[12] For Charles Dickens, Little Dorrit's 'extraordinary repugnance to dining in company' was one of the 'moral phenomena' of his heroine, who would escape company and eat from her lap, or a box, or a mantelshelf. A modern reader might see it as an eating disorder, an attempt to control one part of a motherless life which was hedged about by a whimsical father and the walls and rules of the debtors' prison in which the family lived. The Victorians began to worry about the newly independent woman living, or just dining, alone who chose to eat something from a cupboard or got the servant to bring her a tray with tea, bread and butter and an egg to have in solo comfort.[13] Surely, she owed it to her husband and family to keep her health and spirits up with a 'proper luncheon'.

The master or farmer sat down, ate, drank, talked and sang together with his men with complete freedom on only one day of the year, at the supper to celebrate the end of the harvest. It was sometimes called a 'mell' (from the Old French word 'to mix') supper in recognition of this unusual freedom of mingling. The wives and children joined them for a meal of roast beef, ham, vegetables, plum pudding, but were siphoned off to the tea table when the drinking began in earnest. A family friend, who grew up on a farm in Wales, recalls that the women would prepare a meal for the men, the workers, and only sit down to eat once they had risen. I wonder whether this lies behind the 'moral phenomena' (in Dickens' words) of writer and editor Alice Thomas Ellis, also Welsh, who wrote exuberantly about food, provided food for her family of seven children and huge numbers of guests at publishing parties, a few of whom noticed she never sat down with them to eat.[14]

One of the many ways that the French sociologist Pierre Bourdieu made his readers question ideas of power and class was through his celebration of working-class culture in the 1960s and 1970s. He saw the counter in the working-class café to be a distinctly male space where true companionship flourished. The working diner sat at the counter, where he could shake hands with the patron and other friends, while each chilly table was 'a separate, appropriated territory' left to strangers or women.[15] It was a distinction echoed in most of the pubs of Britain for years, and can still be found in port cities or the dwindling areas of heavy industry, though perhaps no longer in the shires.

Within the family, your social class is still likely to be marked by whether you sit at a table to eat. The middle classes use the dining table to teach their kids 'cultural capital': manners, conversation, openness to new and exotic food, as well as learning to eat vegetables. The working classes are freer in their seating, placing more value on independence and flexibility, particularly in the face of conflicting shift patterns and the demands of the gig economy.

I remember when, aged eighteen, I was invited to Sunday lunch at a friend's house. His stepmother, to mark the culmination of the morning in the kitchen, handed each member of the family a plate piled with chicken, stuffing, potatoes, vegetables and gravy. Everybody in the family of six, including the three-year-old, went off to a different part of the house to eat it. She would have been surprised – and angry – to hear that, because she didn't compel them to sit around the kitchen table, it meant her family was 'what we have learned to call "white trash"'.[16] As a mother of three boys and stepmother to two older children, one living at home, I think, rather, she had made the decision to dispense with the stress of sitting at table. Whatever possible benefits she lost, she certainly did not miss the inevitable squash, the squabbling from the children and resulting bad temper from the father. Many families, and young people starting out their careers in squeezed urban housing, cannot dream of a kitchen table big enough for a family to sit around; and the dining rooms of our pre-war three-bedroom houses are often given over to other uses: a children's playroom, a home office or another bedroom.

The archaeologist Martin Jones describes being obliged by the preferences of his teenage children to eat around the television, rather than the table. A Cambridge academic, he cheerfully glosses this as a change in our domestic 'focus' – the Latin word for 'hearth' – and accepts that the fire has given way to the kitchen table, which has, at least on occasions, given way to the television.[17] South Korean *Mukbang* (eating show) videos are an interactive extension of this. Young and photogenic *Mukbang* stars, who webcast themselves eating from a table which is covered in a massive amount of food, are popular in part because the computer screen gives their fans, living alone, somebody to eat with.

The Centre for Time Use Research in the UK discovered that people with less money and less social capital were more likely to eat solitary meals. They spend less time overall on eating than the managerial or professional classes, and less time around a table with friends, colleagues or family members, teaching their children table manners. People of all walks of life reported the most enjoyment coming from eating together rather than in isolation. Interestingly, however, the working and intermediate classes derived more enjoyment from eating than managers and professionals. For all the pleasure in sitting up at a table and sharing a meal, there are also the stresses from expectations, in the food, in the behaviour of the people, including children, around you – and more chance to be disappointed.[18]

I'm writing this after a big family weekend. At each dinner, I was interested to see, we took the same places as the one before, quickly using habit to ease the decision of where to sit. It was a glorious, sociable weekend. I miss everybody there and those big meals around the table. But, drinking a sneaky pink gin and eating crisps by myself for supper, I can't help thinking, this is no bad life, either.

Eating with family at home provides comfort; yet the context and culture can also be restrictive – particularly as somebody has to make the meal. It is no surprise that before 2020 nearly half of British people ate at restaurants at least once a week, nor, as we shall see, that these establishments have been so influential on what we think we should be eating at home.[19]

The Restaurant: the rise, fall and rise of British food

Why should not the working man take his wife out for a meal sometimes?

Edith Wills, Labour MP for Birmingham,
in Parliament (28 November 1946)

A NEW RESTAURANT OPENS. Is it just a place that sells nice food, or is it a receptacle for a tottering pile of expectations that gets loaded onto it, like a game of Jenga? The food has to be simple, but cheffy; new, but reinvented. We want the marriage of this and that to give birth to something completely fresh. It's all about the raw ingredients. It's all about what you do with them. It's the service, the atmosphere, the buzz... There's a gasp – if we notice – when it all comes clattering down. Who knew that we didn't like the Mongolian barbecue/sharing plates/small plates/square plates/raw food/themed diners or that particular celebrity chef, Cajun blackened fish, foam, or minuscule nouvelle cuisine after all? If you are a foodie family on a long car journey, pass the time by thinking of all the restaurant trends (from A to Z if you want to up the ante) of the last decades, and ask yourself... where did it all come from?

The restaurant is a surprisingly modern invention for the West. There have been places to slake thirst and assuage hunger for travellers, or for the kitchenless poor to eat hot food in the street, since Marco Polo reported on dining out in China, or a tavern in Pompeii was overcome by Vesuvius. Eating out was essential for travellers; in the 1690s, Celia Fiennes travelled the length of Britain, side saddle, for her health, enjoyed fresh salmon and exceedingly good claret in Yorkshire (although she rejects their 'clapped out' bread as it isn't wheaten – see Bread, page 330), apple tarts and clotted cream in the West Country and good ale in Nottingham.[1] Charles Dickens' amusingly gloomy description of Railway Refreshment Rooms or the 'coffee-rooms' of Terminus Hotels with aggrieved and hostile waiting staff and stale, hard, leaden, furry, glutinous, gristly and otherwise indigestible food was probably nearer the mark for most travellers.[2] Most cities had a busy eating-out scene in the eighteenth-century coffee houses, with a limited menu for their masculine clientele, who patronized them for their business or political, rather than culinary, advantages. The coffee houses' best-connected customers disappeared into their private clubs, which became the acme of very private dining. The nineteenth century's most celebrated chef, Alexis Soyer, gained his fame for running the kitchen at the Reform Club; and made the kitchens so famous for their modern innovations of refrigerators and gas cookers that people were given guided tours in the 1840s.

The gap in the public arena was filled by taverns. They catered to the ever-growing classes of merchants and businessmen, writers and intellectuals of different stripes, who didn't quite make it into the clubs, but who had social ambition and a budget to pay for it. Unlike hotels and inns, they were not places to stay. The best had rooms of many different sizes, to allow for cosy meetings or institutional dinners, with the menus arranged in advance.

Taverns gained a reputation for fostering open and egalitarian political debate, or pandering to the chattering classes, depending on how you looked at it. Walter Scott and others founded the Cleikum Club to celebrate the spirit (literally and figuratively) and literature of Scotland at the Cleikum Inn at Peebles in 1798. The journalist Christian Isobel Johnstone played up the idea by taking Scott's fictional Meg Dods and rewriting her as the hostess of the Club in *The Cook and Housewife's Manual* – an excellent recipe book showing the typical skill and attention paid to the food and service of inns and taverns at the time. 'There is nothing which has yet been contrived by man, by which so much happiness is produced as by a good tavern or inn,' sighed Dr Johnson, happily.[3] Imagine that in a restaurant review today.

Taverns made their culinary mark by offering food that was impossible or difficult to make at home, such as fresh, crisp, deep-fried whitebait. Victorian parliamentarians rowed downriver away from Westminster's pressured atmosphere to have whitebait dinners at the great inns of airy Greenwich; Whigs to The Trafalgar and Tories to The Ship. Turtle dinners were an institution; the poor animals were shipped live from the West Indies and kept in tanks fashioned from the taverns' wine cellars.[4] Their heads and legs were chopped off and their shells cracked open, and the meat was made into the iconic turtle soup. Restaurant-quality turtle soup wasn't something to expect in private homes, where cooks were set to make, instead, mock-turtle soup by boiling a calf's head.

Some taverns catered to a more demotic clientele by offering an 'ordinary'. Instead of the menu being arranged in advance, diners could have two or three quite sophisticated courses, at a fixed time and price. They were often found in places of business, such as Simpson's Tavern which opened in 1723 near Billingsgate fish market and offered a 'fish ordinary' – a dozen oysters, soup, roast partridge, three more first courses, mutton and cheese – promptly at 1 p.m.[5] Cheaper still were cookshops, pastrycooks and luncheon bars, with chop houses a little further upmarket for businessmen (see The Sandwich, page 28).

The London Tavern was a centrifugal force in London politics from 1768, whose magnificent banqueting hall on Bishopsgate attracted forces as diverse as the East India Company and the Revolution Society. John Farley, chef of the London Tavern, had Enlightenment aspirations for cookery, insisting that it was an Art (capital A) which all ranks could enjoy. In his book *The London Art of Cookery* (1783), he offered instructions for dishes 'to decorate the Table of either the Peer or the Mechanic'.[6] Long after his time, it was praised for being accommodating about budget and background: 'Jack Snigsly, the commercial traveller, being about to marry, may give a modest little dinner to his bachelor friends, with reasonable port; or De Bouchier may entertain his high-born comrades with cobweb-woven champagne'.[7]

The London Tavern inspired the first 'true' European restaurant, La Grande Taverne de Londres opened by Beauvilliers in 1782 in pre-revolutionary Paris. This, and the restaurants that rapidly followed, heralded a future that belonged, not so much to the Revolution, but to the bourgeoisie and the capitalist. For the first time, the diner could not only choose at what hour to eat, he was also handed choice, in the form of an extensive menu, albeit one carefully curated by the chef. Fixed prices saved embarrassment and aggravation for those on a budget.

For the first time any man (with a sufficiently weighty purse) could discover the kind of foods Paris's aristocrats were eating, and the city's restaurant scene was bolstered when the Revolution provided a stream of out-of-work aristocratic chefs and a commensurate stream of newly enriched *citoyens* who had acquired aristocratic riches, without the corresponding lifestyle and the chef to go with it. Bourgeois gastronomes such as Brillat-Savarin and Grimod de la Reynière, the author of the first restaurant guide, could experience cooking from the kitchens of great houses. Their writing brought it into the middle-class sphere, claiming it for their own as an intellectual endeavour. Critical appreciation declared cookery to be an artistic endeavour, like theatre or literature; Grimod wrote, 'The table is a stage on which there has never been a flop.'[8] Their work also democratized it by educating palates far beyond the restaurants of the capital, argued the great restaurant historian Rebecca L. Spang.

Britain's lively tavern culture, as well as London's gentlemen's clubs, meant the Parisian restaurant wasn't an immediate hit in Britain, until women came knocking softly at the dining room door.

Genteel women never ate in public in Farley's day. In the era of slow and cumbersome coach travel, their host at a hotel or tavern would find them a private room. But improved coaches and coach roads, and then railways, brought families to spas and seaside towns as well as the major cities. As sociability was the point of these refreshing new holidays, the eternal confines of the private room began to seem rather hidebound. Lavish hotels in Cheltenham and Bath and other spas were built with dining rooms. Naturally, they weren't open to other members of the public, lest somebody of the wrong sort be able to dine in the same room as a lady. The separate 'ladies' dining room' took care of that, so long as the ladies in them were accompanied by a man, naturally, or perhaps an older, respectable lady. The other solution, after the disappearance of the male-only coffee house, was the hotel 'coffee-rooms', which offered refreshments 'for Families and Gentlemen' to make it clear upon what terms women might be admitted.

It was the hotel, then, rather than the tavern that gave birth to the restaurant in Britain with hoteliers and chefs joining forces to offer a public alternative to the private members' club. For the first time, they offered what we now expect from every restaurant: a written menu of choices, usually with prices against each dish. Diners might come at any time. Every party had their own table, but the room was public. The French-owned Café Royal was the first to dip its toe in the water in the 1860s and, famously, became the haunt of writers and artists, such as Oscar Wilde, James McNeill Whistler and Aubrey Beardsley. At the end of the century, Célestine Nicols, the then owner and the widow of the founder, realized this impressive list wasn't very 'family-friendly', and redesigned the interior to be softer and more feminine. Even the arch-traditionalist Simpson's admitted women for the first time in 1916. The railway companies brought the first French restaurants to the Midland Hotel in Manchester in 1904 and the Adelphi Hotel in Liverpool in 1914. Gleneagles' Restaurant Fleuri was the first French restaurant in Scotland, opening in 1924.[9]

French restaurants gave the upper classes, for the first time, a place to meet one another and eat well in public, as the middle classes had been doing in taverns for a century or more. The dining rooms were mirrored, golden, carpeted, candlelit; waiters glided; sommeliers recommended burgundies and champagnes from the endless cellars. One dinner might be a dozen or more courses of elegant, rich French food. It was the perfect, opulent arena for what the American sociologist Thorstein Veblen coined, in 1899, conspicuous consumption.

However, it split the dining classes into two, sucking interest, resources and knowledge into a few restaurants catering for a very few people.

The buoyant and cosmopolitan Lieutenant Colonel Nathaniel Newnham-Davis was the key restaurant reviewer in Britain at the turn of the nineteenth century and into the Edwardian era; he refused to depress himself by writing about bad or middling food, and so only his favourite spots got into his column in the *Pall Mall Gazette*. He travelled and wrote about food all over Europe and was deliberately international in his London choices, liking Romano's on the Strand for its Malay curry, Nigerian ground-nut soup and the moussaka – the best he'd eaten outside Bucharest. Generally, though, only French food – with some other international influences – made the cut. Elizabeth David found the menu he had at the Cecil Hotel, to convince his nabob uncle that you could get a good curry outside his hill station or the East India Club:

Hors'd'oeuvre variés
Consommé Sarah Bernhardt
Filet de sole à la garbure
Côtes en chevreuil: Sauce poivrade
Haricots verts à la Villars
Pommes Cecil
Mousse de foie gras et Jambon au champagne
Curry à l'indienne
Bombay duck, etc. etc.
Asperges
Bombes à la Cecil
Petites friandises choisies

The Bombes à la Cecil apparently appeared with an electrically illuminated ice windmill as a background.[10]

Chefs in lesser establishments tried to keep up by adopting a few dishes they were equal to, translating the sort of French menu above into something recognizably English: Brown Windsor Soup, fried sole, boiled beef and carrots, or steak and kidney pudding, fruit with custard, or perhaps an ice cream. The catering trade, like most of its patrons, was middle class and unadventurous, earning for British restaurants a terrible reputation for badly cooked and unimaginative English food, or badly cooked and pretentious French food. Its complacence was shaken by the Second World War and Churchill's insistence that the local-authority-run canteens for workers be known as 'British Restaurants', which gave many working-class people their first opportunity to eat out of the home. When the Caterers' Association called for these to be abolished after the war, the Minister for Food, Evelyn Strachey, noted wryly that 'the catering trade has, on the whole and by and large, catered for the middle class and not for the working class'.[11]

Outside London, particularly Soho and a few high-class French restaurants around the country, Britain's restaurant scene was deplored worldwide. Some public houses were beginning to serve food to encourage respectable customers. Raymond Postgate, editor of the first *Good Food Guide*, reassured his readers that 'a clean-looking British public-house with a menu outside is a place where any respectable woman can go for her lunch without any disquiet'.[12]

The Good Food Guide was a brave endeavour in the post-war situation; it could not be, in the circumstances, a gastronomic tour, Postgate said, rather the charting of unexplored territory. Its aim from the outset was to be inclusive. The first issue appeared in 1951 with reviews elicited from members of the Good Food Club, which Postgate had founded in 1949, and some blank pages at the back, inviting new members (every purchaser of the book was a member) to send in their reports.

And they did. The first guide included enthusiastic reviews of Spanish, vegetarian, Swedish, Burmese, Greek, Austrian, Danish, Czech, Italian, Hungarian, Swiss, as well as French restaurants. One review noticed, 'Mr Chang sells the best spaghetti Bolognese in Soho' (Fava Restaurant, Frith Street). At the same time, Elizabeth David was electrifying post-war Britain with talk of Mediterranean food. A few entrepreneurial amateur cooks cast aside the assumption that only grand restaurants could offer French cuisine, and opened a new type of tiny, cosy restaurant – the bistro – with names such as The Ox on the Roof, on the King's Road, Chelsea, or The Hole in the Wall, in Bath. Menus offered a huge amount of choice; interesting and international dishes with a predominant French accent. Italian, Indian, Chinese restaurants, opening around the country, also began to bring up the standards of cooking; and their cheaper prices and less hidebound atmospheres also allowed couples and families who had never eaten out before to experience restaurant culture.

When I was a student at Oxford in the late 1980s, we ate English stodge in the café in the Covered Market. Restaurants served Italian, Indian, Lebanese or Chinese food or American burgers. The Elizabeth was the restaurant you went to only as the guest of someone's generous parents; I was surprised to discover that, for such an English name and building of wood panelling and old windows, the menu was French and Spanish.

This thriving international scene gave courage and confidence to cooks and diners who wanted to rediscover some non-stodgy English food. Like the old taverns, it was the pub which first offered English food, initially to a political and intellectually minded clientele; the first of what became known as gastropubs was The Eagle in Clerkenwell, which opened in 1991, near the then offices of the *Guardian* newspaper.

Britain's restaurant scene is now lauded (at least by Brits) for being among the best in the world. The Cornish turbot with brassicas, the Kentish lamb with turnips, the steak and ale pie available in the grandest of our hotel dining rooms (Ritz for the first two, Savoy for the pie) owe a debt to the pub, just as the first restaurants in Paris and London owed a debt to the tavern. The restaurant as we know it today, though, was only able to emerge after a complete change in dining styles at the beginning of the nineteenth century, as we'll see in the next chapter.

Small Plates: a return to Georgian dining in miniature

Such getting up of the steam is unbecoming to a literary man who *ought* to have his basis elsewhere than on what the old Annandale woman called 'Ornament and Grander'— The dinner was served up in the new fashion—not placed on the table at all—but handed round—only the desert [*sic*] on the table and quantities of *artificial* flowers but such an overloaded desert!—pyramids of figs rasins [*sic*] oranges—ach!

Jane Welsh Carlyle on dinner with
Charles and Catherine Dickens (1849)

I HAVE NEVER QUITE cracked 'small plates' eating. Every visit to a stripped-back, casual restaurant with butcher-paper menus and stackable tumblers disappoints me with its Lilliputian portions in return for a Brobdingnagian bill. I feel I've had a collage rather than a meal; nothing quite fits together and the proportions are such that there is too much oil, not enough engine. The blessing is that it never takes very long.

The point of small plates eating is sharing; rejecting that clearly makes me a selfish and greedy person, so I kept silent about my shame, until a friend told me how much her generous and courteous husband hates sharing food in restaurants. What if he is taking the last chicken drumstick that someone else had their eye on? He fancies those artichokes, but they are at the other end of the table – can he ask for them without being responsible for a grease-splattering chain of passing on? I was not alone.

Maybe part of my inability to relax with small plates eating is that it has confused two cultures: the eighteenth-century family dinner at home, where all the dishes for one course are on the table at one time, and the more formal restaurant style which emerged in the following century, where each person is given their own plate. Perhaps a bit of confusion is permissible today; it took us nearly 100 years to transition from 'family dinner' to 'restaurant style' for social situations. It shows something about how speeded up our dining culture is today, as new fads appear before we've mastered the previous ones.

There were plenty of changes from the medieval style of dining until the early nineteenth century: ranks became segregated; servants ate separately; forks arrived; pewter and silver gave way to ceramics. One thing that remained constant was the *service*: all the dishes for a meal were placed on the table together.

A Georgian family and guests would enter the dining room to find a table full of dishes of food arranged in perfect order and balance. An even number gave perfect symmetry; or there might be a central one with the others ranged around like the medallion and motifs in a fashionable 'Turkey rug'. The cookbook writer Mrs Rundell suggested five dishes for a family dinner in the early nineteenth century. Thirty years or so earlier, Mrs Raffald suggested twenty-five for an entertainment. Along with other contemporary cookbooks, she included expensive copper-plate engravings to show designs for the layout, with the names of the dishes given in tiny, looped handwriting. A first course might show fish 'at top' and soup 'at bottom', in front of the host and hostess for them to serve. These might be a 'remove', to be taken away and replaced by fish or roasts. The other meats – whole turkeys, legs of mutton or pork, roast beef, some served with vegetables, such as duck with peas – were ranged precisely around, perhaps covered with a dome, to be served by the host or hostess or carved by a male guest (see Carving, page 84) and handed round by servants. After this course was removed, another was borne in by servants. The same number of dishes were set down in the same places, sweet with savoury, so a raspberry tart, orange jelly and lemon cream were served along with lighter roasts such as partridge, lobster or eel, and vegetables such as stewed mushrooms or asparagus. The final 'dessert' course was supposed to have the same number of dishes of fruits, nuts and sweetmeats and, as they became increasingly available, ices.

At the genteel-poor end of the scale, 'You see your dinner' was an apologetic way of explaining to your guests that all you could afford to offer them was on the table in a single course. In Jane Austen's fragment about the genteel-poor family *The Watsons*, 'the entrance of the roast Turkey... formed the only exception to "You see your dinner."'[1]

The art of largesse, in carving and helping your guests, was thought of as the Honours of the Table, used as the title of his 1788 book on etiquette by the Reverend John Trusler. Old-fashioned courtesy had the host or hostess to ask each guest's preference, to carve it for them and then pass the plated meat down the table. William Kitchiner, keener on hot food and no hanging about, growled thirty years later, 'It would save a great deal of Time, &c. if Poultry, especially large Turkeys and Geese, were sent to table ready cut up.'[2]

Kitchiner, along with Launcelot Sturgeon, was already chafing at the British tradition of what they came to call service '*à la française*' (although it was a British variant of the French style of dining). Sturgeon said that the only reason to put twenty symmetrical dishes on the table was to show off. The atmosphere and food would both be warmer if 'Having thus banished symmetry from your table, you will produce nothing on it but what is really meant to be consumed.'[3]

The means of delivery from this cumbersome method, which both men could see on the horizon, came courtesy of the Russian aristocracy. In Moscow or St Petersburg, dinner guests sat down to a table empty of food but laden with lavish decorations, like the crystal decanters, fruit vases and pineapples around which Count and Countess Rostov peer at each other for reassurance at the banquet they give in Tolstoy's *War and Peace* (1869). It was the perfect way for the Russian aristocracy to show off to each other the fruit and flowers they nurtured through all seasons, even the Russian winters, from the hothouses of their country estates. They could call upon their armies of servants to carve the meat on the sideboard and plate it for each diner, while others passed around dishes of vegetables and sauces. When the Russian ambassador to Paris treated his guests to the same style in 1810 it caused a sensation; it became known as service '*à la russe*' and spread through France and Britain and other Western European countries over the century.

In Britain, the greenhouses devised by the garden-loving architect and MP Joseph Paxton made the central display of hothouse fruit and flowers technically possible – at a cost only easily borne by those at the top of society. Those who, like Dickens, believed in their right to be there quickly adopted the style with middle-class variations (and paid for the lavishness of their entertaining with meals of stodge when there was nobody around to impress). Jane Carlyle reported that dinner with Charles and Catherine Dickens in 1849 is 'served up in the new fashion' because it is handed round; it is not this that earned her scorn, though, but the 'overloaded desert!' which she would not have been used to seeing on the table throughout the meal. She also had to remark on the 'quantities of *artificial* flowers', although this wasn't unusual mid-century; fresh flowers became more popular along with service *à la russe* and was yet one more indicator of those who did things properly and those who did not.[4]

Anthony Trollope gives a heartbreaking account, in his 1865 novel *Miss Mackenzie*, of a doomed attempt by the heroine's modest sister-in-law to give a dinner *à la russe*. It is clear she wasn't used to the style or, indeed, to dinner parties at all. 'It was à la Russe, because in the centre there was a green arrangement of little boughs with artificial flowers fixed on them, and because there were figs and raisins, and little dishes with dabs of preserve on them, all around the green arrangement.' But everything is a muddle; the soup and fish are already on the table, while the butler serves the potatoes and seakale. 'The à la Russe construction of the dinner was maintained by keeping the tongue on the sideboard, while the mutton and chickens were put down to be carved in the ordinary way.' The champagne runs out, and nothing is hot, well cooked or well managed and the butler's determined ineptitude reduces the hostess to near tears.

'Why on earth did she perplex her mind and bruise her spirit, by giving a dinner à la anything? Why did she not have the roast mutton alone, so that all her guests might have eaten and have been merry?' Trollope asks.[5] The implicit answer, in 1865, was that one woman – no matter how old-fashioned – could not hold out against the tide of fashion. Being merry together over a joint of meat worked in an eighteenth-century Britain where everybody knew and, generally, kept to their social place. Socially anxious, upwardly mobile Victorian England embraced the new style, where the business of serving food was added to the workload of the servant, and stopped being an important part of the social skills of the hosts and guests. It removed the troubling idea of sharing food with people at dinner who might not be quite the thing. And it drew a clear line between households with sufficient and highly trained servants and those without.

Poor Mrs Mackenzie should have read her Mrs Beeton and been satisfied that 'Dinners à la Russe are scarcely suitable for small establishments'.[6] Even though she is definite that service à la russe is a very particular 'mode of serving a dinner', her menu suggestions show that by 1861 the Georgian two-courses-plus-dessert bill of fare for a dinner party had been stretched to five courses. A first course might offer a choice of soups with some fish, followed by entrées of delicate ragouts or fillets of duck; the second course was the main action – a haunch of venison, a roast loin of veal. The third course was where sweet and savoury dishes rubbed shoulders – tarts, custards, jellies and puddings along with a trifling roast grouse and bread sauce – before the party finished with dessert and ices. (Her plain family dinners, unlike Mrs

Rundell's five dishes on the table at once, have a soup, followed by meat and two veg, plus pudding.)

Mrs Beeton offers these menus of fifteen or twenty dishes to her middle-class readers, while explaining that *à la russe* might be beyond them in its requirements for more servants, more china, glassware and cutlery. Each place setting now required a battery of knives and forks, as well as different glasses for the right wine to accompany each course, of which there might be eight for a club dinner, fourteen for a social statement, yet more for a banquet. Here was further opportunity for more showing off with French terms; the *hors d'oeuvre* made its debut on the British table, often with a nod to its Russian origin with dishes of caviar, smoked or pickled fish; it might be followed by *potage* (soups), *releves* (joints), *entrées* (which might be a main course), *rôtis* (roasts), *salades*, *entremets* (generally pudding), *dessert* (generally fruit) and *fromage*. The terms *entrée* and *entremets* confused everybody; as *The Oxford Companion to Food* says, 'they have ceased to have any real use... Forget them.'[7]

Now that diners did not sit down to a dramatic and impressive display of dishes on the table, the gentlemanly skill of carving was deputed to the butler, or maître d'hôtel, or chef. A plate of food, no matter how beautifully carved, was still a plate of food and people learnt to be more critical of the taste – and the speed of service, to ensure that it was hot. This style and focus on taste lent itself to the growing restaurant culture and the cult of the chef, from the great Carême onwards. It is what we still expect in most English or French restaurants today. The tasting menu, in which the diner delegates all decisions to the chef, is a direct descendant of service *à la russe* and a reversal of a centuries-long hierarchy in which the cook did the bidding of his or her boss.

This unfamiliar, highly codified and formal way of dining had worried guests and hosts turning to etiquette guides to tell them how to handle it. As with many forms of Victorian formality, early twentieth-century taste-makers swept it away in the interest of 'relaxed' and 'informal' stylishness. Established and comfortable parents, who felt they had no need to learn their etiquette from a book, were determined to bring their families around the table to socialize and educate their children (see Etiquette, page 38). Casseroles, pies and salads, then lasagnes and curries and the sort of French peasant food Elizabeth David recommended, began to be the thing, even for dinner parties. Post-First World War, cookery writers started recommending 'oven-to-tableware' which avoided 'that destructive transfer from cosy casseroles to chilly silver or china dishes'.[8] This return to the Georgian English menu brought with it a return to the Georgian way of serving: although there might be some distinction between meals for families and guests, not many people were expecting their servants to plate up each portion individually. Arabella Boxer recalled that in her pre-Second World War childhood, 'Joints of meat were only carved at the table for family meals; for a dinner party they were always carved in the kitchen, and the slices of meat laid on a large dish, surrounded with piles of different vegetables.'[9]

What had become a rejection of Victorian etiquette became a rule itself. A recent edition of *Debrett's* prescribes a form of dining not vastly different from service *à la française*: 'Apart from the first course, which may be plated up individually and set out, do not serve food already on the plate as in a restaurant. Aim to present the food in big dishes from which people may help themselves or be served.'[10]

Debrett's was battling against the powerful influence of restaurants and *MasterChef*, and for some hosts the only acceptable thing to put before your guests came to be a fully *à la russe*, restaurant-style plate of food, frantically plated in the kitchen. Starting from around 2010, there had to be the purée anchoring the design, perhaps a tower, perhaps an odd number of 'flavour bites', or at least meat, carbohydrate and vegetables (suitably colourful) placed as if on the different parts of a clock face, and accent dots or drizzles of sauce, before a garnish so delicate it needed to be precisely plated with tongs.

The individual portion became more about the cook's aesthetic vigilance than the group's shared enjoyment. Nigella Lawson counselled that, if you have guests for dinner, 'It shouldn't be laboriously executed, daintily arranged, individually portioned. It's relaxed, expansive, authentic.'[11] Around the beginning of this century, one or two restaurateurs noticed, and started to offer a shared food experience, inspired by Spanish tapas, or Venetian cicchetti and, quite possibly, Sunday lunch.

'Small plates' or 'British tapas' was a microcosm of service *à la française*. Putting all the plates on the table at once for diners to help one another to brought onto the commercial table ideas of communality and sharing from other cultures and from a long tradition in British homes. The sharing that we loved about a roast with family or huge bowls of pasta and sauce with friends in the home was suddenly on offer to the fashionable, time-poor, snacking diner.

There are differences, though. Service *à la française* loved symmetry and balance and plenty; chefs now are taught that only an uneven number of something looks good enough for Instagram. Tables of two or four are brought three stuffed courgette flowers or five sticks of asparagus and left to figure out the sharing for themselves. Kitchen labour has a basic minimum wage; rents and rates must be paid; food must be served; the only savings that can be shaved off the cost of running a restaurant are in the size of a dish, without a proportionate drop in price. The leisure of sharing food *à la française* is lost when hot or cold dishes leave the pass when it suits their kitchen rather than their customers, and such is the prestige of the chefs, we don't murmur as we are whisked on and off our table in double-quick, increased-profitability, time.

For all our love of novelty and eagerness to try different world cuisines, it isn't easy to iron out nearly two centuries of dining culture. 'Small plates, we were told, would foster social cohesion. Sharing would cultivate our better nature. Pfff! From passive-aggressive cutlery skirmishes across the table as you attempt to secure your share of the food, to the tediously diffident British to-me-to-you over the last plancha prawn, sharing dishes is fraught with problems,' said one journalist, welcoming the foreseeable end to the trend for small plates eating.[12] It was a view waved away as curmudgeonly and mean-spirited by cosmopolitan diners who loved Middle Eastern mezze, Spanish tapas, Indian feasts, Italian antipasti and Chinese banquets. As another journalist said, it had become 'incredibly déclassé to order anything just for yourself'.[13]

In 2020, all those communal plates suddenly looked a bit questionable in a world ravaged by a highly contagious virus. Perhaps future restaurant-goers will view the fans of small plates eating as impossibly pretentious dinosaurs, like the ladies who drank tea with their little finger cocked, or superannuated cranks with medieval ideas of hygiene. Ebay will be flooded with restaurant-quantities of small plates that nobody wants to use any longer, rather as the antique shops were reputed to be flooded with fish knives, as we'll see in the next chapter, after the smart set had condemned them to the social scrap heap.

Fish Knives: and other
ways of being cutting

After John Betjeman's poem 'How to get on in Society' received wide circulation when *Noblesse Oblige* was published in 1956, the antique shops were flooded with fish knives, and the upper-middle and some of the upper classes sat solemnly at breakfast trying to bone kippers with forks.

Jilly Cooper, *Class: A View from Middle England* (1979)

HE SHARP KNIFE in medieval England belonged, not to the cook, but to the male diner of any rank. An image of the Cook in the Ellesmere Manuscript of Chaucer's *Canterbury Tales* shows him with his key tool – a meat hook for roasting joints or whole sides of animals, ready for the diner to carve them at table. In *The Babees Book*, a collection of medieval etiquette guides, well-born young men are instructed over and over again to keep their knives clean and sharp. Unlike modern kitchen knives, theirs had two keen blades as well as a sharpened business end. Weapon, penknife, table knife and companion, young men of all parts of society were learning to carry a knife everywhere, as much a part of them as their teenage hormones, and ready for whatever ego-bruising slights and infringements on their safety or territory they encountered or imagined. Chefs today talk about this emotional relationship with their knives; old friends that, like a wizard's wand, become an extension of them, yet whose potential for aiding and abetting mayhem makes them dangerously exciting.[1]

We worry about knife crime and the way the knife is fetishized today by young men desperate for respect at the bottom of the social and economic order. Medieval society also worried about the capacity for such a large number of teens and young men, seething with hormones and competitiveness, misusing their knives, and dealt with it by hedging about their use with multiple points of etiquette. They were exhorted to take salt with the tip of their knife; to cut (not break) bread; to clean their knife on the napkin (or tablecloth); not to point it at someone; not to pick their teeth with its point; not to put it in their mouth. Etiquette was a way of keeping safe. For a group of boys learning about life away from their parents, it was also a demonstration of tough love by the men who cared for them.

Medieval society expected young men to have this quasi-weapon on them at all times. If they were waiting on the lord and lady, they carved their meat. If they were, themselves, sitting at dinner, they carved meat for themselves and any ladies nearby, and wielding the knife effectively and elegantly at table was as much a part of a gentleman's armoury of accomplishments as Latin or hawking (see Carving, page 84). Medieval paintings show tables crowded with diners, laid with food and some crockery, and with a few, wickedly sharp, knives.

There is a story that, in 1637, Cardinal Richelieu, disgusted by watching Chancellor Séguier picking his teeth with the end of his knife, ordered his steward to have the ends of all his knives ground to a curve, and that Louis XIV made the manufacture of dangerous pointed knives illegal.[2] We can thank the Cardinal and the Sun King for their decorous and peaceable impulses, but it was also the adoption of the fork that did for the dagger-shaped knife at dinner. Diners no longer needed a sharp point to spear food from a communal dish, and round-ended knives, as opposed to carving knives, began to join forks on the table. A few decades later, the English Civil War also had an effect; silver cutlery was melted down to pay for the fighting, and members of the post-war emerging classes, such as Samuel Pepys (see Forks, page 236), keen to add to their domestic silverware, gave a huge boost to the cutlers. Society was keen, too, to eschew Puritanical, warlike functions, and adopt the French ways of the returned King Charles II. Elegance meant round-ended form over savage and pointed function.

Gentlewomen were using table knives too; Hannah Woolley reminds them to 'keep not your knife always in your hand'.[3] As hostesses took on more of an active role, they were expected to wield a smaller, light, sharp carving knife and fork (see Carving, page 84), although the custom of gentlemen carving for the women sitting next to them continued until the introduction of service *à la russe* (see Small Plates, page 223).

Manufacturers experimented with carbon steel cutlery in the early part of the nineteenth century, and it led to a boom in the production of cheaper, non-silver cutlery blades, enabling 'the middling sort' to also acquire extensive sets, with differently shaped knives designed to open oysters and spread butter. Vinegar and citric acid were problematic, though, as they corroded this cheaper steel. The tines of forks and blades of knives for eating fruit and fish were made of silver, and thus began the peculiarly British obsession with fish knives.[4]

The sort of old-fashioned families who inherited their Georgian silver were content to eat fish by pulling the delicate flesh of fish away from the bone with two silver forks, or use a piece of bread to manhandle it onto the tines of the fork. Others, with money to spend on new 'flatware', as cutlery came to be known, viewed the flat fish knife with its scallop-shaped blade as a pleasing step on the road to greater refinement. By 1878, the anonymous etiquette expert who used the soubriquet 'An Aristocrat' warned his or her eager readers, 'Fish should be eaten with a silver fish knife and fork. Two forks are *not* used for eating fish, and one fork and a crust of bread is now an unheard-of way of eating fish in polite society.'[5]

Although the Victorians and Edwardians also loved to have knives for lots of different purposes – oysters, butter, fruit, cheese or dessert – and some were happy to claim that the mark of a true gentleman was someone who used a butter knife when dining alone,[6] it was the fish knife that became a particular lightning conductor of disdain. Like one of those beleaguered women who have married into the Royal Family, it was initially welcomed for its freshness and elegance, until an invisible signal had every social commentator covering it with a heap of invective. Hereditary peers viewed it as the sign of the parvenu who had to buy their own cutlery because their parents and grandparents were too modest of background to have had their own. A generation or two later, their grandchildren saw it as a ghastly Victorian invention whose usefulness has been outlived by its pretentiousness.[7] Interestingly, no such stigma attaches to the steak knife, although its serrated edge and business-like point are equally unnecessary now that technology has refined our steel table knives to be (nearly) always sharp. Sharp is cool; the flat fish knife couldn't keep its glamour in the 1950s when writers and cookware shopkeepers were encouraging home cooks to pay attention to their kitchen tools. It was finished off with a good kicking in John Betjeman's poem 'How to Get On in Society', in which the fish knife introduces a pile-up of lower-middle-class solecisms of the day such as 'phone', 'kiddies' and the dreaded 'serviette'.

The *Daily Telegraph*, reporting in 2017 the groundbreaking news that *Tatler* had decreed that the word 'pardon' was now socially acceptable, reflected that if a nice middle-class girl like Kate Middleton was a senior Royal, then all the old class indicators were up for grabs, except: 'The only thing we can all agree on is that fish knives will never be fine.'[8]

Although the death knell for fish knives is sounded regularly, they never quite go away. For all their associations with the aspirational Victorian middle classes, they still find themselves on well-appointed wedding lists and eagerly collected by lovers of antique silver. They are, after all, elegant and pretty and even a tiny bit useful.

Usefulness is not necessarily a prerequisite for a tool to be accepted onto our tables, though, as the story of the fork shows.

Forks: making a stab

He's the angriest man you'll ever meet. He's like a man with a fork in a world of soup.

Noel Gallagher on Liam Gallagher, *Q* (April 2009)

NO IMPLEMENT HAS drawn as much ire or scorn on its users as the fork, until, perhaps, the fish knife (see Fish Knives, page 232). The attempts by its early fans to bring some degree of hygiene into their eating were seen as either grossly insulting to their fellow diners or a pointless piece of affectation. To this day there is a transatlantic bifurcation and, within Britain, a socio-economic one. Americans happily cut up their food with a knife and fork, and then transfer the fork from left to right hand to eat. An older generation of Brits might indulge Americans (particularly wealthy or influential ones) for an eating style which, in their compatriots, would have been an alarming breach of etiquette. The novelist and critic Adam Mars-Jones recalls his Welsh-born parents meeting his American boyfriend for the first time: 'Mum and Dad weren't hopelessly provincial. They knew that if a dinner guest cut his food up methodically, then transferred the fork to his right hand for the purpose of conveying nourishment to his mouth, there was no cause for alarm. These were standard American manners, deeply embodied aspects of culture.'[1] Our parents' generation prided themselves on knowing that 'correct' behaviour meant squashing everything – even peas – onto the back of a fork held in the left hand. Until the mid-twentieth century, left-handed schoolchildren were rapped for trying to write with their natural hand, so it must have been baffling, but also a relief, to discover they had this one advantage over their right-handed fellows at the dinner table.

From antiquity, forks have been dropped, lost or buried, though rarely; they are unusual finds for archaeologists. In Britain, long, thin two-tined shapes date to the Roman era. They were sharp enough to winkle snails or oysters out of their shells, but too sharp to have been intended to go in the mouth. That innovation, in Europe, is credited to a couple of eleventh-century Byzantine princesses. One, Maria Argyropoulaina, married the son of a Venetian Doge; the other, Theophano, married the son of the Holy Roman Emperor. Both scandalized their adopted societies by their decadent, hygiene-obsessed Eastern ways, including using a two-pronged golden fork to carry food to the mouth. Maria's early death was, obviously (according to Pope Boniface), a punishment from God for her depravity and self-indulgence.[2]

To people used to the wild-fire spread of Instagram-driven trends, it is remarkable how slowly the fork became acceptable. The poor ate bread with their fingers and pottage with a spoon. Even Northern Europe's novelty-seeking aristocracy had no need of another implement. A gentleman-servant would pour water over their hands at the table (see Doilies, Napkins and Tablecloths, page 243); they could cut food with the knife on their right, or scoop up food with clean hands or the bread, to this day, placed on the diner's left. Not everybody had clean hands, though, noticed the English Elizabethan traveller Thomas Coryat. Italians used forks because they could not 'indure' to have their meat touched by others' dirty fingers. This 'curiosity' suggests that even in 1611 they used forks for serving and carving, rather than eating.[3]

Coryat's fork was gleefully seized upon, not for hygiene, but satire. The clown in John Fletcher's Jacobean drama *The Queen of Corinth* (c.1616) pretentiously acts 'th'enamoured courtier/ As full as your fork-carving traveller.'[4] He was, almost certainly, based on Coryat. Around the same time, Ben Jonson gave us an affected character in *The Devil Is an Ass* (1616) who trills about

'The laudable use of forks/Brought into custom here, as they are in Italy/To the sparing of napkins.'[5] Cultured theatre-goers would surely have snorted along with the groundlings, even as they speared berries, quince paste or candied eryngo root with a long, thin-tined sweetmeat fork. Or sipped the sticky syrup of a 'sucket' from the spoon found at one end of a sucket fork, a dual-ended implement with a fork end used to spear the preserved ginger, citron peel or cherries.

An elegant, thin-tined sweetmeat fork, dating from around 1590, was found at the site of the Rose Theatre (now in the Museum of London). Made of iron with a decorated wooden handle, it was a valued piece of kit engraved with its owner's initials, AN. New technology for early, urban adopters such as AN was pretentious enough, but Coryat's suggestion that *everybody* used a fork for a whole meal, every day, was ludicrous.

Specialized forks were known even in Anglo-Saxon times, but they are rare finds and the ones made from modest materials such as copper alloy are rarest of all.[6] Most early forks had two slender silver or iron tines. Makers went to town on the handles, which were exquisitely wrought or cast from silver, or carved from jet, agate, bone or ivory – often stained to a jewel colour; or fashioned from enamel, or Venetian glass, or fashionable porcelain from Meissen, Worcester, Chelsea.

The serving fork caught on first; rather than holding a joint with the two forefingers and thumb of the left hand, 'it will appear very comely and decent' to carve and serve meat with a fork, Hannah Woolley wrote encouragingly to her gentlewoman readers in 1673. The earliest matching sets of knife, fork and spoons for the dinner table are from the Restoration, part of the fashion for elegant living, courtly dress, French food and other rejections of Puritanical plainness. Cutlery sets that survive from the Restoration period show the fork being slowly adopted for the dinner table. Many sets came with a matching travelling sheath, suggesting that people did not necessarily trust their hosts to have clean implements, or even any at all. Pepys, always willing to shell out for something a little bit aspirational, records a payment to his silversmith of £22 and 18 shillings for spoons, forks and a sugar box.[7] It suggests also that he expected to provide cutlery for his guests who didn't bring their own to his dinner parties and indicates that he acquired his cutlery in stages; few people had large, matching services of silverware. As dining became more formalized in the following two centuries, the top cloth would be removed between courses, the dishes and cutlery cleared, and the cutlery would quite likely be washed and brought back to the table by overworked servants.[8]

By the time the third tine came into play after the middle of the eighteenth century, the fork was beginning to have social cachet. Innovations in the great cutlery centre of Sheffield enabled more people to afford a few knives and forks; whole sets became an object of desire for anyone wanting to claw their way upwards. As it became more common, diners had to have the *right sort* of *matching* service; it was considered stylish to lay it face-down to show off the silver hallmark and even more so to keep it in your new dining room in a neoclassical wooden container: a marquetry cutlery urn designed by Robert Adams was just the thing. A new literary genre, the 'silver fork novel', emerged in the 1820s, catering to a public taste for a glimpse into the style of aristocratic life, until Thackeray topped it all with *Vanity Fair* in 1848, an unmatchable apotheosis.

Well-brought-up diners began to expect the right fork for the right food. Mrs Gaskell's genteel characters in *Cranford* (1853) are dismayed to be served duck and green peas with only 'two-pronged, black-handled forks' to eat the dish with. The two old-fashioned ladies struggle to eat the delicious new peas at all. The narrator looks at her host, shovelling them into his mouth with his broad round-ended knife: 'I saw, I imitated, I survived!'[9] 'Copy your host' is advice that was – and still is – discreetly given to the upwardly mobile as the dinner party became more and more girded with social weaponry. Victorian dinner guests entered a weaponized dining room where each place was laid with a phalanx of cutlery with which the upper-class host warded off the ungenteel. There were forks for everything; terrapin, oyster, lobster, snail, fish, sardines, pastry, dessert, berries, even for serving bread (not so crazy perhaps; waiters these days use tongs). Each was supposedly recognizable by the number of tines (three to five), the size, the length of tine, the curve, and whether there was a wide and sharpened left tine for cutting food such as pastry.

By the end of the century, the fork was king, ruling a wide range of dishes alone – vegetable entrées, chopped salads, sweetbreads, rissoles, quenelles, patties, savouries – no matter how much one longed to reach for a helpful knife or spoon. Even if the cook had failed to bring the cheese fondue 'to the requisite firmness of consistency', or you were faced with precariously wobbling jellies and barely set creams, still 'the fork must do', said Mrs Humphrey in *Manners for Men*.[10] She would have been gratified by the lady I saw recently eating her cream tea with a fork. You might use a knife to prepare bananas, oranges, strawberries, though with crystallized cherries it must be the fork alone.

Knives and forks must be used for everything, no matter how fiddly to eat. 'It is only in the lowest grades of society that they are found inadequate,' Mrs Humphrey harrumphed.[11] She might more accurately have said 'expensive'. When schoolchildren began to be offered free school meals in 1906, teachers discovered that they had to teach the grateful beneficiaries how to sit at a table and eat, and how to use a knife and fork.[12] Until stainless steel was invented in Sheffield in 1914 and released for cutlery-making in the 1920s after wartime exigencies, cutlery was too expensive for mass consumption. Manufacturers, realizing the potential of new markets, experimented with cheaper materials; Bakelite and plastic suggested ivory or bone for handles.

And then we decided that eating at a table was too time-consuming for our modern lives, when there is so much television to watch, or driving to be done, or laptops to be hunched over. Much of our food became fast and forkless. Fried chicken, burgers, pizza, chips, a thousand different versions of the sandwich; fast food was hand-held food. Teachers in the 1970s still lamented that children came to school unable to use a knife and fork, though this time they said it was because the only hot food they knew was fish and chips.[13]

Now you can buy a twenty-four-piece cutlery set, made in China, for the price of a couple of coffees (Argos, £5). It might not be an environmentally sustainable model, but it does mean that cutlery has become democratized. *Debrett's* is resolute that 'It may be necessary to use mashed potato to make peas stick to the fork but it is incorrect to turn the fork over and scoop,' which rather counteracts its argument that etiquette is, nowadays, simply about making other people feel comfortable and treads perilously close to the high Victorian neuroticism of class sifting.[14] I confess that I hardly notice what my dining companions are doing with their forks; I might be too busy hoping they are not offended by my habit of eating salad with my fingers.

EIGHTEENTH-CENTURY DUCK AND GREEN PEAS

This recipe is still a classic today. Serve with mashed potato; it goes well and you can use it to help you eat the peas in the approved manner.

MODERN RECIPE

4 duck legs
Two tablespoons of flour seasoned with salt and pepper
A little oil
Bunch of thyme
Handful of parsley
A bay leaf
Small pinch of ground mace
Small pinch of ground nutmeg
500ml chicken or duck stock (or enough to cover)
2 little gem lettuces
450g green peas (fresh or frozen)
1–2 tablespoons chopped mint

This can be done in two parts, braising the duck first, letting it cool (perhaps overnight) so you can skim off the fat, and then finishing off with the vegetables.

1. Preheat the oven to Gas Mark 3/160°C.
2. Dry the duck legs with a paper towel, then dredge them with seasoned flour. Quickly sauté them skin side down in a little oil in a casserole for 10 minutes until the fat starts to run.
3. Clean the fat from the pan (or keep it for roasting), then return the legs, add the herbs, the spices and the stock and braise in a low oven for 90 minutes.
4. If you have time, let the whole dish cool so you can skim off the fat from the top. (Remove the duck legs and keep them in the fridge.) Discard the herbs.
5. If necessary, reduce the gravy over a high heat to a consistency that pleases you.
6. 15 minutes before you are ready to eat, cut the little gem lettuces lengthways. Turn the heat down on the stock and add the duck legs, lettuces and peas to heat through. Another nice option, rather than adding the little gems to the duck, is to cut them, brush the surfaces with oil, sprinkle them with salt and grill them, and serve them separately with a little lemon juice or balsamic vinegar.
7. Remove the duck legs from the gravy and serve with the vegetables, sprinkled with chopped mint and with the gravy in a jug on the side.

ORIGINAL RECIPE: TO DRESS A DUCK WITH GREEN PEAS

From *The Art of Cookery Made Plain and Easy* by Hannah Glasse (1747)

◆

Put a deep stew-pan over the Fire, with a Piece of fresh Butter, singe your Duck and flour it, turn it in the Pan two or three Minutes, then pour out all the Fat, but let the Duck remain in the Pan, put to it Half a Pint of good Gravy, a Pint of Peas, two Lettuces cut small, a small Bundle of Sweet Herbs, a little Pepper and Salt, cover them close, and let them stew for Half an Hour, now and then give the Pan a shake; when they are just done grate in a little Nutmeg, and put in a very little beaten Mace, and thicken it either with a Piece of Butter rolled in Flour, or the Yolk of an Egg beat up with two or three Spoonfuls of Cream; shake it all together for three or four Minutes, take out the Sweet Herbs, lay the Duck in the Dish and pour the Sauce over it; You may garnish with boiled Mint chopped, or let it alone.

Doilies, Napkins and Tablecloths

I made a good pun on Saturday to my lord keeper. After dinner we
had coarse Doiley napkins, fringed at each end, upon the table to
drink with: my lord keeper spread one of them between him and
Mr Prior: I told him I was glad to see there was such a Fringeship
[Friendship] between Mr Prior and his lordship. Prior swore it
was the worst he ever heard: I said I thought so too.

Jonathan Swift, Letter (14 April 1711)

HOW IMPORTANT IS the 'thinginess' of dining? Does a thick,
white tablecloth make a difference to the experience of
eating? Centuries of English and French diners thought it did;
the nicer the tablecloth, the more elegant the glassware, the more
civilized we were. It fitted neatly with the patriotic requirement to
grow the economy and show where you were placed on the socio-
cultural ladder. But does it begin to get ridiculous? Do we need the
doiley? *NON!* said Pierre Bourdieu.[1] In *Distinction*, published in
France in 1979, he batted away centuries of assumptions about
material culture by arguing that those without it – or much of it –
had got it right. The working classes were interested in conviviality
and sharing; dishes, hopefully in generous portions, were all put
on the table at once for people to serve themselves and there was
no changing plates between courses. Material culture, he thought,
was a bourgeois trick to distract the diner from the embarrassment
of the basic and vulgar function of food: to keep us all alive.

In England, we were historically pro-thing but, by the mid-
twentieth century, when the middle classes were earning enough

money to buy plenty of them, those on a higher social plane looked for a subtler way to distinguish between classes. Napkin or serviette? You'll know the story. In 1956, Nancy Mitford set the rabbits running with a teasing essay on 'U' and 'non-U' (U standing for 'Upper Class') language. She had gleefully seized on the terms coined by an academic linguist, Professor Alan S.C. Ross, when she noticed he had mentioned her in a footnote in his paper 'Linguistic class-indicators in present-day English' (1954). Ross wrote that 'perhaps the best known of all the linguistic class-indicators of English' was 'Non-U serviette/U table-napkin'.[2] Mitford's essay, published in *Noblesse Oblige* (1956), made fun of the middle-class worry about seeming vulgar, and their use of indirect, often French-sounding words such as 'toilet' (from the French 'toilette') for lavatory, 'meal' for lunch or dinner, 'sweet' for pudding, and 'pardon?' for 'what?'. The upper classes, confident that everything they said or did was correct, had no truck with such roundaboutness.

Before around 1850, almost nobody used a 'serviette'. The napkin, or 'napkyn', a diminutive of the French *nappe* or tablecloth, was a major part of medieval hygiene, when the hand was used in the way we use a fork today. Like modern-day caterers who use swathes of napery to transform a tent or a church hall into somewhere we associate with festive dining, medieval pantlers (who ran the pantry) or stewards turned the communal hall into a dining room as they did for Sir Gawain returning from a wintry encounter with the Green Knight (see Where We Sit, page 204); the table is laid up on trestles and clad with a cloth of sparkling whiteness (pity the poor launderers), and also a 'sanap and salure and sylverin spones'.[3] 'Salure' was a salt-cellar and the 'sanap' or 'surnap' was a napkin laid on top of the *nappe*.

Etiquette books reminded diners to wipe their hands on their *napkins* (*not* their hair or clothes or bread) and, if necessary, use them for blowing their nose (rather than using the tablecloth). They might also use it as a towel, having washed the grease from dinner from their hands by dipping them into a bowl and rinsing them under a stream of water provided by a servant with a pitcher. Washing your hands *before* a meal wasn't as important.

We know that some peasants had precious napkins and cloths, because there are records that they were stolen.[4] Late medieval images of farmers or yeomen show tables covered with a canvas-like cloth;[5] and the wedding breakfast was served on a glistening white cloth in Pieter Brueghel the Elder's *Peasant Wedding* (1567). By Tudor times the households of farmers and shopkeepers were buying linen or, if they could afford it, damask napery, not just as a display of gentility but as a repository of wealth; linen presses were made to protect it, and it was handed down through the generations like family silver. An unusual portrait of Sir Henry Unton, commissioned by his widow around 1596 to show his life and accomplishments, shows a feast in which the male diners have white napkins thrown across their left shoulders.

These are, like the medieval ones, probably rectangular. As bodies and cleanliness became a matter of privacy, the habit of using the napkin to wash the hands in public became less genteel. Napkins became square to show that they were *not* hand towels; and the Italians further disguised their vulgar function from around the 1550s by inventing the delightful trick of folding them into sculptural shapes or exotic beasts.[6] Samuel Pepys was so mightily pleased with the fellow who came to fold napkins in this way for a dinner he was hosting, he gave him the enormous sum of 40 shillings to teach his wife Elizabeth the skill.[7]

When even a farmer's wife might have a trousseau of snowy white napery, it began to be essential further up the social scale to have, not only tablecloths embroidered, edged with lace, or made from damask, but a succession of them. Oval and circular tables made dining more sociable and cloths more expensive, as huge looms were needed to produce textiles of sufficient width. The Georgian table was dressed like a bishop with layers of fine translucent linens over costly damasks. The top cloth was whisked off after each course, the final flourish revealing a deeply polished dark wood table, on which the dessert course would be placed. It was a theatrical feat, requiring skilled and nimble servants. Jane Austen uses tablecloths as shorthand for her characters' place in life in *Emma*; the old-fashioned Mr Woodhouse 'loves to have the cloth laid' for supper. Emma's former governess is clearly not born into the dinner-giving stratum of society as she doesn't quite have the smooth command of her servants. Her guests 'were called on to share in the awkwardness of a rather long interval between the courses' until the table is again 'safely covered'.[8]

The Victorians liked to layer lace cloths over coloured linen and embraced the openwork or lace doily, not least because it was a way of keeping your needle busy for underemployed ladies. A well-to-do household would be expected to have stacks of linen, with enough napkins for every dinner guest and for the cook to line dishes with. Alexis Soyer in *The Modern Housewife* (1849) wanted to see boiled or fried fish, croquette of beef, lobster gratin and meringues served on a napkin; and dishes such as soufflés, which had to be sent to table in the vessel in which they were baked, should be clothed in a napkin.

Late Victorian society decided against removing the tablecloth for dessert, enabling themselves to buy stacks of yet another new, essential 'thing', the doily or 'd'oyley', named after a famous London haberdasher, and made from lace, crochet-work or cut-out work. These decorative little rounds maintained their association with desserts and cakes throughout the beginning of the following century; decorative but essentially useless, unless it was to show off how much you could afford to pay for your laundry. The paper doilies of our grandmothers' generations failed even to do that but they became a favourite accoutrement for the serviette classes (see Tea, page 45) that John Betjeman satirizes in 'How to Get On in Society'.

Mass Observation records a man remembering how, as a child (in the 1930s) he 'improved the tea laid out in the drawing-room' by adorning each saucer and tea plate 'with a doily carefully cut out from lavatory paper'.[9] The U vocabulary – tea, drawing-room and lavatory – suggests that his U mother hadn't yet socialized him out of such non-U tastes.

The use of napkins by diners began to be codified in the way that has carried on today. Tucking a napkin into a collar so that it *really* protected the clothes became a working-class stereotype. The middles and upwards preferred to hide it and its function on their laps. Napkin rings are déclassé, as they suggest you are going to reuse a dirty napkin (as we did in my childhood, each of us having a bespoke napkin ring with our name on, so at least we were communing with our own germs). Folding a napkin at the end of the meal would imply the same, so you should leave it open on the table (or on your chair if you are only nipping off). As it once served the same function as the fork, the napkin is still also found on the left of the plate; the Victorians loved to hide a bread roll in its folds, presumably to identify the wrong sort who might shake out his napkin and launch his roll at Lady Bracknell or her equivalent.

From the end of the nineteenth century and a few decades afterwards, the upwardly mobile 'serviette' was gaining on the correct 'napkin' in usage. It wasn't surprising to find it in *Etiquette for Ladies* (1894) which felt it necessary to warn the ingénue diner that she would find 'your serviette folded in some fantastic form upon your plate', but even ruggedly masculine writers such as D.H. Lawrence, Arnold Bennett and H.G. Wells fell for its genteel charms in their novels. Fowler in his *Modern English Usage* sternly forbad its use as a 'genteelism' as early as 1926, even before Nancy Mitford lobbed her non-U bomb into intensely socially anxious post-war Britain, whereafter use of the word by anyone claiming an education fell off dramatically. Now, as Kate Fox wrote in *Watching the English* (2004), its use is one of the seven deadly sins of the residents of 'Pardonia', along with pardon, toilet, dinner (instead of lunch), settee, lounge and sweet.[10] Nancy Mitford's list gets taken out and freshened up from time to time: on the non-U side the *Daily Mail*'s favourite 'etiquette expert' William Hanson added toastie, vino, bubbly or Deliveroo; a writer in *Tatler* came down on elaborate gin and tonics, and fruit in plastic. Now that sales of doilies have collapsed, in spite of a few supermarket attempts to revive them by using pictures of celebrities, we can be nostalgic about the place they held on the cake stands of tea rooms and the lower-middle-class lounge. Asda's 'doily buyer' told the *Daily Mail* in 2007, 'We are willing to consider every option to preserve this great British tradition.'[11]

Wait until they become embraced by hipsters. We must be due for a doily revival.

The economist John Maynard Keynes might (or might not) have said, 'When the facts change, I change my mind'; and sometimes our attitudes to foods change quickly, when circumstances change dramatically. I'm thinking, of course, of crises and the tin can.

Food in Tins

A young man from the Bugey had lately returned from a brief visit to the United States and had reported that the food was more foreign to him than the people... good but very strange indeed – tinned vegetable cocktails and tinned fruit salads, for example. Surely, said I, you weren't required to eat them. You could have substituted other dishes.

Alice B. Toklas, *The Alice B. Toklas Cook Book* (1954)

COOKERY LESSONS AT school were often baffling, and not only because they taught us that boys, apparently, needed to learn to make brackets in woodwork, while we girls were treated to visits from home economists who showed us how to make a stew by opening various tins of things and mixing them together. Having been brought up on home-made everything, I was half-intrigued and half-appalled by this idea that using tinned food was *cooking*. I tested the hypothesis with a different teacher in my next school, in pie week. It failed. A tin of pineapple was not, in the eyes of my doughty domestic science teacher, adequate for a fruit pie. I was lucky not to really need to be taught how to make a pie – but I had learnt an interesting lesson about the snobbery around tinned food.

Transforming food by fire is sometimes attributed to humankind's ascendance over other animals; to that we could also add the preservation of food. Humans have used smoke, salt, desiccation, fermentation and heat to change the nature of meat and fish and, sometimes, plants, so that they are available to eat all year round. Until the nineteenth century most cookbooks had recipes for curing meat (with salt and spices), preserving or conserving with sugar to make pastes or 'marmelades' or the candied fruits in syrup known as 'suckets', curdling milk to make cheeses, or salting fish. Smoking was perhaps the one transformation that was left to the specialist. Preserving food took time, salt (which was sometimes taxed) and sugar and was essential in making at least some protein – salted fish, bacon or cheese – available over the winter months. Cooks understood something of the role that air played in making food decay, and used long-keeping clarified butter to fill up the gap left in pastries once the filling had cooked and shrunk, or to act as a plug on cooked food in jars, to make potted fish, seafood or meat.

Gardeners competed with each other to produce the first asparagus or peas or strawberries for their customers and fresh, out-of-season produce was often crazily faddy (see Peas, page 124). Nicolas Appert, a one-time brewer, chef and confectioner in Napoleonic France, spent thirty years experimenting with ways of preserving food in a way that made it seem fresh. He figured out, fifty years before Pasteur demonstrated why it should be so, that if he heated the food in sealed glass containers – he started off using champagne bottles – it was preserved with limited change to its taste. He sent some peas and beans to the French navy in 1806 and earned himself a prize of 12,000 francs that Napoleon had established, in 1795, for ways of preserving food – on condition that he published his findings so that all France might benefit. The result, *L'Art de conservir* (*The Art of Preserving*; 1810), described how to delicately process the products of the kitchen garden – the juices of herbs, cherries, raspberries and mulberries, spinach and succory, truffles and chestnuts – as well as preserve some elegant ingredients such as refined Julienne soups, rounds of beef, mutton, fowls and partridges, and grape juice or must for making wine.

Although his recipes are more for the bourgeois housewife, the government committee that awarded him the 12,000 francs – which included Antoine-Augustin Parmentier (see Parmentier Potatoes, page 183) – was clear that Appert's innovation was founded on good Republican principles. It should bring good food to people on ships and in kitchens on land, whether that be in France, India, Mexico, Africa or Lapland – and would, in return, bring new foods into France. The committee noticed, with some frustration, that big business was not developing Appert's ideas, however, and even the government itself seemed to be thwarting them (his canning factory was requisitioned as a hospital).

There were no such inhibitions hampering the commercial and military exploitation of his discoveries in England when his method was translated into English in 1811. The publishers, who were tied to the East India Company, instantly saw the benefit of preserved food for 'the health and comfort of the floating defence of the country, as well as of that numerous and meritorious class of men, to which the nation owes so much of its prosperity', meaning the merchants and sailors of the East India Company.[1]

Appert's free-for-all system was encountered by an English broker, Peter Durand, who patented it and, after a bit of experimenting, sold his patent for £1,000 to an engineer, Bryan Donkin. Donkin translated it to tin cans, instead of bottles, and opened the first tinned food factory in Bermondsey, which began to produce more basic provisions than those envisaged by Appert; generally a combination of beef and mutton and vegetables. Almost immediately the factory was supplying quantities to the Navy; in 1813 the Duke of Wellington praised the preserved beef made by the firm Donkin, Hall and Gamble, and sailors quickly christened their rations of *bouilli* – or boiled – beef 'bully beef'. Tinned food was taken on expeditions, and the lordly Sir Joseph Banks, celebrated botanist and long-term President of the Royal Society, professed himself happy to recommend the firm's 'embalmed Provisions' in 1817.[2]

Tinned food was not an immediate hit in civilian life, though. Cans were thick and heavy, and had to be opened with a hammer and chisel, until the first rudimentary can opener was invented in around 1855.[3] The contents became putrid if they weren't properly sealed.

They were prized, however, by military and administrative families in the colonies, desperate to keep up their 'civilized'

British culture, who hoped that tinned food would enable their cooks to recreate French cuisine, or cosy British supper dishes. Memsahibs worshipped tinned food as luxuries, choosing leathery white mushrooms from an English tin, when the fresh equivalents were available in the market, greatly to the exasperation of the doyen of Anglo-Indian cookery, Colonel 'Wyvern':

> There will be times and places, when and where you will be obliged to fall back upon Messrs Crosse and Blackwell, and be thankful. Until those evil days come upon you, however, do not anticipate your penance, but strive to make the food you can easily procure, palatable and good by scientific treatment.[4]

Most of the welcome for tinned food came because it hugely extended the range of food available to domestic cooks. Mrs A.B. Marshall admitted in her cookery book of 1890 that she used tinned chestnuts for *Timbale de Marrons a la Cannes*. Marketing stories spun tinned foods as high-living that everyone could afford. *The Hotel World* in December 1895, reviewing tinned sauces such as *espagnole, allemande* and *italienne*, enthused that 'all this luxury is to be placed within the reach of the great middle class and of the ordinary cook'.[5] Tinned sardines were also, optimistically, marketed as the luxuries of the patrician class to the middle-class readers of *Woman's Life*: 'Oh Tomkins, this is your evening out, is it not? Just lay the table for supper and put out the tin of Skippers (there's a tin in the cupboard). We'll open it ourselves.'[6]

One of the problems of tinned food that no amount of colourful graphic labels could overcome was that you couldn't *see* what was in it. Upton Sinclair's novel *The Jungle* (1906), although written to draw attention to the terrible treatment of industrial workers in the meatpacking plants of Chicago, succeeded mostly in alerting the American – and British – buyers to the diseased, rotten and contaminated horrors that might lurk inside a tin of corned beef. It fuelled the panic that tinned food was a fake copy of fresh food, where the nutrients had been destroyed and that it was in turn destroying the health of the working classes, who had come to rely on it.

The pro-eugenics journalist Arnold White worried that Britain was slipping down the league table of world powers, as the health of the industrialized 'great masses' of the population was diminished by, among other evils, their diet of tinned fish and frozen meat. The Empire, 'won by a hardy people, fed on their own beef and bread, will scarcely be held by invalids'.[7] The Great War had only been possible because of tinned food, according to George Orwell; but the result was it carried off the best of the male population, and the physically diminished figures it left were yet further weakened by their diet. 'We may find in the long run that tinned food is a deadlier weapon than the machine gun,' he predicted gloomily.[8]

If tinned food could not properly nourish the body, it followed by some kind of unstated logic that it was also responsible for starving the soul. The critic of literary Modernism John Carey curated an impressive list of writers who use the image of 'tinned food, to tell us something about the debased cultural life of the masses':

> E.M. Forster's Leonard Bast eats tinned food, a practice that is meant to tell us something significant about Leonard, and not to his advantage... T.S. Eliot's typist in The Waste Land 'lays out food in tins'. John Betjeman deplores the appetite of the masses for 'Tinned fruit, tinned meat, tinned beans'. Tinned salmon is repeatedly a feature of lower-class cuisine in Graham Greene... One of Jerome K. Jerome's most famous comic scenes in Three Men in a Boat is constructed round a tin of pineapple. The Morning Post cited Jerome K. Jerome as an example of the sad results to be expected from the over-education of the lower orders.[9]

In point of fact, tinned, and then frozen food, brought protein and a range to the working-class diet not seen in centuries. Australia started to export tinned boiled beef and mutton in the 1860s, of mixed quality but, at 5d to 7d per pound, it was half the price of fresh meat. It was followed by factories in Chicago and Cincinnati – and then Fray Bentos in Uruguay – which started canning and exporting cheap meat. By the First World War, less than half of Britain's total meat requirements came from British farms.[10]

Second World War rationing soothed the population's repugnance to tinned food. Jack Drummond, the nutritional advisor to Lord Woolton, Minister for Food, put tinned food at the heart of his ambitious (and successful) programme to use rationing to level out the standards of nutrition between classes. Partly through fascination, partly through desire to prove the validity of tinned food, he published a curious little book called *Historic Tinned Foods* (1939), which told the stories of heroic and adventuresome tins such as those of roasted veal and of carrots taken by Sir Edward Parry on his Third Expedition in search of the North West Passage in 1824, and which were still in existence. It reconnected tinned food with the image of brave and stalwart Brits, akin to the Home Front enthusiasm to Dig for Victory, and the stoical embrace of rationing as part of the war effort.

The mood of the time extended to tins as part of good, as well as necessary, food. Ambrose Heath, with twenty or so books on Good Food behind him, snorted at the gastronomic super-snob: 'One of his greatest affectations is to despise tinned food'[11] – although he agreed that fresh food was better if procurable. His list of hundreds of types of food available in cans ranged from whortleberries to guavas, sea kale to okra, enchiladas to poppadoms, whole roast grouse to tripe and onions.

A speciality of the first bistro, The Ox on the Roof on the King's Road in Chelsea, in the early 1950s, was tinned kidneys with a wine and mushroom sauce, served with rice.[12] After the war, families were delighted to have tinned peaches and tinned cream for Sunday lunch and not even the most self-regarding of chefs seemed to mind using tinned tomatoes as a key ingredient in newly fashionable Italian and French peasant cuisine.

The honeymoon between the middle-class consumer and the tin lasted perhaps a couple of decades. While millions of families were eating cheap suppers of baked beans on toast, others were frowning at the amount of added sugar and salt (which food labelling laws oblige us to see), forgetting perhaps that the original recipe relied on salted pork, brown sugar and/or black treacle to make it both palatable and long-lasting. The huge amounts of salt needed to preserve meat and fish, and sugar for fruits, was reduced by canning – and later by freezing – at a stroke. As frozen, then air-freighted out-of-season vegetables became first wildly fashionable, then widely available, and then eschewed by taste-makers as being 'unseasonable' (which included implications of unnatural and ecologically unsound), tins were again consigned to the shelves of the working classes.

One woman in 1988 whose husband earned £65 per week, explained how she managed her budget: 'Well first of all we sort out all the bills when he brings home his wages and whatever's left out of his wages I get the tinned stuff. When I get my family allowance on a Monday that goes on meat and things like that for the week.'[13] Cheap, reliable and with an almost infinite shelf-life, tinned meat, fish, fruit and pasta sauces are an essential part of the Trussell Trust's emergency parcels for people finding themselves in food poverty.

For luckier cooks, tinned goods have settled into a social hierarchy. Anything in a glass jar, particularly with a nice label or looking as though it has been home-made, could be given as a present. Tinned luxuries such as caviar, and tins with replaceable lids – for biscuits, coffee, tea – are also eminently giftable. Parents rapidly became suspicious of tinned baby food, often prepared with salt, sugar, preservatives and thickeners (and sometimes nitrites or MSG), so manufacturers threw out the tins along with the additives and turned to jars and then (non-recyclable) vacuum-pouches to advertise their '100% organic' ingredients. Raw ingredients in tins – tomatoes, sweetcorn, chickpeas – all form part of the middle-class larder. A friend told me that her teenage friends thought she was spoilt to get tinned peaches or tinned fruit salad, as pudding every day; thirty years later, tinned fruit was now also déclassé. Kate Fox listed it as one of her 'Foods with class warning labels', adding that, if secure uppers and upper-middles eat tinned fruit it is viewed as charmingly eccentric. 'The more class-anxious should take care to pick their charming eccentricity from the very bottom of the scale (chip butties) rather than the class nearest to them (tinned fruit in juice), to avoid any possibility of a misunderstanding.'[14]

This infuriated the cook and poverty campaigner Jack Monroe so much, she wrote *Tin Can Cook* (2019), 'partly as a food-bank cookbook, but also as a rebuttal to tiresome snobbery that we have around food'. [15] Although written for people struggling with food bills, there is also an unexpected market for people who have never had to learn to cook with tinned food, but have started to stockpile in the face of geo-political uncertainty and potential trade wars, in a way not seen in this country since the 1950s.

Writing this chapter has made me realize that I've had a pointless snobbery about tinned food, perhaps since my bruising encounter with my domestic science teacher. I hadn't bought a tin of pineapple since then, but Brexit, nuclear war, disastrous trade deals, a global pandemic and Jack Monroe's Pina Colada bread, using tinned pineapple and coconut milk, might just make me change my mind.

POTTED SHRIMPS

◆

In the seventeenth century cooks filled thick rye pastries with clarified butter, to seal the venison pasty, which we look at in the next chapter. In the following century the same technique was adapted to pot salmon, smelts, chars, eels, lobsters, shrimps and also some kinds of meat. Commercially potted meats and fish generally had a low-class reputation in the nineteenth century, although one company ingeniously marketed its potted anchovies as 'The Gentleman's Relish' and continued to appeal to the upper classes. This potted shrimp recipe, from 1769, is so simple and so good.

MODERN RECIPE

150g unsalted butter
Good squeeze of lemon, to taste
Pinch of salt
Good grind of mace
Good grind of white pepper
150g cooked and peeled shrimps
Sprinkle of paprika – if desired

Straight-sided dish or a couple of ramekins or small pots

1. Start by clarifying the butter. Heat it very gently without stirring, skimming off the foamy residue on top with a spoon. Add the lemon, salt, mace and white pepper and stir.
2. In a bowl, mix your shrimps with about 1–2 tablespoons of the butter so that it's dispersed throughout. Press it into your containers. Pour the remainder of the butter over the mix and place in the fridge for a couple of hours, or until the butter has formed a solid crust on top.
3. Take it out of the fridge about 20 minutes before serving. Sprinkle over some paprika.
4. Serve with toast.

ORIGINAL RECIPE: TO POT SHRIMPS
From *The Experienced English Housekeeper* by Elizabeth Raffald (1769)

◆

Pick the finest shrimps you can get. Season them with a little beaten mace, pepper and salt to your taste, and with a little cold butter pound them all together in a mortar till it comes to a paste. Put it down in small pots and pour over them clarified butter.

NB To clarify butter: Put your butter into a clean saucepan, set it over a slow fire. When it is melted, scum it and take it off the fire, let it stand a little, then pour it over your lobsters. Take care you do not pour in the milk which settles to the bottom of the saucepan.

PART FIVE

◆

Disappearances and Reappearances

The Venison Pasty:
too posh to last

Come, we have a hot venison pasty to dinner: come, gentlemen,
I hope we shall drink down all unkindness.

William Shakespeare, *The Merry Wives of Windsor*

HISTORIES OF THE Cornish pasty like to point out that there are references to pasties going back to *Le Ménagier de Paris* (*The Goodman of Paris*; c.1393), Shakespeare's *The Merry Wives of Windsor* and, especially, to Pepys, who loved a pasty. They glide over the inconvenient fact that these are not Cornish but venison pasties. While the Cornish pasty (see The Cornish Pasty, page 117) is thriving in Britain, its aristocratic forebear, the venison pasty, has disappeared. The name is now oxymoronic; venison is served at tables of privilege, while pasties are for anyone to eat on the hoof.

The closest living relative of the venison pasty is the game pie. There are some impressive examples raised from a hot-water crust pastry and imbued with the spirit of its noble ancestor, such as the 'game pie decorated musically and inscribed with the words of *Così Fan Tutte*' made for a Glyndebourne picnic.[1] More within the reach of home cooks, a hot stew of venison with red wine, juniper and bay and covered with a puff pastry top isn't too shabby either. But who has eaten all the (venison) pasties?

The Elizabethan traveller Fynes Moryson was struck by the unique English predilection for them: 'In the seasons of the year, the English eat fallow deer plentifully, as buck in summer and does in winter, which they bake in pasties, and this venison pasty is a dainty, rarely found in any other kingdom.'[2] A huge pasty, encasing a whole shoulder of deer, exquisitely decorated with pastry trees, scrolls and a stag, was a magnificent gift; and rural landowners kept deer parks not just for their own amusement but to cultivate important people. For Restoration Londoners such as Pepys, after the supposedly egalitarian rations of Cromwellian England, how luxurious it was to show his fellow diners that he was well connected enough to have venison sent from his aristocratic patron, Edward Montague of Hinchingbrooke. Pepys immediately gives the gift of half a buck (smelling a little strong, but no worse for that) to his mother to make into a pasty.[3] In *The Queen-Like Closet*, his contemporary, Hannah Woolley, suggests serving her venison pasty not only as one of the many dishes for the summer feast of 'Great and Noble Houses' but also as part of the 'Bill of Fare for Gentlemen's houses of lesser quality'.[4] It would have hurt Pepys to think it, but she probably had men of his sort in mind for the latter.

Venison's extraordinary, almost mythological, status in England dates back to 1066. The new Norman overlords outraged Saxons with their wasteful demands for the meat of baby animals, and their forest laws – a land-grab of around a third of England's well-wooded terrain for royal deer parks. Eating 'froth' or baby animals never really caught on this side of the Channel; to this day, veal is seen as a Continental aberration, and it took an agricultural revolution to turn a nation of mutton-eaters into lamb-lovers. However, game, especially venison, was desired, fetishized and fought over by natives and incomers, old and new, imperious high and resentful low. The new masters kept Saxon peasants well away by devising draconian laws against poaching; a man taking a deer or hart could be blinded, according to the anti-Norman 'Rime of King William' from 1087. Three hundred years later Richard II's game laws fell over themselves in an attempt to close every possible loophole:

No artificer, labourer or layman which hath not lands or tenemented to the value of 40/- a year, nor any priest or clerk, if he be not advanced to the value of £10 per annum, shall have or keep from henceforth any greyhound, hound or other dog to hunt, nor shall use fyets, nets, harepipes nor cords nor other engine to take or destroy deer, hares nor conies nor other gentlemans game upon pain of one years imprisonment.[5]

The Normans and their medieval successors ritualized every part of the hunt, down to the cutting up of the stag. Their cooks, entrusted with the valuable saddle or haunch, must have fretted over how easily the lean meat dried out on the spit in front of a huge fire without a jacket of pork fat. They learnt also to bake each huge, whole joint long and slow in fat-enriched pastry, which larded the lean meat and kept it moist. They added pepper, spices, perhaps red wine for flavour, and discovered how to fill up the air holes with clarified butter for better keeping properties. The pastry itself, of sturdy rye flour, would often become so hard – or stale – it would be discarded. Venison pasties were the Fortnum & Mason hamper of the Christmas gift season, until the game pie edged it off the Victorian Christmas sideboard: more towering, more dramatic and with more room for Gothic Revival images created in pastry that evoked a fashionable nostalgia for an era when everybody knew their place (the time, in fact, of the outmoded pasty).

Writing in the mid-twentieth century, Dorothy Hartley explained that good Anglo-Saxons had an atavistic prejudice against venison because of its associations with the aristocracy. She is tickled to find that it is ignored by a queue of local shoppers in a country town, even in wartime when meat was scarce; the butcher then sold it for half as much again in a more upmarket store to urbane evacuees. Once deer farming started in the 1970s, middle-class home cooks began to think of the meat as fair game. Ironically.[6] The need for butchers to have a game licence disappeared in 2007 and the market is said now to be growing at about 10 per cent per year.[7]

Venison, subject to game laws and hard to get hold of, has been imitated down the centuries. Pepys was derisory when his 'Cosen' Thomas passed off 'palpable beef' for venison in a pasty for a Twelfth Night dinner.[8] That it was, in Pepys's words, 'not handsome' didn't stop entirely reputable cookbook writers such as Gervase Markham from matter-of-factly giving recipes 'To make beef or mutton for venison' with the dye turnsole to make it appear blue-blooded.[9] Robert May thought that, with the right spices, salt and a bay leaf or two, after eight hours' cooking time 'a very good judgement shall not know it from red Deer'.[10] Even in the early twentieth century, Alice B. Toklas is enthusiastic about a hilariously byzantine recipe from a local medic which subjects a leg of mutton to injections of brandy and orange over several days to make it taste of venison.[11] It would be extraordinary to Markham, May or even Toklas that it was not the venison pasty that became protected by EU law from imitation, but the humble swede, potato and beef Cornish pasty.

If the venison pasty has, perhaps, disappeared from off the top of the scale, a more humble kind of meat could be said to have disappeared from the bottom. Which brings us to tripe.

Tripe: a social outcast

Do not let the word tripe deter you. Let its soothing charms win you over and enjoy it as do those who always have!

Fergus Henderson, *Nose to Tail Eating* (1999)

A ROUND THE TIME a Californian businessman was discovering how to turn chicken into mass market food, a Manchester consortium was attempting the same capitalist magic with tripe. In the 1920s, a union of fifteen or so tripe dressers banded together to become United Cattle Products (Manchester). There were already shops dedicated to tripe throughout the North West – 260 in Manchester by 1906 – and UCP went on to build an empire of tripe restaurants which still numbered 146 in the 1950s. The *Wigan Observer* reported ecstatically in 1917 on the new Tripe de Luxe Restaurant and Tea Room with its lavatory accommodation ('provided on the most scientific lines'), daintily placed palms, and ladies' orchestra which 'dispensed' music.[1]

UCP's trick was to elevate a food which, like fried fish, had image problems (see Fish and Chips, page 377); the 1875 Public Health Act designated tripe dressing an 'Offensive Trade' subject to public health scrutiny. Tripe, which might be any one of four bovine stomachs (called, in stomach order, blanket, honeycomb, thick seam, reed tripe), needed thorough washing – even bleaching – to be rid of the traces of its contents; and several hours' boiling before it was soft enough to eat. Although taken as something of an insult by the profession, this scrutiny acted in its favour; unsanitary backyard tripe dressers, the premises smeared with rotting offal, had to clean up their act. 'Chatchip', the pen-name for William Loftas whose column in the *Fish Trades Gazette* cheered on fish friers, recommended that they sell tripe, too, because in a better-class neighbourhood people who might be ashamed of going to the chippy would happily admit they were 'off to the tripe merchant's'.[2]

Although tripe was appreciated by northern millworkers with little time and money up to and throughout the First World War, UCP realized that it must overcome the prejudices of the aspirational housewife to raise the dish to a higher level of social acceptability. It engaged the services of Florence B. Jack, the cookery editor of *Good Housekeeping*, no less, to show in ninety-nine recipes how cheap and easy it was to feed the whole family with tripe: tripe steak (baked with onion and rice) for the tired husband; tripe with macaroni for the fussy child; tripe soup to cosset the invalid; or, of course, the classic, comforting, milk-seethed tripe and onions. Like chicken, it is protein-rich, easily digested and bland (or has 'outstanding nourishing value and purity' as UCP had it). In spite of vaunting its remarkable history, the flowery introduction isn't quite sure how much to acknowledge that tripe had an image problem: 'Prejudice has been replaced by Prestige,' UCP declared, prematurely, as it ushered in a new era of eating this 'right delicious food for all classes'.[3]

UCP seems to have backed the right horse but in the wrong race. The evidence suggests that, for centuries, tripe had no social stigma and it could even be rather grand. The Romans set great store by it (there is a haggis-like recipe for stuffed tripe in Apicius), and it was greeted enthusiastically by Shakespeare, Lamb, Burns and Dickens. The Goodman of Paris, the male Mrs Beeton of the Middle Ages, giving domestic instructions to his young wife around 1393, says that mock-hedgehogs of mutton tripe are too much expense and trouble for people of their bourgeois station. Poor Katherine in *The Taming of the Shrew* is tormented by the servant Grumio who offers her 'a fat tripe – finely broiled', a dish she likes well, she says; he also suggests a neat's (cow) foot and beef and mustard – before withdrawing every offer because they are too 'hot'. The aim of this abuse is to tame her, like a hawk, with starvation but also to teach her not to like this strong, hot, masculine food. Presumably she will learn to nibble at dainty junkets or sweet 'cates', as Petruchio punningly refers to cakes. Pepys boasted that the most excellent dish of tripes 'covered with mustard... of which I made a very great meal' was made at his direction to copy a dish served at 'my Lord Crew's'.[4]

Prejudice crept in as people became aware that it was the food of the 'labouring population of this country', as a political economist in Dickens' Christmas book *The Chimes* (1844) describes it, complaining at the same time that it was the most uneconomical of foods.[5] One-time chef to Queen Victoria, and self-appointed instructor of the poor, Charles Elmé Francatelli has a similar view; he includes a recipe in case one of his working-class readers wants it as a treat, but it 'is not exactly a cheap commodity for food'.[6]

By the time UCP was attempting to overcome this double hurdle of the perception that tripe was for poor people, and yet not cheap enough, it had started a steady, forty-year decline, weighted down by the other meaning of 'tripe' as 'nonsense'. George Orwell, lodging in a Lancashire 'tripe and pea' shop, recounts how ageing tripe lurked in a basement of horrors, where it is attended to by a man with filthy hands and a swarm of black beetles.[7] It never shook off this comically ghoulish image of mill-town misery and none of its champions have ever managed to remake it in a different image such as, for example, fish and chips' reinvention as a seaside holiday treat for the middle classes; haggis's canny association with a newly respectable Scottish nationalism; or black pudding's cheffy introduction into restaurant society. One or two contemporary offal-loving chefs hold a torch for its charms. Fergus Henderson, remembering tripe and onions from his Lancastrian mother, revived it at St John in London and, together with the financial crash of 2008 when people began to be interested in offal and cheaper cuts of meat again, was responsible for a sprinkle of interest among food writers. However, in the years since, its reputation in the English-speaking world has been against it; in spite of reminders of the French, Turkish or Chinese use of the dish, or exhortations by Tripe Adviser[8] (yes, really) for people to embrace its English history, it is still a minority taste.

People will probably always complain of its soft, shivery, slithery texture; but is it this or tripe's lowly connections that make it so unloved in this country? After all, the oyster is soft, shivery and slithery and, like tripe, has been valued by both rich and poor throughout history. Yet, at the same point in its story, the oyster has a reputation as the food of privilege.

Oysters: from national treasure to rarity value

I never shall forget the indulgence with which he treated Hodge,
his cat: for whom he himself used to go out and buy oysters, lest
the servants having that trouble should take a dislike to the poor
creature.

James Boswell, *The Life of Samuel Johnson* (1791)

IF YOU FIND yourself on Whitechapel High Street, in need of a
cholesterol laden snack of, say, fried chicken, a short walk, or
waddle, will offer you a wide choice of adjectives... Kentucky,
Whitechapel, Perfect, Dixie, Royal, or nouns... Chicken Shop, Hut,
Job or Shack. Not only the endless junk food joints, but businesses
such as betting shops, tanning salons and payday lenders betray a
particularly well-resourced kind of urban poverty. Such windows
onto short-termism and obesity earned the street the dubious
honour of being the 'unhealthiest' high street in London in a 2015
survey by the Royal Society for Public Health.

In 1837, Whitechapel was similarly marked by poverty.
Dickens' funniest character, Sam Weller, chaperoning his boss, Mr
Pickwick, through its crowded and filthy streets, remarks on the
proportion of oyster stalls to houses: 'Blessed if I don't think that
ven a man's wery poor, he rushes out of his lodgings, and eats
oysters in reg'lar desperation.'[1] Poverty and oysters were Victorian
London's partners in crime as much as poverty and fried chicken,
burgers, chips and deep-fried saveloys are now. How have we let

the first, high in nutrients, protein and low in calories and as fast a food as you could wish, slip away into gleaming restaurants and plush oyster bars for the wealthy, to be replaced on the streets by junk?

Oysters are perhaps unique in food history, as both the fortunate and the needy have adored that indecently shivery texture and elusive taste of mineral sweetness, and relished (or at least put up with) their peculiarly asymmetric and secretive packaging. Even in Ancient Rome, the English oyster was prized as a luxury as much as it is in Britain today, where 'Natives' rub shoulders with caviar and champagne in restaurants which boast of their 'celebrated history' (Wheeler's) or 'iconic' status (J.Sheekey), or that they once obliged the waitresses to behave as nannies to make their aristocratic clientele feel at home (Wilton's). Roman foodies also fetishized the English oyster. Juvenal scoffed in Satire IV that a gourmand could tell whether his oyster fed on the 'Rutupian or the Lucrine Bed'. The shells of plump English 'Rutupian' oysters from Richborough and other parts of England's east coast have been found on middens in Rome, although it's a mystery as to how they might have arrived there, fresh. In the holds of ships, perhaps, or as Seamus Heaney surmises in his poem 'Oysters', 'packed deep in hay and snow' and hauled over the Alps.

The Romans might have taught the Anglo-Saxons to appreciate the oyster as food; certainly, by the first sightings of them in medieval records they were valued for being nutritious, plentifully available and for providing a good livelihood. An impressive network of careful cultivation, local laws and taxes regulated dredging and sales, such as the medieval edict in Ipswich which ordained 'for common benefit (of poor men as well of rich men)' that oysters should be sold only by the people who catch them, meaning no middleman could hike up the prices. Richard I's Royal Charter, in 1189, granted rights to the Colne oyster fishery to Colchester; and the town's corporation protected local livelihoods by requiring all oyster-men to be licensed. It kept the beds rejuvenated by enforcing a closed season and demanded that local hunger should be satisfied before a quick buck was made on the London market. In return, local dignitaries were given enormous oyster feasts (the cost of them carefully kept out of the town accounts), which survive in some form or other to this day.

The huge numbers of oysters consumed have made them a by-word for cheap plenty in English gastronomic history. The urban poor probably ate the millions of oysters they consumed, pickled, like their salmon (and, the joke went, themselves). One recommendation to alleviate the Irish Famine of 1845–9 was that the Irish should collect and pickle oysters, not to assuage their own hunger, but to sell to the voracious London market.

Henry Mayhew said that the more expensive fresh oysters were luxuries to tittle rather than assuage the appetite. It wasn't until 1848 when what the costermongers called 'scuttle-mouths' – oysters with a thick shell but small meat – started to be brought up from the Sussex coast, that the fresh-oyster trade boomed in the streets. Even then, an oyster-seller explained that, although 'two penn'orth is a poor gentleman's dinner', the very poor, with only a penny to their name, wouldn't spend it on oysters when it could buy a penny loaf, or a ha'porth of bread and a ha'porth of cheese or, of course, a half-pint of beer.[2] Eating on the street was not a respectable thing to do, and the trade in oysters took off at night when darkness hid the shame of 'lofty-minded' customers.[3]

Fresh oysters were a ubiquitous kitchen ingredient, relished for the umami tang they brought to a leg of mutton or when slipped into a meat pie. They made a lush cream sauce for cod, were stewed with wine and herbs, or baked into spiced mince pies instead of beef suet.[4]

This plenty was destroyed around the turn of the century by a series of mostly man-made environmental fiascos, particularly over-dredging of the oyster beds which Victorian laissez-faire economics did nothing to prevent. Local councils could be criminally stupid; the one in Emsworth, Hampshire, proudly opened a sewage system which released untreated sewage over the local beds. Fresh Emsworth oysters supplied to two different banquets on 10 November 1902 caused sickness for all who'd eaten them and four deaths, including the Dean of Winchester who died after contracting typhoid.

It was a far cry from the careful preservation of oyster beds and livelihoods of medieval Colchester. 'The oystermen faced an authority that was perpetrator, judge and jury. The councils closed the oyster beds in the name of public safety – locked them up and threw away the keys,' said the food writer and former editor of *The Good Food Guide*, Drew Smith.[5]

Oysters in English waters were also devastated by disease in the 1980s, so their rarity value and prestige soared. To some extent their new status has been their saviour; the restaurant trade has done more than anybody to find new sources, such as Scottish sea-lochs. Rarity has removed oysters from the streets of Whitechapel; for some their rarity value enhances the experience. For Seamus Heaney, though, knowing about their exclusivity gets in the way of the simplicity of eating and sharing when a food is so weighted down with what he calls, in 'Oysters', the 'Glut of privilege'.

We all know that a bad oyster can have a ruinous effect on health, and yet it has never affected our admiration for them. It makes an interesting contrast to fruit, which was feared and neglected for many centuries.

Fruit: the raw and the cooked

Good apple pies are a considerable part of our domestic happiness.

Jane Austen, letter to her sister
Cassandra (17 October 1815)

UNTIL A FEW years ago, the quince was a stranger to restaurant and dinner tables in its English state, although a few had been on holiday to Spain and come back tanned a deep maroon colour and taking on the name Membrillo. Quince paste, made for centuries in England and then largely forgotten, had been made fashionably exotic served with salty Manchego or, on retrieval of a folk-cooking memory from down the back of the collective sofa, perhaps even with roast game. Its fruit cousins, however, led by the apple, have gone on from strength to strength, reflecting our changing views of raw and cooked fruit.

From the earliest records of our diet, raw fruit provoked anxiety in physicians and diners. The idea that fruit – or too much fruit – gave rise to fevers came directly from the ideas of the second-century AD Greek physician Galen, but the twentieth-century food scientist Jack Drummond points out that this also tallied with observations that summer fevers and diarrhoea, particularly in children, coincided with the season of fresh fruit.[1] And, of course, unwashed and uncooked fruit might harbour many kinds of microbes. Sir Thomas Elyot, author of the influential *Castel of Health* (1534), said that it was 'noyfulle' (noisome), would 'ingender ylle humours' and, when eaten after meals, acted as a laxative.[2]

Raw fruit was appreciated for its luscious looks and equally feared for its ability to destroy life; it was piled into fruit bowls or strewn across a table in the Vanitas paintings of the sixteenth and seventeenth centuries. A winged insect might shimmer between a plate of strawberries and cherries, or a maggot wriggle motionlessly in an apple, to remind the viewer that also in life was decay and death.

Most fruit was grown for the kitchen where, in medieval times, it could be cooked and balanced in terms of the theory of the humours: a hangover from Roman times, which believed that foods were hot, cold, wet or dry and too much of one or the other was damaging to the body. Raw fruit was blamed, not only for engendering fevers, but for being too 'cold', which could be balanced by the warmth of wine and spices. Although the results, pears in spiced wine, say, were doubtless excellent, anybody who couldn't afford wine and spices to counteract the dangers of fruit probably simply never ate it. The early sixteenth-century *Boke of Kervynge* instructed the cook, 'Beware of green sallettes and rawe fruytes for they wyll make your soverayne seke', which suggests that fruit was only expected on the table of the 'soverayne' or master.[3]

As sugar became more commonly imported in the sixteenth century, it was poured into preserving pans to turn fruits into pastes, marmelets or marmalades, suckets and conserves, and to candy roots, fruits or flowers, so that they might be available all through the year. Tarts and pies made from fresh or preserved fruit were decorated with exquisite cut-out or leaf-and-flower designs in the pastry; in the 1600s and 1700s they formed part of the second course, along with lighter meat and fish dishes (see Small Plates, page 223), while preserved and fresh fruits, when they were served, might be offered at the end of the meal, as chocolates are today.

The names and the trees of many of our cooking fruits have all but disappeared in these days of the fruit bowl. Hard, cooking pears, such as Wardens, were common pie ingredients; they 'must have saffron to colour the Warden pies' for the sheep-shearing feast in Shakespeare's *The Winter's Tale*.[4] Cooks painstakingly made verjuice from crab apples. Apple recipes called for codlins to stew, pearmains for pies, the versatile pippins for everything – pies, tarts and creams – and biffins to cook long and slow to a cake form. The anonymous author of *A Proper New Booke of Cookery* (1545) and Robert May, in *The Accomplisht Cook* (1660) both give a recipe for a rich, treacly medlar tart. 'Take medlars when they be rotten', the former says, before simmering them with sugar and cinnamon and adding a thick egg yolk custard.[5] It's a cross between a treacle tart and a sticky toffee pudding with, if any more reason is needed to make it, considerably less added sugar. The flesh of the medlar, which needed to be rotten or 'bletted' before it could be used, could not survive the weight of imagery – of overripeness, prostitution and death – it was laden with. Thomas Dekker, looking for suitable insults in his play *The Honest Whore, Part II* (1630), uses their flesh as a metaphor for sexual ruin and venereal disease, often known as 'rot'; 'women are like Medlars (no sooner ripe but rotten)'.[6] Even in the twentieth century, D.H. Lawrence was describing them as 'Wineskins of brown morbidity/Autumnal excrementa' in his poem 'Medlars and Sorb-apples'.

The great virtue of the quince was that it was ideal for preservation; indeed, it could not be eaten raw. The work involved took place in bigger, wealthier kitchens which could afford the sugar, the work and time in cutting and boiling the quince with its skin and pips (wherein lay the pectin which is the source of its magical setting properties) and then straining the jelly. Indeed, turning classical quinces into rosy, scented quidinia (or jelly) was one of Sir Hugh Plat's Elizabethan *Delights for Ladies*. John Nott, who cooked for a series of aristocrats before writing his excellent *Cook and Confectioners' Dictionary* in 1723, gives endless recipes for quince marmalade, plus cakes, 'composts' (which we know as compotes), cream, jelly, pudding, 'quiddany' (a jelly or paste), tart, syrup, 'pyes' – far more than for apples.

Apples were the most classless of fruit and sweetened the diet of all but the poorest. William Ellis noted that they were available all around the agricultural land of his native Hertfordshire and that labourers, carters or craftsmen working outdoors might be given an apple pasty, or dumpling, as a portable snack. At home they and their families ate apples in fritters, pies, tarts and puddings. One lord, 'a true Œconomist', obliged his servants to eat apple pudding, to save himself the expense of the ingredients for plum pudding.[7] Naturally sweet apples were valued for baking, as they spared the use of costly sugar, although it was becoming more affordable throughout the seventeenth and eighteenth centuries, sweetening the lives of the labouring classes in Britain, to the devastation of their enslaved counterparts in the West Indies.

Attitudes to fresh fruit changed for some in society because the Enlightenment swept away the pseudo-science of Galen. For urban families with income but no land of their own, expanding market gardens and orchards around cities such as London brought apples, pears, cherries and plums more readily to their kitchens, but town-dwellers such as Pepys, although pleased to serve strawberries and asparagus, were slow to admit uncooked tree fruits to their tables. Fresh fruit as a dessert became wildly popular at the top of society once gardening became a fashionable hobby (see Vegetables and Vegetarians, page 314) and producing hard-to-grow fruit such as peaches or apricots, grapes or figs, from a south-facing wall of an enclosed kitchen garden, became an icon of the modern landowner. Just as a love of the French *ragout* damns one of Jane Austen's male characters, a liking for fresh fruit (and the financial wherewithal to produce it) indicates a gentle authorial approval; when Elizabeth Bennet meets her future sister-in-law at Darcy's magnificent country estate, Pemberley, we are assured the meeting is a happy one because 'the beautiful pyramids of grapes, nectarines, and peaches soon collected them round the table'.[8]

Not many years after *Pride and Prejudice* invoked the spirit of Chatsworth, the young Joseph Paxton became head gardener there; his new hothouses grew pineapples and bananas and the competition among the beau monde to grow exotic fruit was ratcheted up a notch. Paxton himself cultivated the Cavendish banana at Chatsworth House in the 1830s, and named it after the Duke of Devonshire, William Cavendish: an aristocratic beginning for what is now the most common of all banana cultivars. Soon, every fashionable Victorian dinner or supper table had to feature a towering mound of hothouse exotics, preferably topped with a glamorous pineapple, as much a decorative craze as a fruit. It was said that people who weren't quite the thing *hired* pineapples for show. The society chef and philanthropist Alexis Soyer delighted in retailing a rumour that the same pineapple was spotted first at an 8 p.m. dinner and then at a supper at a civic ball at midnight. 'Memoirs of a Pineapple in London' would be a bestseller, he mused, 'having had the advantage of mixing in so many different societies'.[9]

Horticulturalists began to become interested in developing the strains of apples we know today, separating, for the first time, the function of cooking from eating apples, such as Cox's Orange Pippin, developed in 1830 by Richard Cox. Improved transport brought these new cultivars to the city markets, bringing fresh apples into easy reach, for the first time, of urban artisans, clerks and tradesmen and their families.

The fruit bowl in many middle-class homes might be a cornucopia of variety and lushness of which the Duke of Cavendish, showing off his first hothouse-grown bananas, would be proud. Today, it is common to have apples, oranges, tangerines, bananas, grapes, melons, peaches, nectarines, pears, figs... with punnets of berries and cherries in our fridges. The display has moved from its towering status at the centre of the grandest dessert to the sideboard in the well-resourced kitchen, from which children are encouraged to eat one of their 'five a day' in place of sweets, cakes and biscuits. Research suggests that some people of lower socio-economic status, particularly men, still do not see fresh fruit as a food for them. They don't eat or enjoy or rate it in status as much as their middle-class counterparts, partly because they don't view it as good value or filling enough, even just for a snack, and partly because it has never been part of their diets.[10] Cooked apples are the fruit most likely to be consumed, as they were for William Ellis's Hertfordshire neighbours in the eighteenth century; these days in the guise of a McDonald's apple pie, a pastry, a danish or a turnover.

The Spanish have reminded us of the value of quince paste, and Middle Eastern cooks such as Honey & Co and Ottolenghi reintroduced us to the quince as a dessert. French medlars occasionally make it onto the cheeseboard, along with quince paste, as a dense fruit 'cheese'. But with the lushness and variety of fresh – and frozen and tinned – fruit available, the quince, the medlar and the warden, no longer valued for their longevity, have been all but forgotten.

QUINCE PYE

◆

If you see quinces, buy them! Or grow them. Make mahogany quince paste, or rose-coloured Quince Pye, after Robert May's seventeenth-century recipe. Like most early recipe book writers, May is endlessly flexible, offering a number of different ways to make 'pye' for quinces and all kinds of 'curnel'd' or cooking fruit. His book is particularly charming for pie-artists as he offers several intricate designs to cut into the pastry lid.

MODERN RECIPE
SERVES 6

100g golden caster sugar for the syrup, plus extra for the apples; I suggest between 50–100g to please your taste
600ml water
2–3 quinces
Optional – cinnamon stick, a little lemon peel or a vanilla pod
Approx. 750g cooking apples
650g shortcrust pastry

22cm pie dish

1. Make the poaching syrup by gently heating the sugar in the water until it dissolves. Add your flavourings, if you'd like to use them. Keep it simmering very gently.

2. Using your sharpest knife, peel, core and slice the quinces, putting the slices into the syrup as you go so they don't discolour. Cover the pan and simmer the quince on a very low heat until they give to the point of a knife. It could take anything from 30 minutes to 2 hours.

3. You should end up with cooked quince slices and a sticky, rose-coloured syrup. If necessary, fish the slices out with a slotted spoon and continue to reduce the syrup until it is thick enough to serve as a pouring sauce.

4. Preheat the oven to Gas Mark 4/180°C.

5. Take about two thirds of the chilled pastry, roll out to about 3mm and line a pie dish, leaving an overhang.

6. Roll out the remainder on a sheet of baking paper, to a circle about 24cm wide. Cut out a pattern.

7. Peel, core and slice the apples, pile them into the pie dish, sprinkle the extra sugar on the apples, and then arrange the quince slices on top.

8. Pick up the pastry lid on its baking paper and carefully slide it on top, pressing the pastry edges together to seal. Bake for 40–45 minutes.

9. Serve the quince syrup separately, or swirl it into thick or whipped cream to serve alongside.

ORIGINAL RECIPE: TO MAKE A QUINCE PYE OTHERWAYS

From *The Accomplisht Cook* by Robert May (1660)

◆

Take Quinces and preserve them, being first coared and pared, then make a sirrup of fine sugar and spring water, take as much as the quinces weight, and to every pound of sugar a pint of fair water, make your sirrup in a preserving pan; being scumm'd and boil'd to sirrup, put in the quinces, boil them up till they be well coloured, & being cold, bake them in pyes whole or in halves, in a round tart, dish, or patty-pan with a cut cover, or in quarters; being baked put in the same sirrup, but before you bake them, put in more fine sugar, and leave the sirrups to put in afterwards, then ice it.

Thus you may do of any curnel'd fruits, as wardens, pippins pear, pearmains, green quodlings, or any good apples, in laid tarts, or cuts.

Saloop: comfort for outsiders

This is *Saloop* – the precocious herb-woman's darling – the delight of the early gardener, who transports his smoking cabbages by break of day from Hammersmith to Covent-garden's famed piazzas – the delight, and, oh! I fear, too often the envy, of the unpennied sweep.

Charles Lamb, 'In Praise of Chimney Sweeps', *Essays of Elia* (1823)

WE STILL ENJOY the bark of the cinchona tree (or a synthetic substitute), the bitter quinine taste in tonic water; however, there are many more tree roots, barks and saps we once used for their distinctive flavourings but which have disappeared from our drinks menu. In the pages of *Sylva; or, a Discourse of Forest Trees* (1662), by the Restoration diarist, gardener and arboriculturist John Evelyn, can be found a recipe for 'a most brisk and spiritous drink' of spiced birch sap.[1] Hannah Glasse gives recipes for birch and elder wine (Benjamin Franklin scribbled down the spruce beer recipe from a later edition of *The Art of Cookery* – it isn't in the 1747 one – and was credited with introducing it to America). Jane Austen and her circle used to joke about their friend Martha Lloyd's penchant for spruce beer – made from the new tips of the fir branches. The 'choice purl' that so delights the mistreated little servant in Dickens' *The Old Curiosity Shop* was a beer made from artemisia, or wormwood (reputedly the green fairy in absinthe).[2] The Pilgrim Fathers, noticing how the Native Americans used the resources of the wooded land they first occupied, begat a more systematic use of root and branch for soft and alcoholic drinks which is still evident in American root beer and sodas such as sarsaparilla.

The new and old worlds collided in Britain in the drink called saloop. It was originally made from the twin tubers of the early purple orchid. The root was ground and dried, then mixed with hot milk or water and sugar. Its shape gave rise to its Latin name – *Orchis mascula* – *orchis* meaning 'testicle'. Nicholas Culpeper, who brought together ideas of medicine, botany and astrology in his book *The Complete Herbal* (first published under the title *The English Physitian* in 1652), thought that the roots could 'provoke lust exceedingly'; it became associated, principally, with energy, although there was also a whiff of virility if you looked for it – Brillat-Savarin was beguiled by a Parisian pharmacist who prescribed saloop-flavoured chocolate for body building.[3] Unlike chocolate or coffee, it was strangely cheap, given its exotic provenance. On the basis of a price of 8d or 10d a pound for the powdered root, Sir Frederick Eden, whose survey of the economic and social lives of Britain's lowest-waged and unemployed was published as *The State of the Poor* in 1797, recommended it to the poor because it contained 'the greatest quantity of vegetable nourishment in the smallest bulk', which made the root powder 'extremely convenient as a portable soup'.[4] Maria Rundell, who wasn't above using demotic ingredients in her cookbook, recommended mixing it with wine and lemon peel as a sort of milk pudding for the sick.[5]

It became a favourite drink for working men, in the days before the coffee cart brought a more caffeinated lift to the streets of London. Porters, coalmen, market gardeners and workers of all kinds, particularly those up late and in the early morning, were its customers, reckoned the botanical illustrator Anne Pratt.[6] Its most famous literary outing, though, was probably with the lovable Romantic essayist Charles Lamb who urged his readers, finding themselves in the city at dawn, to press a penny onto a chimney sweep, so that the child might have a 'fragrant breakfast' of saloop; without their charity he would hang his sooty head over the intoxicating steam, like a cat purring over valerian.[7]

Lamb thought that his chimney sweep's drink was made, not from orchid, but from the sweet wood of sassafras. He might have been right. As the supply of Indian or Turkish purple orchid roots was patchy they seem to have been replaced by a flour made from the aromatic sassafras tree from America's East Coast. Nobody knows exactly which drink was made from the root and which the branch; nor what it was called. It wasn't a beverage that much troubled culinary scholars – and it was rendered salep, saloop and salop.

Online histories, taking their cue from Wikipedia, gossip that saloop gained itself a reputation as a cure for syphilis and that this whiff of indecency put an end to its popularity. It's a nice story but it's hard to find contemporary corroboration; given that it was reckoned a cheap food for the poor, it is unlikely that it was also sold as a medicine. However, its humble customers might have suggested something disreputable about it. In 1820, the cartoonist Thomas Rowlandson sketched a soldier, a crone and a woman (whose visible décolletage, flash of ankle and close proximity to the soldier might suggest her profession), all enjoying a saucer of saloop. And, lest we be in any doubt as to Rowlandson's class palette, his cartoons were gathered together by Samuel Leigh under the giveaway title *Rowlandson's Characteristic Sketches of the Lower Orders of the British Metropolis*.

Henry Mayhew, writing forty years later, remarked regretfully that saloop had been edged out by coffee stalls, which were not much in demand until 1824 when duty on coffee was reduced from 1 shilling to 6d in the pound, and consumption trebled. He remembered saloop being used by the hackney-carriage man and chimney sweep, who hopped from one foot to another in an attempt to keep them warm, 'his white teeth the while gleamed from his sooty visage as he gleefully licked his lips at the warm and oily breakfast'.[8]

We see a last, fleeting glimpse of it in Dorothy Hartley's mid-twentieth-century *Food in England*, not in England at all, as though it had been pushed away to the margins: 'In Cardiganshire I had it at an old seaman's cottage after a long, wet sea crossing; it was made very thick and hot and served with a spoon and sugar. In Scotland I had it laced with spirit in a glass. In Ireland it was served in a teacup, thickened with cream and egg yolk.'[9] Sadly, she doesn't mention what it tastes like. If we wanted to reconstruct the taste, we might hunt it down in the markets of Istanbul, or look to sarsaparilla, a vine rather than a tree, the taste of which was brought to Britain by West Indian immigrants. Sassafras, though, has disappeared from our drinks as the US Food and Drug Administration ruled against it, worried that its essential oil was carcinogenic. It is now reconstructed artificially, but there are also versions with natural flavourings from wintergreen, sweet birch, black cherry bark, cinnamon, liquorice, balsam, cassia and acacia. A toast to the trees.[10]

While cuisines from all over the world have encouraged us to expand our range of herbs and spices in our cooking, we still have some hurdles to overcome when we think about them as flavouring for drinks; saloop might have slipped quietly away but there are signs that the once-prized and then despised mead and metheglin are coming back to life.

Metheglin and Mead:
champagne or alcopop?

He sente hire pyment, meeth, and spiced ale,
And wafres, pipyng hoot out of the gleede,
And, for she was of towne, he profreth meede.

Geoffrey Chaucer, *The Miller's Tale*

THE WORD 'BOTANICALS', which for a long time seemed to belong to herbalism, has come back into the gin-lover's vocabulary. It has jumped species from gin to botanical beers, some made with berries, aromatics and flowers, and to soft drinks such as ginger beer. Every herb and flower of the garden is now available as a herb tea; and turmeric has been brought to the party by coffee. But metheglin? Botanical mead? Are either ever going to trouble us again? When I first tried a bottle of dry, sparkling mead, it was almost impossible not to think of sparkling wine, and the flavour was simply wrong, until I realized I was tasting it with my expectations, not my taste-buds. Replace the thought of grapes with a meadow of wild flowers and the humming of bees, and you will find that your mouth is full of the dreamy aromatic taste of honey.

Most of us think of mead, if we do at all, as an oversweet sort of honey liqueur with ecclesiastical top notes and an antiquated finish, a Drambuie for monks. In fact, as well as a sticky dessert-wine, mead can, depending on the honey to water ratio, be a dry, slightly sherry-like wine; it can also be sparkling. There was a long tradition of spicing it with herbs and spices, often called 'metheglin' from the Welsh *meddyglyn* or 'medicinal liquor', particularly in the South and West of England. The Tudors, reflecting their Welsh origins, popularized the Welsh word, though it was often used interchangeably with mead (or meed, or meeth, or meath, etc.). The spelling, like the recipes themselves, was a free for all.

The world's oldest alcoholic drink, the first batch of mead almost certainly made itself from fermented honey and rainwater in our most ancient cultures. By the time it swims into view in Northern European culture, it had considerable status. The 'medoful', the mead cup, is the figurative honeypot around which the court of Hrothgar buzzes in the 'meodhuhealle', the mead-hall, in *Beowulf*, and King Hrothgar's wife, the gold-bedecked Wealhtheow, is in charge of protocol, offering first to the king, then veterans and then the younger warriors in a feasting scene stuffed with symbols of power and hierarchy. Mead had potency as an image and as a drink in reinforcing social and hierarchical bonds. To the medieval Welsh poet (or poets) Taliesin, 'Sweet mead, a reward from the horn at a feast' was not only sweet to the taste, it was a gratifying sign that he was secure in the favour of his lord.[1]

Who knows how much honey cost in the early Middle Ages; but by the time records began to be kept, it was clear that its cost was steadily rising along with the progressive cultivation of land, which led to fewer fields of wild flowers. The price of honey versus the price of malt and, after around 1400, hops (when they were introduced into British brewing) kept mead as a drink for the wealthy, along with the few cottagers who could afford to keep hives but who seldom made it into the records. The mead-hall in *Beowulf*, although thought of as a celebration of masculinity, makes it clear that Wealhtheow is Queen Bee. Chaucer was quite clear that it was a genteel and elegant drink, with a strong feminine role; in *The Knight's Tale*, it is Emelye who sacrifices to Diana, goddess of chastity, with 'hornes fulle of meethe, as was the gyse [custom]'.[2] The bawdy *Miller's Tale* also gossips about a priest who tries to seduce a lady with fancy drinks – pyment (a fruit mead), meeth (metheglin) and spiced ale. Because she's an urban sophisticate, he sends her pure 'meede' or mead, like a modern-day sugar daddy hedging his bets with chi-chi liqueurs and champagne.

Charles Butler, the Elizabethan priest, bee-keeper and author of *The Feminine Monarchie*, reminded his readers that, although the ancients had assumed the Bee 'Governour' to be male (or 'the worthier' sex, as he puts it), in fact 'the males here beare no sway at all, this being an Amazonian or feminine kingdome'.[3] Butler then segues smoothly into a celebration of Elizabeth I, our 'renowned Queene of happie memorie', and seizes the opportunity to give a recipe for her favourite metheglin.

Butler's recipe involved seething sweet-briar, thyme, rosemary and bay leaves before straining, adding honey and ale or beer (for the yeast), and leaving it to 'work' (ferment) in the barrel. It was a standard method, but as the century wore on, recipes got more rather than less elaborate and spices were often added during the fermentation. French and Southern European wines were becoming far more available than they had been in medieval England. The English particularly liked sweetened, or reinforced wine, such as sack, malmsey, bastard (yes, really), etc. For the first time sugar, rather than honey, was added to spiced wine called Hippocras – oddly named after Hippocrates – and the forerunner of our mulled wine. The mead-makers responded with more honey to make a sweeter drink flavoured with a range of herbs which only a large garden could supply.

The handbook for Restoration-era bartenders was *The Closet of Sir Kenelm Digby Opened*, published posthumously in 1669. The title invites the purchaser into the secrets of a post-Commonwealth aristocracy which was reviving the good life. His hundred or so recipes for mead and metheglin were a roll call of the great and the good: 'My Earl of Denbigh's Metheglin', flavoured with rosemary and ginger; 'My Lady Bellaisses Meath' with raisins of the sun and cardamoms. Many of the recipes, such as the Countess of Dorset's for white metheglin, are, depending on how you look at it, a skilful mélange of botanicals, or the equivalent to weeding the estate grounds and throwing it all in one pot.

> Take Rosemary, Thyme, Sweet-bryar, Peny-royal, Bays, Water-cresses, Agrimony, Marshmallow leaves, Liver-wort, Maiden-hair, Betony, Eye-bright, Sabious, the bark of the Ash-tree, Eringo-roots, Green-wild-Angelica, Ribwort, Sanicle, Roman-worm-wood, Tamarisk, Mother-thyme, Sassafras, Philipendula.[4]

Mead and, even more, metheglin did not lend themselves, as did ale and beer, to the growing potential of mass production and remained confined to those who had estates – or cottage gardens – big enough to produce their own honey and botanicals. Town-dwelling Pepys, always with an eye to conspicuous consumption, doesn't get to taste metheglin until after the Restoration of 1660; when he is at the palace and 'had metheglin for the King's owne drinking' it's not surprising that the privilege 'did please me mightily'.[5]

In the following century, more French and other wines became available to those who could afford them and the grape started to displace mead from fashionable glasses. The beau monde preferred their sweet alcohol to have the sophistication of a foreign label: port, sherry, madeira, Constantia from South Africa. Mead became old-fashioned; the references petered out and are confined to those country people who make and drink it themselves. Mr Dennison in Smollett's *The Expedition of Humphry Clinker* rejects urban life for self-sufficiency and rural society, hiding from callers who come to the gate with 'gay equipage' but receiving modest neighbours; he is delighted when one teaches him to brew beer, and to make 'cyder, perry, mead, usquebaugh, and plague-water'.[6] While her brothers drank French wine, Jane Austen, her sister and mother lived a life of genteel domestication in a Hampshire village, sharing with guests their home-made fruit wines and around 20 gallons (91 litres) of mead a year. In a late letter to Cassandra, Jane laments that there will be no honey to make mead that year: 'Bad news for us.'[7]

Bee-keepers were unanimous in praising their bees for the qualities they admired in human society. Charles Butler celebrates their ordered government, their art and industry, their loyalty and magnanimity. The satirical philosopher Bernard Mandeville challenged that classic view in his much-studied *Fable of the Bees* (1714), arguing that bee – and human – communities only thrive if the individual members are self-interested (see Gin, page 290). George Cruikshank, best known for his illustrations of Dickens' novels, turns to the idea of bee orderliness and the industrial structure of the beehive as a taxonomy of British classes with the Queen at the top in an etching called *The British Bee Hive* (1840).

Bee-keeping and mead-making appealed to religious orders that were, for a long time, the caretakers of centuries of mead knowledge and custodians of its image, as it seemed to be falling off the edges of life, pushed to the Celtic and religious fringes. It was kept alive in the twentieth century by a handful of religious figures, such as the sublime Benedictine Brother Adam of Buckfast Abbey, in Devon, who became an internationally renowned apiarist. Both religious and secular organizations loved the idealized structure of the beehive, and bees themselves were venerated as a pure and particularly rural form of society, which couldn't survive with industry and smoke. No wonder country-dwellers identified with them. The additional herbs and spices of metheglin began to fall out of favour with the few mead-makers left, who wanted, instead, a direct honey hit. Flora Thompson notes that mead, at the end of the nineteenth century, was 'a drink almost superstitiously esteemed, and the offer of a glass was regarded as a great compliment'. In her Oxfordshire village it was far west enough to be called 'metheglin' although clearly it was simply 'mead'. One old neighbour who made it said that the folks who 'messed up their metheglin with lemons, bay leaves, and suchlike... didn't deserve to have bees to work for them'.[8] It seems likely that as mead-making became solely a cottage industry, country bee-keepers made it sweet to suit themselves, rather than to the taste of a dry-wine-drinking class of privilege and influencers. In 1948 a mead-lover lamented 'the liquor degenerated more and more, until the present product made of herbs, hops, spices, honey and even raisins, arose – a shabby pretender never drunk by the gods in Valhalla or by the nobles in Tara's halls'.[9] Whether the taste of the drink had 'degenerated' or not, its reputation certainly did over the second half of the twentieth century. It was not because people had lost the taste for sweetness, per se – honey continued to be prized and some, such as Manuka honey, is ascribed near-magical health-giving properties and is priced to match. All sweet drinks, however, were swept down a reputational chute with the arrival of oversweet fruit or nut liqueurs, cream-based cocktails, sweet sherries and alcopops. In the words of anthropologist Kate Fox, these were only considered socially acceptable for 'working-class and lower-middle-class females'; they were vulgar if ordered by middle-middle to upper-class females, and beyond the pale for nearly all males.[10]

The sweet and heavy meads, some sold with a swirly Celtic-looking label, joined these tawdry ranks in the public estimation. It probably didn't help that some were not in fact mead but wine or 'fermented grapes' sweetened with honey (technically a 'pyment' if you want to be charitable). We could draw a parallel with sherry, whose fortunes fell as it was judged to be a sweet, unsophisticated and outmoded drink; it became fashionable again with a concerted effort to make and market well-made, bone-dry Fino, Oloroso and Manzanilla sherries.

There are signs of a mead resurgence, though, thanks to the craft-brewing community, who embrace the very things that made mead so unfashionable: its reliance on bees and on the wild flowers, heather and orchards we have to cherish lest agribusiness uproot them for good. Fantasy fiction such as *Game of Thrones* and Neil Gaiman's *American Gods* are the impetus for some converts. Makers and enthusiasts are manoeuvring mead out of the category of kitsch sweet liqueur and into one of artisanal product, with an emphasis on skill and dedication, wild flowers and happy bees. Dry, sparkling, champagne-like, or a – literally – honeyed dessert-wine, they are a long way away from the alcopop meads of a decade or two ago. And who knows, someone might start to make metheglin again. It could be the craft gin of the future.

Gin: how it drove
everyone crazy

We hear that a strong-water shop was lately opened in Southwark
with the inscription on the sign:
Drunk for 1d.
Dead drunk for 2d.
Clean straw for nothing.

Old Whig newspaper (26 February 1736)

FOR A RECENT big birthday (OK, fifty), two of my close friends
gave me bottles of craft gin. I was surprised; I thought they
knew my tastes well enough to know that gin wasn't my drink
(it made me weepy). In fact, they knew me better than I knew
myself; a couple of ice-fuelled, lime-twisted gins with fancy tonics
later and I was as addicted as any eighteenth-century gin-crazed
slum-dwelling ruined mother. I couldn't guarantee there were no
more tears, but it turns out that any alcohol makes you weepy,
if you drink it fast enough and have something to weep about.
Now, matching the 'botanicals' – the juniper, angelica, cardamom,
coriander, orange – in different kinds of hand-crafted mother's
ruin to tonics containing citrus or elderflower or angostura is a
favourite way to welcome the weekend.

Gin had the terrible and, mostly, deserved reputation for being
the inner-city hell-raiser of the English drinks family, before
it met tonic, moved out to the suburbs and settled down. It
leapfrogged the aristocracy almost entirely, coming into Britain

via soldiers who encountered it fighting in the Low Countries.[1] Farmers and landowners, having a surplus of corn to sell in the late seventeenth century, were served by William III, and his Act of 1690 'for encouraging the distilling of brandy and spirits from corn' and successive punitive taxes on imported French brandy, on 'Hollands', that is, Dutch gin, and also locally produced beer. This neatly gave landowners a market for their surplus grain and shifted the burden of taxation away from their income and onto consumers.

The history of gin is a lesson in fiscal economics. Daniel Defoe, writing in 1726 in support of those 'Publick Spirited People', the distillers, defended them on the basis of the extraordinary sums they generated through tax for the 'Publick credit'. He divided up the different classes of people that gin benefited into 'Gentlemen or Landed Interest', 'Tenant and Farmer', and the 'Poor' who found work through the trade. He skated over the problems of alcoholism for which he mainly blamed imported Dutch gin, complaining, somewhat contradictorily, that the Dutch then got the profits, 'leaving us nothing but the Poverty and the Crime'.[2] Bernard Mandeville, the early economist and philosopher we met in the previous chapter, who was to influence Adam Smith, agreed. His eccentric and paradoxical *Fable of the Bees* also argued that 'Private Vices' such as gin drinking led to public benefits, including work for the poor and revenue for the public purse. (Mandeville is the first to use the word 'Gin'; initially known as 'genever' or 'geneva' after an approximation of the Dutch word for 'juniper', it was, as he said, then 'shrunk into a Monosyllable'.)

'Intoxicating Gin' had already earned a reputation for being destructive of the Health, Vigilance and Industry of the Poor, particularly those living in the inner city. London's Covent Garden, Soho and Westminster were the areas where the 'gin craze' most upset observers, probably because it was in their backyards. The gin-drinking port cities, further from Parliament's febrile anxiety, forged their own relationships with gin, the most lasting being Plymouth, which began distilling in 1697.[3]

The first half of the eighteenth century saw five Gin Acts which attempted to tread a course between public morality, vested interests and the riotous demands of gin's inner-city fans by balancing the cost of licences and the imposition of duty. Making and selling continued whether it was legal or not; unlicensed vendors might have their fines paid by the bigger distillers.[4] The wildly unpopular 1736 Act, which increased licences and duty, was repealed by the 1743 Act in favour of the free market; the Exchequer benefited as taxes and duties were easier to collect. As one opposition politician thundered: 'It is an experiment to discover how far the vices of the population may be made useful to the government, what taxes may be raised upon a poison, and how much the court may be enriched by the destruction of the subjects.'[5]

From the end of the seventeenth century it was both possible and profitable for anyone to distil the spirit in the morning and have it on sale by the afternoon. Consumption quadrupled from an annual 2 million gallons (9 million litres) in 1710 to a peak of around 8 million (36 million litres) in 1743.[6] The juniper and botanicals used by the Worshipful Company of Distillers were replaced by back-room gin-makers with cheap chemicals: oil of turpentine, oil of almonds (instead of coriander) and 'oil of vitriol' – sulphuric acid. As it was drunk neat, sugar took the edge off and made it more appealing to the ladies. Gin shops had no shortage of ragged customers among the intemperate, uneducated urban poor, eager to be transported to a happy gin haze, or at least have their woes benumbed for a while, or their existence enlivened by a quarrel, while in a less public back room servant-maids and 'the Wives of middling Sort of People who live thereabouts' refreshed themselves with their Juniper Water in more privacy.[7]

While the poor drunk themselves to wretchedness and Parliamentary landowners happily collected the grain profits and taxes, the moral majority, including bodies such as the Society for the Promotion of Christian Knowledge, the legal profession, writers and artists, began to intervene. For some, the problem was simply the wretchedness of gin-crazed lives, and the challenging sight of women drinking openly in public; but it wasn't until the prevailing argument on the 'public benefit' of taxes was challenged with an equally hard-hitting economic counter-proposal that things began to change.

How could the working population benefit the economy as workers or defend the nation as soldiers when they were crippled by foetal alcohol syndrome, and brought up to gin-soaked lives of crime, misery and intemperance? Gin also threatened the very size of the urban population; christenings in London declined by about 5,000 over twenty-five years, in spite of an increase in immigration.[8] Daniel Defoe, still espousing the importance of trade, changed tack two years after his *Case of the Distillers*. In his pseudonymous *Second Thoughts are Best* (1729), gin was now 'accursed Geneva'. Far from being the route to prosperity it was 'the bane and ruin of our lower class of people'.[9] Defoe was less worried about the health of individuals, and more concerned about the economy of the nation overall, arguing that, unless the lower orders were fit enough to work in manufacturing, trade and commerce, then the whole nation would fail to thrive.

Henry Fielding, as a magistrate, blamed gin for many of the petty crimes brought before him on the bench, which inspired his friend Hogarth to produce his famous *Gin Lane* and *Beer Street* prints. One focuses on a mother so addled by gin she is unaware that her baby is plunging to its death. Behind her is physical ruin, idleness and collapsing buildings at Seven Dials in Covent Garden. In the other, the sturdy residents of an economically thriving Westminster refresh themselves with honest beer at the end of the working day. Hogarth admitted frankly that his work was done 'to reform some reigning Vices peculiar to the lower Class of People', adding that it was 'in hopes to render them of more extensive use'.[10] Though whether he wanted his prints – or the lower orders – to be of extensive use is not made clear by his punctuation. Hogarth's xenophobic dislike of 'Hollands' had a degree of sociological grounding. The gin craze has been compared to crack cocaine; both were new drugs pumped into equally new, unsettled inner-city populations, which don't fit into established patterns of consumption and sweep social inhibitions and taboos before them.

Parliament finally listened and produced the Gin Act of 1751, which eliminated back-room distillers by insisting on a huge minimum still size, and cooled the gin craze for 250 years. The result was two-fold: a rapid dampening of consumption, by about a third within the year, and the birth of the large distilleries, beginning with Gordon's in 1769, which are still big names today.

Political memories are short, however; an Act of 1825 intending to reduce smuggling lowered the duty on English spirits from 11 shillings 8¼d a gallon to 7 shillings. It gave a huge boost to the major distillers that were building plate-glass, gilded, gas-lit 'gin palaces', which were jostling for custom with existing taverns and ale houses, particularly as beer was being priced out of reach. Designed for a quick in and out drink, with scant seating, food or comforts, they operated on a model of volume over quality of wares or experience.[11] Like the gin craze, they were an urban phenomenon, springing up in the cities of Manchester, Birmingham, Leeds, Liverpool and Hull as well as London; honeypots for factory workers and the disapproval of teetotal reformists. Tavern-loving Charles Dickens took a pop at both the 'epidemic' of gin palaces and the misplaced zeal of the Temperance movement in 'Gin-shops', one of his *Sketches by 'Boz'* (1835): 'If Temperance Societies would suggest an antidote against hunger, filth, and foul air… gin-palaces would be numbered among the things that were.'[12]

The gin palace rapidly became an image of kitsch and immorality. George Eliot, in an essay entitled *Authorship*, believed that the author of work which tries merely to be entertaining, without being morally beneficial, was writing 'on the principle of the gin-palace'.[13] Even as new distilling methods saw the creation in the 1830s of a purer 'London'-style dry gin and companies such as Gordon's and Tanqueray (the latter founded by the son of a Protestant Huguenot family) promoted their products as a respectable ingredient of punch, the drink beloved of the Victorian 'middling sort', gin's sordid reputation clung on. Thackeray's clumsy young James Crawley in *Vanity Fair* believes he is successfully ingratiating himself with his rich aunt – until she is presented with his bar bill. 'Had he drunk a dozen bottles of claret, the old spinster could have pardoned him... Gentlemen drank claret. But eighteen glasses of gin consumed among boxers in an ignoble pot-house – it was an odious crime and not to be pardoned readily.'[14]

Juniper's affinity with other flavours began to make it new friends at home. Makers began experimenting with a menu of 'botanicals' which, according to an 1868 list written to enable 'manufacturers' to counterfeit the genuine stuff, included oils of sweet fennel, orange peel, orange flower water, coriander seed, angelica root, calamus root, cassia buds, lemon peel, cardamom, oil of cedar, sweet almonds, nutmegs, mace, caraway seed, wintergreen and honey.[15] The distillers of what is now 'London Gin' started to add them at the second distillation.

The Plymouth style of gin (often now described as fruitier or less dry than London Gin) was being exported via the Navy, which had begun to issue rations of gin to its officers (the ratings were given rum) and a more alcoholic 'Navy Strength' gin was carried on board its ships. With the obligatory Vitamin C-carrying lime, it made a Gimlet. When a new commercial 'Indian quinine tonic' was launched by Schweppes in 1870, it did its bit for the Empire, counteracting the bitter taste of the quinine which helped Brits in the colonies to ward off malaria.

Young James Crawley was ahead of his time. His descendants embraced dissolute gin as a form of rebellion against Victorian stuffiness, fired up by imports from America and its love of the cocktail. Dickens, happy to bow to British archetypes in the gin-sozzled character of Mrs Gamp in *Martin Chuzzlewit*, acknowledged the gin cocktail on his trip to the States where, in the Boston theatres, 'the stranger is initiated into the mysteries of Gin-sling, Cock-tail, Sangaree, Mint Julep, Sherry-cobbler, Timber

Doodle, and other rare drinks'.[16] Cock-tail, at the time, was not a portmanteau term, but its own thing of spirit, bitters and syrup. By the end of the century, the highly respectable *Cassell's Dictionary of Cookery* gave recipes for Gin Punch, Gin Sling and Mint Julep,[17] obviously believing its civilized readers had developed habits of self-control to cope with its fiery embrace, whereas it would, the editors thought, be 'cruel' to leave an open bottle of the stuff within reach of the working man.[18]

Brits were impressed by sophisticated Americans who took gin's dissolute image as part of its attraction, and began to party with cocktails in defiance of Prohibition. Americans made amusingly self-mocking claims to gin addiction; T.S. Eliot claimed 'gin and drugs' as his wellspring of inspiration.[19] Perhaps America's best Prohibition export was out-of-work barman Harry Craddock who came to London and gave us the *Savoy Cocktail Book* of 1930. In Britain, less sophisticated 'angry young men' were enthusiastically drinking spirits and rejecting the reverence around wine (although they drank that too). The Martini, said to have been invented in a New York cocktail bar in 1910, became a dumb-bell for a kind of intellectual machismo to see who could lift the most potent one; Kingsley Amis boasted that he made the best Martini by flicking in a few drops of vermouth;[20] Noël Coward that 'a perfect Martini should be made by filling a glass with gin, then waving it in the general direction of Italy'.

Returning colonialists brought back their taste for gin and tonic and shared it with their suburban neighbours, an effervescent combination throughout the war (if you could get it) and the 1950s. But the taint of Empire-and-tonic, the bombast suggested by Beefeater gin or the dusty green Gordon's bottle went down badly with the 1960s generation, who were rediscovering the glamour of European food and wines. George Orwell's imagined 'Victory Gin', which numbs Winston in his final subjugation to Big Brother in *1984* (1949), suggested an unhappy pairing of totalitarianism and colonialism. Gin's colonial legacy was cleverly repackaged, however, by the marketers at a drinks company which was descended from the makers of Gilbey's Gin. Bombay Sapphire was launched in 1986 with a vivid blue glass bottle and a convincing story about botanicals and history.

But gin truly came back to its London home with the launch of the new gin craze. It began with the founders of Sipsmith Gin who, wanting to distil small quantities of craft gin, had to challenge HMRC, which, following the 1751 Gin Act, was still only giving licences for stills of over 1,800 litres. In the last decade, Britain has become intoxicated with gin; London went from one gin-maker, Beefeater, to twenty-four.[21] Distillers and mixologists around the country have dusted down old copper stills and old techniques to make batches of 'hand-crafted gin', marketed on the botanicals, on the names and types of the stills, and all varieties of local flavours and lore.

With my two bottles of hand-crafted small-batch birthday gin, I've joined the second gin craze. This has a very different consumer profile from the first. In Holborn, down the road from the last surviving gin palace, now simply a pub, is the Gin Bar at Holborn Dining Room, selling 500 different types. There are online gin clubs for enthusiasts. There are specialist gin stalls at farmers' markets, parading vintage bottles, promises of the nation's herb gardens and the world's spices, and offering a dirty flirtation with the past and a clean finish.

Bread and Butter: tea-time essential to pre-dinner bagatelle

Though I asked most distinctly for bread and butter, you have given me cake. I am known for the gentleness of my disposition, and the extraordinary sweetness of my nature, but I warn you, Miss Cardew, you may go too far.

Oscar Wilde, *The Importance of Being Earnest* (1895)

WHEN PEOPLE ASK me what foods from the past have disappeared, I usually say something about mutton, saloop or rosewater, but perhaps I should say 'bread and butter'. Nobody would believe me, of course. There is bread. There is butter. You are entirely free to spread the one on the other and eat it. But it has moved from an indispensable part of afternoon tea, to something we are given before a meal in restaurants. And you are lucky to have good, fresh, unsalted butter rather than oil and balsamic vinegar. To some, such as the restaurant critic Giles Coren, it's a waste of a precious appetite: 'Bread is not a first course, it is a breakfast food which will ruin your whole damn meal.'[1] He isn't expecting his readers to be ravenous from a day's manual labour. I think those first crumbs of bread and butter, when you are hungry, are like the first sip of a drink: relaxing, promising and satisfying.

When Thomas Twining opened what became known as Tom's Coffee House on the Strand (still there under the name of Twinings) in 1706, the only food to be offered alongside the various alcoholic drinks for sale was bread and butter. The business morphed into

The Golden Lion when it focused on tea and coffee so that, without the alcoholic component, ladies could, for the first time, come into the shop and buy their tea for home consumption; they did not expect to drink it on the premises.

Some of the earliest places where ladies as well as gentlemen *could* drink tea together in public were the pleasure gardens. Ranelagh Gardens in Chelsea, opening as a 'place of public entertainment' in 1742, soon came to rival the famous Vauxhall Pleasure Gardens through the great attraction of 'the Elegant Regale of Tea, Coffee, and Bread and Butter' included in the admission price of half a crown.[2] Artisans, shopkeepers, merchants and their apprentices could easily escape the dirt and noise of the city for the gardens abutting the northern districts, such as White Conduit House built in an open field in Islington in the 1750s; it offered 'hot loaves and butter; milk directly from the cows; coffee and tea and all manner of liquors in the greatest perfection'.[3] Tea gardens offered refreshments, music, fireworks, medicinal waters, walks, ponds and the all-important 'arbours' for 'gallantry', plus the thrill of celeb spotting, particularly Vauxhall and Ranelagh, which had the reputation for the most royal and aristocratic of patrons.

No matter how many shady arbours on offer, the attraction of the pleasure gardens was their apparent innocence; everything was above board and in the public eye, and bread and butter and tea formed an important part of the image. It was said that if a gentleman wanted to attract a lady's attention, he would tread on her skirt and, as part of his profuse apology, entreat her to take tea with him.[4] A 1772 print of the Long Room at Bagnigge Wells (present-day Clerkenwell) shows two affected young men with 'Macaroni'-style hair and dress (see Macaroni, page 186) flirting with a courtesan. It is entitled, slightly satirically, the 'Bread and Butter Manufactory', although the only refreshments on offer, from a young servant, is tea.[5]

When the thrill of a slight brush with disrepute started to become less fashionable, the gardens offered more tawdry entertainment to compete with one another for their dwindling visitors, until their reputations degraded and they closed one by one during the early years of the nineteenth century.

The term 'bread and butter' came to mean one's finances; it is first recorded in 1732 in a letter from Jonathan Swift attempting to reconcile the Duchess of Queensberry with his friend and the beneficiary of her patronage, John Gay. It did not appear, yet, to have the meaning of 'everyday' or 'ordinary' which we now also associate with it. Tea with bread and butter became an indoors institution; in the Yorkshire of Dickens' *Nicholas Nickleby* (1839), Nicholas, underfed at the miserable school he finds himself teaching in, is invited to a 5 o'clock tea-party where he is more interested in 'making fearful ravages on the bread and butter', than he is in flirting with the young lady who invited him. Charlotte Brontë explains in *Shirley* (1849) that, among the customs of a Yorkshire rectory tea, 'It was essential to have a multitude of plates of bread and butter, varied in sorts and plentiful in quantity.'[6] Bread, supplied in generous portions, was still significant enough to indicate plenty. In *Hints on Etiquette and the Usages of Society*, the hostess is advised to make sure her bread is cut at least an inch and a half thick because 'There is nothing more plebeian than *thin* bread at dinner.'[7]

In all these 5 o'clock tea-times, bread and butter is the desirable luxury. In *Shirley*, set in Victorian Yorkshire, it is a feature of the only evening meal, but fifty years later, in the social circle of *The Importance of Being Earnest*, it is merely a stop-gap between lunch and a late dinner (see Afternoon Tea, page 54). One Scottish visitor to London in the nineteenth century discovered for herself this conspicuous abstemiousness: 'in the vera [sic] best houses' in London, 'only plain, flimsy loaf bread and butter is served – no such thing as shortbread, seed-cake, bun, marmlet or jeely to be seen'. Perhaps overlooking the fact that it demonstrated that the occupants of the 'best houses' were also expecting a large dinner in the evening, she applauded it as an 'okonomical plan, and well worthy of adoption in ginteel families with narrow incomes'.[8] For the majority of families with narrow incomes, tea, bread and butter (or dripping) was their only tea-time food; the butter made it something of a success; sweet, cheap jam or margarine were more usual, particularly for children. George Orwell describes encountering unemployed men in London who stood at street corners, 'slightly underfed, but kept going by the tea-and-two-slices which the Londoner swallows every two hours'.[9]

Bread and butter continued to be offered for tea-time and took a bit part in women's emancipation through the Aerated Bread Company, opened in the 1860s. It rapidly graduated from a bakery to the ABC tea-shop chain, second only to the Lyons Corner Houses, when it began to offer tea as a way of persuading lady customers to sample the bread and butter before buying its new kind of bread, made from the patented aerated process (see Bread, page 330). They became among the first places for women to stop and have tea without being accompanied.

Aerated bread, heralded as an improved and hygienic food, was put out of business by the Chorleywood Process. Bread-lovers now see this as the start of the degradation of commercial bread, and bread made on an industrial scale ceased to be an alternative or supplement to cake for afternoon tea – only sandwiches would do.

Bread and butter has graduated – or been demoted – from the mainstay of afternoon tea to an optional filler before a meal. The bread or roll on your left-hand side and the little pats of butter in a dish represent, not the satisfaction of hunger, but a test of upbringing. If you are the 'right' sort, you will not slice and then spread butter on the whole lot before eating it. Instead, you will butter each piece of crust or crumb in turn, perhaps to demonstrate that you aren't ravenous, but can afford to eat in a deliberative and leisurely way. And you are certainly not expecting to be served sliced bread.

WIGGS

If bread and butter is teetering on the edge of extinction, its cousin the wigg (or wig, or whigg, probably from the Old German word for 'wedge') has been pushed over the cliff completely. Wiggs were a type of enriched tea bread or bread roll or bun, usually with the addition of caraway seeds and sometimes other spices as well.

MODERN RECIPE: SAMUEL PEPYS'S LENTEN WIGGS

450g extra-strong white flour
½ teaspoon salt
7g (or 2 good teaspoons) easy bake yeast
60g butter
60g sugar
1 dessertspoon caraway seeds
220ml milk

1. Mix the flour, salt and yeast together in a large bowl; rub in the butter until it looks like fine breadcrumbs. Stir in the sugar and the caraway seeds.
2. Warm the milk to blood heat and add it to the dry ingredients to make a soft but not sticky dough. Add more flour if it is too sticky to knead easily.
3. Knead the dough on a floured work surface for 10 minutes or so, or for about 4 minutes with a dough hook and an electric mixer.
4. Cover the bowl with a damp tea towel or cling film, and leave to rise in a warm place, until it is doubled in size (it could be 1–2 hours).
5. Punch the air out of the dough; and divide it into two rounds on a floured baking sheet; score each into 4 wedge shapes with a sharp knife.
6. Cover with oiled cling film or a damp cloth again to rise in a warm place for 45–60 minutes until they have, approximately, doubled in size.
7. Preheat the oven to Gas Mark 6/200°C.
8. Glaze with milk or egg and bake for 15–20 minutes.
9. Eat them warm with or without butter, or split and toasted, like teacakes.

ORIGINAL RECIPE: TO MAKE LONDON WIGS

From *The Cook and Confectioner's Dictionary* by John Nott (1723)

◆

To half a Peck of Flour put a Pound of Sugar, and Carraway Seeds according to your liking, set them before the Fire to dry; then melt three Pound of Butter over a slack Fire, stir it frequently, and put to it three Pints, or two Quarts of Milk or Cream, when they are warmed together, put in a Quart of Ale Yeast, and a little Canary; mix all well into a Paste, lay it before the Fire to rise, make your Wigs, lay them on Tin Plates and bake them.

PART SIX

◆

Fads, Fasts and Health

Almond Milk: why fasting fell out of favour

Growing Good

Slogan of the Almond Board of California

Y OU PROBABLY KNOW somebody like Alice. The big house in rural Suffolk; the busy kitchen which somehow produces meal after meal for an extended, hungry household; dietary requirements that vary by the day. At the moment, everybody is off cows' milk. Why? It's partly spiritual, partly environmental; it has become the norm. Instead Alice uses almond milk – or 'mylk' as fashion has it. It's an ideal source of protein for the non-meat-eaters; and super versatile in the kitchen for sweet and savoury food. She buys local food as much as possible, but almond milk isn't sold in the local shops, so instead she buys about 40lb (18kg) of almonds a year from the market in neighbouring Stourbridge; it's not cheap but it's easy to make at home by mixing blanched and ground almonds with water and straining it through a muslin.

We know this about Dame Alice de Bryene because her household account books from Acton Hall in Suffolk, covering a year from 1412 to 1413, have survived. Like everybody in pre-Reformation England, she observed 'fast' days. These were getting a little more relaxed; a century before her time no 'flesshe' was allowed on three days of the normal week (or permanently for some religious orders), but for Dame Alice just

Friday was the 'fysshe' day, with some other particular days in the year. Although the medieval diet was heavily based on meat, it would be forsworn for up to a third of the year. The forty days of Lent were the most stringent: out went meat, as with the other fast days, and also eggs and dairy. Dame Alice, using Arabic techniques brought back by the Crusaders, would use almond milk in their place in soups and pottages, creamy fish dishes, and custards or sauces thickened with rice flour. If she added vinegar to the process, the acid, working on the almond protein, would have made a thicker, yogurt-like cream. If she was entertaining someone of note on a fast day, she might have got her cooks to tackle the sort of 'fast' dish found on the king's table, such as the 'loseyns' or lasagne served with a sweet, spiced almond sauce; or 'Furmente with Porpays' made with 'Almandes'.[1] Porpoise, along with barnacle goose, whalemeat and beavers' tails, was one of the ingredients that those wealthy enough to eat it insisted was a 'fish'.[2] If you were desperate for an egg in Lent, you could 'make' one in a cleaned-out shell, with almond milk, set with isinglass, and a saffron-coloured yolk.[3] Monks and members of the clergy might use almond milk with 'herbs' – spinach and leeks – to bring some body to the eternal fast-day soups and pottages.

Almonds were prized for their whiteness and ability to make glossy and pure-looking food, for 'fish' and 'flesshe' day recipes, too. Rice, seethed in almond milk and mixed with the whitest of flesh such as capons or white fish, became a 'Blank Mang'.[4] They took colour well; a white pudding could be dyed one part yellow with saffron, another green with parsley.[5] Flour mixed with almond milk made pastry in the shape of hats, which might be filled with creamed fish, rather like vol-au-vents.[6]

The workers on Alice's estate, without a chance in hell of affording almond milk, lost their basic protein of bacon and cheese at Lent. They had to rely entirely on the same old same old: grains, onion and leeks, and windy worts (cabbage and greens). Any protein they might get would come from salted herring or salted and dried 'stockfish', which was also a standby for their wealthier neighbours and unpopular with everybody. One recipe advises the cook to beat it with a hammer for an hour before soaking it in warm water, to try to make it tender.[7]

Why, in Lent, was fish permitted but eggs and dairy forbidden? Knowledge of husbandry in medieval times was basic; with hardly enough cereals to see the human population through the winter, most animals were slaughtered in the last two months of the year, their meat eaten in a last glorious blowout at Christmas, or salted to last until Shrove Tuesday. The Lenten fast was something of an ecclesiastical cloak for the real, basic need of a much-reduced livestock to breed and feed their young. It was the same for the human population. Sex and weddings were forbidden in Lent. Whitsun, the seventh Sunday after Easter, was the traditional time to marry, so that first babies were likely to be conceived soon after and born the following year when the grass started growing and the spring crops, eggs, milk and meat were available for nursing mothers.

When the power of the Church was unquestioned, people might grumble but they didn't question that meat and dairy were off the menu. The confusion of the Reformation allowed people of all ranks to revolt against six weeks of salted herring and worts. The whole idea of 'fysshe' days was, after all, distinctly Popish for a country learning to define itself by its Protestantism. Henry VIII re-allowed milk and eggs around 1538, but the country was running into problems of supply of its beloved 'flesh'. A number of statutes in the time of Edward VI and drives by Sir William Cecil, advisor to Elizabeth I, tried to steer the population to eat more fish, both to support the fishing industry (a nursery for the Navy) and because 'by the eating of fish much flesh is saved to the country'.[8] As late as 1687, James II issued a proclamation ordering abstention from meat.

Puritans, inclined to fasting by temperament, attempted to reframe it as a matter of personal dedication or civic duty rather than Catholic ritual, but the old, strict bans on eggs and milk had broken down. The growing numbers of households with their own supplies put butter and eggs on well-to-do tables throughout Lent, in dishes such as tansies (a sort of rich, sweet omelette or pudding coloured green with spinach juice), a quaking pudding (a sort of set, wobbly custard) and buttered shellfish or fish. The agricultural revolution of the early part of the following century brought more hay and turnips to feed livestock over the winter months, and the strict necessity for meat-free Lent was eased, and it became a matter of personal choice. Cookbooks of the late seventeenth and early eighteenth centuries continued to offer bills of fare for fish and fast days. Hannah Glasse has a whole chapter of vegetable, dairy and fish recipes for 'A Fast Dinner'.[9]

Almond milk, once it had less of an essential role to play, started to acquire a reputation as a health food for pampered or delicate palates. It was 'a comfortable meat, meet for weak folks such as have lost the taste of meats by reason of much and long sickness'.[10] The politician and poet Andrew Marvell joked that some women are too delicate to eat anything other than the thick hot drinks known as cawdles, almond milk and broth. Famous for his Cromwellian politics, there might have been a touch of anti-Catholicism in the line.[11]

The eighteenth century did not lose its taste for almond milk; but in most cases it ceased to be a substitute for dairy and had more of a starring role on the dinner or supper table. Marchpane, the stiff paste of sweetened almonds, had long been a glamorous dish, moulded into highly elaborate 'subtleties' – Elizabeth I was given one in the shape of St Paul's Cathedral, and poor Leonardo da Vinci was horrified to see the marchpane sculptures he designed for the Milanese court actually being *eaten*.[12] A century or more later, the recipes have merged almonds and dairy; Hannah Glasse has a playful recipe for an almond cream, thickened with eggs, cream *and* butter and made into the shape of a hedgehog, with slivered almonds for the bristles and two currants for the eyes, nestling in grass made of jelly.[13] Almond blancmanges were also moulded into fabulous shapes. The famous white soup, the savoury descendant of blancmange, was made of white meat such as chicken and veal, and thickened with almonds to give it the right degree of elegant paleness. It was illustrious party food, served at ball suppers such as the one that the good-natured Bingley in *Pride and Prejudice* promises to the young ladies in the neighbourhood 'as soon as Nicholls has made white soup enough'.[14]

By the end of the Georgian period, courses were no longer an amalgam of sweet and savoury; recipes for savoury pies ceased to be strewn with sugar, or finished off with a dash of orange juice. In the dessert course almonds were served whole, along with dried and fresh fruit, or fashioned into almond cream in puffed pastry shells, biscuits and macaroons, reunited with the rosewater flavours of the Middle East.

Almonds were democratized by that new culinary innovation, cake (see Cake, page 400). Recipes for almond cakes rapidly filtered down from the court cooks such as Patrick Lamb to the household cooks of country squires and yeoman farmers. Regional specialities blurred the line between pudding and cake, such as almond cheesecakes with lemon or the original Bakewell Pudding of pastry, fruity jam and an eggy almond custard. Marchpane became a marzipan dress for the rich fruit Bride Cakes and Twelfth Cakes which might be shared amongst a whole community. Some recipes stipulated 'sweet' or 'Jordan' almonds. Bitter almonds were also used when a stronger almondy flavour was desired. This comes in part from deadly hydrogen cyanide; these days bitter almonds aren't available to buy, but are used to make commercial almond essence, but with the toxicity removed.

While the almond was in demand all over the cake kingdom, almond milk disappeared from culinary view for 200 years or so. Butter, cream and milk made from the nut came creeping back into notice as a useful ingredient in the 'meatless meals' John Harvey Kellogg propounded as the root of healthfulness at his Battle Creek Sanitarium (*sic*). His wife, Ella Eaton, used them in her 'Healthful' recipes for creams, pie crusts, dessert fillings and cream of almond soup; and almond butters started to be made commercially.

Americans love the versatility of almonds as much as the medieval English had done, and the last century has seen almond trees spreading over half a million acres of California, which now provides 80 per cent of the world's almond crop. As with avocado (see Avocado, page 347) and chicken (see Roast Chicken, page 102), supply has driven demand. Almond milk is marketed as a healthy alternative to cow's milk to hipsters, vegans and the lactose intolerant. There is, however, an accompanying chorus of controversy over the amount of water used in the drought-hit state, and the vague acquaintance most milks have with the nut – usually around just 2 per cent plus sugar and other additives. Arguments rage the other way about the water-intensive and cruel dairy industry.

Then and now, almond milk was a symbol of whiteness and purity, of a cleansed body and mind. It shows we are putting the needs of the wider environment above the human. Unlike many elite medieval foods, instead of spreading out through the population, it disappeared and reappeared in a different kind of elite. The Californian almond industry can only cajole, not force, us into drinking almond milk in the way that the medieval Catholic Church did. But are its reasons as good? The Church needed to allow cows to nurture their own calves in Lent. The nut industry simply wants us to buy almonds, at whatever cost to the environment that might be. Some small part of the educated choices we make are not really choices at all, any more than they were for Dame Alice.

QUAKING PUDDING

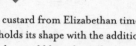

There are recipes for this rich custard from Elizabethan times onwards. I have found it best holds its shape with the addition of ground almonds, but gives the best wobble without the 'penny loaf' that most early recipes included. It's quite shy about quaking when it gets cold, so be brave and turn it out when it is just cooked. It would go well with some nicely sharp stewed fruit, such as plums, or with berries with some good acidity, such as raspberries.

MODERN RECIPE

300ml double or single cream
2 whole eggs plus 2 yolks
80g caster sugar
50g ground almonds

Any one of the following flavourings:

A few drops of almond essence
Grated zest of 1 lemon and/or orange
Spices: a few gratings of nutmeg; 1 blade of mace; plus 1 cinammon stick
A few drops of rosewater

A small (approx. 500ml) pudding basin, thoroughly buttered and floured. Put a circle of greaseproof paper at the bottom.

1. Pre-heat the oven to Gas Mark 2/150°C.
2. Put the cream in a small pan; if you are using the whole spices add them at this point and bring it just to boiling. Take off the heat and let the cream cool to blood heat.
3. Whisk the eggs and sugar until light and frothy. Add the ground almonds and continue beating until thick and custard-like.
4. Pour the cream onto the egg mixture (through a strainer if you have used the whole spices), beating it well. Add any alternative flavourings at this point, and the ground almonds, mixing well so they are dispersed throughout the cream.
5. Pour into the prepared pudding basin and bake for approximately 30 minutes. After 25 minutes, check every 5 minutes. When the centre is set but still a little wobbly, run a palette knife around the rim of the bowl, clamp a plate on top of the bowl and swiftly turn it out.

ORIGINAL RECIPE: TO MAKE A QUAKING PUDDING

From *The Compleat Housewife: Or, Accomplished Gentlewoman's Companion*
by Eliza Smith (1727)

Take a pint of cream, and boil it with nutmeg, cinnamon and mace; take out the spice, when it is boiled; then take the yolks of eight eggs, and four of the whites, beat them very well with some sack then mix your eggs and cream, with a little salt and sugar, and a stale half penny white-loaf, one spoonful of flour, and a quarter of a pound of almonds blanch'd and beat fine, with some rose-water; beat all these well together; then wet a thick cloth, flour it, and put it in when the pot boils; it must boil an hour at least; melt butter, sack and sugar for the sauce; stick'd blanch'd almonds, and candied orange-peel on the top.

Vegetables and Vegetarians: unpopular cranks, revolutionaries and proselytizers

'It is vegetarian hotpot,' said Miss Schofield. 'Would you like to try it?'

'I should love to,' said Ursula.

Her own dinner seemed coarse and ugly beside this savoury, clean dish.

D.H. Lawrence, *The Rainbow* (1915)

THERE IS A family story about my grandfather who, as a young socialist in the 1930s, came home with a nut cutlet, and announced that he was going vegetarian for the benefit of society. Society, in the shape of his siblings, was derisory rather than grateful. As a second-generation Jewish immigrant, his sister Lily was interested in *belonging* to British society, not in 'doing it good'. As George Orwell jibed, at about the same time, being vegetarian was *alienating*: 'the food-crank is by definition a person willing to cut himself off from human society in hopes of adding five years onto the life of his carcase; that is, a person out of touch with common humanity.'[1]

Nearly a century later, vegetarianism has become almost mainstream. The Orwells and Lilys of today would probably transfer their disdain to veganism; as, famously, did the journalist Piers Morgan who tweeted to the bakery chain Greggs in January 2019: 'Nobody was waiting for a vegan bloody sausage, you PC-ravaged clowns'. He was wrong. Its success pushed the company's sales up by 11 per cent in one year. Why has it taken four centuries of British vegetarianism for it to become socially acceptable? And why does it still make the Orwells and Morgans of this world so angry?

A pre-Reformation Piers Morgan, wealthy and entitled though he might be, would have been a flexitarian himself, thanks to the Church's enforced fasts (see Almond Milk, page 306). Orwell's 'common humanity' would have gone without meat, particularly fresh meat, far more often and relied on a palette of vegetables coarser and more limited than today.

Think of all the other things lacking in the average vegetable rack before the Columbian exchange. Potatoes and tomatoes, capsicums and maize were in undiscovered America; it wasn't until the end of the sixteenth century that the cauliflower came via Europe, and the sweet orange carrot came to replace its tough, yellowish predecessor. Celery and courgettes were eaten in Europe but not in Britain. Aubergines and avocados were unknown. Mushrooms were eaten by all nations with trepidation, until they began to be cultivated in France around the 1600s.

Medical treatises and those whose budgets ran to fresh meat found reasons why vegetables and coarse grains should be left to peasants. Medicine in Italy, France and therefore Britain was still strongly influenced by Galen's trick of uniting philosophy and physiology, which fostered the idea that as peasants were coarse and rustic, their bodies must be too. The birthright of a ploughman and his family was their diet of unrefined grains (see Bread, page 330); members of the onion family (onion, leek, garlic); leaves such as 'spynoches' (probably close to spring greens); worts (close to a cabbage) and 'erbes'; dried greens and peas. It didn't go unnoticed that it was a fairly flatulent diet, altogether unsuitable for delicate and refined digestions.[2]

A diet of plants, intrinsic to the state of being poor, only crept up the social chain when times were tough. Good harvests meant cheaper bread and more money left over for luxuries such as education, and a proliferation, over the sixteenth century, of more comfortable artisanal and trade classes who could afford meat. But by the 1640s, a series of poor harvests, an economically ravaged kingdom, radical Protestantism and the turmoil of the Civil War were the background to the first, tentative exercises in vegetarianism as a choice.

The pre-Reformation attitude to meat was straightforward; it would be ungrateful and immoral to refuse this gift from God, unless the Church demanded a fast. Some radical Protestants, eager to find biblical evidence to repudiate everything Catholic, pointed out that Adam and Eve were given command over all the animals – but only herbs to eat; and it wasn't until the story of Noah that there was any explicit permission to eat animals. Protestant sects such as the Ranters, Shakers, Diggers and Muggletonians began to see eating plants as a route to prelapsarian grace. They rejected consumption of meat (as well as alcohol and strong condiments such as mustard) in favour of a simple life which brought them closer to God. They invoked the wisdom of Pythagoras, the first philosopher to argue that animals had souls, who lived on millet, honey and vegetables so that his purified soul would come closer to the gods. British 'Pythagoreans' were also making a political statement about the worth of the humble poor, those who grew their own vegetables, compared to the luxury-loving, corrupted, landowning rich whose land was given over to grazing. They were also sometimes called 'Brahmins' after European travellers to India were shaken by two aspects of the 'Hindoo' world-view: a social hierarchy predicated on the *avoidance* of meat; and the Indian doctrine of non-violence to living things, which was a challenge to the Christian assumption of human primacy.[3]

An early 'Pythagorean' was Thomas Tryon, son of a poor tiler, he had worked from the age of five, first at spinning and carding wool and then as a shepherd; he educated himself, became an Anabaptist and took to writing books on popular health-care and self-help, showing that 'Pythagoras's Mystick Philosophy' offered an honourable route to prosperity, health and self-improvement. He wrote what could be thought of as the first 'vegetarian cookbook', for the 'Sons of Wisdom, or such as shall decline that depraved system of eating flesh and blood'. *Wisdom's*

Dictates: or, Aphorisms and Rules: Physical, Moral and Divine was published in 1691 and its 'Bill of Fare of Seventy five Noble Dishes' are mostly for boiled vegetables, but in combinations that would please us today: 'spinnage and the young buds of colworts' or 'spinnage, endive and young parsley' – mostly eaten with bread, butter and salt.

His few converts included, impressively, Benjamin Franklin but not his own wife. He presented vegetarianism as a personal choice for artisans and educated workers as a means of self-improvement, but it had less appeal with the relative peace, prosperity and religious homogeneity of the eighteenth century, and the Pythagorean diet disappeared.

A century later, poor harvests and the Enclosures brought hunger and political restlessness, and vegetarianism began to be talked about as 'the natural diet'. It was enmeshed in an emerging world-view in which all men (and sometimes women) had what Thomas Paine called 'natural rights', held by virtue of being human and which could not, therefore, be either granted or revoked by government. Some thinkers, such as Percy Bysshe Shelley, began to argue that other animals had inalienable rights too, to a life without the unnatural cruelty of livestock farming. This moral position was backed by an economic argument, that feeding animals in order to provide meat to the most privileged in society, rather than sharing a 'natural diet' among everybody, was hardly an efficient or just use of land resources. It challenged the established values which prized meat, particularly meat produced from your own land. This vegetarianism was not simply a personal choice, it was part of a web of radical ideas which threatened the political order based on landowning. Perhaps it still is.[4]

Shelley's long poem *Queen Mab* (1813), showing what the world would look like without inequality and exploitation, became a text of working-class radicalism. An elderly Chartist told George Bernard Shaw that the poem 'was known as the Chartists' Bible'.[5] Shelley looks forward to a virtuous circle in the world when men, freed from oppression themselves, also free animals from the same cruelty; when 'no longer now/He slays the lamb that looks him in the face'.[6] His notes to the poem, *A Vindication of a Natural Diet*, lobs argument after argument at the reader. Some feel outdated; few proselytizers now argue that we are closer to the plant-eating orang-utang than carnivorous beasts. The claim that the vegetable diet made people more civilized and peaceful was quietly dropped when it was discovered that Hitler was a vegetarian. But many of Shelley's arguments for the 'natural diet' are forcefully contemporary. It is a practical solution to the problem of food scarcity – you can feed six times as many people on land given over to vegetables as to livestock (his statistic). It is the only feasible moral response to the cruelty visited on animals. The ruling classes' insistence on a diet of meat is to the detriment of their own physical and moral health, and it impoverishes the people who work for them.

Shelley's radical suggestion that the diet of the landowners was responsible for the hunger of the poor was hardly going to make him popular with the ruling classes, and the 'middling sort' who emulated them. The intellectual response framed 'the natural diet' as something outside of society – what Orwell came to call 'the food crank'.

Vegetarianism, if it had a home anywhere, belonged to the uneducated, the low-waged and unemployed whose dietary problems were due to the ill-informed choices they made, according to a popular conservative view. Shelley's contemporary, the Scottish physician William Buchan, writing in all sympathy with the 'distress of the poor, occasioned by the high price of provisions', recommended that they be educated from childhood to eat vegetables and wholegrains, rather than expensive meat, bread and tea.[7] This would benefit not just the poor but the whole state for 'Nor can economy in living, be deemed a trivial virtue, in a country where the riches depend on the cheapness of labour.'[8] He didn't expect 'our ladies of fashion and fine gentlemen' to eat less meat but he did argue that, if they would 'make use of their limbs, instead of being dragged about in carriages', there would be fewer horses and more grain for everyone else.[9]

The diet of the upper and bourgeois classes was beginning to change, not in response to political hectoring, but to fashion. At the end of the seventeenth century, John Evelyn helped inspire the gentlemanly pastime of growing fruit and vegetables, in a substantial kitchen garden attached to the substantial house. Jane Austen's General Tilney knows that he must have a kitchen garden to impress visitors to Northanger Abbey, no matter what his own tastes: 'He loved a garden... he loved good fruit – or if he did not, his friends and children did.'[10] Evelyn considered gardening to be an art but also a science in which new ideas of observation played a part in determining what was healthful about 'sallets' (broadly meaning leaves and herbs that could be eaten raw), rather than blindly following the precepts of the vegetable-phobic Galen. He noted, for example, that the cucumber 'may be mingl'd in most sallets, without the least damage, contrary to the common opinion; it not being long, since cucumber, however dress'd, was thought fit to be thrown away, being accounted little better than poison'.[11]

The vegetables that were most prized – then as now – were those that were difficult to grow and transport and which lost their freshness quickly, such as peas, sallets and asparagus (it takes many years for an asparagus bed to become productive). The old way of serving fresh vegetables as accompaniments to meat dishes or in a rich 'ragoo', complicated with cream, wine, butter, nutmeg, mace and sweet herbs, started to disappear. By 1816, Mrs Rundell was telling her readers to boil them simply but not so much that they 'lose their beauty and crispness' and conditioning them out of the duck-and-peas kneejerk reflex of the previous century: 'Bad cooks sometimes dress them with meat; which is wrong, except carrots with boiling beef.'[12]

British travellers couldn't help but notice how much vegetables were prized in Italy and France, too, and Eliza Acton took care to let her 'young housekeepers of England', to whom she addresses herself in *Modern Cookery for Private Families* of 1845, know what to learn from Continental cooks. She draws on her own experience of cooking in France to hint as to how French cooks serve artichokes,[13] gives 'the Belgian mode' of serving 'this excellent vegetable, the Brussels sprouts',[14] and laments that another excellent vegetable, salsify, should 'be so little cared for in England', although her instructions for boiling it for an hour might explain why this should be so.[15]

When a new society was launched in 1847 to promote a non-meat diet, for the first time it put vegetables front and centre of its identity, and vegetarianism was born. Much of the first literature of the Vegetarian Society set out to proselytize to the labouring classes and use ethnography to convince them that the diet produced healthy, rugged working men. Dr Anna Kingsford (who took her degree in France because in Britain it was illegal for women to study medicine) described labourers in Mexico, Egypt, India, Scandinavia and Japan who lived on unfamiliar foods such as rice, tortilla, chickpeas, lentils and hardly or never ate meat, and who were impressively robust, strong and admirable men (she rarely mentioned the women). She extended her sympathy to all hard-working men and to butchers whom she considers to be victims of class injustice: 'Is it morally lawful for cultivated and refined persons to impose upon a whole class of the population a disgusting, brutalising, and unwholesome occupation...?'[16]

There were also attempts to get the working classes to forswear other corrupting influences such as alcohol and highly flavoured food. One patrician Victorian vegetarian set about converting some 'horny-handed sons of toil' that he meets on the Metropolitan railway with arguments similar to Anna Kingsford's about the nutritional value of the natural diet, plus a new one of his own: 'If flesh meat be so tasteful, how are we to account for the ever-increasing demand and supply of sauces and pickles to be added thereto, and of which the working classes are great consumers?'[17]

George Bernard Shaw, although famously himself a vegetarian, wasn't keen on the way vegetarians dangled the promise of health and strength in front of the working classes. You can't just convert people with 'the blazing lie that vegetarians are free from disease', he warned the founder of the American Vegetarian Party, Symon Gould. 'Today people are brought up to believe that they cannot live without eating meat, and associate the lack of it with poverty.' Quoting his friend, Henry Salt, he said what London needed were vegetarian restaurants 'so expensive that only the very rich could afford to dine in them habitually, and people of moderate means only once a year as a very special treat.'[18] Salt and Shaw might dine together on the champagne risottos, Périgord truffles, New Forest mushrooms, own-grown rooftop herbs and flowers in restaurant vegetarian dishes today, and crack their knuckles with glee. Shaw added that 'the so-called simple life is beyond the means of the poor'. It seems that they agreed with him; there were almost no members of the Vegetarian Society who identified as working class.[19] Meat was still such an occasional luxury; giving it up would be pointless for most.

Perhaps the reason that the first waves of vegetarian proselytizing were largely unsuccessful is that it was mostly addressed to working-class men, probably the least influential category of people in dietary terms. The fashionable palate was not formed by the tastes of the few labouring men who accepted the Pythagorean, or Natural Diet, or Vegetarian challenge (or advice) given by radical Protestants, or Romantics, or Chartists. The most influential people, in those centuries, were male chefs in aristocratic households or in commercial kitchens, and pragmatic female cooks catering to households of the 'middling sort'.

The difference in the twenty-first-century resurgence of vegetarianism was not the arguments, but the influencers. People converting to veganism tend to be female (though there is a more balanced gender split for vegetarianism). Their points of influence are no longer aristocratic hostesses, but friends and celebrities.

In university cities and cultures where globalism and diversity brought cachet rather than suspicion, foods from Buddhist, Hindu or Rastafarian cultures produced a vastly wider vegetarian palate. An array of stir-fries, jackfruit burgers, dal, vegetable curries and falafel means that vegan takeaways have increased four-fold in four years.[20] The accompanying corporate marketing is carefully multi-cultural. Its message is that the right food – and alcohol if you want it – is the way to a group of like-minded and ethnically diverse friends. It's a contemporary version of the centuries of social messages which have persuaded us that the right eating habits are the way to climb a rung of the social ladder.

The vegan pound attracted the notice of corporations that decided to bring vegetarianism and veganism to the customers of burger and fried-chicken chains with ultra-processed vegan sausage rolls, 'impossible' plant-based burgers, faux-cheese pizzas. Vegetables, once the sine qua non of the vegetarian diet, ceased to seem so essential, and traditional British vegetarian dishes got rather lost with such attention-seeking competition; who would think, any longer, of turning to pease puddings, carrot fritters and herb pies?

If the first waves of vegetarianism were a response to troubling social conditions and hunger, the same could not be said of the countercultural resurgence in the well-fed 1960s and the first decades of the twenty-first century. There is so much food available that we can no longer define ourselves by what we eat, as Brillat-Savarin said, so much as by what we *don't* eat. If climate change, trade wars, political isolationism and global pandemics drive up food prices, so that meat is a rare luxury, will the current wave of vegetarianism and veganism recede into the past, along with the Pythagoreans, the Brahmins, the Chartists and the Natural Dieters?

A POOR MAN'S PEASE PORRIDGE

Pease porridge can be an excellent vegetarian recipe, though the eighteenth-century 'poor man's family' this recipe comes from would think us mad for passing up any opportunity for a bit of meat. It's a great side dish with pig meat of any kind; the urchins in the musical version of *Oliver Twist* dream of 'pease pudding and saveloys'. Most of the recipes you'll find today for 'pease pudding' are actually for pease porridge or pottage; the puddings were boiled, usually in a cloth, so that they came out a nice spherical shape.

MODERN RECIPE

500g yellow split peas (or dried green peas)
1 litre ham or vegetable stock, or water and a ham or beef
bone
A bay leaf (optional)
A little butter
Salt and pepper to taste
To serve: mint, parsley, marjoram
Malt vinegar

1. Soak the peas overnight if directed to on the packet.
2. Put the peas, the stock (or water and meat bone) and the bay leaf, if using, into a large pot.
3. Bring to the boil and skim off any white scum on the surface. Partially cover and let it blip away gently on the stove until the peas are cooked, adding more water as needed. It can take anything from 1 to 3 hours.
4. Remove the bone and the bay leaf.
5. Victorian recipes had you pushing it through a sieve. You can purée it with a blender, if you wish.
6. Season with salt and pepper. Serve hot with butter, chopped herbs and a little vinegar.

Pease pudding:
To turn it into a pudding, when the peas are cooked, add 50g butter and an egg, pepper and salt (if it needs it). Butter a heatproof bowl, add the porridge, cover it with greaseproof paper and/or foil with a fold in to allow for expansion, tie it all tightly with string and steam it for an hour.

ORIGINAL RECIPE: A POOR MAN'S
FAMILY PEASE-PORRIDGE

From *The Country Housewife's Family Companion* by William Ellis (1750)

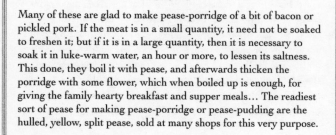

Many of these are glad to make pease-porridge of a bit of bacon or pickled pork. If the meat is in a small quantity, it need not be soaked to freshen it; but if it is in a large quantity, then it is necessary to soak it in luke-warm water, an hour or more, to lessen its saltness. This done, they boil it with pease, and afterwards thicken the porridge with some flower, which when boiled up is enough, for giving the family hearty breakfast and supper meals... The readiest sort of pease for making pease-porridge or pease-pudding are the hulled, yellow, split pease, sold at many shops for this very purpose.

Rationing: making the class war obsolete

Your butter is going to be rationed next month. It would be scarcely possible – even if Dr Goebbels were asked to help – to devise a more harmful piece of propaganda for Great Britain.

Daily Mail (November 1939)

A TRICK USED BY enterprising teachers, when telling school-children about rationing, is to show a plate of food for an adult in 1941: 2oz butter, 2oz cooking fat, 4oz margarine, 2oz cheese, 4oz bacon, 8oz sugar, 2oz tea and 1 shilling 10d of meat, which could buy a chop or two, some minced meat or a very small steak (before it fell to 1 shilling; there were fluctuations in the other foodstuffs too). It looks OK, even generous, for a day's rations. Only, of course, it is for a whole *week*.

Kids could not only see exactly what their grandparents and great-grandparents ate, but also, for the first time in the history of food, their voices shout louder in the record than those of commentators, cooks and political or social leaders. Thanks to Mass Observation, Wartime Social Intelligence reports, oral histories, family archives and letters to newspapers, we know a lot about what people thought about rationing. Suddenly, the food you had to eat didn't just depend on how much you could afford to pay and people began – vocally – to negotiate a new set of hierarchies.

A Food Department was set up in 1936 to avoid the mistakes of the First World War, when the government, with an ideological allergy to rationing, didn't introduce it nationwide until April 1918 when it could no longer ignore the hunger and lengthening queues. The Minister for Food, plus the Scientific Advisor (Jack Drummond; see Food in Tins, page 249) and a cascade of offices, committees and officers endeavoured to implement a system that deliberately set out to make nutrition egalitarian. Even the low-waged and unemployed, who had spent the 1930s in hunger, were to have exactly the same protein, vitamins and fats as everyone else. The Home Front needed a well-fed and healthy population; not one weakened by rickets, dental caries, tuberculosis and anaemia.[1] Ration books were printed and the system was ready to go when it was launched, initially with bacon, butter and sugar, on 8 January 1940.

Brits did not have a history of quietly accepting restrictions on what they could eat, nor taxes on types of food, and it is remarkable that rationing was generally accepted in spite of thundering by the *Daily Express* and *Daily Mail*. It succeeded because it was generally agreed to be a *fair* and well-structured system, blind to income and social standing, imposed on a prepared population, with, eventually, a popular and communicative Minister of Food in Lord Woolton. There had to be grumbles, and these mostly became focused on the tiny differences of allocation. These were mainly to provide children and nursing or expectant mothers with sufficient milk; to allocate rare Vitamin C-rich oranges to children; and to ensure that people working in the heaviest industries had enough nutrition.

Men employed in heavy industry complained throughout the war that they did not get enough meat to be fit and well. In a few decades before the 1930s, as imported meat had become more available, workers, in particular, had changed their view of it from luxury to physical necessity.[2] In fact, the need was more psychological; workers reported not *feeling* fit and well from a lack of meat although the medical evidence is that everyone had sufficient protein. As one ex-prisoner of war pointed out acidly, try a life of manual work on black bread and cabbage soup, and you'll think you are not so badly off after all.[3] And in fact, the rationing system was calibrated so that animal protein was well shared out; but that protein also came in other guises, such as the unpopular National Loaf, made from wheat whose extraction-rate was raised to 85 per cent (leaving in more nutrients including protein) and with added calcium and vitamins (see Bread, page 330). Early in the war, people began asking for *more* rationing, because supplies of food disappeared so quickly from the shops. In 1941 the Ministry of Food introduced, instead, a points-based system which allowed consumers to choose a limited quantity from a range of useful foods, including tinned meat, fish and fruit; and later dried fruits, tapioca, rice, dried peas and beans and breakfast cereals.

Complaints that it wasn't fair were usually accompanied by suggestions of a finely tuned version of rationing that would, in the complainants' view, be entirely judicious, but was usually, in fact, tailored to their own precise preferences. Some older people were particularly aggrieved that children should be given extra milk rations and oranges. Why give bananas to children, one wrote, when they have never tasted them and don't know what they are missing? One mother complained that her child had never had a banana, as mothers from other districts queued at her local shops before she got the chance.[4]

Food in restaurants was not rationed. Organizations employing over 250 people were required to provide a canteen; school-children were similarly catered for and for other workers a system of 'Communal Feeding Stations' was set up to provide a hot, cooked meal in the middle of the day. Churchill disliked the socialist connotations of the name, and had them renamed 'British Restaurants'. By the middle of 1943, 2,115 British Restaurants were serving 615,000 midday meals.[5]

It was the restaurant rules which made for the greatest discrepancy among different social classes. On the one hand, rural workers who weren't near a British Restaurant probably got the worst of it. There were various subtle adjustments which gave miners, foresters, townspeople who helped with the harvest or the Women's Land Army an extra ration of cheese. Wild rabbits supplemented some rural diets. Although there was a perception that country-dwellers fed themselves well from their allotments, this was an option mostly only available to families with money, space and leisure. They might grumble that you could no longer get a good restaurant meal in London, but were just as likely to entertain friends with their home-grown vegetables and eggs laid by their chickens.

Restaurant rules, at least initially until a 5 shilling upper limit was introduced in 1942, allowed a very few at the top of the social hierarchy to eat well-cooked seafood, game and fresh fruit, which were never rationed, but generally disappeared from shops. It was one of the few inequalities of the system, which led to one British Eighth Army infantryman complaining, 'one class gets the sugar and the other class gets the shit'.[6]

Rationing carried on after the war because of worldwide food shortages but also because of the Exchequer's balance of payments, which was politically very unpopular. Bread and potatoes were rationed for the first time, at the expense of the 'poorest of the community' in industrial centres without access to gardens or allotments, complained Herbert Butcher, MP for 'Holland with Boston' (Lincolnshire).[7]

Housewives and working mothers were tired of long queues, and trying to please their families with vegetable pies. Whereas in the 1940s rationing and price controls were welcomed as a way to keep the distribution of food equitable, in the late 1940s and 1950s the middle classes just wanted better food and more choice, even if the increased cost meant the poorest 40 per cent of the population lost out.[8]

When rationing and price regulations were finally lifted in 1954, with the last restrictions on meat and bacon lifted on 4 July to the jubilation of shoppers, it left a population wearied with austerity, but with the most equality in terms of nutrition ever in our recorded history. There was little difference between the classes in terms of their consumption of butter, milk and meat; the population all had roughly the same calories and the huge pre-war differences in terms of protein, fat, vitamins and minerals effectively disappeared. Diseases of malnutrition such as rickets were almost eradicated among children born during the war.

This ironing out of differences between the classes allowed Harold Macmillan, upon becoming Conservative Prime Minister in 1959, to declare 'the class war is obsolete'. And for a decade or two, as shops became full of cheap, imported food, as supermarkets were established and sold shelves of tins and convenience foods, and the kitchen table increasingly belonged to two-income families as women entered the workplace, it really seemed so.

And yet, in the years since, it has become apparent that cheap food has not helped to make 'the class war obsolete'. For centuries it was believed that cheap bread was the answer to the problems of poverty. Bread is now the cheapest it has ever been in real terms; but we are realizing that levels of nutritional inequality are now the highest they have been since the 1930s, and the poorest in our society are paying a price with their health.

Bread: white or brown?

For centuries the working man envied the white bread of the privileged. Now he may very soon grow to envy them their brown wholewheat bread. This is certainly every bit as inaccessible to the majority as was the fine white manchette bread of the sixteenth century, perhaps more so.

Elizabeth David, *English Bread and Yeast Cookery* (1977)

OUR WORD FOR 'lord' comes from the Anglo-Saxon *hlafward* (loaf guardian), and for 'lady' from *hlaefdige* (loaf maker or maid). It's a nice bit of etymology that wraps up ideas of social hierarchies and the centrality of bread in the Anglo-Saxon world-view. In some ways this is surprising, given how complex bread is to make. Its chain of labour and expertise starts with farmers selecting grain varieties, harvesting at the right time, the back-breaking work of threshing. The miller needed perfectly dressed and aligned millstones, so the grooves scissored the grain without getting chips of stone into the flour; sieving – known as bolting – was done through linen or woollen cloth. The baker needed to keep his yeast going, either mashing it from potatoes, or taking liquid yeast from the brewing process, or using an existing leaven. It took skill and experience.

In spite of this, from the early Middle Ages, the population bound itself, physically and emotionally, to a single crop that our small, wind- and rain-battered islands couldn't reliably provide. Wheat needs a long, dryish growing season, which has ruled out much of the north and west of the country from growing it at all.

Its failure to grow or to ripen because of frost, rain or drought has punctuated the successive centuries with hunger, localized famines and food riots. We could have, like Germanic and Nordic countries, privileged rye flour and sourdough as the leavening process. Or put oats at the centre of every kitchen, instead of regarding them as food for the northern fringe. Wheat, however, with its high gluten content, tends to make the lightest breads. And the whitest. Our peculiar obsession with which has driven its history – and ours.

Breadmaking was a skill apart from the usual kitchen activity; there are no recipes for it in the earliest cookery scrolls. Mills and bread ovens worked best at scale; in the feudal period the mill or bakehouse was often part of the manor. Bakers and millers had a captive market as few people were wealthy enough to have ovens in their houses; and, as the oil in the wheatgerm goes rancid after a while, people were obliged to return to the local miller to have freshly ground flour. From the peasant's perspective, there was always somebody else to pay – and to mistrust. And certainly, there was lots of room for cheating. You gave the miller your wheat to be ground; he gave you back, minus a tithe for him and one for the landowner, what he *said* was the right quantity and quality of your wheat. The temptation to degrade the flour or steal some of the dough given to them to bake was, for many bakers, irresistible. History books are full of the colourful punishments given to millers and bakers who short-changed their customers. Pelting the miscreant as he was pulled around the cobbled streets on a wooden crate, with mouldy bread tied around his neck, was a favourite. It was a way for the people at the bottom of the bread chain to vent their frustration at neighbours who seemed to be enriching themselves.

Much was made of the three different grades of flour. The most prized was ground fine and 'bolted' through the finest cloth perhaps multiple times. It made the Chaucerian 'pandemain' which we assume was the same as the 'wastell bread' that his shockingly extravagant Prioress fed to her dogs. This easy-to-eat white bread came to be known as 'manchet' in the fifteenth century. Wheaten bread, also called 'cheat bread', was bolted with a coarser cloth or sieve to remove much of the bran but left in the germ. The grain for household bread might be sieved once to remove dead insects and the biggest shards of bran. Even so, much of the bran stayed in, its bitter taste and sharpness making it universally unpopular. Even the lord and lady of a great household would supplement the labour-intensive and finickety 'wastell' bread with 'household' bread. In the earlier medieval period, some of this might become the 'trencher' – a slab of dried bread (which might also be made specially from unbolted flour) which was used as a personal plate by anybody above a certain level to eat in the communal hall. Once finished with, the gravy-soaked trencher was distributed to animals or the poor.

The long-standing 'Assizes of Bread', in place from the thirteenth century to the early 1800s, dictated that smaller loaves of wheat bread were sold by value rather than by weight, so the weight of your loaf changed with the scarcity of corn but the price was always consistent; which is why people bought 'a penny loaf' for centuries, in spite of inflation. Whatever the penny white loaf weighed, the 'wheaten bread' weighed one and a half times as much and 'household bread' weighed twice as much.

Ideas of social status and the colour of your bread went back to Roman times or before. Juvenal wrote that the lord's bread was snowy white and it was up to the rest of the household to 'know the colour of their bread' and therefore their place. The language of bread was highly graded to include, not just the type of flour, but how it was proved and baked. Gervase Markham's 1615 instructions to *The English Housewife*, one of the earliest full recipes for bread that we have, make explicit the distinctions between the different types of bread, their raising agents, how they were made and who they were fit for: 'Your best and principal bread is manchette'. The finest flour is ground on the hardest, black millstones, and sifted through the closest bolting cloth. It is raised with the superior 'ale barm' or yeast from the brewing process. Barm gave the loftiest rise; but it was unstable and unreliable – literally 'barmy' – and needed a skilled hand. Next in fineness comes 'household' bread, which Markham still calls by its medieval name of 'cheat bread'. He made it with wholewheat flour, or with some rye and barley mixed in. It is raised, not with ale barm, but with 'leaven', some yeasted dough kept (perhaps in salt) from the last breadmaking batch.

At the bottom of his hierarchy is 'brown bread' made for the 'hind' servants, the lesser household servants or farm workers. The flour is a mix of barley, pease (dried peas) and malt, with the gluten being provided by some wheat or rye. It is proved by what we would recognize as the 'sourdough' method: the sponge gets left to the work of residual yeasts in a 'sour trough' and left overnight. Sourness was not a desirable taste in bread, either from the method, or from the slight rancidity of gone-off wholewheat flour.[1]

This catch-all 'brown bread' for the lowest servants and workers was baked in enormous loaves – quartern (4lb 5oz/nearly 2kg), half peck (8lb 11oz/nearly 4kg) or peck (17lb 6oz/7.8kg) loaves were common.[2] There were some advantages to eating labourer's bread. The size of the loaf and the moisture content meant that it would have dried out less quickly than the finer wheat breads. It was also highly nutritious and, although the arguments raged about whether or not bran was a gut irritant, most writers came to agree that it was good for the digestion. Nutritious it needed to be. Bread formed around 80 per cent of the labourer's diet until well into the nineteenth century. The disadvantages of such a fibrous and purgative foodstuff were obvious to everybody obliged to eat it and cope with rudimentary sanitation. It was a tough proposition without butter, cheese or something to help it slip down, and was unforgiving on delicate or painful teeth. Many cottagers, particularly in the South and South East, who were proud to grow some of their own grain and make their own wheat bread, lost it all overnight when their land was enclosed. After this, they might only taste wheat bread made from the gleanings after the harvest.

One step down, even from 'brown', was Hogman bread or horse bread – a rough cake of hay, chaff, ground beans and peas, fed to horses and, in desperate times, eaten shamefully by the poor. Samuel Johnson's oft-quoted dictionary definition that oats are 'a grain, which in England is generally given to horses, but in Scotland support the people' is so taunting, not because the Scots didn't grow and eat oats, but because he's implying that the important division between the food of animals and people has broken down. A constant grumble against bran in bread was because it was used by country people as hog swill and was therefore unfit for human consumption. Being reduced to eating animal food was a humiliation; 'horse beans' (a small variety of broad bean) were used to feed 'heathens' on the slave ships between Africa and America, William Ellis observes, because they are nutritious although 'somewhat bitter and strong tasted'. He thinks the same would be apt for bread for 'the poor common' Christians, or fed to pack horses, to keep them 'in heart and from catching cold'.[3] After being told for centuries that white bread, in its various forms, was too good for the likes of them, it isn't surprising that easy-to-eat, comforting, white bread is what 'the poor common' people wanted.

The agricultural advances of the eighteenth century saw more wheat being grown across the country, particularly in East Anglia; and the move towards the cities gave many urban workers access to white bread for the first time. An official who was considering what bread should be subject to regulations in 1773 remarked of the poor who had come to towns and cities to find work: 'They see how the opulent live; and they can emulate the wealthy only in the quality of *bread*, and of this they are particularly tenacious.'[4] In the burgeoning factory towns 'the meanest artificer in the woollen manufacture' insisted on the 'modern luxury' of white bread.[5] This urban libertarianism infected the more rule-abiding countryside, too, until 'The ploughman, the shepherd, the hedger and ditcher, all eat a white bread as is commonly made in London.'[6]

White bread had become an obsessional mark of identity for families who felt their kind had been denied it for centuries.

Disapproval of it became an opposing obsession for the gentry whose forebears had considered it their birthright. One after another, commentators, doctors, self-appointed medical experts and disgusted correspondents published pamphlets, tracts, arguments and letters to the press to disabuse 'persons in the lower class of life' of their misapprehensions. Every published argument marshalled empirical and anecdotal 'proof', involving stories of dogs in scientific trials, mariners, or other nationalities who thrived on wheatmeal bread or languished on white. It was clear to many self-appointed advisors that bread, along with salty foods such as bacon and cheese, was driving labourers to the inns – another scourge of their class. Although their advice might be couched in compassionate terms, it generally rested upon the conviction that it was up to the poor to manage themselves better. If only they could learn to eat more vegetables and less bread, their troubles would be over. The poor, when they had the chance, replied that their troubles would be over if their employers paid a living wage which bought adequate food, clothes and shelter for them and their families. The kindly advice was also tinged with fear; hunger made men reckless and dangerous. Wartime inflation and terrible harvests had led to vertiginous food prices and bread riots in Britain in the 1790s. Landowners looked anxiously at the wretchedness of their agricultural labourers, aware that the French Revolution was fuelled by hunger.

In addition to this flood of genteel rhetoric, there started to be a movement of educated people who sought to understand the state of the poor *quantitatively*. Reverend David Davies collected data through household surveys to present *The Case of Labourers in Husbandry* (1795). He showed that 'the lower denominations of people' spent 75 per cent of their income on food – as a contrast, in Britain today we spend 8.4 per cent of our *consumer spending* on food[7] – and argued that at the most basic they should earn enough to buy 'wheaten bread'. He was unusual in acknowledging that the diet of labourers was not simply a problem that needed to be solved, whether that be through their own better housekeeping or the state; they were the people who produced the country's food, and, without them, there would be no white bread for the people of rank and wealth who would rather keep it for themselves. He challenged his readers to 'give a reason why they, whose hands have tilled the ground, and sown and reaped the grain, are not as well entitled to eat good bread, as manufacturers?'[8] Another painstaking compiler of statistical information was Sir Frederick Eden (*The State of the Poor*, 1797). His tables of income and expenditure demonstrated that agricultural labourers in the South, mostly owing to the effect of the Enclosures, were far worse fed than their northern counterparts where food and fuel were cheaper, and housewives were more likely to bake at home;[9] there was also more milk available, and people were content to eat oatmeal and potatoes.

In spite of Dr Johnson's disparagement, all the pamphleteers held up the diet of the North Country and Scottish labourer for admiration. Yorkshire was praised for its wheat and rye 'maslin', a medieval word for 'bread' from the Old French word for 'mixed', referring to the combination of grains. To translate it today we would reach for the contemporary French *pain de campagne*. The area north and east of the Pennines was admired for its hasty pudding of any kind of grain, and the whole of the North for oats, which were a forgiving crop for high, cold and wet fields. 'Oatcake' might be similar to the thin biscuit we eat today, but it could also be raised with sourdough, like the one in Charlotte Brontë's *Shirley*, which is toasted over the fire. It is rejected by the French tutor for being 'like bran, raised with sour yeast' but preferred by Shirley's Yorkshire friends over the 'proper luncheon laid out in the dining room' for 'proper people'.[10] William Ellis, recording country life in eighteenth-century Hertfordshire, is tickled to find that when Manchester people come to Hempstead market they bring their own coarse brown bread with them, preferring the taste to that of the Hertfordshire bread which, although it is wheaten, reportedly tastes 'corky, bitter' due to being made with yeast from strong hopped beer, rather than strong mild ale.[11] Barley, although acceptable in Scotch broth as a regional curiosity, fell out of favour as a bread flour in the 1700s, perhaps because it became so strongly associated with deprivation. Ellis remembers the poor of Hertfordshire resorting to barley-meal after the great frost of 1740 destroyed the wheat crop.[12] The ensuing century crushed its reputation irrevocably, as Henry Mayhew discovered when he talked to some London street traders, bruised from their attempt to sell bread baked with barley and wheat flour. They told him that they had been 'met with abuse, from street buyers especially, for endeavouring to palm off "brown" bread as "good enough for poor people"'.[13]

Charlotte Brontë's joke against the refined taste of the French tutor is partly a reference to what was called at the time 'French bread'. White loaves could be made even softer with the addition of some fat, which has found its way into many modern bread recipes. Urban bakers began making bread with milk for fancier customers at the end of the eighteenth century and rich, brioche-like 'French bread' was the ultimate status symbol on the breakfast table. When Jane Austen's young heroine Catherine Morland returns from her stay at Northanger Abbey, her mother reprimands her for becoming a little spoilt: 'I did not quite like, at breakfast, to hear you talk so much about the French-bread at Northanger.'[14]

The white penny loaf was traditionally half the weight of brown household bread (until the end of the 'Assizes of Bread' in the early 1800s), and this size distinction continued. The upper classes served white bread rolls at their dinner parties. A defining form of etiquette was whether you knew to work your way through your roll piece by piece, buttering each piece before eating it, rather than slicing the whole thing before buttering it all, as if you had only encountered slices from a loaf (see Bread and Butter, page 298).

The millers and bakers were particularly keen on pushing white flour into the market because it was popular, they knew it would sell, and it was easy to adulterate. Lime, chalk and alum (and, it was rumoured, powdered bones) were easy to add to flour as makeweights. Many medics pointed out the toxicity of the adulterants; and many more pointed out that the bread-reliant poor were the ones to suffer. The medical journal *The Lancet*, running a campaign against adulterants, found that every single loaf the report's author bought at random in London contained alum. The millers and bakers responded by denying that alum was toxic, but Eliza Acton drily pointed out that, 'as their education generally does not qualify them to form an opinion worthy of respect upon the subject, it is unwise of them to make such an assertion'.[15] However, the victims were more vociferous in their hatred of brown bread than of adulteration. The obsessive search for ever whiter bread had brought together those oldest of enemies – the millers and bakers on the one hand, and the poor whom they exploited on the other. The hatred of millers soon began to move up a class. The Tory-leaning Thomas De Quincey, inviting his friend Charles Knight to stay with him in Grasmere in 1829, tempted him with bread 'made of our own wheat... rich, lustrous, red-brown, ambrosial bread', unlike the dirty-looking stuff the millers 'doctored and separated'.[16]

People like De Quincey were turning to brown bread; maybe they read the many pamphlets urging its nutritional qualities. Perhaps they were, as George III urged them to by Proclamation on 3 December 1800, abstaining from wheaten flour in pastry, and remembering not to feed grain fit for humans to their horses, so that there was bread for the poor. The king set an example by eating brown bread at his 1 p.m. dinner, and earned himself the scornful epithet 'Brown George' from the people he was hoping to help.[17] Rather as architects and designers invented a fictional medieval past in Victorian Gothic, brown bread came to represent a bucolic innocence which was greatly attractive in the fast-changing social world of the nineteenth century. Sir Walter Scott was an early influence. In contrast to General Tilney's fashionable and modern breakfast in *Northanger Abbey*, a typical breakfast in Scott's novel *Waverley* (1814) has this:

> [Waverley] found Miss Bradwardine presiding over the tea and coffee, the table loaded with warm bread, both of flour, oatmeal, and barley-meal, in the shape of loaves, cakes, biscuits, and other varieties,

together with eggs, rein-deer ham, mutton and beef ditto, smoked salmon, marmalade, and all the other delicacies which induced even Johnson himself to extol the luxury of a Scotch breakfast above that of all other countries. A mess of oatmeal porridge, flanked by a silver jug, which held an equal mixture of cream and butter-milk, was placed for the Baron's share of this repast.[18]

The Corn Laws were introduced in 1815 to protect the income of farmers and landowners by blocking grain imports when the price fell below 80 shillings a quarter, keeping bread prices high for the first half of the nineteenth century. They were repealed in 1846, thanks to the potato blight, opening the way to a rush of imports of the new, harder wheats grown in America, Canada and the Ukraine. At first British millers struggled to grind them sufficiently finely, until roller mills were introduced in the 1870s and 1880s.

Towards the end of the century, the anarchist Russian prince Peter Kropotkin was calling for 'Bread for All' as a sign that his utopian revolution had triumphed.[19] It was, he said, an idea the middle classes hated because 'it is not easy to keep the upper hand of a people whose hunger is satisfied'. Had he looked at the state of the milling industry, he would have realized that it was meeting his demands, not through a utopian redistribution of income and assets, but because bread had suddenly become industrialized.

New porcelain rollers could rip off the entire husk, fibrous bran, nutritious germ and all, leaving flour made from the starchy endosperm; it was *almost* white, except for a yellowish tinge which went as the flour oxidized with age. As the many old-fashioned millstones around the country suddenly became redundant, the new owners of the roller mills could only hope to recoup their huge capital outlay by selling a *lot* of white flour. Fortunately for them, ripping off the bran and oil-rich germ meant that it could be sold as highly nutritious animal feed, leaving, for human consumption, almost inert white flour with a dramatically longer shelf-life. Without the inconvenient fibre, the carbohydrate of roller-milled bread turned rapidly to sugar, an attractive quality for hungry workers wanting an immediate hit of energy. On the down side for the industry, rising standards of living around the turn of the century meant that bread became a lower proportion of food eaten by the families of skilled workers, small tradesmen and administrative clerks who were no longer on the breadline. The millers were now competing with cheap imported meat for satisfying, high-status food and sugary cakes and biscuits for the quick, carb kick. One study reckoned that, in the hundred years before the 1930s, bread was an equivalent price but consumption had halved. By contrast, the price of sugar had halved over the same period, and consumption had risen by five times.[20] The millers responded by competing against each other to make their flour cheaper and whiter, both achieved by bleaching the slightly yellow flour to an even snowier perfection with agents such as chlorine and peroxide (illegal now in the EU, but permitted in the States).

What their refined white bread now ceased to provide was some of the B vitamins (B1 and B3 – nicotinic acid and riboflavin) and iron. The medical profession quickly realized that incidences of heart disease, diabetes and anaemia were rocketing in industrial populations; the latter affecting girls and women in particular with a hard to shake off lethargy and a wan, sickly look. By the time the British Army realized that working-class recruits to fight in the Boer War were 5 inches (12cm) shorter than their public-school fellows, it was clear that diet was responsible. The solution in both succeeding world wars, partly for health and partly to make imported wheat go further, was to raise the extraction level of wheat, meaning that more of the wheat was extracted from the grain – the higher the level, the browner the flour. From the time the first 'war bread' was introduced in November 1916 the extraction rate varied from 78 to an even more unpopular 92 per cent.[21] In the 1930s Great Depression, white bread (and margarine) was again the central pillar of the diet of the low-waged and, particularly, the unemployed. George Orwell, running through the budget of an unemployed miner's family who lived on white bread and margarine, corned beef, sugared tea and potatoes, forestalled the inevitable objection to this 'appalling diet': 'The ordinary human being would sooner starve than live on brown bread and raw carrots. And the peculiar evil is this, that the less money you have, the less inclined you feel to spend it on wholesome food. A millionaire may enjoy breakfasting off orange juice and Ryvita biscuits; an unemployed man doesn't.'[22]

Bread still formed the emotional heart of most British families' diets and so wasn't rationed during the Second World War (although its rationing was introduced after the war in response to world grain shortages). Instead, the extraction rate was set at around 85 per cent and locally grown wheat, with less gluten than imported hard wheats, was used as much as possible. The 'National Loaf' was often somewhat stale, brown or grey, and with less airiness and, once it lost its subsidy, was readily abandoned by a population eager to embrace the comforts of a luxurious pre-war extraction rate of 70 per cent. The ingenious solution of the government and public health bodies was to 'fortify' this highly processed flour with the missing B vitamins, iron and calcium carbonate.

For a while, the Aerated Bread Company, founded in 1862, dominated the cheap, industrial bread market with its healthy, modern method. This abolished unhygienic kneading and yeast needed for leavening the bread, for carbon dioxide which was forced into the dough under pressure. It was outmoded by the infamous Chorleywood Process, developed in the 1960s, which could produce a loaf of bread within four hours. The secret was low-cost, low-protein flour, the gluten being made up for by huge amounts of standardized yeast and high-speed mixing instead of kneading and proving time, plus various chemicals to emulsify, counteract the taste of the yeast, preserve the flour and 'enhance' the almost negligible flavour of the bread. It brought the reputation of bread to its lowest ever point. When Elizabeth David came to write her seminal book *English Bread and Yeast Cookery* (1977), it was full of barely suppressed rage that the industrial millers and bakers had taken choice away from most people by passing off white bread with added colouring and a little added bran as 'wholemeal'. The consumer response was mostly passive. It was seen as family food; even revered food writers such as Nigel Slater, at the end of the twentieth century, nostalgically prescribe 'factory-made plastic bread' for a bacon sandwich. Nevertheless, up to a third of factory-made bread ended up in the bin. Some people, learning about the evils of carbohydrates, repudiated it altogether.

Another response came from the twenty-first-century equivalent of the Elizabethans who believed that peasants were physically suited to eating low-status brown bread (see Vegetables and Vegetarians, page 314). They began to discover 'wheat allergies' that made them physiologically intolerant of proletarian, sliced white loaves. Food allergies started off as a phenomenon of educated, media-savvy, upper-middle-class women (mostly), until, as Kate Fox says, 'the lower classes cottoned on and started using it as an excuse for being overweight... there is no point in having a wheat intolerance if all those common people who say "pardon" and "serviette" have one too'.[23]

Around the same time, from San Francisco, came the perfect excuse for everybody to go back to eating lovely, white bread: sourdough. The method had supposedly reached the West Coast with the pioneers who couldn't bring fresh yeasts with them, and their leavens and starters have bubbled away ever since. It was adopted enthusiastically by nerdy young men in the tech industries, who loved the endless breaking down of the method into scientific units and the competitive 'crumb shots' on social media. To the British food-conscious classes, it was a revelation. We have learnt to think of sweetness as the infantile taste of those who haven't been educated to enjoy the bitterness of coffee, dark chocolate, even vegetables, or the tang of fermented foods. The sourness of the dough, once the taste of the despised 'sour trough', is a welcome contrast to the refined-carb sweetness of factory bread. Thanks to seventy years of NHS dentistry, most of us have teeth strong enough to deal with its chewy crust. We welcome any amount of previously despised grains and seeds, which seem to be processed as much by our progress in dietary knowledge as the digestive tract. And, for a bonus, some of us can quietly put our wheat intolerances behind us because there is something about sourdough – no amount of scientific trials have identified quite what – that makes it more likely to be acceptable to the wheat intolerant.

One of those strong and bitter tastes that really shows what you are made of, from the mustardy *Brassica* family, is the Brussels sprout about which opinion is bitterly, natch, divided.

Brussels Sprouts and Brassica Cousins

The success of the cabbage continues so obstinately here, where it adorns the tables of both the great and the poor, and medicine has not been able to dissuade people from regularly consuming it.

Jean Bruyérin-Champier, sixteenth-century French physician

I LOVE THE CHRISTMASSY taste of sprouts and so, I discovered at Christmas one year, do my sister's family; only theirs are made from chocolate and wrapped in pretty green foil to resemble the real, earthy, bitter thing – a lone bowl of which was placed beside my plate at Christmas dinner. They were slightly mushy, reminding me of the joke that the Brits' way of boiling Brussels sprouts is 'until they are uncountable'. We associate sprouts with Christmas, not only because they are available when summer vegetables are not, but they taste better then; the chemicals which produce their distinctive bite are milder in the cool, dark and wet of winter.[1]

Brussels sprouts are something of a mystery; there are fleeting mentions of them in medieval market regulations and on the menus of fifteenth-century feasts; and then nothing until the late eighteenth century. They are soon thereafter, grudgingly, allowed to ascend 'to the dignity of the table', if civilized with butter, pepper and perhaps nutmeg.[2] In the 1970s they were considered to be a staple, and included in the basket of goods used to calculate inflation.[3]

In contrast, the grandfather of the brassicas has had a whole 2,500 years since domestication; plenty of time to build up an entire dossier of complaints, resentment and disdain against it. But it didn't start out that way. Pliny in his *Natural History* quotes Cato the Elder on a huge list of diseases and maladies that can be cured by cabbage, including joints, wounds, carcinoma and melancholy, and recommends washing little children in the urine of somebody who's had a cabbage-rich diet, so that they may never be weak and puny.

Yet as other foods were bred and refined, cabbage could never quite be cleansed of its faults. As the Italian chef Pellegrino Artusi said airily in the late 1800s, its family members are the 'children and stepchildren of Aeolus, god of the winds', and well-named as the *Cruciferae* family, as for those of delicate make-up, they 'are truly a cross to bear'.[4] Wind has long been associated with the labouring classes, by those who could afford not to eat the cruciferous vegetables. Few people, like A.A. Gill, associate it with the upper-class experience of 'floggings, polish, Latin and buggery', before his taste-buds are opened to its charms in an Alsatian restaurant in Paris.[5]

Yet its main fault seems to be that it is good-tempered in the garden. It was quickly adapted, along with potatoes, by Irish peasants, as part of their subsistence diet in the eighteenth and nineteenth centuries and familiarity bred contempt. Samuel Taylor Coleridge, returning the loan of Mrs Rundell's cookbook to a friend, harrumphed that it was 'some sausage-wife's receipt scrawl' who had never lifted her eyes from a 'Battersea Cabbage Garden' (with a 'Potato Field in the distance, and an occasional glimpse of a Turnip Waggon') and knows nothing of the glories of Covent Garden's fruit and vegetable market.[6]

It loses its manners, though, as we all do, when it is overboiled; which is easy to do if thrift encourages you to throw the thick stems, which need long cooking, in with the leaves, which do not. The sulphurous smell of overcooked cabbage taints Orwell's buildings in *1984*, where it gangs up with bad lavatories and rag mats to haunt cities of decaying and dingy buildings. It was part of the rural life of Victorian nature-writer Richard Jefferies, who described how, at dinner time, the road leading to the labourer's cottage was also, euphemistically, scented with its 'powerful odour'.[7] It became associated with poverty, subsistence and poor cooking.

Poverty. Bitterness. Sulphurous smells. Wind and discomfort. The prosecuting counsel seems unanswerable, until the defence produces examples of experimentation and careful preparation. Hannah Glasse has a charming, if rather eccentric, recipe for forced (stuffed) cabbage.[8] Away from our prejudiced shores, civilizations have been built on coleslaw, sauerkraut and kimchee, and there are medieval equivalents closer to home such as 'Compost' made from cabbage, parsnip and pears in a sweet and sour vinegar mixture.[9]

Photogenic cauliflower and broccoli, curly kale and its dark and handsome Italian cousin cavolo nero all found their way onto pictorial media and chefs' recipes. Consumption of Brussels sprouts, which fell by four fifths between 1974 and 2013,[10] is creeping up again, now that chefs have discovered how to fry – or even deep-fry – them, and serve them with their Christmas friends: bacon, chestnuts and cranberries. Cabbage has few additional merits, but it is at least one of those 'green, leafy, vegetables' which have become a signifier of health, worthy of a place on the middle-class worry list. How much time, patience and will-power will it take to coax the children into educating their palates to accepting their bitter and unusual tastes? The solution to making your child eat something green might, however, be provided by the smooth and buttery avocado.

The Avocado:
the middle-class signifier

In America the avocado is just something that grows on trees; here
it is *posh*.

Anne Boyer in conversation (2019)

THE AVOCADO HAS a strange fame in the fruit and veg world of
the twenty-first century; where it pops up, who it hangs out
with, and what that *means*, has become a fixture in whatever
is the edible equivalent of the gossip columns. Why, though, does
it always come with the prefix 'middle-class'? When the British
Association of Plastic, Reconstructive and Aesthetic Surgeons
warned of the dangers of stabbing yourself when trying to get the
stone out, 'avocado hand' was hailed as 'the most middle-class
injury ever'.[1] When Mumsnet asked its readers what made them
feel middle class, having avocados in the fridge (and no tattoos in
the family) scored top.[2] *The Sun* announced, 'They mashed them up
and spread them on toast, and now the latest trend for middle-class
millennials is to use avocados in wedding proposals.' (Apparently
you put the ring in the empty stone hole and open the avocado
as if it was a ring box... ta daaa... A diamond engagement ring
and a rapidly browning container more usually used for prawn
cocktail. What could be more romantic?) Wealthy Australians
began criticizing millennials for spending money on smashed
avocados, rather than saving for their first home. 'We're at a point
now where the expectations of younger people are very, very high,'

said one millionaire.[3] For those with an international, economic outlook, CNBC has reported that Americans are beginning to worry that Mexican suppliers are supplying an increasingly large middle-class Chinese market, and that they will increase the cost.[4]

Although we think of the avocado as a recent introduction, they were first mentioned in the same breath as potatoes and tomatoes by Spanish observers in the New World in the 1520s, who all commented favourably on its smooth, flavoursome flesh.[5] William Dampier, pirate and explorer (depending on your view), wrote about them in his wildly successful *A New Voyage Around the World* (1697), enthusing about their buttery texture, excellent taste and 'wholesome' nature, and including the usual titillating idea that they were an aphrodisiac (knowing that his sideswipe at Spanish sensibilities would go down well with his English audience): 'It is reported that this fruit provokes to lust, and therefore is said to be much esteemed by the Spaniards'.[6] Perhaps these supposed aphrodisiac qualities, and certainly the shape as they hang in pairs from the tree, suggested their original name in the Aztec Nahuatl language – *ahuacatl*, meaning 'testicle' – which was elided with the respectable and lawyerly Spanish *avogato* or 'advocate'. A wise move; who now eats the 'open-arse' or 'cul de chien', the Anglo-Saxon and French names for the medlar?

The succeeding centuries were dark ages for the avocado, and they troubled neither herbals nor cookbooks in Britain. There are glimpses of them on banqueting menus in the 1920s and a little flurry of interest after 1926 when Rudolf Hass, a retired postal worker in California, accidentally produced a Mexican-Guatemalan hybrid and patented it in his name in 1935. (It now dominates the avocado market, with the smooth-skinned, green, lower fat Fuerte an honourable second.) Elizabeth David was surprised to find a 1930s recipe for avocado salad (to accompany pressed beef) in *The Pleasures of the Table* by Sir Francis Colchester-Wemyss.[7]

America got to the avocado a decade ahead of Britain. Sylvia Plath adored them – in her semi-autobiographical novel *The Bell*

Jar (1963) her beloved grandfather steals them for her from the country club where he worked, and they have a supporting role in a comically dramatic scene about food poisoning with crab and mayonnaise. For our British parents and grandparents, the avocado comes into the culinary light in the 1960s and the age of the bistro and cautiously adventurous home cooking; Sainsbury's modestly took the credit for introducing them to Britain in 1962, in a 2009 advert.[8]

For a while, the avocado looked as if, like the Black Forest gâteau, it was heading towards a fall, tugged towards the museum of retro-curiosities by its frequent dalliance with the prawn cocktail in 1970s dinner parties. At the end of the century, Nigella Lawson thought an avocado salad was 'very seventies', and gaily invited her readers to pair it with potato skins because 'if you're going to go seventies wine bar you might as well go all the way'.[9]

It was cleverly and deliberately saved by the California Avocado Commission which was set up in 1978. The Californian avocado industry (followed by the Floridian version) mobilized its growers to form a united front with the California Avocado Association (now Society) in 1915 to promote both worldwide consumption and 'industry value'; one of its effects was to export the industry to Israel, Chile, Brazil, South Africa, Australia, the Dominican Republic and the highlands of Kenya, and between 1961 and 2004 global production grew fourfold[10] and then doubled again up to 2018.[11]

'Industry value' meant the careful positioning of the avocado to US and worldwide consumers as *healthy* and therefore, well, *middle-class*; and for Americans both of those categories meant *not* Latino. The California Avocado Commission positions the fruit as part of a healthy *Mediterranean* diet, glossing over the fact that Europe was neither the cradle of the avocado nor is a main producer, but the Mediterranean image helps the Commission to pull the avocado up from its humble Mexican roots, like an arriviste who does everything to hide their origins in 'trade'. The Commission's recipes for avocado hail from chefs and cuisines from South East Asia, Australia, Canada and California; the guacamoles are described mostly as 'Californian', but other adjectives are 'all-American', 'Italian'; the closest they get to their unmentionable origins are 'autentico' and 'south of the border'. Its Californification was helped along when Gwyneth Paltrow and her fellow connoisseurs of *wellness* launched 2 million avocado Instagram pictures and said, with an interesting choice of tense, that avocado toast 'will always be a diet essential'.

However, we should be careful of attributing too much agency to the California Avocado Commission as the avocado is, after all, simply following the same pattern of introduction as its tomato and potato cousins, although on a vastly different timescale: years of neglect (although without the abuse that was thrown at both potato and tomato), before becoming seen initially as suitable only for 'the gentry' and finally as food of the people. The avocado is now in the 'gentry' stage of its life, albeit in a modern middle-class equivalent. The signs are that this is already beginning to enter phase three; the industry is huge, dependent on a genetically narrow crop, and the middle classes will eventually realize that its ecological footprint is a potentially damaging one, and be troubled about its reputation as 'blood guacamole', a cash crop on which Mexican drug cartels are imposing their own 'taxes'.

Californian farmers' markets are already promoting other cultivars, grown on a smaller scale; eventually the Hass and Fuerte avocados in today's supermarkets will soon be seen as ordinary, a little common, perhaps environmentally and ethically irresponsible, and our media will stop prefixing the generic avocado with 'middle-class'. The future avocado could, like bread, have two images: lesser-known, Californian-grown cultivars such as the Pinkerton or Wilson Popenoe as the pricey equivalent of the hipster sourdough; and monocultural and probably Mexican fruits seen as the ethically and environmentally unhealthy sliced white.

This is what has happened in the world of the tomato.

The Tomato: whose heritage?

There was once a priest from Romagna who stuck his nose into everything, and busy-bodied his way into families, trying to interfere in every domestic matter. Still, he was an honest fellow, and since more good than ill came of his zeal, people let him carry on in his usual style. But popular wit dubbed him Don Pomodoro (Father Tomato), since tomatoes are also ubiquitous.

Pellegrino Artusi, *Science in the Kitchen and the Art of Eating Well* (1891)

NOBODY EXPRESSES THE omnipresence of the tomato better than that gossipy Italian cook of the late nineteenth century, Pellegrino Artusi. Imagine a diet without the tomato. Would Mediterranean cuisines have conquered the hearts of the West without the sweet tang of the paste on pizza, the sauce to give pasta a lift, or eye-catching flashes of red in salads with green basil and white mozzarella? Would fish fingers and beefburgers have become quite so acceptable to young palates without the zip of tomato ketchup? Would Andy Warhol's repeated images of Campbell's soup tins have worked without the iconic, reassuringly constant tomato soup?

It seems we have tired of the tomato with its round, red homogeneity and ubiquity, and we now want our tomatoes to be anything but the same old 'fiery colour', which Pablo Neruda celebrated in his poem 'Ode to Tomatoes'. Black, green, yellow, purple, shaped, striated and ridged tomatoes are now worthy of a place on a restaurant plate in their own, raw, right. These are 'heritage' varieties ('heirloom' in the US), which begs the question, for the awkward food historian, anyway: whose heritage?

Although they found their way to Europe in the 1520s, so slow were they to catch on, you only have to set your time machine to take you back 200 years to encounter the British plate as a near-complete tomato-free zone. It took us even longer to learn to love this nutritious and versatile introduction from the Americas than we did the potato (see Parmentier Potatoes, page 183). Now it comes second only to the potato in US and UK vegetable consumption.

It wasn't until the mid-twentieth century that its botanical origins were traced to the coastal highlands of western South America, where wild plants can still be found and are the likely ancestors of the cultivated version which was encountered by the conquistadors in Mexico. The Franciscan friar Bernadino de Sahagún, rather lovingly describing Aztec life at the capture of Tenochtitlan in the 1520s, was impressed by this intriguing new fruit. He meticulously enumerated its variety of shapes: thin, serpent, nipple-shaped; the types of fruit: coyote, sand, leaf; and he was especially taken by the variety of colours: yellow, very yellow, quite yellow, red, very red, quite ruddy, bright red, rosy-dawn coloured. He noticed how it lent itself to chicken and shrimp casseroles and the salsas that the tortilla sellers offered in the marketplace. From Spain it was introduced to Italy and given the name of 'golden apple' or *pomi d'oro* by the Venetian herbalist Pietro Andrea Matthioli in the 1550s, which of course survives in the lovely Italian name *pomodoro*. Matthioli classified it along with nightshade and mandrake, both feared for their poison; the latter also thought to have magical and aphrodisiac properties. It is true that it comes from the same family (*Solanaceae*) as petunia, tobacco and potato; some attribute its botanical family relationship to deadly nightshade, stinkweed, henbane or woody nightshade to the popular belief that it was, as the English botanist John Gerard describes it in his *Herball* (1597), of 'rank and stinking flavour [yielding] little nourishment to the body and the same naught and corrupt'. Gerard acknowledged it was eaten in Spain and hot regions as a sauce, mixed with oil, vinegar and pepper, but if he had a stock of disaster stories about its corrupting effects, he didn't share them.[1]

When it came to England it was under the name 'apple of love', the term which first surfaced as *poma amoris* in Konrad Gesner's Swiss herbal of 1553.[2] The idiom lasted until well into the nineteenth century, although there is a disappointing absence of anecdotes about its supposed aphrodisiac powers. It did, however, earn a place in the herb garden for its reputed benefits to a compendium of ailments; and also in ornamental gardens, as attested by its presence in horticultural lists of the seventeenth and eighteenth centuries, including that of Thomas Jefferson. Meanwhile, the debate about whether it was poisonous rumbled on. Richard Bradley, the professor of Botany at Cambridge, said in 1728 that it was agreeable to look at but he was quite certain that the fruit was 'dangerous'.[3]

Some must have been eaten, though. As early as 1615 Gervase Markham counts sowing 'apples of love', which must be done at the full moon in March or April, as one of the *English Housewife*'s skill in cookery, rather than 'physic', although after that she is on her own and he doesn't include them in any of his 'sallat' recipes.[4] Over a century later, though, it still hadn't caught on. John Hill noted in his gardening manual *Eden* (1756–7) that 'few eat this, but it is agreeable in soups. Those who are us'd to eat with the Portuguese Jews know the value of it',[5] although his mild and inclusive words might hide another black mark that was harboured against the tomato, given our traditional culinary anti-Semitism (see Fish and Chips, page 377). Claudia Roden explains that some old Italian classic tomato dishes were designated *alla mosaica* (meaning 'of Moses') because the Marrano Jews from Spain and Portugal were among the first to bring the vegetable to Italy.[6]

Tomatoes were cautiously admitted to the British culinary lexicon as a 'tomata' or 'love-apple' sauce because of their affinity with red meats, both of which share glutamic acid, the natural version of MSG.[7] The lone tomato sauce in all of Catherine

Dickens' otherwise inventive suggestions for *What Shall We Have For Dinner?* (published pseudonomously under the name 'Lady Maria Clutterbuck'; 1851) accompanies a veal cutlet, following the recommendation of Maria Rundell who gives an interesting recipe for a cross between roasted tomato sauce and ketchup, made with capsicum vinegar, garlic, salt (so far so good) and, oddly, ginger, to be served 'for hot or cold Meats'. Its forgiving nature with tins and bottles, and the British love of pickling everything, also endeared the tomato to cooks and housewives laying in stores for winter. Early ketchup recipes used mushrooms, walnuts or fish to replicate the umami hit from the first 'ketchup' – a fish sauce encountered by European traders in South East Asia; but it didn't take long for cooks, including Mrs Beeton, to realize that the 'tomata' or 'love-apple' – both green and red – worked well, and that it was a useful participant in soups, sauces and gravies. The 'love-apple' came burdened with confused reputations for being ornamental, herbal and toxic, and the shift to 'tomata' and then 'tomato' reflected its increasing use in the kitchen.

The fresh tomato was quite another matter. Flora Thompson, recalling the first time she encountered one in *Lark Rise to Candleford*, unaware of their (then) 300-year history, said that they had not long been introduced into this country and were slowly making their way into favour. The carter who brought them said they were 'Love-apples, me dear. Love-apples, they be; though some hignorant folks be a callin' 'em tommytoes. But you don't want any o'they – nasty sour things, they be, as only gentry can eat.' Thompson's character Laura insists on buying a tomato rather than the orange the carter presses upon her, which creates a sensation among the onlookers. '"Don't 'ee go tryin' to eat it, now," one woman urged. "It'll only make 'ee sick. I know because I had one of the nasty horrid things at our Minnie's."'[8] Flora's neighbour, however, clearly had lived to tell the tale.

It's true that the Victorian 'gentry' were beginning to broach the idea of eating a raw tomato; it was the sort of responsibility that colonials had to shoulder – the white man's burden – which came with a good dollop of machismo, rather as, for some men, hot curry or chilli does today. 'Wyvern' in his Anglo-Indian *Culinary Jottings for Madras* gives a refreshing recipe for fresh tomato chutney (with onion, celery and mint) and a tomato salad; both would have been unheard of back home and he hints that (partly owing to the fellow ingredient of a 'Bombay Onion') it is only a dish that 'the sterner sex' should attempt to eat, although not when he's expecting to be on intimate terms with one of his frailer counterparts until they are safely in wedlock (when, presumably, it is too late for her to object to his onion breath). It is not, he warns, a dish to be partaken of 'just before a ball, on his wedding day, or at all during the halcyon period which generally precedes that ceremony'.[9]

The world wars, particularly the second with its emphasis on growing your own food, sealed the tomato's respectability in British dining rooms. Helped by Elizabeth David's love of Mediterranean and seasonal food, the fresh tomato must have had a blessed decade or two of summers in salads, stuffed with rice *à la grecque*, served *à la provençale*, or on a tart. And then, thanks to the tin and the jar, it was ubiquitous as tinned soup and tinned plum tomato, peeled, and, of course, ketchup. Ketchups of every kind transformed the spiced sauce from a symbol of culinary prestige, which it had been from medieval times onwards, to the most demotic of condiments.

Just as our growing love of Mediterranean cuisine helped the raw tomato take off in British dining rooms, industrial growers began to debase it. Growers in the Netherlands and the US, and to some extent in Spain, raced to develop high-yield, low-price, perfectly round, grainy-textured and insipid varieties. Those which are picked and refrigerated before they are ripe have a soft, mealy texture from cold-damage to their cellular structure; cold also inhibits the enzymes which enable them to ripen. The supermarket tomato has become a byword for everything that is wrong and tasteless about industrial food; signs in supermarkets now boast that some of their tomatoes are 'selected for taste', implying (presumably unwittingly) that the others are selected for tastelessness. It also attracted the attention of scientists working with the GM industry who worked out you could 'turn off' the gene which was responsible for the enzyme that ripened and aged the fruit, so all tomatoes could be harvested at the same time mechanically and ripened with ethylene gas, just before they hit the supermarket shelves; this is now standard practice in the United States. Cheap GM tomato paste went on sale in UK supermarkets in 1996; it outsold the more expensive versions, but was withdrawn after two years of media outrage and an alliance of ecological campaigners, who convincingly presented themselves as on the side of nature and tradition against Frankenfoods, even if they were more affordable.

After all the neglect and abuse the tomato has been through over the centuries, it has found equality of opportunity in the kitchen in any of its cooked guises, but there is now a hierarchy of raw tomatoes. According to the anthropologist Kate Fox, sliced tomatoes in a green salad 'come with invisible labels warning of lower-class associations', although whole cherry tomatoes would be acceptable, she thinks. But 'the class-anxious would be advised generally to keep tomatoes, eggs and lettuce away from each other'.[10]

Heritage tomatoes have all been bred in Europe or America and one or two in Russia, mostly in the twentieth century, but some, such as the yellow pear tomatoes, hail from the eighteenth century. Tomato enthusiasts now bring together the best of the eighteenth-century focus on the aesthetic appeal of the plant – celebrating pear shapes, the huge pleated beefsteak, plum and banana shapes; their colours: golden, the shade of a purple bruise, orange, tiger-striped, green and sometimes even red – with a twenty-first-century appreciation of a range of natural sweetness, juiciness and texture for eating raw; and varieties particularly appropriate for stuffing, stewing and cooking.

Although its Aztec origins barely get a mention in the celebration of our 'heritage' varieties, after 500 years of neglect and abuse, horticulture and industrial science, we aren't very far away from where Sahagún was standing when he was first impressed by the diversity of the tomatoes and the delicious street food of the Aztec markets in 1521.

Sahagún was also one of the earliest European tasters of *xocoatl*, which he considered a refreshing, morale-boosting health food. It came to be known, in the Old World, as chocolate.

Chocolate: my health drink, your drug

The Confection made of Cacao called Chocolate or Chocoletto
which may be had in divers places in London at reasonable rates,
being taken in substance, or as is more usual relented in Milk,
is of wonderful efficacy for the procreation of Children; for it
not only vehemently incites to *Venus*, but causeth Conception in
Women, and hastens and facilitates their delivery, and besides,
that, it preserves health, it makes such as drinke it often to become
fat and corpulent, fair and amiable.

William Coles, *Adam in Eden* (1657)

WHY DO WE care so much about chocolate? Although I
acknowledge its fine ability to lift the spirits, I don't have
a painted wooden sign in my kitchen declaring my love
for it; chocolate cake gives me an unpleasant head-rush; those
praline shells are cloying; I don't like the way Dairy Milk, Britain's
bestselling chocolate, covers the tongue with vegetable fat. Like a
rabid xenophobe, I want to keep it out of our native sweet things.
White chocolate chips push an Eton Mess into parody; chocolate
chips besmirch the good name of an honest shortbread. Conversely,
the alien tastes of Earl Grey or pepper or Marmite should never
be invited into an artisan-craft bar or truffle. And as for chilli in
chocolate? Don't get me started. Or rather, do...

Chilli and chocolate have a long-standing marriage, contracted
first by Olmec, Mayan and Aztec Meso-Americans, who used

the hard-to-grow cacao beans as a form of money, tribute and ceremony. The Aztecs roasted and ground the beans into a paste, mixed with water and flavoured it with chilli or vanilla. Seeing that it was drunk by the emperor Montezuma and the warrior caste,[1] the Spanish were impressed by its elitism, its suggestion of vigour and sexuality (it was, they were told, an aphrodisiac) and its use in religious ceremonies where, like communion wine, it symbolized blood, emphasized by adding the red colouring achiote (anatto). Early Europeans weren't, however, impressed with its bitterness; it was more fit for pigs than men according to the Milanese Girolamo Benzoni in his *History of the New World* (1564). Although Benzoni's view was parroted throughout Europe for some time – the Elizabethan John Gerard described it in his *Herball* as having an 'astringent and ungrateful taste' although it is unlikely he ever tried it[2] – *chocolatl* caught on in first the Spanish courts before finding its way to Italy, France and finally Northern Europe.

As they did later with potatoes and tomatoes, Europeans began to expunge chocolate's barbarian Aztec origins, mainly by replacing chilli with sugar and exploiting cacao's complex chemical structure by pairing it with complementary flavourings of the time. Seventeenth-century European views of health were still heavily influenced by Galenic humours, so the Spanish nobility who first began experimenting with this Aztec drink Europeanized it by adding wholesome spices such as cinnamon and nutmeg to balance what they considered to be its 'cold and dry' characteristics. Its popularity was also helped by Jesuits (who traded in it) and who argued that it was a drink which could be taken during fasts (the Dominicans disagreed).

Thus began its double European career as a popular health aid and a sure road to physical ruin, but as only a very small segment of the population took chocolate, these competing ideas could be found within one society, even within one individual. The mercurial Marquise de Sévigné wrote to her daughter in 1671 that it was only fashion that had led her astray into taking such a terrible drink which 'flatters you for a while' before leading to fever and death. She knew for a fact that 'The Marquise de Coetlogon took so much chocolate during her pregnancy last year that she produced a small boy as black as the devil, who died.'[3] Three days later she was drinking it to nourish her and aid her digestion. Pepys, too, enjoyed drinking it with friends as a health drink, and a sociable stomach settler after a debauched night celebrating the coronation of Charles II.[4]

A French fan, writing in the 1720s, blamed the Spaniards for burdening chocolate with the false science of Galenic humours and responsibility for a variety of ills, including the dread Consumption, and was pleased to prove the contrary by argument: chocolate was temperate and nourishing, it repaired exhausted spirits and prolonged life.[5] The lawyer and gastronome Brillat-Savarin also stood as council for defence, recommending a Parisian apothecary who mixed it with saloop (see Saloop, page 279) to build you up, and with orange blossom for an anti-spasmodic. Milk chocolate with almonds was for the irritable (must remember that one); however, Brillat-Savarin admitted he liked it best drunk as it was at breakfast, and as a flavouring for creams, ices and sweets at dinner and supper.[6] The French court was careful to keep it as an elite drink: Louis XIV granted a country-wide royal monopoly for chocolate to one maker.

Initially, the British seemed to be immune to chocolate-induced hysteria. The early London chocolate houses, such as White's Chocolate House and The Cocoa Tree, were so exclusive they disappeared into the private gentlemen's clubs. Most houses preferred to name themselves after the cheaper and more demotic coffee, although they also served chocolate, making it, unlike in France, available to the 'middling sort' of businessmen and scholars.

The Quakers recognized in chocolate a health benefit that was of supreme importance to their Temperance beliefs: it was not alcohol. Anxious to give the poor and working classes a path out of drunk and disorderly hell, from the beginning of the nineteenth century Fry's in Bristol, Cadbury's in Birmingham and Rowntree's in York worked towards offering an affordable drink that, made with boiled water, was safe and sweetened the lives of the toiling masses. Developing a luxury for the working classes in this way was unheard of, but it laid the commercial stage for Britain's mass consumption of cheap chocolate bars. The technical groundwork was done by Fry's, which adopted a Dutch-originated technology that separated cocoa butter from cocoa powder, developed the first solid chocolate bar in 1847 and launched the first mass-produced chocolate bar in 1866.

Associating the product with health and ethical working conditions in Britain (and quietly erasing the country of origin) became the driving message behind the companies' considerable marketing budgets. Over the years, in Cadbury's adverts, African workers disappeared to be replaced by athletic young Brits, women working in hygienic conditions and healthy children who were benefitting from the glass and a half of milk that became its slogan in 1928. People preferred to believe that their chocolate came from clean and civilized Switzerland or Belgium, rather than troubled African or Latin American hotspots. One way that contemporary chocolatiers claim authenticity, in opposition to the industrial giants, is to emphasize their direct connection to the grower in the Ivory Coast or Ecuador.

Chocolate had a military application, too, which helped to spread its popularity. The Swiss firm Suchard, eager to promote the idea that its product was necessary for the most active of young men, began sending 'military chocolate' to soldiers, and sold chocolates in the shape of bullets, which George Bernard Shaw lampooned in his anti-war play *Arms and the Man* (1894), with his adorably pragmatic and peaceable Swiss hero, the chocolate cream soldier who carried chocolates instead of bullets. After it was used as rations for soldiers in the First World War, generations of young men brought back their newly acquired taste to the Home Front.

The usual story of mass production and mass taste led to a cheaper, debased and less nutritious product, which didn't stop spurious advertising slogans about chocolate bars helping you work, rest and play; in fact, the messaging of the big corporations in the second half of the twentieth century began to be that it was good for you because it made you feel good – whether that was because of its supposed aphrodisiac qualities (the 1980s Flake commercial), romantic appeal (Milk Tray), or sociable qualities (Quality Street). Would the Quaker chocolate-makers be pained to see that their confection, designed to sweeten the lives of people on the poverty line, was now being blamed – with some justification – for making their descendants obese, unhealthy and often unhappily guilty about eating that last Kit-Kat or Twix? Meanwhile, wellness bloggers are putting raw, unsweetened cocoa powder into avocado for 'frosting', artisan chocolatiers are hand-making silky truffles and glossy mendicants. Ethical chocolate companies are, like the Quakers before them, aiming to spread good fortune and sweetness, this time to the poor of the source countries.

In Roald Dahl's *Charlie and the Chocolate Factory* (1964), the first bar of Willy Wonka's chocolate Charlie gets to eat isn't just a hedonistic titbit, it's 'rich solid food' for a starving boy.[7] We identify with his experience of it, even though it's unlikely we have lived on starvation rations of bread and cabbage soup. The same chocolate just goes to show how spoilt, greedy and brattish are the pick'n'mix assortment of children who come to a sticky end in the factory tour. Chocolate has always had a double career: healthful for the deserving (ourselves) and a sure road to ruin for the uneducated or morally idiotic (others).

PART SEVEN

◆

Country and Town

The Pork Pie: class-free
but not unclassy

The pork pie now seems sacred to railway refreshment-rooms, picnics and race-courses.

Lieutenant Colonel Newnham-Davis,
The Gourmet's Guide to London (1914)

PORK PIES ARE delicious at the first bite, but a whole one is always a bit too much. I'm sure it's because they are such sturdy little fellows; that adipose hot-water crust pastry, hand-raised over substantial chunks of chopped fresh and well-fatted pork (which turns grey-pink on cooking; bright pink pork in a pie means that the meat has been cured), and, let no cook forget, the savoury jelly. By the end – no matter how 'picnic' the size – I feel I've gone two rounds with a rather solid pugilist. This, of course, is the point; it punches above its weight in terms of sustenance and it doesn't disintegrate. It is rugged outdoor food for rugged outdoor people.

The sturdy pork pies baked by workers and servants were quickly talent-spotted by their aristocratic, hunting employers in need of a portable snack. The middle-class tendency to attempt to instruct the one or ape the other was not part of its early history. This is what makes it such an intriguingly socially adaptable little pie, equally at home in a hamper next to champagne flutes at Henley, a backpack on a mountainside, a plastic bag on the local green, or in a hunter's pocket.

Pork was a cottager's meat. Early recipe books, by definition for the educated and wealthy (and their cooks), don't give recipes for pies made wholly from pork, but add it, as does Robert May in *The Accomplisht Cook*, to other meat, game or, oddly, eels. Where pork is the only meat in a pie, he titivates it with a fine title – 'a Maremaid Pye' – and an even finer array of spices, herbs, gooseberries, grapes or barberries (from the berberis plant), butter, verjuice and sugar.[1] He does, however, give a recipe titled 'To make Paste for thin bak'd Meats' for a hot-water crust pastry which paved the way for a sturdy pie case that preserved the contents but could also be eaten.[2] Made with the last fresh pork of the year, it became a Christmas treat for village families, such as Pip's in *Great Expectations*, who don't get to eat the 'beautiful round compact pork pie' which he has guiltily filched to feed the convict Magwitch.[3]

An early 'Pork Pyes' recipe in William Ellis's *Country House-wife's Family Companion* (1750) is recommended for harvest time for being 'portable, wholesome and satiating' when done the Hertfordshire Housewife's way. It's a bit of county history, which might be galling for the (rightly) proud pork pie producers of Melton Mowbray, as it pre-dates early Leicestershire records. However, theirs have aristocratic pedigree which has shaped the reputation of the whole pork pie tribe.

Pork pie historians begin with the *terroir*, the lush countryside around Melton Mowbray in Leicestershire, which was ideal for the rich milk needed to make cheese (see Cheddar and Stilton, page 367); pig farming grew up alongside the dairy and cheese industries, as the pigs feasted on the whey which was discarded in the churning process.

The eighteenth-century Enclosures gave landowners not only more wealth, but – with hedges and ditches instead of open lands – more exhilarating horse-riding. Three hunts, the Quorn, Cottesmore and Belvoir, thrived, offering employment to whole stables-full of grooms, all fed by kitchens-full of maids and cooks. As grooms set off to meet their masters and mistresses with fresh horses, they would tuck a resilient pork pie into a handkerchief or a deep pocket.

The very nature of hunting meant that the middle classes could never afford to elbow their way in, and their social anxieties about eating the same food as the servants weren't shared by the aristocracy, particularly in the outside rough and tumble of the hunt; by the 1780s, it was recorded that hunting folk had adopted their servants' pork pie for themselves.[4] *The Melton Breakfast* by Scottish artist Sir Francis Grant (1839) shows ten red-coated members of the Quorn hunt waiting for their day's sport while one finishes his breakfast, a little pile of pork pies on an elegant plate before him.

About this time, the first commercial pork pie businesses started, taking advantage of the Leeds–London stagecoach which stopped at Melton Mowbray to send the pies to London for sale. Businesses handed down through generations have been bought, sold and expanded, but the people running them have consistently and successfully fought for their product's 'artisanal' qualities and pulled up both the reputation and (in many but not all cases) quality of even those pork pies not lucky enough to be born in this corner of Leicestershire. The 'Melton Mowbray Pork Pie' is a protected food name under EU law – at least at the time of writing. Campaigning by local makers and businesses was rewarded with a Protected Geographical Indication in 2009, meaning that only makers in that area of the county can claim for their pork pies the quality and the history that have made it a favourite food for outdoor eating for an impressively wide range of social occasions.

It's a nice irony that it is the lobbying of middle-class entrepreneurs which has preserved the heritage of a food that has come to us from the worker's cottage and the most aristocratic of pastimes.

Their cheesemaking neighbours have been equally successful in making Stilton one of the most celebrated – and legally protected – of English cheeses.

Cheddar and Stilton:
a tale of two cheeses

I shouldn't like to think of your father eating cheese; it's such a strong-smelling, coarse kind of thing. We must get him a cook who can toss him up an omelette, or something elegant. Cheese is only fit for the kitchen.

Mrs Gaskell, *Wives and Daughters* (1866)

OFFERED A CHEESEBOARD which might consist of Brie, or goat's cheese, or smoked cheddar (the height of sophistication in the 1980s, I assure you), my father always said, 'Just give me some mouse-trap.' He meant, of course, cheddar.

Cheddar and Stilton are Britain's most famous cheeses, although Cheshire – mentioned in the Domesday Book – is almost certainly the oldest. Cheddar, which makes up more than half our cheese buying in this country, is, apparently, 'an unpretentious cheese that goes well with bread and ale'.[1] It can be made anywhere and to any quality – and is. We all know the stuff: shrink-wrapped, reliable; good for sandwiches and cooking as a sharp knife or grater slides easily through its oily and homogeneous mass; its strength goes from 'mild' which is bland and sweet, to 'extra strong' which is as salty as a packet of crisps. It is 'cheddar' simply if it is made by a 'cheddaring process', whether this has taken place in a factory in New Zealand or the US, from pasteurized milk of any quality, churned out (literally) after three months or 'matured' (i.e. kept) in plastic for longer. There is a half-way nod to the fact that this stuff should really be called 'cheddar-style' by the EU, which has agreed to a Protected Designation of Origin for 'West Country Farmhouse Cheddar', which can only be made on farms in Somerset, Dorset, Devon and Cornwall.

Stilton, on the other hand, is not an 'unpretentious cheese'; its natural fellow is port, and it is admired for its nobility. *Larousse Gastronomique* not only acknowledges its existence (unlike cheddar) but admits it to be 'Considered one of the best cheeses in the world'.[2] It is the only British cheese to have full EU protection (alongside its neighbour, the Melton Mowbray Pork Pie; see The Pork Pie, page 364). And certainly a good Stilton is a fine, tangy, crumbly thing, the cheese equivalent of royal blood running through its blue veins. Yet a beautifully made cheddar is equally worthy of a place on a cheeseboard: flinty, well textured, changing on the palate from spirited and salty to clean and sweet.

Cheddar is incomparably older than Stilton. It was so esteemed at Charles I's court that the whole cheeses were sold to aristocrats even before they were made.[3] Daniel Defoe, touring through the Mendip Hills, was quite certain that it was 'the best cheese that England affords, if not, that the whole world affords', and that this was down to its famously communal method of creation. All the town cows grazed on the rich common pasturage in the village; the milk was measured according to the cow's owner and then pooled to make the huge, hundredweight cheeses. Each inhabitant got one in turn, according to how much milk he had contributed – 'And thus every man has equal justice'.[4] In 1697 a political poem mocked a ministry 'whose composition was like Cheder-cheese, in whose production all the town agrees'.[5] It was a method that could only have been devised before the Enclosures; Cheddar's common land was enclosed by the Act of 1811, after which the town and village people who didn't own land could no longer afford to graze their cows.

Stilton, on the other hand, was very much a private-enterprise cheese; it seems to have started life as a pressed, white cheese, enriched with cream, but how and when it became its current open-textured (i.e. unpressed) blue-veined self isn't recorded with any clarity. There are claims from several quarters about the individuals who 'invented' it on farms or manorial dairy houses in the town of Stilton, a staging post a day's ride from London, where it was brought for sale at The Bell Inn. One enterprising local historian deploys feminist sociology to prove that his preferred originator, a cheesemaker named Frances Pawlett (or Paulet), was the first to produce the famous cheese in the 1740s. It seems unlikely, though, as twenty years before, Defoe had remarked that Stilton was already famous for cheese 'which is call'd our English Parmesan'. His description of it is not appetizing: 'it is brought to table with the mites, or maggots round it, so thick, that they bring a spoon with them for you to eat the mites with, as you do the cheese'.[6] Perhaps he was there on an off-day; in his *Imitations of Horace* (1738), Alexander Pope tells the story of the country mouse who entertains his town friend, offering him Suffolk cheese 'But wish't it Stilton for his sake'.[7]

There are seven permitted makers of Stilton now who have fought off industrial competition for the name and unique characteristics, although none of them are in the Cambridgeshire town itself, but in Derbyshire, Leicestershire and Nottinghamshire. Cheddar, on the other hand, was seen as such public property that when a local man, Joseph Harding (1805–76), from a cheese-making family in Somerset, pioneered a process by which cheese could be made in industrial quantities, it was entirely open to exploitation (or democratization, depending on your view). The technique was quickly copied and adapted, particularly in America whose cheeses were sold alongside their British counterparts by London costermongers in the mid-nineteenth century.

Cheese was the mainstay of farm labourers: for centuries their main protein and part of their payment in kind. The dairymaid of 1550 was granted grain, beans, cheese and 2d per day; the reeve or bailiff got in addition six whole cheeses and an extra at both Easter and Christmas. In the summer it would have been fresh – known as 'white meat'; winter milk would have been too thin to make cheese, so the matured summer cheeses were the main protein in the cold months, supplemented with bacon. Piers Plowman, trying to appease an allegorical hunger, has no meat – not even a scrap of bacon – but does have:

Ne neyther gees ne grys, but two grene cheses,

A fewe cruddes and creem, and an haver cake,

And two loves of benes and bran ybake for my fauntis[8]

[a couple of green [fresh] cheeses, a little curds and cream, an oat-cake,

and two loaves of beans and bran which I baked for my children]

At the end of the 1700s, Sir Frederick Eden reported in *The State of the Poor* that the poorest labourers in the South of England were 'habituated to the unvarying meal of dry bread and cheese from week's end to week's end'.[9]

A century later, labourers were eventually benefiting from cheese deflation, as blocks of the stuff were unloaded from refrigerated container ships from the US, Canada and Australia and sold far more cheaply than anything Britain could produce, even in its newest factories. But what was an advantage to the worker, hungry for protein, was disastrous for the artisan and farmhouse cheesemakers and their customers. Cheesemaking was hit further by the Milk Marketing Board, established in 1933 in order to guarantee a minimum price to farmers for milk, further lancing the incentive to produce more expensive cheese. This was swiftly followed by the Second World War, which left precious few skilled cheesemakers in the farms and dairies. As a result, Stilton disappeared completely; block cheddar was government approved because it could be cut into neat 2oz blocks for rationing. In 1954 Dorothy Hartley lamented, 'The industrial revolution of the dairy is complete! And our really fine cheeses are lost to England.'[10]

She would have enjoyed witnessing the demise of the Milk Marketing Board and the cheese renaissance of the 1980s, spearheaded by Neal's Yard Dairy and other small cheesemongers, and which is flourishing in shops and farmers' markets around

Britain. You are unlikely to find Stilton there, though; the makers' association insists on their cheese being pasteurized, which makes it a rather predictable, one-note experience, compared with raw-milk cheddar made in dairy farms around the British Isles. In some ways the two cheeses have swapped places; it is cheddar's artisan and farmhouse producers who are admired and sought out, leaving Stilton to the time-poor supermarket shopper, where it sits beside plastic-wrapped mousetrap and the other mass-produced cheeses which, together, make up 90 per cent of Britain's cheeses.

With hand-made and 'artisan' cheeses, their names give away a sort of fierce pride in their origins, reminding us that the specifics of the soil, the weather, the geology, the breed of cows, sheep or goats – and their wellbeing – and the people who make it are key to the taste. Kirkham's Lancashire, Cornish Yarg (the maker's surname backwards), Ogleshield all incorporate makers' names; Hafod, Gubbeen, Tunworth, Rollright are a homage to places. One of the most evocative names is Lincolnshire Poacher; it pits the lone cheesemaker against the commercial behemoths, drawing on a centuries-old folk image of the defiance and cunning of the underdog against the power of the landowner. Which brings us to poaching.

Rabbit: a poacher's tale

It seems hard to punish people for stealing bread or turnips,
though one must, of course; but I've no sympathy with poachers.
So many of them do it for sheer love of sport!

John Galsworthy, *The Country House* (1907)

F YOU ENCOUNTER a dish of rabbit in a country pub whose swirly
carpet might smell of chip fat and beer, it will likely be half-jokingly
called 'poacher's' something – pie, stew, pot – an invocation of
something earthy, proudly transgressive, good on its own terms and
fancy urban food be damned. And if it is good, it will be delicate
and juicy, its high bone to meat ratio giving it tenderness and a
slightly wild flavour, though the meat is most likely to be white,
farmed rabbit. The genuinely poached article might be a bit tough;
and few commercial or domestic kitchens these days will want to
take the trouble to find the right recipe for the rabbit in question, as
did country cook Dorothy Hartley. She had far more sense than to
ask awkward questions about provenance; she could see if a rabbit
had died in a trap from starvation and pain and wouldn't eat it.
Her recipes in *Food in England* are tailored to the *age* of the rabbit:
young to be grilled with peas and potatoes, middle-aged should be
oven-fried 'Dorset fashion', the elderly rabbit goes into a pie with
bacon; the *season*: harvest-time rabbits make brawn; and *place*: a
mountain or Welsh rabbit is likely to be a toughie, while a Norfolk
bunny is probably a softie.[1]

There is scant evidence for the popular belief that Romans
introduced rabbits to England, although they certainly bred them

in softer climates. If they did, the diseases that leporine populations are prone to, and a few hard winters, must have wiped them out. The Normans brought rabbits over and bred them in warrens for their black and silver fur, but also as a superior, white meat for a lord's table. In *The Forme of Cury*, the first English cookbook, from the 1390s, they appear as frequently as chicken (or 'capons') with expensive spices and syrups. They also find a place alongside swanne, crane, heron, pecocke, in the list of terms in *The Boke of Kervynge*. The carver is directed to 'unlace that cony' – a cony being over a year old, rabbit being the young.

Andrew Boorde, a sixteenth-century Welsh physician, traveller and writer, said that a warren, along with the stew-pond, the dovecote and the deer park, was an essential accoutrement for the gentleman's estate.[2] They were particularly useful on the sandy soils of the South East; here rabbits could turn themselves into protein where sheep and goats would have struggled. There was a 'cunegeria' (roughly translating as 'conygarth') at Petworth House in Sussex from the thirteenth century.

The trouble was that the wretched bunnies didn't *stay* on the gentleman's estate. In spite of clear boundary markers on warrens, escapees merrily helped themselves to corn-shoots, vegetables and crops that medieval peasant tenants were attempting to grow on their awkward strips of land, or they competed with sheep and cattle for grass on common land, and devastated young trees so that forest areas became heathland populated by bracken, which rabbits turn their twitchy noses up at.

Peasant farmers claimed that these escaped rabbits, encroaching and devaluing common land as they did, were fair game and, although it didn't suit landowners, there grew a clear differentiation in the folk mind between rabbits and conies and other game which could be equally destructive, such as deer or pheasant. Rabbits, it was felt, belonged to the common, and when the common began to be enclosed, such as the 830 acres of common woodland at Harting Combe in East Sussex, some of the most violent protests came from poachers, one such being a gentleman neighbour who was also a notorious poacher and deer stealer.

Poaching became a war between landowners, for whom shooting protein they didn't need was a gentlemanly pursuit, and, often, the landless poor or, sometimes, more lawless members of the yeomanry, for whom shooting the same animals as food they and their families needed was a crime. Farmers, somewhere in the middle, would often turn a blind eye to poachers who were helping rid them of a crop-destroying pest.

Sometimes it was a violent conflict; William Cobbett, in his championing of the dispossessed land-worker, told the story of two young poachers, Charles Smith of Romsey and James Turner of Andover, who were hanged in Winchester in 1822 for their part in the death of a gamekeeper. While he acknowledged the illegality of trespassing, he abhorred the taking of a man's life because of the false belief that 'any particular set of individuals should have a permanent property in wild creatures'.[3] Punishments only worked, he stressed, if the community at large believed that justice had been properly served; the community of Hampshire had been appalled at sending two poachers to the gallows. The Reverend Sydney Smith was similarly sympathetic: 'For every pheasant that flutters in a wood,' he told a public meeting at Taunton in 1831, 'one English peasant is rotting in gaol.'[4] To Parliamentary grandees, the rabbit was guilty by association with the company it unwittingly kept. 'The Radical,' observed Albert Pell, the Tory member for Leicestershire, 'had no better friend in the world than the Rabbit.'[5]

Radical and rabbit were held alike in contempt. Recipe writers began to suggest ways to pass rabbits off as chickens by cutting the heads off and covering them with 'White Sellery sauce, or Rice Sauce tossed up with Cream';[6] or deploying black pepper, allspice, port and vinegar 'To make a Rabbit taste much like Hare'.[7]

These stories of conflict between the greedy powerful and the hungry poor, living on their wits and country knowledge, have given us the lone and lovable poacher, quietly hiding in his coat a rabbit or two 'for the pot' to feed a growing family. It is an image from a pre-Welfare State past, when gamekeepers were too busy making love to Lady Chatterley in the woods to notice the cunning Roald Dahl heroes, outwitting the local landowners to poach pheasants with ruses involving raisins and sleeping pills.

Shooting thousands of birds was the entertainment landowners offered to their own circle at their country estates; in the evening over cocktails or dinner, the talk might be of the iniquity of their landless neighbours who poached, not for need, but for the thrill of it.

In the twenty-first century this has been given a different cast – 'psycho poaching' – to show it as a cruel abuse of defenceless wild animals; a crime against the common good rather than against the wealthy landowner. It has been redefined as a 'wildlife crime', and is likely to be committed by gangs, using methods such as blinding lights to stun their prey, and dogs to chase them. As *The Independent* headlined, 'Modern-day poaching is no longer about taking one for the pot. Increasingly, it's carried out by gangsters with links to organized crime for money or just for the sick thrill.'[8]

One such gang, using the latest equipment, raided land on the South Downs outside Brighton, attacked and disabled two wildlife wardens before making off with 700–800 rabbits for the London market. This was, however, the 1620s; the latest equipment being dogs, ferrets and nets, rather than arc-lights, but otherwise the details haven't changed much in 400 years, in spite of the folk myth of the solitary poacher.

In the Second World War, although the real thing was off ration, tinned rabbit from Australia and New Zealand was available (for 16 ration points per lb, meaning that 1lb of tinned rabbit cost the 20 points each consumer was given in a four-week period). Rural families during this time ate better than their urban counterparts, if they had the wherewithal to keep chickens and rabbits in hutches and could cope with PTSD in children forced to eat their pets.

For all its ubiquity in our countryside, rabbit is a rare visitor to the table and cookbook. Some people from that wartime generation associate rabbit with wartime privation and wouldn't countenance eating it by choice. We have always been uneasy about its associations, and a couple of Benjamin Bunny and Peter Rabbit stories were enough to switch it from pot to pet in the collective mind.

Urban-dwellers, sufficiently divorced from rural pragmatism on livestock and slaughter, cannot dissociate the rabbit from the cute pet. We aren't so hungry that we need to. As our society's growing wealth opens us up to the possibility of caring for other species, perhaps the social prestige our society gains by *caring* will outweigh the social prestige we gain by eating. If enough of us keep chickens as pets, perhaps, in time, we'll start to feel as queasy about eating battery-farmed birds as we do about tucking into Peter Rabbit. And what about that other great environmental problem of our day, overfishing? It isn't likely that we'll foster a sense of responsibility for the overfished stocks of cod or haddock, through keeping sleek 10kg cod as pets in the bath. However, our attitude to fish and chips – and to friers – has changed so much over two centuries, it's not impossible that we can draw on the history to find a way to rethink the whole supply chain, before the shoals disappear from the sea, and cod and chips disappears from our national menu.

Fish and Chips:
a mixed-race marriage

A few customers are queuing for their 'chippy teas', still perhaps the ultimate working-class comfort food. I remember that when I was a very small boy, some people would arrive with bowls from home to collect their chips in, thus ensuring a larger portion. We never did this, as it was thought slightly common.

Stuart Maconie, 'Little Boxes', *Common People* (2019)

THERE MUST BE more descriptions of fish and chips than any other meal, all with eager words like *crispy* and *golden* for the batter; *succulent, sweet* and *flaky* for the fish; *chunky* or *fluffy* for the chips. Is this the same dish I've tried over the years? Indigestible and oily batter; flabby, pale and rapidly cooling (or cold) chips; only the fish, if lucky, approaching anything like its description? If you are a fish and chip fan, you might tell me I am simply doing it wrong; that I haven't had them from your favourite shop, covered in salt and vinegar, hot and fresh in their paper packaging. That my appetite should be seasoned with the salt air of the coast; or I should enjoy them as a Friday-night indulgence for the family which lets everybody off the cooking; or after a long Saturday night boozing, where they soak up the alcohol and revive the taste-buds. This is how they are lodged in our collective consciousness: a traditionally British phenomenon which has for years been a key mainstay for workers and their families; every works canteen in the land offers fish and chips on Fridays, and they have now become a staple seaside holiday treat.

Fish deep-fried in batter and potatoes cut into strips and deep-fried are both surprisingly modern inventions; the serving of them together even more so. Recipes for curry, for example, pre-date both, the first appearing in Hannah Glasse's famous 1747 cookbook; it's not great but you can see where she's going with it. Whereas her recipe for proto-chips is seriously unattractive: fried potatoes covered with melted butter, sack (a sweet wine) and sugar; a version of salt and vinegar, perhaps, that surely was never tried and tested.[1]

Hannah Glasse's 1781 edition included a recipe for fried and pickled fish, which she describes as 'The Jews way of preserving Salmon and all sorts of fish'. Other recipes for fried fish, such as Alexis Soyer's in *A Shilling Cookery Book for the People* (1854), suggested cooking and serving it cold in the 'Jewish Fashion', which he probably took from an interesting 1846 cookbook, *The Jewish Manual*, the first of its kind in England, which was written anonymously by Judith, Lady Montefiore for young Jewish housewives.

The fish was prepared on a catering scale too as evidenced by the 'fried fish warehouse' in *Oliver Twist* (1837), on Saffron Hill in Farringdon, which Dickens calls a 'commercial colony' of 'filthy shops' in a dismal alley whose air was 'impregnated with filthy odours'. Well into the twentieth century, descriptions of fried fish are united in agreement that it stank. Lady Montefiore recommends 'Florence oil' (meaning olive oil), but commercially it would have been cottonseed or rapeseed – unrefined and probably used multiple times. The fish that made it into the frying pan had likely been passed over by the previous days' shoppers; hygiene and ventilation were noted, by appalled visitors, by their absence. Fish friers were not popular neighbours; one costermonger told Henry Mayhew that 'a gin drinking neighbourhood suits best for people hasn't their smell so correct there'.[2]

It suits societies, in many ways, to have sections of it who are so poor and so ostracized that they will pick up all the jobs that nobody else wants to do. Frying was such a job – the bottom rung on the ladder of culinary acceptability; before the advent of purified oils and ventilation, people were happy to leave it to the Jews in London, particularly because they might enliven their recipe with a dash of spice or pepper. The Jews were, although ostracized, a settled community; their predilection for fried fish could be traced back to Portuguese Marrano refugees of the sixteenth century.[3] Incoming Irish immigrants had the edge over the Jews, though, for these toughest of jobs. They were used to hard living and a very limited diet, particularly in the years of the disastrous potato famine, from 1845 onwards, when their numbers radically increased in London and other cities, especially around the North West.

The chippy first surfaces in the North West, tracked down by an enterprising fish-and-chip historian, Gerald Priestland, to Mossley, where John Lees turned his pea-soup and pigs' trotters hut into an emporium of 'chipped potatoes in the French and American style' in 1863, after he was inspired by a man he met in Oldham selling 'Chipped Potatoes in the French style'.[4] The fictional adjective 'American' anticipated a later fully realized fact. A delightful photo of 1902 shows it describing itself as 'Lees's Chip Potato Restaurant Oldest Esta in the World'.

Nobody knows exactly when or where fried fish and fried chips came together, though Malin's in the East End of London has the boldest claim. However, from the end of the nineteenth century it was a marriage that began to produce thousands of offspring, selling hot food to workers, particularly in industrial and mining districts. There were estimated to be 25,000 fish and chip shops in Britain in 1910; a further 10,000 ten years later. (There are now around 10,500.)[5]

In many local authorities, fish and chips were deemed an 'offensive trade' from 1907, along with industries such as gut-scraping and tallow-melting, and had to keep themselves away from residential areas and respectable high streets. Cooking it at home wasn't an option for most families, who had neither the equipment nor the fuel budget; it was easy for public inspectors to overlook the economics of time and equipment and see shop-bought fish and chips as an extravagance, a misallocation of resources and a replacement for proper home-cooked food, by working women who were too thriftless or harried or uneducated to look after their children properly. A school medical officer in Blackpool wrote in 1928: 'A few of the poorer and less thrifty parents supply fish and chips, a food... which is indigestible and unwholesome, for their children's dinners.'[6]

Fridays and Saturdays were the big days for friers, as workers spent their pay packets on a hot and welcome meal. It's a tradition that carries on today in office canteens around the country (and has little to do with Catholic ideas of fasting on Fridays). Many friers in working-class neighbourhoods reported selling chips early on in Friday and Saturday evenings as the children of big families were given chips and batter scraps for an early tea; and more fish later on in the evening for the adults. Late-opening fish and chip shops earned the trade a reputation for sleaze, serving Friday-night drunks and women of loose morals, in search of refuge, refreshment and companionship, as J.B. Burnley noted in Bradford in 1880: 'girls whose every feature betokened deplorable depravity could here prolong their excesses, and put themselves beyond the reach of the law'.[7] In 1880 the image was meant to appal and titivate in equal measure; 100 years later, *Viz* comic wanted us to laugh at 'The Fat Slags' when Sandra's major concern, while having sex against a wall, is that she's dropped her chips.

The fish friers themselves, a broadly homogeneous group of very hard-working families, started to hit back at the characterization of their wares, often through their unofficial spokesperson, William Loftas, who, having run his own fish and chip shop and been President of the National Federation of Fish Friers, wrote a popular column in the *Fish Trades Gazette* under the pen name 'Chatchip'. When *The Pall Mall Gazette* ('written by gentlemen for gentlemen') complained about the smell of fish and chip shops, he thundered back: 'The abominable stink created by many readers of *The Pall Mall Gazette* as they rush through the streets of our cities and our country lanes in their motor cars... ought to be stopped too.'[8] He had a point.

George Orwell thought that the sanctimonious classes should be grateful to fish and chips (along with tinned salmon, cut-price chocolate, the movies, the radio, strong tea and the Football Pools) for averting a revolution among the put-upon poor who have 'neither turned revolutionary nor lost their self-respect; merely they have kept their tempers and settled down to make the best of things on a fish-and-chip standard'. He wonders whether the ruling classes have deliberately allowed this to happen, as a sort of 'bread and circuses' soporific, but concludes that this would attribute more artful intelligence to the governing class than they are likely to have, and that the whole thing is an unconscious process whereby manufacturers looking for a market and the half-starved people looking for cheap palliatives find a product that satisfied both needs.[9]

'Self-respect' is a very relative term; there were plenty of the respectable working classes who would not dream of eating fish and chips. Sheila Dillon, who presents Radio 4's *The Food Programme*, recalls her Lancashire Methodist grandmother saying, 'We are better than those people who go to the fish and chip shop.'[10]

One powerful PR message from the fish friers came with the insistence that fish and chips were a culinary symbol of Britishness, 'a national institution' as a correspondent to the *Hull Daily Mail* had it in 1929, conveniently ignoring the fact that many chip shops had been taken over by Italians in Scotland and Wales, the Cypriots and then Chinese in the main cities. Orwell wasn't alone in attributing the aversion of a national catastrophe to what Churchill called 'the good companions'; 'Chatchip' pointed out that fish and chip shops kept a wartime population well fed with hot and nutritious food. Partly in acknowledgement of this, and certainly because of advances in technology such as ventilation and oil-purification, shops ceased to be deemed an 'offensive trade' in 1940.

Perhaps the man who did most to bring fish and chips upmarket was Leeds' own Harry Ramsden, who rapidly moved from serving in a wooden hut in Guiseley in 1928, to a restaurant with fitted carpets, panelled walls and chandeliers; and the company continues to run smart and contemporary-looking restaurants, particularly in coastal towns, where they have become a holiday fixture.

The debate goes on. 'What would thousands of people do in Hull for supper if it was not for fried fish shops?' asked our *Hull Daily Mail* correspondent. The answer echoes down over the years: they should eat a healthy diet and not be poor or fat. As *The Times* reported in 2004, 'high levels of obesity are strongly linked to class', quoting a report that found ten fish and chip shops in the centre of Kingston upon Hull, whereas there was none in Kingston upon Thames.[11]

But the forces of Harry Ramsden, patriotism and gentrification mean that the focus of concern about health has now moved away from shops selling fish and chips to those selling chicken and chips (see Oysters, page 268). The residents of Kingston upon Thames allow themselves fish and chips every now and then, so long as it is done correctly, as an occasional seaside treat, with an eye to the health of marine fish stocks and proper cognizance of our NHS-sapping arteries. As a British seaside dish it belongs somewhere in most of our lives; it was, after all, born from that most British of phenomena – mixed-race parentage, with fried fish from Portuguese Jews and French (or Belgian)-inspired Irish potato chips.

Some food can be made acceptable in our minds, not because the ingredients have changed, but because of where we eat it. We have convinced ourselves that open-air eating is healthy eating, no matter how many pork pies or chocolate biscuits it involves; this is one of the reasons we love to picnic.

Picnics: wandering lonely as a cloud... or being sociable?

One spirit animating old and young,
A gipsy-fire we kindled on the shore
Of the fair Isle with birch-trees fringed—and there,
Merrily seated in a ring, partook
A choice repast—served by our young companions
With rival earnestness and kindred glee.

William Wordsworth, *The Excursion* (1814)

BRITISH PICNICS – at least the writing and remembering of them – come accompanied with a knowing but competitive doughtiness. Picnic writing is the Olympics of the soggiest sandwiches; the most abysmal weather (gold usually going to holidaymakers in Scotland); the most ludicrous ducking of a family member (sometimes canine) in lake or river; the worst flesh wounds on attempting to open the most intractable of tins. Medals are earned for the parents who marched or boated a complaining family to the most out-of-the-way spot – only to discover that the backdrop was a sewage works or rubbish tip; the seat bestrewn with sheep dung or ants. The upside to all this was the picnic: Thermos-infused coffee and a squashed Twix; 'Sand in the sandwiches, wasps in the tea', as John Betjeman reminds us in 'Trebetherick'; and the feeling of achievement. To those of us dedicated to picnicking as an endurance sport, the people who chose to eat comfortably next to their car, or on regimented benches, were unfortunates who were missing out, due to a paucity of education or culture, in an uplifting experience of the *real* natural world. I was shocked when, as a young adult, I was taken to Henley Regatta for the first time, to discover fields and fields of posh (and therefore, presumably, *educated*) people picnicking, not only right next to their cars but, horror, within champagne-cork-popping distance of the next group along.

The ancestor of Henley, an outdoor meal of aristocratic leisure rather than workers' convenience, could be found at the hunt. George Gascoigne's *The Noble Art of Venerie or Hunting*, first published in 1575, tells us the perfect conditions for what the author describes as an 'assembly': in addition to a 'gladsome greene', sunbeams and wild flowers, there should be a skilful butler and staff dispensing wine and cold meats, spiced tongue, ham, pigeon pies, sausages and 'savery knackes'. An accompanying woodcut shows nearly thirty people, men sitting or reclining around cloths and plates on the grass, being served with drinks from pitchers and barrels, and from large joints of meat. It isn't only the doublet and hose and the horses, though, that differentiate it from the Ascot of today. It is clear that beyond this gladsome greene there is no other group of people dining likewise; it is eating *al fresco* for an assembly of the *very* few.

Except for the highly ritualized and hierarchical hunt, eating outside in rural areas was too close to the life of an agricultural labourer for comfort. Cities, though, offered a civilized structure that made eating outdoors less socially ambiguous. Pepys records sharing claret, bread and butter and botargo (a type of cured fish roe) with his neighbour on the leads of their building,[1] while taking a boat on the Thames offered a safely elegant way for him to enjoy cold meat, wine and songs under the stars.[2] Urbanites took their rural pleasures in tea gardens or, if sufficiently well connected, in the palladiums, grottoes, temples and banqueting houses that were popping up on aristocratic country estates.

Agricultural workers ate outside less than we might suppose, unless compelled to by being far from home or the farmhouse, or the all-engrossing urgency of harvest time. The 'common ploughman' in William Ellis's eighteenth-century Hertfordshire expected to have his dinner at home and to be provided with a snack for he 'thinks himself not rightly provided, if he cannot carry a piece of pickled pork and apple-dumplin into the field, to bite on till he comes home to dinner'.[3] Although the bread, ham, cheese and beer of agricultural labourers is very close to many modern-day picnics, they didn't use 'picnic' as a noun or verb; William Ellis gives instructions for 'victualling' men at harvest time. In *Lark Rise to Candleford* it is called 'bavour'; in Yorkshire, 'lowance' of currant pasty, bread, cheese and 'ham cake' (a sort of pasty) was brought from the farm to the workers in the field.[4] In the West Country, men called their midday bread and cheese or saffron cake 'namett'.[5] The miners in D.H. Lawrence's Nottinghamshire had 'snap'.[6]

The word 'picnic' was probably brought by émigrés fleeing the French Revolution at the end of the eighteenth century, but changed in form and meaning in its trip over the Channel. The French 'pique-nique' was a meal to which everybody contributed – a sort of potluck supper – but its early use in English was fluid. The word was seized on by a racy group of London society who staged amateur theatricals and music and earned themselves a reputation for rakish morals as the 'Pic Nic Club'. Their short-lived literary periodical, *The Pic-Nic*, established in 1803, was in some ways a manifesto of class war: a defence against the fake news – 'the wilful and envenomed falsehoods' – of the gossip columns which were making a false impression on the public mind and 'exposing exalted characters to obloquy, and the superior classes of society to contempt and detestation'.[7] Whatever the definition, the picnic was posh. The *Annual Register* in 1802 recorded, 'the rich have their sport, their balls, their parties of pleasure and their *pic-nics*'.[8] It isn't clear that this meant a picnic in the modern sense – but in a few short years that is how it began to be defined and, since this was Britain, along with the pigeon pies and cold meat there came a tussle over what sort of class of person the picnic belonged to.

The battleground was marked out as the Lake District. Although full of the joy of, and reverence for, the natural world that marked the Romantic project, the earliest diaries and letters of Dorothy and William Wordsworth show no social eating outdoors and only a few occasions when they might put some cold meat and bread into a pocket to fuel them on a walk of many miles.

Then the Wordsworths began to picnic. William was oblique in his references. In his Lakeland poem *The Excursion* several characters boat to an island and make tea on a 'gipsy-fire', and he hints at something edible brought by two boys in a basket, although sadly doesn't give us a menu. Dorothy, describing a similar occasion in her letters, tackles this new idea head on. Writing to her friend about a picnic for nineteen upon Grasmere island that was rained off, she asks, 'Bye the bye, what is the origin of the word picnic? Our Windermere gentlemen have a picnic almost every day. They call them always by that name.'[9] Dorothy's friends are gentlemen in this context, not because they are *genteel* in the Georgian sense, but because they have a moral connection to the natural world.[10] The Romantic picnic took the idea of outdoor eating from the landowning and land-labouring classes, and used it to connect themselves to the land in a way that expressed something about the virtues of the intellectual and artistic middle class.

In *Emma*, written a year or two later, Jane Austen makes it plain that a large group of people picnicking in the open air, in a way that the Wordsworths were beginning to enjoy, was not *genteel*. Emma's ideal outing is highly controlled and selective in order to be in *good taste*: 'Two or three more of the chosen only were to be admitted to join them, and it was to be done in a quiet, unpretending, elegant way, infinitely superior to the bustle and preparation, the regular eating and drinking, and picnic parade of the Eltons.'[11] Sure enough, when the picnic at Box Hill takes place with all the 'picnic parade' she had been dreading, civilization is left behind with the table, chairs and dining room. Emma is rude to Miss Bates! Her behaviour, Mr Knightley reminds her, is both unmannerly and immoral because Miss Bates, having fallen on hard times, is no longer Emma's 'equal in situation'.

Jane Austen was voicing an anxiety of the upper-middle class that the wrong environment could have a negative impact on behaviour. The new century disagreed. Victorian societies, dedicated to improvement and enjoyment through rambling, exploration, discovering antiquities, bicycling or – as with Dickens' Pickwick Club – the noble art of drinking and having a good time, all enthusiastically took to picnicking.

At the top end of the social scale, picnics became a part of the 'London season': the Harrow and Eton cricket matches, Henley Regatta, Cowes Regatta, the Epsom Derby, Ascot. Mrs Beeton gave her middle-class readers an exhaustive bill of fare for a picnic for forty people which would equip them for this new upper-class sport, without losing any of the trappings of civilization: 'It is scarcely necessary to say that plates, tumblers, wine-glasses, knives, forks, and spoons, must not be forgotten; as also teacups and saucers, 3 or 4 teapots, some lump sugar, and milk, if this last-named article cannot be obtained in the neighbourhood. Take 3 corkscrews.'[12]

Like Elizabethan hunting parties, Victorian picnics were safe when they were organized with the full 'picnic parade' and there was a visible difference between the well-organized social excursion and the piece of pickled pork and apple dumpling in the pocket of the field labourer. Their urban, industrial counterparts, however, took the Victorian mass picnic and adapted it to suit their communities. Rail travel enabled entrepreneurs such as Thomas Cook to charter trains for collective day trips for the moral and physical good of his economically modest customers; his first was to a Temperance Rally in the Midlands in 1841. Sunday School picnics, chapel outings and Temperance societies brought workers out from under the polluted skies of their homes and workplaces into the benefits of fresh air and the countryside. Miners' picnics – particularly in Durham, Sunderland and parts of the North East – were established to celebrate the urban, industrial communities that the middle classes were so anxious to escape. Guest speakers were selected to make a show of political strength; there were games to bring people together, a colliery band for entertainment; people brought their own food or bought sandwiches and cakes from local bakeries. It has far more in common with the Elizabethan hunt than the picnic on Grasmere island. The current revival of local miners' picnics, despite the lure of 'food and drinks stalls', gives more expression to ideas of community than to the pleasure of eating food in the open air.

That pleasure is often given as the reason for picnicking, although it is just as frequently noted that British weather does not lend itself to the experience. However, solid, indestructible British food does. The sandwich, the meat pie, the pasty, cold roast beef, ham, cheese and beer stay the course from Gascoigne's 1575 treatise on hunting through to the nineteenth century. Sam Weller unpacks a familiar menu for a shooting picnic in *The Pickwick Papers*:

> 'Weal pie,' said Mr Weller, soliloquizing, as he arranged the eatables on the grass. 'Wery good thing is a weal pie, when you know the lady as made it, and is quite sure it an't kittens... Tongue; well that's a wery good thing, when it an't a woman's. Bread – knuckle o'ham, reg'lar picter – cold beef in slices, wery good.'[13]

And, seventy years later, in another famous picnic in *The Wind in the Willows* (1908) the names become a litany for Rat as he unpacks cold chicken from a 'fat, wicker luncheon-basket' followed by:

> coldtonguecoldhamcoldbeefpickledgherkinssaladfrenchrollscress sandwichespottedmeatgingerbeerlemonadesodawater[14]

Kenneth Grahame, keen to swap the Bank of England where he was Secretary, for the river bank, and London-dwelling Mr Pickwick were both discovering that educated urbanites could form their own, personal and leisured relationship with the countryside which would feel more familiar to members of the National Trust today than to their rural contemporaries. The picnic brought the lakes, woods and hills of 'England's green and pleasant land' into the circle of the town-dweller. No matter whether it was a Thermos of tea, cheese salad sandwiches and pork pies, or punch, lobster salad and a lump of roast beef, picnics and picnic fare gave us a way of thinking of both the food and the meal itself as particularly British, rather in the way that our Christmas dinner unites food and setting in a unique way.[15]

Claudia Roden, whose bestselling cookbooks have been bringing Middle Eastern cuisine to her readers in Britain since the late 1960s, notes that huge, formal picnics were exported to the Middle East, Africa and Asia by colonialists, who, desperate to be as English as possible, ignored the kebabs or sweet and sour ribs being grilled over a fire by the local cooks for their own lunches, in favour of the traditional lobster salad and pies. Contemporary picnickers are happy to be more eclectic; those who have absorbed the predilection for the barbecue from the Americans are just as likely to borrow dishes from the East to cook on it.[16]

The wicker hamper with its fitted crockery and cutlery became an upmarket extra, as cheap and portable paper and plastic plates and crockery brought the individual picnic within reach of almost everybody. The affordable motor car and relatively unaffordable train travel did more than anything to democratize the family picnic. Now that strawberries and cream, fizzy wine and any kind of sandwiches are hardly upper-class luxuries, writers reached for the material culture of picnics to distinguish between different classes of picnickers. Charles Moore, the well-connected journalist and biographer, said that the 2019 Extinction Rebellion protests in Trafalgar Square 'reminded me of the Fourth of June at Eton, with ordinary parents in ordinary tents and nouveaux riches ones in huge picnic tents with pseudo-Georgian plastic windows'.[17] The *Metro* newspaper signalled its mass appeal by announcing that taking 'actual glasses' to a picnic was a sign that you were 'too middle class for words'.[18]

While I'm in no position to argue with Charles Moore's definition of 'ordinary parents', not having been to the Fourth of June at Eton, I'm not sure that *Metro* is entirely right. It is neither the food nor the material objects that make you 'too middle class for words' but where you choose to enjoy them. The too-middle-class-for-words family will wander lonely as a cloud for hours to find the most isolated spot on beach, or hillside, or island, and is *outraged* when somebody else, with acres of empty space to choose from, comes and parks themselves right next to them.

Now that the urban middle classes have laid claim to rural spaces, there is a certain amount of competitiveness about who gets to be there, as the story of foraging shows.

Foraging: the knowledge economy

The bitter-sweet of a white-oak acorn which you nibble in a bleak
November walk over the tawny earth is more to me than a slice of
imported pine-apple.

Henry David Thoreau, *Wild Fruit* (1859)

THE JOY OF picking blackberries. One for me, one for the
empty ice-cream carton. The challenge of discovering the
juiciest ones just out of reach; the scratched skin, stained
hands (and mouths), the competition to see who had picked the
most. As a child I didn't know I was 'foraging', or that gathering
'wild food' was a quasi-political act that makes a statement about
my relationship with the land and my right to be there. I was just
thinking about blackberry and apple crumble.

Anthropologists and historians have often wondered why,
sometime between 5,000 and 10,000 years ago, some people
became farmers, rather than hunter-gatherers and effectively
invented a lower caste for themselves. The powerful remained
hunters; their reward was the thrill of the chase and a protein-
rich and varied diet.[1] The famous list of carving terms in *The
Boke of Kervynge* shows just how varied a wild food diet could
be: deer, swan, heron, crane, mallard, curlew, bittern, woodcock,
plover, as well as fish and farmyard animals. It might be the other
way round, of course. Perhaps caste pre-dated agriculture. Our
new high-caste Stone-Agers kept the fun and the nutrition of the

hunt for themselves, forcing weedier members of their group – including women – to discover that gathering without hunting wasn't going to keep them alive. Agriculture became a necessary curse. The ploughing and tilling and harvesting they were forced to do sunk them into an eternal state of peasantry.

John Lewis-Stempel's account of living off wild food for a year in Herefordshire in the first decade of the twenty-first century shows how much – barring a few dandelion roots, corn salad or nettles – meat and alcohol were the principal sources of calories in the winter months. Both are still icons of Northern European culinary culture, their pedestals hardly lowered by centuries of imports and politics. The earliest medieval records of the peasant diet suggest a limited palette of peas, beans and worts (cabbage or other leaves) which went into the ubiquitous pottage; bread and cheese were a step up, and meat prized most of all. There are scant records of foraging by the poorest in almost any period; not, presumably, because it didn't happen, but because it either wasn't considered worthy of notice or it was slightly shameful, a sign of destitution. Foraging for plant food was subcontracted to livestock. Acorns, pignuts (a sort of wild carrot), tubers and fungi in woodland and hedgerows were transformed, through some porcine magic, into all sorts of good things such as bacon, pork, sausages and black pudding. Cattle and sheep transubstantiated the edible grasses of the commons into 'white meat' (dairy), beef and mutton. Flocks of geese grazed on the grain left after harvest and on commonland, a Michaelmas treat for their owners or, more likely, a source of cash (each was identified with a punch on their webbed foot).[2] For villagers hungry for protein, it seemed axiomatic that this was the most effective use of wild food. This is why they were so badly hit by the Enclosures which began to trickle through the countryside in Tudor times up to the reign of Queen Anne, then swept away the livelihood of villagers throughout the second half of the eighteenth century; 3 million acres were enclosed in the long reign of George III (1760–1820).[3] Overnight, landless families lost the grazing for their cattle and sheep, and the wherewithal to forage for fuel. Many sought to replace their protein deficit with poaching, and all the draconian punishments that entailed. What did people forage? The Scottish food historian F. Marian McNeill said that when people were evicted from South Uist and elsewhere, 'they fell back on certain wild vegetables, most of which were used only in emergency – wild spinach, wild mustard, the goose-foot, and the root of the little silver-weed'.[4]

For the official record, the principal value of most wild plants lay not in the kitchen but in their medical application. Monastic gardens were early horticultural laboratories, where beneficial strains were brought into cultivation, ready to be turned into the cures or 'simples' for the infirmary. By the seventeenth century, Nicholas Culpeper, in *The English Physitian* (later known as *The Complete Herbal*), objected to the word 'simples' as 'vulgar', suggesting that the knowledge of how to use them spread throughout all levels of society, although practitioners didn't all enjoy the same reputation; local herbals suggest that My Lady's knowledge was valued more than a villager's. Physic was the principal virtue of an English housewife, according to Gervase Markham's book of recipes and instructions aimed at her, but 'the depth and secrets of this most excellent art of physic is far beyond the capacity of the most skilful woman, as lodging only in the breast of the learned professors'.[5] The learned professors themselves didn't seem quite so certain that their authority would go unquestioned, and were at pains to validate their work with higher powers. William Coles promised that the 'Art of Simpling' would bring the reader to a prelapsarian closeness to God, in his *Adam in Eden* of 1657. For Culpeper, herbalism gained its scientific respectability from Astrology, and his descriptions of 'the vulgar herbs of the nation' are starlit with planetary influence. He isn't above guiding his 'vulgar' (that word again) readership who might simply want a cure, for example, for a woman who has miscarried because of wind.[6] John Gerard invokes classical wisdom for the pedigree of his 1597 *Herball*. Everybody genuflected to Galen, the Greek physician of the second century AD, still the highest authority on the 'vertues' of each plant – the herbal version of morality and character.

There is little distinction in early cookbooks and herbals between what was grown or gathered; it is estimated that over fifty plants which were valued members of the kitchen garden have reverted to the wild.[7] Alexanders, orache, the species of dock known as 'Monk's Rhubarb', sorrel and tansy were all once cultivated. Recipes for 'tansy', a sort of pudding or omelette coloured green with spinach juice and flavoured with the bitter juice of the herb, were found throughout the aristocratic cookbooks of the seventeenth century. Country people in the North used bistort, known also as 'ledges', in an Easter-time pudding, also known as Dock Pudding. It was revived in 1971 with the World Dock Pudding Championship in West Yorkshire.[8]

The East Anglian farmer Thomas Tusser lists a range of kitchen garden plants which are today considered not only wild but inedible: Betony, Penny Royal, Mercury.[9] Anything leafy was usually called a 'wort' in medieval English and the word gradually changed to suggest only a herbal use, giving way in the fifteenth-century kitchen to 'potherbs'. Eventually the word 'vegetable' edged out the portmanteau 'potherb', signalling an almost thorough move from the wild to the garden. Throughout John Evelyn's *Acetaria: A Discourse of Sallets* (1699) he is much concerned with the art of the kitchen garden, advising his readers to get the best seeds for (rock) samphire from France. He doesn't dismiss foraging, 'every hedge affords a sallet', he says,[10] but it is something done by other people; the more frugal French and Italians gather the tops of nettles and brambles; Jack-by-the-hedge is gathered by country people as it grows wild 'under *their* banks and hedges' (my italics).[11] Like Gerard and Culpeper, he gives a strong classical dressing to his salads; the wisdom of Pliny, Galen and 'the Poets' are more valuable to him than English folklore.

Evelyn would have been astonished by the Victorian scholars and botanists who followed him, discarding his precious Galen altogether, and drawing on the knowledge of 'the people'. As the antiquarian William Hone said, 'Hagbush-lane is well known to every botanizing perambulator on the west side of London. The wild onion, clownwound-wort, wake-robin, and abundance of other simples, lovely in their form, and of high medicinal repute in our old herbals and receipt-books'.[12] He would not have called it 'foraging', though, as the word at the time was reserved for the slightly disreputable gathering of food by soldiers on military campaign. Further into the heart of the city, Charles Elmé Francatelli, 'Late Maître d'hôtel and Chief Cook to Her Majesty the Queen Victoria', was suggesting to the working classes that they look to country practices of foraging to improve their city-bound diet. He advised young Londoners to be like the 'Industrious and intelligent boys who live in the country', and catch some small birds with which their mothers can make 'a famous pudding' for supper, without suggesting where or how such small birds were to be caught.[13]

The English Folk Cookery Association suggests that foraged plants had slipped out of most kitchens but lingered in the still room: cowslip wine, elderflower wine, mulberry, dandelion, blackberry and coltsfoot.[14] Some were gathered and became cash crops, while quantities of maidenhair fern were imported from Ireland when it became the chia seed of Victorian dining. The seashore offered foragers a meal of salty oysters, mussels, cockles and winkles, followed by candied eryngo roots; the sea holly was semi-cultivated on shorelines (by forcing them with piles of stones, rather like rhubarb);[15] and marshmallow was gathered by fishermen's wives in the dykes and salt marshes of the east coast.[16]

In the Second World War, the government promoted foraging as a national benefit with pamphlets such as 'Hedgerow Harvest', containing the simplest of recipes for jams and jellies and rosehip syrup. Pounds and pounds of rosehips were gathered to make Vitamin C-rich syrups, and schools laid down friendly challenges to one another as to who could pick the most. One Cotswold school awarded itself the crown for picking an average of 43.2lb (19.5kg) per child in 1945.[17]

Lark Rise to Candleford, Flora Thompson's record of life in rural Oxfordshire around the turn of the century, was published during the war. Her recollections of the village women who made jam with wild fruits and berries, and children foraging on their way to school, resonated with her ration-strapped readers, many of whose children were evacuated to the countryside.

Indeed, David Lloyd George hoped that the war would enable people to relearn lessons from our once 'thriving and prosperous peasantry': 'Our people have grown more sophisticated, but less wise; intellectually more elaborately taught, but practically less widely competent.'[18]

However, the balance between town and country that Lloyd George was hoping for was pushed even further away from 'Our people' by the massive post-war expansion of agribusiness and convenience food. Advertising persuaded people that ready-made food – Smash, Spam, Angel Delight – was at the centre of the cosy home. It was a challenge to this 'domesticity as much as domestication' that inspired Richard Mabey to publish his ground-breaking guide to foraging, *Food for Free* (1972). It was only later that he realized it might also be a way of 'reconnecting with the wild'.[19] It is this idea, though, that is the one most often cited for the mushrooming (forgive the pun) of foraging in the years since, and the chefs and restaurants that have brought the taste of 'wilderness' to diners so sophisticated there seemed to be no truffle or caviar left untried. It caught the attention of people who have no physical *need* to turn to wild food and are confident (even if wrongly) of a never-ceasing supply of a global range of foodstuffs. It rapidly caught on, and Britain is now well supplied with foraging programmes on the television and experts offering courses. Urban-dwellers can connect with the natural world; can take back control from multinational food corporations; can discover the salinity of marsh samphire, the lemony bitterness of sorrel, the delicacy of nettles, and the joy of picking them oneself. A more sinister arm of foraging comes with survivalism and people prepping for the end of the world, studying how to make acorn burgers and turnip bread, make a shelter and purify water, and all the other knowledge they'll require when the rest of civilization has been destroyed.

One of the things people say they value most about foraging has more in common with Tudor herbalists than deracinated peasants, and that is *knowledge*. As part of an urban generation who will never have the pleasure of living off the produce of our own land, nor, I hope, the anxiety of wondering where their next meal is coming from, we all share the value of knowledge. As Hugh Fearnley-Whittingstall says, 'An understanding of wild food is therefore, in part at least, an education about food history, and food safety.'[20] Expertise and field guides have turned mushroom picking from Russian roulette into a treasure hunt. Those stories of organ failure and a lifetime of poor health from making a single mistake, which, I confess, send a shiver down my spine and have me reaching for boring, cultivated mushrooms, have been a boon for mushroom-picking guides. Foraging offers a legitimate relationship with the natural world *through* the process of discovering, learning and reading. Mushroom-pickers fight like cats over their territory. It isn't only the question of whether an incomer (particularly a *Londoner*) has the right to pick mushrooms in the New Forest, for example, it is a question of whether they do it in the right way. Is their culture, their education, their knowledge up to that of local people?

While wild meat always had a very high status because it implies ownership and control of land (or poaching), foraging for wild fruit, vegetables and herbs has never been as prized as it is now. Its status comes from the people who, in Britain's huge, urban landscape, have access to the countryside, and the luxury of time and education for this most calorifically inessential of activities. For most of us, our recipes for hedgerow jelly or sloe gin come from the internet or a book, rather than our grandparents. We have no connection left with the land, but foraging helps to give us one. There is no more intimate relationship in the food chain than eating something; so the most astringent of herb salads and the sweetest of blackberry and apple crumbles, and the wood-taste of chanterelles and morels, have come to suggest that we, too, have a right to the meadow, the forest and the hedgerow.

NETTLE SOUP

◆

Eating foraged food began to lose its stigma in the Second World War, aided by recipe writers such as the aristocratic Frenchman Vicomte de Mauduit, sharing the secrets of 'Nature's larder'. Armed with his book, he said, you could live 'in comfort, in plenty, and in health even if all banks, all shops, and all markets be closed for indefinite periods'.[21] These were powerful words to read in the middle of the Coronavirus lockdown of 2020, when I picked the nettles for this excellent, mild, herby soup.

MODERN RECIPE

1 large onion
Knob of butter
1 large floury potato
1 litre light stock (chicken or vegetable)
About 150g nettle leaves (not stalks) – you could include other green leaves such as sorrel, wild garlic, young dandelion leaves, wild rocket, wild chervil, watercress
150ml full-fat milk
Salt to taste
Croutons, made with bread fried or baked with oil, with rosemary and garlic

1. Chop the onion and fry it softly in a little butter until it starts to soften.
2. Peel and chop the potato, add to the onion; cover and let it stew over a low heat until it is soft but not coloured.
3. Add the stock and boil for about 10 minutes.
4. Add the nettles and other green leaves and cook for up to 5 minutes – don't let them lose the fresh green colour.
5. Add the milk and liquidize with a stab mixer. Taste and add a little salt, if need be.
6. Serve with croutons.

ORIGINAL RECIPE: NETTLE SOUP

From *They Can't Ration These* by Vicomte de Mauduit (1940)

◆

Pick, wash, and dry a pint potful of nettles and put them in a pint of salt water. Stir well and cook for 10 minutes. Melt 1oz bacon fat, stir in 1oz of flour, add the nettles and water, and cook for another 5 minutes slowly, stirring all the time. Add a little boiling milk and serve with croutons.

Cake: a regional lexicon

It's scone as in 'gone' not scone as in 'bone'.

YouGov poll (2016)

H OW DO YOU pronounce 'scone'? It's such a divisive question it even had a YouGov poll dedicated to it in 2016. The pollsters concluded that if you are either middle class, from Scotland or northern England, you are far more likely to pronounce it to rhyme with 'gone'. I didn't learn, until I left my northern, middle-class home, that there was a whole parallel universe of people who rhyme it with 'bone', comprising some (not all) southern and Midland folk, Americans and what the pollsters call 'the C2DE' social grade.[1] In the 1950s John Betjeman gleefully rhymed 'scones' with 'stones' as part of his vivisection of the lower middle classes in 'How to Get On in Society'.

The great scone schism is only one of the regional and social divisions in the history of Britain's cakes, buns and biscuits, and what we call them.

The word 'cake', related to the Germanic *Kuchen*, came to us in the early thirteenth century from Old Norse *kaka* or Germanic *kokon*, which is where our 'everyday' words tend to come from (see French Food, page 166). The Germanic root suggests that recipes for cake emerged from the farmhouse kitchen as treats – and fuel – for workers, unlike their French cousins, the pastry or tart, which were devised by chefs to sweeten the days of the Norman overlords and their aristocratic descendants.

A little bacon fat, or lard, or butter transformed oatmeal into our first cakes. The fourteenth-century *Froissart Chronicles* attributed the hardiness of Scottish soldiers to their carrying sacks of oatmeal and a griddle pan;[2] Piers Plowman feeds oatcakes to the allegorical Hunger to stop him destroying the people. Wheat was a cut above oats, but even for the wealthiest, there was little available to make their wheaten cakes into anything other than bread until the explosion in trade in the sixteenth and seventeenth centuries that bought currants (the word and thing coming from Corinth in Greece) and raisins of the sun, which bakers wrapped with the pillowy arms of their bread dough to produce the first fruit cakes.

Trade and technology (and, later, slavery) pushed the price of sugar and flour downwards, so that even ordinary people began to punctuate their monotonous diets with the occasional cake, sanctioned by the fêtes and festivals of the Church, which so closely followed the agricultural year.

Housewives used up their rich animal food – butter and eggs before the Lenten fast, a Church stricture which mirrored agricultural needs to allow animals to breed and feed their young (see Almond Milk, page 306). Pancakes are the best-known example, but the Shrovetide cooking of Baldock in Hertfordshire has left us the earliest known recipe for doughnuts, fried in hogs' lard; while Norfolk families ate a spiced bun called a Cockerells (or perhaps Coquilles or Cookeels). If it sounds like 'cockerel', it is probably because cock-throwing and cock-fighting were entertainments for labourers at this time of year.[3] Pepys has a Lenten supper of wiggs and ale; named 'wigg' for their wedge-shape, these were spiced and always contained caraway seeds, and were not just a cheap version of fruit cakes (although that was true) (see Bread and Butter, page 298). At Easter and funerals caraway cakes symbolized death and rebirth; at harvest festival they signified fertility, while the gift of a seed cake to a young man or woman carried with it a strong hint of sexual interest. A rich caraway seed cake or Simnel cake was a welcome respite from the Lenten fast; it emerges into the light of the 1640s courtesy of the poet Robert Herrick who was fascinated by popular traditions (as well as by food and sex). In a collection of poems called *Hesperides* from 1648, we find this:

> I'll to thee a simnell bring
> Gainst though go'st a mothering.[3]

There are still three competing claims for the original Simnel cake recipe, from Shrewsbury, Devizes and Bury. Parkin, made in Yorkshire and Cumbria, is still eaten around Bonfire Night; hot cross buns at Easter. I much regret the passing of 'Dumb cakes' which young women would make and eat at St Agnes Eve or Midsummer, to dream of whom they might marry. Suggested ingredients, besides flour, include salt, soot and your own wee. Yes, wee.[5]

The edible map of Britain shows a grassroots force of local bakers, all working with a similar palette of ingredients, who conjured up different shapes and tastes that proudly announce their place of origin: Banbury cakes, Eccles cakes, Bakewell tart, Dundee cake, Chelsea buns, Ecclefechan tart, Welsh cakes, Devon splits, Chorley cakes, Coventry God cakes. Others tell us something about the ingredients, perhaps in dialect or Celtic: lardy cake from the southern counties and fat rascals from Yorkshire announce that they are made with the luxury of white animal fat or butter. Saffron buns from Cornwall mark one of the few places where crocuses were grown commercially for their saffron (a baking opportunity missed, surely, by the Essex town of Saffron Walden). The *Oxford English Dictionary* tells us that Yorkshire parkin comes from the families of Perkin. Singing hinnies from Northumberland are supposed to sing when the fat sizzles. Barm brack from Ireland and its cousin bara brith from Wales both (probably) mean 'speckled bread', owing to the smattering of currants or dried fruits. Every baker, village, town and region had its own currant bread for holidays; as the Scottish writer 'Margaret Dods' explains, 'under some such name as "Lady Bountiful's loaf", "Mrs Notable's cake", "Miss Thrifty's bun"…

the formula is endless – and they are all good.'[6] Housewives who couldn't afford an oven – which was most – sent their cakes to the bakers', pricking their initial or mark into the pastry or dough, to identify it as theirs, as in 'Pat a cake', the nursery rhyme dating back to the seventeenth century.

Whereas we might use chocolate or money, cake was used to bribe or reward children. The lure of Grasmere gingerbread is what got children to take part in the local saint's day 'rush bearing'. On the evening before All Souls' Day (on 2 November), children went from house to house singing for 'soul cakes'; the festival has elided with Halloween and the newly reinvigorated tradition of trick or treating. Cake was a unit of currency in public schools, too. George Osborne in Thackeray's *Vanity Fair*, desperate to be in with the popular boys at Dr Swishtail's famous school, writes to his mother to send him 5 shillings and a cake ('Please not a seed-cake, but a plum-cake').[7]

The published cookbooks and cookery manuscripts kept by the noble ladies of the seventeenth century followed local recipes but generally dispensed with the geographical appellation (although 'Banbury cake' seems to be an honourable exception). John Evelyn, who was born and lived in the South East, is probably unaware his 'Cakes of Currance' are what we would now call Eccles cakes.[8] Sir Kenelm Digby, who liked to demonstrate his grand connections in the names he gave to his recipes, such as 'The Queen's Hotchpot' or 'My Lord Lumley's Pease-Porage', does not bestow any of his cakes with knighthoods or any kind of hint as to their origins. Mostly they are 'cake', 'another cake' or 'an excellent cake'.[9]

But what was a cake? Cakes could be as flat as a pancake (or an oatcake). Digby and Evelyn's large cakes were coaxed to rise with 'ale-yest' or yeast, the barm or yeast taken as a side-product of brewing (see Bread, page 330), though it was notoriously unstable or 'barmy'. It gradually became replaced with eggs, which, well beaten, reliably held the air within the mixture. Hannah Glasse's cake recipes have the cook beating the mixture for one, sometimes two hours. Elizabeth Raffald warned her readers to beat the eggs well and use them immediately or else 'your cakes will not be light'.[10] And then a British chemist called Alfred Bird changed everything in 1843 when he started to sell baking powder.

The names of the articles themselves, though, haven't necessarily kept up with technology but have clung on to an earlier incarnation or place of origin. Stotty cake, barm cake, bread cakes are all northern terms for bread rolls. Shortbread, gingerbread, Shrewsbury cakes and Aberffraw cakes aren't bread or cakes at all but biscuits. No matter how many expeditions it has been on, Kendal mint cake is just a sweet. The Tunnock's Teacake, made in Glasgow since 1956, is its own proud, marshmallowy thing; it is nothing to do with the fruited yeast buns we love to eat toasted with melted butter, which in turn is nothing to do with the Georgian 'tea-cake' which was rolled out and cut out. The border between 'biscuit' and 'cake' is not strictly policed, although HMRC once famously tried to rule that the Jaffa Cake was a biscuit (and therefore liable to tax). In an excellent use of the country's legal resources, the court agreed with the manufacturer in 2016 that it was a tax-free cake.[11]

The great age of cake-making in Britain coincided not just with the rise of 5 o'clock tea (see Afternoon Tea, page 54) but Alfred Bird's magical powder. Without relying on the cook's aching arm or unreliable yeast, kitchens in country houses ramped up the production of seed cake, orange or lemon cake, ginger cake, sand cake and, eventually, chocolate cake. The Edwardians renamed the fruit cake 'luncheon cake' to distinguish it from the plainer 'breakfast cakes'. The pound cake, an easy-to-remember recipe in which every ingredient – flour, butter, sugar, eggs – weighed the same, sounds rather solid to us but was quite modest compared with recipes of the previous century, calling for several pounds of dry ingredients and twenty or thirty eggs, and designed to fuel enormous households. Although they are part of the country house tea, the aristocratic food writers of the nineteenth and twentieth centuries rarely drew on their local specialities. Books with titles such as *When the Cook Is Away* or *Lady Sysonby's Cook Book* gave recipes for Victoria sponges (named for the queen) or madeira cake (named for the wine): large, sociable cakes, designed to be cut up. They were not the kind of cakes like Banbury cakes (dried fruit inside a pastry) or hot cross buns which were sold by bakers, at fairs, or from a basket to be enjoyed hot and fresh as you walked along, because well-brought-up people *never* ate in the street. They might, however, eat a slice of fruit cake, with a glass of sherry or a 'stirrup cup', on horseback, as the Melton Hunt cake attests.

The cake was at the centre of every celebration, wedding, Christmas, birthday, saint's day, festival and festivity; an association which has given it a higher social status than its biscuitty inferior, which survives to this day. A biscuit might be absent-mindedly dunked into a mug of builder's tea, but it is never the centre of a wedding ceremony, nor invited onto the tiered cake stand of the afternoon tea. A study of 'Women, Food and Families' in 1980s Manchester saw that the members of working-class families all rated cake above puddings, biscuits or sweets.[12] The cutting of it and sharing it out make it part of a social occasion which is a meal, and not just a snack. The study showed that all 'high-status' foods – red meat, alcohol, cake – were consumed more by men, particularly working-class men, than their partners and children. Their partners made sure that there was a good, solid slice of fruit cake, or lemon drizzle, or chocolate cake in the packed lunches they made them, because cake was more like 'proper food' than a snappy little Rich Tea biscuit.

The one-per-person bun, too, was admitted into the pantheon of 'proper' food because of its appeal for reliable, working appetites. This did not, apparently, include Elizabeth David, who quoted a friend as describing the Chelsea bun as 'rather large and bucolic', which gave it, she thought, 'little place in our lives today'.[13] She was out of step, not only with working men but also with earthbound recipe collectors such as Florence White who determined to 'capture the charm of England's cookery before it is completely crushed out of existence'.[14] Her English Folk Cookery Association gathered together recipes from the people who still had a place in their lives for Barnstaple Fair Gingerbread, Cornish

Fairings, Ripon Spice Bread, Devonshire Chudleighs, Scarborough Muffins and Kent Huffkins.

Although her Association sadly died with her, Florence White, in many ways, succeeded. Since the end of the twentieth century, local and home baking has had a resurgence thanks to people who, eager to capture English traditions, have painted their rooms in heritage colours and flocked to National Trust tea rooms, happily fuelled their days out with tea-shop pit-stops and watched as the *Great British Bake Off* bakers – just sometimes – draw on regional classics. People all over Britain now are proud to be home bakers in the unshowy tradition of the cottage or farmhouse kitchen, to make regional cakes without feeling the need to explain them away as 'folk' or 'bucolic', or to aspire to the gâteaux and tortes of the Grande Café. The food industry has given the home baking classes something else to define themselves against: a Mr Kipling Battenberg laden with sugar and laced with preservatives, emulsifiers, acidity regulators and added colours or a tooth-aching Fondant Fancy sitting on a doily for tea-time (see Doilies, Napkins and Tablecloths, page 243). Or the processed fat and sugar in Greggs' doughnuts, yum-yums, rocky road or triple chocolate muffins. These sometimes make it into middle-class shopping baskets as an occasional guilty pleasure. In Yorkshire cricket, which proudly draws together players, families and fans from all social backgrounds, the home-made cake of the traditional tea supplied by the home team has sometimes morphed into Mr Kipling's Fondant Fancies. These, a cricketer tells me, are welcomed wholeheartedly by urban and rural working and lower-middle classes, and with ironic pleasure by the middle classes as a 'quaint' custom. The kids, of course, love them.

Children's hankering for the sugar hit of synthetic cakes (and sweets and biscuits) is treated differently across the social classes. Studies suggest that women with more status in their own families (because of their perceived background, their education or their income) were more confident about imposing healthier choices on their partners and children rather than putting the family's pleasure first and buying them the highly processed cakes and biscuits they might have chosen for themselves.[15] They are more likely to bake at home with their kids, partly for fun and to teach them baking skills, but also in part to control the amount and kinds of sugars and fats the family consumes.

Home bakers and local bakeries are often the most active of food historians, recreating recipes from across the British Isles. There is a regional and historical democracy in the home kitchen which I find particularly pleasing; some basic ingredients and a good cookbook (or an online search), and I can taste my way into the cottage and farmhouse kitchens of any county or era that I choose. Here, the attempts to assert ownership over various recipes – gingerbread or Sally Lunns, or the trademarking of the traditional fat rascal which means only one chain of tea shops can now sell it – have no sway.

For reasons best known to pâtissiers, the joys of British cakes do not miniaturize well, or perhaps it is that curd tarts, muffins and tea breads are considered too lowly to trouble the tiered plates of the fanciest of afternoon teas. The exception, of course, is the scone. These plain and doughty little characters have rubbed shoulders with so many petits fours, éclairs and macarons that the French have admitted them to their godly pantheon of pâtisserie and offer 'Parisian scones' at exclusive *salons de thé* in Paris and London. Perhaps in a few years, YouGov polls will be working out our social background according to whether we pronounce 'scone' with a French accent.

MRS MACNAB'S SCONES

After a lifetime of greed-fuelled trial and error, this is the best recipe for scones I know. They are so light that you'll need to weigh them down with jam and cream to ensure they don't blow away. Mrs MacNab was a Scottish farmer's wife living near Balmoral Castle. Distinguished royal guests such as King Frederick of Prussia would, understandably, insist on going over to have tea with her, early proof of the scone's adaptable social skills.[16]

MODERN RECIPE

250g plain flour
I level teaspoon bicarbonate of soda
I level teaspoon cream of tartar
Generous pinch of salt
50g butter
I dessertspoon caster sugar
Approx. 200ml buttermilk (or I egg whisked into 150ml
buttermilk). Note – the buttermilk is acidic, which enables you
to use less raising agent, which can give an unpleasant metallic
taste. If you can't find buttermilk, use ordinary milk with a
squeeze of lemon juice.

1. Preheat the oven to Gas Mark 6/200°C.
2. Mix together the flour, raising agents and salt. Rub in the butter. Stir the caster sugar through the mixture.
3. Bind with buttermilk until you have a dough which comes together but is not sticky. Do not knead or roll it out.
4. Turn it onto a floured board and lightly pat it down until it is about 4cm thick. Cut into rounds 4 or 5cm across, pulling the leftovers together to use up all the dough, but handle it as little as possible.
5. Bake in the oven for 8–12 minutes until they are golden brown on the top.

ORIGINAL RECIPE: MRS MACNAB'S SCONES (ABERDEENSHIRE)

From *The Scots Kitchen: Its Lore and Recipes* by F. Marian McNeill (1929)

◆

*Flour ◆ butter ◆ salt ◆ bicarbonate of soda
cream of tartar ◆ egg ◆ buttermilk*

Mix thoroughly a pound of flour, a teaspoonful of salt, a small teaspoonful of bicarbonate of soda and two small teaspoonfuls of cream of tartar. Rub in two ounces of butter. Stir in gradually a beaten egg and half a pint of buttermilk. Turn out the dough on a floured board, flour the top, and knead with the hand as little as possible. Cut off pieces of dough and flatten them with the knuckles, but do not roll out at all. Prick with a fork and cut into quarters. Bake in a pretty quick oven for from ten to fifteen minutes.

Conclusion

Though we are many we are one body, because we all share in one
bread.

The Book of Common Prayer

WHEN I AM looking for old recipes to recreate, perhaps to
illustrate a culinary or historical point, or just for fun,
I usually find myself ending up in the 'long eighteenth
century' (1688–1815), the period from the Glorious Revolution
of 1688 to the Battle of Waterloo in 1815. It is then that the
British palate was laid down; the roast meat, fish with sauces,
vegetable soups, stews, fruit pies, jellies, sweet and savoury
puddings, family cakes and yeast buns from that period are
familiar. Usually it is easy to look at a recipe and translate it
into something recognizably modern. True, it is very meaty, as
British food has been throughout the centuries, but there are
many vegetable gems to be had, too, such as Hannah Glasse's
whole stuffed cabbage, or Maria Rundell's herb pie. Most people
expected their meat and dairy, grains, fruit and vegetables to
come from somewhere close by; people of all classes grew and
reared it themselves and might only depend on their grocer for
dried goods such as tea, coffee, flour and dried fruit and exotics
such as lemons. They knew what was in it, how it had been
grown, how it had lived and died.

The national taste had moved on from the lavish spice
combinations of medieval and Tudor times (which can be nice,
it's true), the conspicuous consumption – the peacocks and boars'
heads – with which a very small and very powerful stratum of

society used to clash antlers and show off to each other. The century was feeling a way to what the French would call a bourgeois cuisine; but it was an open, expansive and quite flexible one. Old recipes can be frustratingly vague in terms of quantities and cooking time, but that also made them very adaptable to the equipment, ingredients and level of the cook's skill. Most recipe compilers suggested 'and another way...' of making an apple tart or oatmeal pudding or a chine of beef; there was no real 'right' or 'wrong'.

It wasn't a halcyon time; it was a century of deep division and injustice as well as enlightenment. There was human slavery, cruelty to animals, periods of economic depression and unemployment and, particularly at the end of the century, widespread famines in which tens of thousands of people on low and perilous incomes went hungry. Social mobility, particularly for women, could only happen if you married well. There might have been general agreement about what the best food was, but for the majority of families it was an aspiration never to be realized. There was a commonly held idea of what 'good food' was, though, and, in theory, the raising of incomes over the succeeding period of industrialization could have brought it to a wider range of people.

But something happened to change the idea of good food in the Victorian period that followed. It wasn't simply the impact of the Industrial Revolution and the difficulty of bringing fresh, unadulterated produce to smoky, urban centres. Even as the income of the country as a whole was rising, the left-behind scrabbled around in urban slums for whatever they could afford or find. Everybody more fortunate than this mass of the population wanted to be on the way up, to distance themselves from the *lower orders*, and join the *higher ranks*. It was an unsettling form of social mobility, and one of the strongest – and in some ways strangest – marks of it was the growing preoccupation with French food, or, rather, a British conception of French gastronomy. Many French attitudes to food, matching sauces to meat, being clever with techniques, an abhorrence of waste, had informed and inspired (and sometimes infuriated) professional cooks throughout the previous century. In Queen Victoria's reign, particularly the latter decades, a certain type of French food, haute cuisine, became not just an enthusiasm but a mania, leaping off the pages of cookbooks and spreading throughout the kitchens of the urban basement, the suburban villa, the country house. Hosts with even quite limited resources were tantalized by 'La Blanquette aux Concombres', 'Les Peuillantines de Pommes', or 'Les Poulardes trûffées à la sauce Périgueux', as they were served to Her Majesty by her then cook, Charles Elmé Francatelli.[1] Or, if the menu of a royal banquet was too much, then the most everyday of ingredients could be glorified by the right treatment and the right name: 'pig's feet, à la Périgord',[2] or 'black-puddings, à l'anglaise'.[3] It was an obsession we didn't shake off for some time; in the 1930s Bertie Wooster was still looking forward to a menu of 'Le Bird of some kind' and 'Le Ice Cream'.[4] Good English food was, people thought, just *there* and didn't need much attention.

French grand cuisine had moved away from the relaxed 'and another way' instructions of earlier recipe books. The great nineteenth-century chefs Marie-Antoine Carême and Auguste Escoffier are said to have codified French haute cuisine, breaking the process down into a simpler series of procedures, preferably with a number of highly trained assistant chefs to execute them. There was a 'right' and 'wrong' way to do things, which didn't make it a remotely suitable way of cooking for any but the best trained of chefs and the best equipped of households. But for a century or so, that is where the energy and focus in cooking at home and in restaurants lay, and what taste-makers and influencers valued. Nobody in Britain was celebrating peasant dishes of beans or peas, and the sensible approach to cheap cuts and available vegetables, by cooks such as Eliza Acton, was changed, by the century's end, to a fashion for shiny food, with aspic, glazes, confections, ices, moulds. If you couldn't afford to worry about status, an increasing number of commercial operations came on stream to fill the gap with sliced bread, margarine, potted meat, tinned milk. The focus changed from a question of how to produce a good dinner, to a question of how to serve a statement dinner. Many of the foods in this book, with no champions, became what you ate if you couldn't afford something better. That obsession with French cuisine perpetuated and normalized a gulf of inequality which rising incomes and living standards should have ironed out, and yet hasn't been closed to this day.

No food-lover could be oblivious to the lure of haute, bourgeois and peasant cuisines or fail to be aware of the debt we owe to their practitioners. We have, similarly, learnt estimable lessons from Indian, Italian, Chinese and many immigrant cuisines, and these have been particularly valuable in kickstarting a more democratic restaurant culture. The problem lay, not in the food itself, rather in our attitude to it. The quality of the food available to the majority of the population, already in the doldrums, was debased further by the post-war impetus to produce as much food as cheaply as possible. Government departments helped kill off regional specialities from local dairies and bakeries and it was common to deny that we had ever had a 'peasant' or even a 'British' cuisine. Some of our 'peasant' dishes such as pottage or pease pudding – or at least the taste for them – fell out of the mainstream or were treated as regional curiosities, and we became more likely to celebrate the rusticity of French cassoulet or open a tin of beans, baked in the Boston style. We are, rightly, proud to be a culinary 'melting pot', but in reaching for the exotic, the international, the new, we risk overlooking or undervaluing what is under our noses.

I'm writing this in the spring of 2020; we are in lockdown because of Covid-19. Our newspapers and social media feeds are full of talk of a renaissance in baking, of instructions for nurturing a starter to make sourdough bread, and our shop shelves are empty of flour and yeast. It brings to mind a crumb of food history which sounds counterintuitive to our contemporary sense of the North/ South divide. Up to the twentieth century, the most immoveable commitment to white, wheaten bread was among the agricultural workers in the South of England; in the North and in Scotland, workers and their families were far more ready to bake with the humble – sometimes despised – oats, and grow and eat potatoes, and were better fed as a result. During the 2020 pandemic, the Prime Minister of Sint Maarten (in the Dutch Caribbean) told her nation, 'If you don't have the bread you like in your house, eat crackers. Eat cereal. Eat oats.'[5] It is a hard lesson to learn. I *want* to make sourdough bread and send pictures to my friends, family and work colleagues; I'm a sourdough kind of person, not a crackers kind of person. But starting with the food that is easily available could help, not just during a pandemic, but to ease our vexed relationships with food and identity within our, still, omnipresent class structure.

When I started writing this book, I set out to explore how ideas of social class have been most influential and most damaging over a thousand years or so of history. Three common threads have emerged: the first is that we use food, and the manners and material culture surrounding it, to be exclusive; to say that this belongs to us but not to you. The result is that society has come to think that it is natural and inevitable that different social classes eat foods of significantly varying type and quality.

The second is that we have learnt to discount the idea that one of the characteristics of 'good food' is that it should be easily available to everybody.

We seem to ask the wrong questions about food; we want to consume it or abjure it as a way of saying something about us, our identity, our status. As centuries of food fights show, while we put too much focus on the wrong questions, there are plenty of businesses that are very happy to make money for themselves by selling food that does not feed people well; from the nineteenth-century bakers who put alum into flour to contemporary manu-facturers of highly synthetic food. The food of privilege in Britain is no longer French; it doesn't really have a name and it might be influenced by cooking from all over the world, but it shares particular characteristics – and adjectives – which have become part of the vocabulary of 'cultural capital': fresh, good, local, home-made, healthy, organic. You'll recognize the vocabulary, too, of the food of mass consumption: ultra-processed, industrial, pre-packaged, unhealthy, fast food, sliced white.

Perhaps we can only start narrowing the gap between these two positions if we start with different questions which take us, the consumers, out of the equation altogether and put the focus back on what we are consuming. Is it good food? It is not an easy question; the answers are enmeshed in other issues, involving the environment, the food system, food security, imports, farming. But it is possible to answer. And if it is good food, then is it – or can it be made – available to as many people as possible? To all of us? It's an idea inherent in our language: 'companionship' means sharing bread. Eating together is what bonds us. If we wish to be a society with genuinely equal opportunity, there should be equality about what is on our plates.

The third thread to emerge is that, not surprisingly in a history of the last thousand years, there has been a lot of change and an acceleration in the pace of change. There have been practical considerations, such as discoveries from around the globe, agricultural revolutions, technological innovations. Cooks and consumers have responded with new recipes, new ways of dining, new attitudes. It isn't impossible that we can change the way we systematize and think about food, so that it becomes axiomatic that we have the same chance of nourishment and enjoyment. I hope that some future reader will take this book off a dusty shelf, read the title and the subtitle, and scoff at it for the antiquated and superannuated concept that it has become.

Bibliography

Primary Sources

Acton, Eliza, *The English Bread Book for Domestic Use*. London, Longmans & Co., 1857

— *Modern Cookery in all its Branches* (later retitled *Modern Cookery for Private Families*). London, Longman, Brown, Green & Longmans, 1845

Aldrovandi, Ulisse, *Aldrovandi on Chickens: The Ornithology of Ulisse Aldrovandi*. 1600. Tr. L.R. Lind. Norman, University of Oklahoma Press, 1963

Allen, Darina, *Forgotten Skills of Cooking*. London, Kyle Books, 2009

Amis, Kingsley, *Everyday Drinking: The Distilled Kingsley Amis*. London, Bloomsbury, 2008

Anonymous, *The Boke of Kervynge*. London, printed by Wynkyn de Worde, 1513

Anonymous, *The Court and Kitchen of Elizabeth, Commonly Called Joan Cromwel*. London, printed by Tho. Milbourn, for Randal Taylor, 1664

Anonymous, *The Epicure's Almanack*. London, Longman's & Co., 1815

Anonymous, *An Essay on Modern Luxuries, Tea, Sugar, White Bread and Butter, etc.* Salisbury, 1777

Anonymous, *Etiquette for Ladies*. London, Ward Lock & Co., n.d.

Anonymous, *The Good Huswife's Handmaide for the Kitchin*. Richard Jones, 1594

Anonymous, *The Jewish Manual, Edited by a Lady*, London, T. & W. Boone, 1846

Anonymous, *Le Ménagier de Paris (The Goodman of Paris)*. c.1392. Ed. Eileen Power. London, G. Routledge & Sons, 1928

Anonymous, *A Proper New Booke of Cookery*. London, 1545

Anonymous, *Sir Gawain and the Green Knight*. C.late 14th century. Tr. Simon Armitage. London, Faber & Faber, 2007

Appert, Louis, *The Art of Preserving*. France, 1810. London, printed for Black, Parry and Kingsbury, booksellers to the Honourable East India Company, 1811

Arnot, Sandford, *Indian Cookery*. London, London Oriental Institution, 1831

Artusi, Pellegrino, *Science in the Kitchen and the Art of Eating Well*. 1891. Tr. Murtha Baca and Stephen Sartarelli. Toronto, University of Toronto Press, 2003

Austen, Jane, *Emma*. London, Nelson, 1816; London, Macdonald, 1974

— *Mansfield Park*. London, printed for T. Egerton, 1814; London, Macdonald, 1974

— *Northanger Abbey*. London, John Murray, 1818; London, Macdonald, 1974

— *Pride and Prejudice*. London, T. Egerton, 1813; London, Macdonald, 1974

— *The Watsons*. Begun 1805; Oxford, Oxford University Press, 1990

— *Jane Austen's Letters to Her Sisters and Others*. Ed. R.W. Chapman. Oxford, Oxford University Press, 1932, reprinted 1979

Austin, Thomas, ed., *Two Fifteenth-century Cookbooks*. London, N. Trübner & Co., 1888

Austen-Leigh, J.E., *A Memoir of Jane Austen, and Other Family Recollections*. London, Richard Bentley & Son, 1871

Austen-Leigh, William and Richard Arthur Austen-Leigh, *Jane Austen, Her Life and Letters: A Family Record*. London, Smith, Elder & Co., 1913

A.W., *A Booke of Cookerie*. London, printed by John Allde, 1584

Beeton, Isabella, *Book of Household Management*. London, S.O. Beeton, 1861

Betjeman, John, 'How to Get On in Society' in *A Few Late Chrysanthemums*. London, John Murray, 1954

Borrow, George, *Wild Wales: Its People, Language, and Scenery*, Volume III. London, John Murray, 1862

Boswell, James, *The Life of Samuel Johnson*. London, 1791; London, Penguin Books, 1986

Boxer, Arabella, *Arabella Boxer's Book of English Food: A Rediscovery of British Food from Before the War*. London, Hodder & Stoughton, 1991

Bradley, R., *The Country Housewife and Lady's Director*. London, Woodman & Lyon, 1727

Breton, Nicholas, *Fantasticks*. London, Printed by Miles Flesher for Francis Williams, 1626

Brillat-Savarin, Jean-Anthelme, *The Physiology of Taste*. 1825. Tr. Anne Drayton. Published as *The Philosopher in the Kitchen*. Harmondsworth, Penguin Books, 1970

Brontë, Charlotte, *Jane Eyre*. London, Smith, Elder & Co., 1847; London, Penguin Books, 2006

— *Shirley*. London, Smith, Elder & Co., 1849; Oxford, Oxford University Press, 1981

Buchan, William, *Observations Concerning the Diet of the Common People*. London, printed for A. Strahan, T. Cadell jun. and W. Davies; and J. Balfour and W. Creech, Edinburgh, 1797

Buckland, Anne Walbank, *Our Viands: Whence They Come and How They Are Cooked*. London, Ward & Downey, 1893

Buonaiuti, B. Serafino, *Italian Scenery; Representing the Manners, Customs, and Amusements of the Different States of Italy*. London, Edward Orme, 1806

Butler, Charles, *The Feminine Monarchie*. London, printed by John Haviland for Roger Jackson, 1623

Carlyle, Jane, and Thomas Carlyle, *Letters*. http://carlylelettersdukeupress.edu

Carlyle, Jane, *I Too Am Here: Selections from the Letters of Jane Welsh Carlyle*. Eds Alan and Mary McQueen Simpson. Cambridge, Cambridge University Press, 1997

Cassell's Dictionary of Cookery. London, Cassell, Petter & Galpin, [1875, 1876]

Chaucer, Geoffrey, *The Canterbury Tales*. 1387–1400. London, Penguin, 2005.

Chélus, D. de, *The Natural History of Chocolate*. Tr. Richard Brookes. London, J. Roberts, 1724

Chesterfield, Lord Philip Dormer Stanhope, *Letters to His Son*. First published as *Principles of politeness, and of knowing the world; by the late Lord Chesterfield. Methodised and digested under distinct heads, with additions, by the Reverend Dr. John Trusler: containing Every Instruction necessary to complete the Gentleman and Man of Fashion, to teach him a Knowledge of Life, and make him well received in all Companies. For the improvement of youth; Yet not beneath the Attention of any*. London, John Bell, and York, C. Etherington, 1775

Cibber, Colley, *The Lady's Last Stake; or, the Wife's Resentment*. London, 1732

Cobbett, William, *Cottage Economy*. London, C. Clement, 1822; Cambridge, Cambridge University Press, 2009

— *Rural Rides*. London, 1830; London, Penguin Books, 2001

Cockburn, Henry, *Memorials of His Time*. Edinburgh, Black, 1856

Coles, William, *Adam in Eden or Natures Paradise*. London, printed by J. Streater for Nathaniel Brooke, 1657

Collister, Linda, *The Great British Book of Baking*. London, Michael Joseph, 2010

Conan Doyle, Arthur, 'The Adventure of the Naval Treaty', *The Complete Sherlock Holmes*. London, Vintage, 2009

Cooper, Jilly, *How to Survive Christmas*. London, Methuen 1986

Coren, Giles, *How to Eat Out*. London, Hodder & Stoughton, 2012

Coryat, Thomas, *Coryat's Crudities, Hastily Gobbled Up in Five Months' Travels in France etc.* Printed by William Stansby for the author, 1611

Creevey, Thomas, *The Creevey Papers: a selection from the correspondence and diaries of the late Thomas Creevey, M.P. born 1768–died 1838*. Ed. Sir Herbert Maxwell. London, John Murray, 1903

Culpeper, Nicholas, *The English Physitian, or, an Astrologo-physical discourse of the vulgar herbs of this nation. Being a compleat method of physick, whereby a man may preserve his body in health; or cure himself, being sick, etc.* London, printed by Peter Cole, 1652

Curye on Inglysch: English Culinary Manuscripts of the Fourteenth Century (including the 'Forme of cury'). Eds Constance B. Hieatt and Sharon Butler. London, published for the Early English Text Society by Oxford University Press, 1985

Dahl, Roald, *Charlie and the Chocolate Factory*. London, Allen & Unwin, 1967; London, Penguin Books, 2016

Dallas, E.S., *Kettner's Book of the Table: A Manual of Cookery*. London, Dulan & Co., 1877

Dampier, William, *A New Voyage Around the World*. London, printed for James Knapton, 1697. London, Penguin Books, 2020

David, Elizabeth, *English Bread and Yeast Cookery*. London, Allen Lane, 1977; Harmondsworth, Penguin Books, 1979

— *French Country Cooking*. John Lehmann, 1951; London, Penguin Books, 2011

— *Italian Food*. London, Macdonald, 1954; London, Penguin Books, 2011

— *An Omelette and a Glass of Wine*. Harmondsworth, Penguin Books, 1986

— *Spices, Salts and Aromatics in the English Kitchen*. London, Penguin Books, 1970; London, Grub Street, 2017

Day, Charles William, Writing as Ἀγωγός (Agogos), *Hints on Etiquette and the Usages of Society, with a glance at bad habits*. London, printed for the Booksellers, [1834]

Debrett's Handbook: British Style, Correct Form, Modern Manners. Ed. Elizabeth Wyse. London, Debrett's, 2014

Dekker, Thomas, *The Honest Whore, Part II*. 1630

Defoe, Daniel, *A Brief Case of the Distillers, and of the Distilling Trade in England, shewing how far it is the interest of England to encourage the said trade… Humbly recommended to the Lords and Commons of Great Britain, in the present parliament assembled*. London, T. Warner, 1726.

— *A Tour Through the Whole Island of Great Britain*. London, printed by G. Strahan, 1724–27

— [as Andrew Moreton, Esq.] *Second Thoughts are Best: or, A Further Improvement of a Late Scheme to Prevent Street Robberies*. London, printed for W. Meadows by J. Roberts, 1729

Díaz del Castillo, Bernal, *The Conquest of New Spain*, translated by J.M. Cohen. Harmondsworth, Penguin, 1963

Dickens, Charles, *American Notes*. London, Chapman & Hall, 1842; London, Penguin Books, 2000

— *Bleak House*. London, Chapman & Hall, 1853; Harmondsworth, Penguin Books, 1985

— *The Chimes*. London, Chapman & Hall, 1844; reprinted in *Christmas Books*, London, Heron Books, 1970

— *A Christmas Carol*. London, Chapman & Hall, 1843; reprinted as *A Christmas Carol and Other Christmas Writings*, London, Penguin Books, 2003

— *Dombey and Son*. London, Chapman & Hall, 1844–6; London, Penguin Books, 2002

— *Great Expectations*. London, Chapman & Hall, 1860–61; London, Penguin Books, 1996

— *Martin Chuzzlewit*. London, Chapman & Hall, 1843–4; London, Penguin Books, 1999

— *The Old Curiosity Shop*. London, Chapman & Hall, 1841; Oxford, Oxford University Press, 2008

— *Our Mutual Friend*. London, Chapman & Hall, 1865; London, Penguin Books, 1997

— *The Pickwick Papers*. London, Chapman & Hall, 1836–7; London, Penguin Books, 2003

— *Sketches by 'Boz'*. London, Chapman & Hall, 1839; London, Heron Books, 1970

— *The Uncommercial Traveller*. London, Chapman & Hall, 1860; Oxford, Oxford University Press, 2015

Digby, Sir Kenelm, *The Closet of Sir Kenelm Digby Opened*. 1669. Eds Jane Stevenson and Peter Davidson. Totnes, Prospect Books, 2010

Disraeli, Benjamin, *Sybil, or The Two Nations*. London, Henry Colburn, 1845; Oxford, Oxford University Press, 2017

Dodd, George, *The Food of London*. London, Longman, Brown, Green, and Longmans, 1856

Dods, Margaret, *The Cook and Housewife's Manual*. Edinburgh, Oliver & Boyd, 1829; London, Rosters, 1988

Dumas, Alexandre, *Dumas on Food: Selections from Le Grand Dictionnaire de Cuisine*. Trs /eds Alan and Jane Davidson. London, Michael Joseph, 1978

Duncan, Daniel, *Wholesome advice against the abuse of hot liquors particularly of coffee, chocolate, tea, brandy and strong-waters. With directions to know what constitutions they suit; done out of the French*. London, H. Rhodes, 1706

Eales, Mary, *Mrs Mary Eales's Receipts, Confectioner to her late majesty Queen Anne*. London, 1718

Eden, Sir Frederick Morton, *The State of the Poor, or, An history of the labouring classes in England*. London, printed by J. Davis, 1797

Edlin, Abraham, *A Treatise on the Art of Bread-Making*. London, 1805; reprinted Totnes, Prospect Books, 2004

Eliot, George, *Essays and Leaves from a Notebook*. Edinburgh, Blackwood, 1885

Ellis, William, *The Country Housewife's Family Companion*. London and Salisbury, 1750; Totnes, Prospect Books, 2000

Elyot, Thomas, *The Castel of Helth gathered and made by Syr Thomas Elyot Knyghte, out of the chiefe Authors of Physyke, wherby every manne may knowe the state of his owne body, the preservation of helth, and how to instructe welle his physytion in syckenes that he be not deceyved*. London, 1539

Escoffier, Auguste, *A Guide to Modern Cookery*. London, William Heinemann, 1907

Evans, George Ewart, *Ask the Fellows Who Cut the Hay*. London, Faber & Faber, 1956, 1965

Evelyn, John, *Acetaria: A Discourse of Sallets*. London, printed for B. Tooke, 1699; Totnes, Prospect Books, 1996

— *John Evelyn, cook: the manuscript receipt book of John Evelyn*. Ed. Christopher Driver. Totnes, Prospect Books, 1997

— *Sylva, or A discourse of forest-trees, and the propagation of timber in His Majesties dominions. By J. E. Esq; As it was deliver'd in the Royal Society the XVth of October, MDCLXII... To which is annexed Pomona; or, an appendix concerning fruit-trees in relation to cider*. London, printed by J. Martyn and J. Allestry, printers to the Royal Society, 1664

Farley, John, *The London Art of Cookery*. London, printed for J. Fielding, 1783

Fearnley-Whittingstall, Hugh, *A Cook on the Wild Side*. London, Boxtree, 1997

— *The River Cottage Meat Book*. London, Hodder & Stoughton, 2004

Fiennes, Celia, *Through England on a Side Saddle*. London, Field & Tuer, 1888

Fisher, M.F.K., *Consider the Oyster*. New York, Duell, Sloan & Pearce, [1941]

Fletcher, John, *The Queen of Corinth*. c.1616

The Forme of Cury, a roll of ancient English Cookery, compiled, about A.D. 1390, by the Master-Cooks of King Richard II. Ed. Samuel Pegge. London, printed by J. Nichols, 1780

Forster, E.M., *A Room with a View*. London, Edward Arnold, 1908; Harmondsworth, Penguin Books, 1986

Francatelli, Charles Elmé, *A Plain Cookery Book for the Working Classes*. 1852; Stroud, History Press, 2010

Freeman, Laura, *The Reading Cure: How Books Restored My Appetite*. London, Weidenfeld & Nicholson, 2018

Furnivall, Frederick J., ed., *Early English Meals and Manners: John Russell's Boke of Nurture, Wynkyn de Worde's Boke of Keruynge, The Boke of Curtasye, R. Weste's Booke of Demeanor, Seager's Schoole of Vertue, The Babees Book, Aristotle's ABC, Urbanitatis, Stans Puer ad Mensam, The Lytylle Childrenes Lytil Boke, For to serve a Lord, Old Symon, The Birched School-Boy, &c. &c., with some forewords on education in early England*. London, 1868

G.V., *Dinners and Dinner Parties, or the Absurdities of Artificial Life*. London, Chapman & Hall, 1862

Gascoigne, George, *The Noble Art of Venerie or Hunting, Wherein is handled and set out the vertues, nature, and properties of fifteene sundry chaces, together with the order and manner how to hunt and kill every one of them*. London, printed by Thomas Purfoot, 1611

Gaskell, Elizabeth, *Cranford*. London, Chapman & Hall, 1853; Ware, Wordsworth Editions, 1993

Gerard, John, *The Herball, or Generall Historie of Plantes*. London, John Norton, 1597

Gill, A.A., *Table Talk: Sweet and Sour, Salt and Bitter*. London, Weidenfeld & Nicolson, 2008

Glanville, Philippa, and Hilary Young, eds, *Elegant Eating: Four Hundred Years of Dining in Style*. London, V&A Publications, 2002

Glasse, Hannah, *The Art of Cookery Made Plain and Easy*. London, printed for the author, 1747

— *The Compleat Confectioner: or The whole art of confectionary made plain and easy, etc*. London, J. Cooke, [c.1765]

Grahame, Kenneth, *The Wind in the Willows*. London, 1908

Gray, Patience and Primrose Boyd, *Plat du Jour*. Penguin 1957. London, Persephone Books, 2006.

Grigson, Jane, *The Mushroom Feast*. London, Michael Joseph, 1975

— *Vegetable Book*. London, Michael Joseph, 1978

Grosseteste, Robert, *Rules for Countess of Lincoln, in Walter of Henley's Husbandry, together with an anonymous Husbandry, Seneschaucie, and Robert Grosseteste's Rules*. Tr./ ed. Elizabeth Lamond. London, Longman's and Co., 1890

Gunter, William, *The Confectioner's Oracle, containing receipts for desserts on the most economical plan for families*. London, Alfred Miller, 1830

Hales, Stephen, *A friendly admonition to the drinkers of gin, brandy, and other distilled spirituous liquors*. London, printed for B. Dod, Bookseller to the Society for Promoting Christian Knowledge, 1751

Hansard, HC Deb. 29 April 1874 vol. 218 col. 1387

— HC Deb. 28 November 1946 vol. 430 col. 1800

— HC Deb. 10 November 1947 vol. 444 col. 156

Hanway, Jonas, *Essay on Tea* in *A journal of eight days journey from Portsmouth to Kingston upon Thames... in a series of sixty-four letters: addressed to two ladies of the partie. To which is added, An essay on tea... With several political reflections; and thoughts on public love... By a gentleman of the partie [i.e. Jonas Hanway]*. London, printed by H. Woodfall, 1756

Hartley, Dorothy, *Food in England*. London, Macdonald, 1954

Heath, Ambrose, *Good Dishes from Tinned Foods*. 1939

Herrick, Robert, 'To Dianeme, A Ceremonie in Glocester', *Hesperides*. London, printed for John Williams and Francis Eglesfield, 1648

Hill, John, ed., *Eden, or a compleat body of gardening* (from the papers of Mr Hale). London, T. Osborne, 1757

Hogarth, William [?], *A Dissertation on Mr Hogarth's Six Prints lately publish'd, viz. Gin-Lane, Beer-Street, and the Four Stages of Cruelty... Being a proper key for the right apprehension of the author's meaning in those designs*. London, B. Dickinson, 1751

Holland, Lady Saba, *A Memoir of the Reverend Sydney Smith, by his daughter Lady Holland*. London, 1855

Hone, William, *The Everyday Book*. London, William Tegg and Co., 1826

Humphrey, Mrs C.E., *Manners for Men*. London, Ward, Lock & Co., [1897]

Jaffrey, Madhur, *An Invitation to Indian Cooking*. London, Jonathan Cape, 1976

Irving, Washington, *Bracebridge Hall*. London, John Murray, 1822; London, MacMillan & Co, 1877

— 'Christmas' in *The Sketch-Book of Geoffrey Crayon, Gent*. New York, 1819–20. Reissued as *Old Christmas*, London and Glasgow, Collins Clear Type Press, 1907

James, Henry, *The Portrait of a Lady*. London, Macmillan, 1881; London, Penguin Books, 1988

Jarrin, G.A., *The Italian Confectioner*. London, John Harding, 1820

Jekyll, Agnes, *Kitchen Essays*. London, Thomas Nelson & Sons, 1922; London, Persephone Books, 2001

Jerome, Jerome K., *Three Men in a Boat*. Bristol, 1889; Harmondsworth, Penguin Books, 1985

Jonson, Ben, *The Devil Is an Ass*. 1616

Keats, John, *Complete Poems*. Harmondsworth, Penguin, 1973.

Kingsford, Anna, *The Perfect Way in Diet: A Treatise Advocating a Return to the Natural and Ancient Food of Our Race*. London, 1881

Kitchiner, William, *Apicius Redivivus; or, The Cook's Oracle*. London, printed for Samuel Bagster by J. Moyes, 1817

Kropotkin, Peter, *The Conquest of Bread*. Paris, 1892; London, Penguin Classics, 2013

La Chappelle, Vincent, *The Modern Cook By Mr. Vincent La Chapelle, Chief Cook to the Right Honourable the Earl of Chesterfield*. London, 1733

La Rochefoucauld, Françoise de, *A Frenchman in England*. 1784. Cambridge, Cambridge University Press, 1933

Lamb, Charles, *Elia. Essays which have appeared under that signature in the London Magazine*. London, 1823

Langland, William, *Piers Plowman*. [1370?]

Larousse Gastronomique, with the assistance of the gastronomic committee president Joël Robuchon. Paris, Larousse, 2007; London, Hamlyn, 2009

Lawson, Nigella, *How to Eat: The Pleasures and Principles of Good Food*. London, Chatto & Windus, 1998

Leyel, Mrs C.F. (Hilda), *The Gentle Art of Cookery*. London, Chatto & Windus, 1929; London, Quadrille, 2011

Listowel, Judith, *The Modern Hostess*. London, Odhams Press Ltd, 1961

Mabey, Richard, *Food for Free*. London, Collins, 1972; London, HarperCollins, 2012

Mandeville, Bernard, 'The Evils of Gin' in *The Fable of the Bees: or, Private vices publick benefits. Containing several discourses, to demonstrate that human frailties… may be turn'd to the advantage of the Civil Society, etc.* London, printed for J. Roberts, 1714

Markham, Gervase, *The English Housewife, Containing the inward and outward virtues which ought to be in a complete woman*. 1615. Ed. Michael R. Best. Montreal, McGill-Queen's University Press, 1986

Marshall, Mrs A.B., *The Book of Ices, Including cream and water ices, sorbets, mousses, iced soufflés, and various iced dishes, with names in French and English*. London, Robert Hayes, 1898

— *Fancy Ices*. London, Marshall's School of Cookery, 1894

— *Mrs A.B. Marshall's Cookery Book*. London, Marshall's School of Cookery, [c.1887]

Mars-Jones, Adam, *Kid Gloves: A Voyage Round My Father*. London, Particular Books, 2015

Martin, Edith, *Cornish Recipes, ancient and modern*. Truro, Cornish Federation of Women's Institutes, 1929

Marvell, Andrew, 'To his Worthy Friend Doctor Witty Upon his Translation of The Popular Errors'. 1650

Massialot, François, *The Court and Country Cook: giving new and plain directions how to order all manner of entertainments… Together with New instructions for confecioners… And, how to prepare several sort of liquors. Translated by JK*. London, A. & J. Churchill; M. Gillyflower, 1702

Mauduit, Vicomte de, *They Can't Ration These*. London, Michael Joseph, 1940; London, Persephone Books, 2004

May, Robert, *The Accomplisht Cook or the Art and Mystery of Cookery*. London, printed by R.W. for Nath. Brooke, 1660; Totnes, Prospect Books, 2012

Mayhew, Henry, *London Labour and the London Poor*, 4 volumes. London, 1851–61

McGee, Harold, *On Food and Cooking: An Encyclopedia of Kitchen Science, History and Culture*. London, Hodder & Stoughton, 2004

A Member of the Aristocracy, *Manners and Tone of Good Society: or, solecisms to be avoided*. London, Frederick Warne and Co., 1879

Menon, *La Cuisinière bourgeoise*. Paris, 1746

Mikes, George, *How to Be an Alien*. London, André Deutsch, 1946; reprinted in *How to Be a Brit*, London, Penguin Books, 2015

Ministry of Information, *Rationing of Food in Great Britain*. [1944?/1945?]

Misson, Henri, *M. Misson's Memoirs and Observations in His Travels over England*. London, 1719

Mitford, Nancy, *Pigeon Pie*. London, Hamish Hamilton, 1940; reprinted in *The Penguin Complete Novels of Nancy Mitford*, London, Penguin, 2011

— ed., *Noblesse Oblige: An Enquiry into the Identifiable Characteristics of the English Aristocracy*. London, Hamish Hamilton, 1956; Harmondsworth, Penguin, 1959

Moran, Mollie, *Aprons and Silver Spoons: The Heartwarming Memoirs of a 1930s Kitchen Maid*. London, Penguin, 2013

Moryson, Fynes, *An Itinerary: containing ten yeeres travell through... twelve dominions*. 1617. Glasgow, James Maclehose & Sons, 1907

Moubray, Bonington, *A Practical Treatise on Breeding, Rearing, and Fattening All Kinds of Domestic Poultry*. London, Sherwood, Neely & Jones, 1816

Moxon, Elizabeth, *English Housewifry Exemplified in above four hundred receits, never before printed; giving directions in most parts of cookery... With sculptures for the orderly placing the dishes*. Leeds, J. Lister, 1748

Muffet, Thomas, *Health's Improvement: or, rules comprising and discovering the nature, method, and manner of preparing all sorts of food used in this nation*. London, printed by Thomas Newcomb for Samuel Thomson, 1655

Napier, Mrs Alexander, ed., *A Noble Boke off Cookry ffor a prynce houssolde or eny other stately houssolde*. London, Elliot Stock, 1882

Newnham-Davis, Lieut. Col., *The Gourmet's Guide to London*. London, Grant Richards, 1914

Nicholson, George, *On Food*. Poughnill, 1803

Ninety Nine homely and delicious ways of preparing and serving U.C.P. Tripe and Cowheels. Manchester, United Cattle Products, 1924

Nott, John, *The Cook and Confectioner's Dictionary: Or the Accomplish'd Housewife's Companion*. London, C. Rivington, 1723

Nutt, Frederick, *The Complete Confectioner, or, The whole art of confectionary, made easy; with receipts for liqueures, home-made wines, &c., The result of many years experience with the celebrated Negri*. London, printed by J. Matthews, 1789

O'Callaghan, R.E., *The Best Diet for a Working Man. With month's dietary*. London, London Vegetarian Society, 1889

Orwell, George, *Down and Out in Paris and London*. London, Victor Gollancz, 1933; London, Penguin Books, 2001

— *Nineteen Eighty Four*. London, Secker & Warburg, 1949; London, Penguin Books, 2013

— *The Road to Wigan Pier*. London, Victor Gollancz, 1937; London, Penguin Books, 2001

Panton, J.E., *From Kitchen to Garret. Hints for young householders*. London, Ward & Downey, 1888

Parmentier, Antoine Augustin, *Observations on such Nutritive Vegetables as may be substituted in the place of ordinary food in times of scarcity. Extracted from the French*. London, John Murray, 1783

Paulli, Simon, *A Treatise on tobacco, tea, coffee and chocolate*. London, printed for T. Osborne, 1746

Pepys, Samuel, *The Diaries of Samuel Pepys: A Selection*. London, Penguin Books, 2003

Pierpoint Johnson, C., *The Useful Plants of Great Britain*. London, 1862

Plat, Sir Hugh, *Delights for ladies, to adorne their persons, tables, closets, and distillatories. With, bewties, banquets, perfumes and waters*. London, printed by Peter Short, [1600?]

Pliny the Elder, *Natural History, Book X: The Natural History of Birds*. Trs/eds John Bostock and H.T. Riley. London, Henry G. Bohn, 1855–7

Pope, Alexander, *An Imitation of the Sixth Satire of the Second Book of Horace, the first part by Dr. Swift, the latter part and first added [by A. Pope.]*. First published London, 1738. Reprinted *Pope: Poetical Works*, Oxford, Oxford University Press, 1966, reprinted 1985

Postgate, Raymond, ed., *The Good Food Guide*. London, Cassell & Co., 1951–2

Powell, John, *The Assise of Bread*. London, John Windet, 1608

Pratt, Anne, *Flowering Plants, Grasses, Sedges and Ferns of Great Britain*. London, Frederick Warne & Co., 1891

Rabisha, William, *The Whole Body of Cookery Dissected*. London, printed for George Calvert and Ralph Simpson, 1682; facsimile edn, Totnes, Prospect Books, 2003

Rack, John, *The French Wine and Liquor Manufacturer: A Practical Guide and Receipt Book for the Liquor Merchant*. New York, Dick & Fitzgerald, 1863

Raffald, Elizabeth, *The Experienced English Housekeeper*. Manchester, J. Harrop, 1769; Lewes, Southover Press, 1997

Ridell, R., *Indian Domestic Economy and Receipt Book*. Bombay, Bombay Gazette Press, 1852

Ritson, Joseph, *An Essay on Abstinence from Animal Food as a Moral Duty*. London, R. Phillips, 1802

Roberts, Patricia Easterbrook, *Table Settings, Entertaining, and Etiquette*. London, Thames & Hudson, 1967

Roden, Claudia, *The Book of Jewish Food: An Odyssey from Samarkand and Vilna to the Present Day*. London, Viking, 1997; London, Penguin Books, 1999

— *Coffee: A Connoisseur's Companion*. London, Faber & Faber, 1977; London, Pavilion Books, 1994

— *Picnics and Outdoor Feasts*. London, Grub Street, 1981; reissued 2001

Ross, Alan S.C., 'Linguistic class-indicators in present-day English', *Neuphilologische Mitteilungen*, Volume 55, 1954, pp.113–49. Reprinted in Mitford, Nancy, ed., *Noblesse Oblige*

Rowntree's, *A Jelly for all Seasons*. 1978

Rundell, Mrs Maria Eliza, *A New System of Domestic Cookery*. London, John Murray, 1806; London, Persephone Books, 2009

Santiagoe, Daniel, *The Curry Cook's Assistant; or Curries, How to Make Them in England in Their Original Style*. 1887. 3rd edn: London, Kegan Paul, Trench, 1889

Shakespeare, William, *The Complete Works of William Shakespeare*. London, The Literary Press, 1923

Shaw, George Bernard, Letter 1948 [author to provide details when Brit Library reopens]

Shelley, Percy Bysshe, *Queen Mab: A Philosophical Poem: With Notes*. 1813

Short, Dr Thomas, *Discourses on Tea*. London, T. Longman, 1750

Simon, André L., *Soups, Salads, Souses: Wartime fare for the fastidious*. London, The Wine and Food Society, 1942

Sitwell, Osbert, 'Picnics and Pavilions' in *Sing High! Sing Low! A Book of Essays*. London, Macmillan, 1944

Slater, Nigel, *Eating for England: The Delights and Eccentricities of the British at Table*. London, Fourth Estate, 2007

Smith, Eliza, *The Compleat Housewife, or accomplish'd gentlewoman's companion*. London, J. Pemberton, c.1732

Smollett, Tobias, *The Expedition of Humphry Clinker*. London, printed for W. Johnston and B. Collins, 1771; Oxford, Oxford University Press, 1998

Society of Antiquaries of London, *Household Ordinances, A collection of ordinances and regulations for the government of the Royal Household, made in divers reigns, from King Edward III to King William and Queen Mary. Also receipts in ancient cookery*. London, 1790

Soyer, Alexis, *A Shilling Cookery Book for the People*. London, George Routledge, 1855

— *The Modern Housewife or Ménagère*. London, Simpkin, Marshall & Co., 1849

Spry, Constance, and Rosemary Hume, *The Constance Spry Cookery Book*. London, J.M. Dent & Sons, 1956

Stempel, John Lewis, *The Wild Life: A Year of Living on Wild Foods*. London, Doubleday, 2009

Sturgeon, Launcelot, *Essays, Moral, Philosophical and Stomachical, on the Important Science of Good-Living*. London, printed for G. and W.B. Whittaker, 1822

Swift, Jonathan, *Directions to Servants*. Dublin, George Faulkner, 1745

Taliesin, *The Book of Taliesin: Poems of Warfare and Praise in an Enchanted Britain*, translated by Gwyneth Lewis and Rowan Williams. London, Penguin Books, 2019

Thackeray, William Makepeace, *The Book of Snobs*. London, Bradbury and Evans, 1855

— *Vanity Fair: A Novel without a Hero*. London, Bradbury and Evans, 1848; London, Penguin Books, 2001

Thomas Ellis, Alice, *Fish, Flesh and Good Red Herring: A Gallimaufry*. London, Virago Press, 2004, 2006

Thompson, Flora, *Lark Rise to Candleford: A Trilogy*. London, Oxford University Press, 1945; London, Penguin, 2000

Tóibín, Colm, 'Christmas Pudding', *The New Yorker*, 22 November 2010

Toklas, Alice B, *The Alice B. Toklas Cook Book*. London, Michael Joseph, 1954; London, Serif, 1994

Trollope, Anthony, *Miss Mackenzie*. London, Chapman & Hall, 1865; Harmondsworth, Penguin Books, 1993

— *The Warden*. London, Longman, Brown, Green, and Longmans, 1855; Harmondsworth, Penguin Books, 1984

Troubridge, Lady Laura, *The Book of Etiquette*. London, Associated Bookbuyers' Co., 1931

— *Etiquette and Entertaining*. London, Amalgamated Press, 1939

Trusler, John, *The Honours of the Table, or Rules of Behaviour During Meals, with the Whole Art of Carving*. London, 1788

Tryon, Thomas, *Wisdom's Dictates; plus Bills of Fare*. London, Thomas Salisbury, 1691

Tusser, Thomas, *Five Hundred Points of Good Husbandry*. London, printed for the Company of Stationers, 1614

Ude, Louis Eustache, *The French Cook*. London, printed by Cox & Baylis, 1813; 10th edn: London, J. Ebers, 1829

Verral, William, *A Complete System of Cookery*. 1759. Republished as *The Cook's Paradise*. London, The Sylvan Press, 1948

Walker, Thomas, *Aristology, Or The Art of Dining*. London, G. Bell & Sons, 1881

Waugh, Evelyn, 'Open Letter to the Honble Mrs Peter Rodd (Nancy Mitford) on a Very Serious Subject', in Mitford, Nancy, ed., *Noblesse Oblige*

White, Arnold, *Efficiency and Empire*. London, Methuen & Co., 1901

White, Florence, *Good Things in England*. London, Jonathan Cape, 1932; London, Persephone Books, 2010

William of Malmesbury, *Deeds of the Kings of England/Gesta Regum Anglorum*. 2 volumes. Oxford, Clarendon Press, 1998, 1999

'W.M', *The compleat cook: expertly prescribing the most ready wayes, whether Italian, Spanish, or French, for dressing of flesh, and fish, ordering of sauces, or making of pastry*. London, printed by J.G. for Nath. Brook, 1665

Wodehouse, P.G., *The Code of the Woosters*. London, Herbert Jenkins, 1938; London, Penguin Books, 1985

— *Jeeves and the Feudal Spirit*. London, Herbert Jenkins, 1954; London, Arrow Books, 2008

— *Right Ho, Jeeves*. London, Herbert Jenkins, 1934; reprinted in *Life with Jeeves*, London, Penguin Books, 1983

Woodforde, James, *The Diary of a Country Parson 1758–1802*. 5 volumes. Ed. John Beresford. Oxford, Oxford University Press, 1924–31; Norwich, The Canterbury Press, 2003

Woolley, Hannah, *The Gentlewoman's Companion or A Guide to the Female Sex*. London, printed by A. Maxwell for Dorman Newman, 1673; Totnes, Prospect Books, 2001

— *The Queen-Like Closet or, Rich cabinet stored with all manner of rare receipts for preserving, candying & cookery*. London, Richard Lowndes, 1670

Wordsworth, Dorothy, and William Wordsworth, *Letters of William and Dorothy Wordsworth: The Middle Years, Volume 1, 1806–June 1811*. Ed. Ernest De Sélincourt. Oxford, Clarendon Press, 1937

'Wyvern', *Culinary Jottings for Madras, a treatise in thirty chapters on reformed cookery for Anglo-Indian exiles, based upon modern English, & continental principles, with twenty-five menus for little dinners worked out in detail*. Madras, Higginbotham & Co., 1878

Yates, Lucy, H., *The Country Housewife's Book: How to make the most of country produce and country fare*. London, Country Life, 1934; London, Persephone Books, 2008

Secondary Sources

Appelbaum, Robert, *Dishing it Out: In Search of the Restaurant Experience*. London, Reaktion Books, 2011

Ayto, *The Diner's Dictionary: Food and Drink from A to Z*. Oxford, Oxford University Press, 1993

Bannerjee, Abhijit, and Esther Duflo, *Poor Economics: Barefoot Hedge-fund Managers, DIY Doctors and the Surprising Truth about Life on Less Than $1 a Day*. London, Penguin Books, 2012

Barkas, Janet, *The Vegetable Passion: A History of the Vegetarian State of Mind*. London, Routledge and Kegan Paul, 1975

Barnett, Richard, *The Dedalus Book of Gin*. Sawtry, Dedalus, 2011

Battiscombe, Georgina, *English Picnics*. London, Harvill Press, 1949

Black, Maggie, *The Medieval Cookbook*. London, The British Museum Press, 1992, 1996

Black, Maggie, and Deirdre Le Faye, *The Jane Austen Cookbook*. London, The British Museum Press, 1995

Black, Maggie, *et al.*, *A Taste of History: 10,000 Years of Food in Britain*. London, The British Museum Press and English Heritage, 1993, 2003

Bloch-Dano, Evelyne, *Vegetables: A Biography*. Chicago, Chicago University Press, 2013

Bolitho, Hector, ed., *The Glorious Oyster*. London, Alfred A. Knopf, 1929; London, Sidgwick & Jackson, 1960

Boulton, William B., 'London's Tea Gardens' in *The Amusements of Old London*. London, John C. Nimmo, 1901

Bourdieu, Pierre, *Distinction: A Social Critique of the Judgement of Taste*. Tr. Richard Nice. London, Routledge and Kegan Paul, 1984

Braudel, Fernande, *Civilization and Capitalism 15th–18th Century: Volume I: The Structures of Everyday Life*. Tr. Miriam Kochan. London, Collins, 1981; Berkeley, University of California Press, 1992

Brears, Peter, *Jellies and their Moulds*. Totnes, Prospect Books, 2010

— *Traditional Food in Yorkshire*. Edinburgh, John Donald, 1987

Brown, Peter, ed., *British Cutlery: An Illustrated History of Design, Evolution and Use*. London, Philip Wilson, 2001

Burnett, David, and Helen Saberi, *The Road to Vindaloo: Curry Cooks and Curry Books*. Totnes, Prospect, 2008

Burnett, John, *England Eats Out: A Social History of Eating Out in England from 1830 to the Present*. Harlow, Longman, 2004

— *Plenty and Want: A Social History of Diet in England from 1815 to the Present Day*. Harmondsworth, Pelican, 1968

Cannadine, David, *Class in Britain*. Yale, Yale University Press, 1998; London, Penguin, 2000

Capatti, Alberto, 'The Taste for Canned and Preserved Food' in Flandrin and Montanari, eds, *Food: A Culinary History*

Carey, John, *The Intellectuals and the Masses: Pride and Prejudice Among the Literary Intelligentsia, 1880–1939*. London, Faber & Faber, 1992

Charles, Nickie, and Marion Kerr, *Women, Food and Families*. Manchester, Manchester University Press, 1988

Cheke, Val, *The Story of Cheesemaking in Britain*. London, Routledge and Kegan Paul, 1959

Chevalier, Natacha, '*Rationing Has Not Made Me Like Margarine*': *Food and Second World War in Britain: a Mass Observation Testimony*. PhD thesis, University of Sussex, 2016

Coe, Sophie, and Michael Coe, *The True History of Chocolate*. London, Thames & Hudson, 1996

Coffin, Sarah, ed., *Feeding Desire: Design and the Tools of the Table, 1500– 2005*. New York, Assouline with Smithsonian Cooper-Hewitt, National Design Museum, 2006

Collingham, Lizzie, *Curry: A Tale of Cooks and Conquerors*. London, Chatto & Windus, 2005; London, Vintage, 2006

Colquhoun, Kate, *Taste: The Story of Britain Through Its Cooking*. London, Bloomsbury, 2007

Cooper, Jilly, *Class: A View from Middle England*. London, Eyre Methuen, 1979; revised edn, London, Corgi, 1999

Counihan, Carole, and Penny van Esterik, eds, *Food and Culture: A Reader*. London, Routledge, 1997; London, Routledge, 2008

Dalby, Andrew, *Cheese: A Global History*. London, Reaktion Books, 2009

Dalby, Andrew, and Maureen Dalby, *The Shakespeare Cookbook*. London, The British Museum Press, 2012

Dalby, Andrew, and Sally Grainger, *The Classical Cookbook*. London, The British Museum Press, 1996, 2000

Davidson, Alan, ed., *The Oxford Companion to Food*. Oxford, Oxford University Press, 1999

Day, Ivan, 'The Etiquette of Dining' in Peter Brown, ed., *British Cutlery: An Illustrated History of Design, Evolution and Use*

— *Ice Cream*. Oxford, Shire Publications, 2011

— ed., *Over a Red-Hot Stove: Essays in Early Cooking Technology*. Leeds Symposium on Food History 'Food and Society' Series. Totnes, Prospect Books, 2009

Dickens, Cedric, *Drinking with Dickens*. Published by the author, 1980

Driver, Christopher, and Michelle Berriedale-Johnson, *Pepys at Table: Seventeenth-century Recipes for the Modern Cook*. London, Bell & Hyman, 1984

Drummond, J.C., *Historic Tinned Food*. Greenford, International Tin Research and Development Council, 1939

Drummond, J.C., and Anne Wilbraham, *The Englishman's Food: Five Centuries of English Diet*. London, Jonathan Cape, 1939

Elias, Megan, *Lunch: A History*. Lanham, MD, Rowman and Littlefield, 2014

Elias, Norbert, *The Civilizing Process: The History of Manners and State Formation and Civilization*. Tr. Edmund Jephcott. First published in German, 1939. Oxford, Blackwell, 1994

Feirstein, Bruce, *Real Men Don't Eat Quiche*. Sevenoaks, New English Library, 1982

Fernandez-Armesto, Felipe, *Food: A History*. London, Macmillan, 2001

Fielding, Helen, *Bridget Jones's Diary*. London, Picador, 1996

Flandrin, Jean-Louis, and Massimo Montanari, eds, *Food: A Culinary History*. Tr. Clarissa Botsford, English edn by Albert Sonnenfeld. New York and Chichester, Columbia University Press, 1999

Fox, Kate, *Watching the English: The Hidden Rules of English Behaviour*. London, Hodder & Stoughton, 2004, revised edn 2014

Freedman, Paul, ed., *Food: The History of Taste*. London, Thames & Hudson, 2007

Gayre, G.A., *Wassail! In Mazers of Mead*. London, Phillimore & Co, 1948

Gentilcore, David, *Food and Health in Early Modern Europe: Diet, Medicine and Society, 1450–1800*. London, Bloomsbury, 2016

Germov, John, and Lauren Williams, *A Sociology of Food and Nutrition: The Social Appetite*. Melbourne, Oxford University Press, 1999; 3rd edn 2008

Gershuny, Jonathan, and Oriel Sullivan, eds, *What We Really Do All Day: Insights from the Centre for Time Use Research*. London, Pelican, 2019

Goody, Jack, *Cooking, Cuisine and Class: A Study in Comparative Sociology*. Cambridge, Cambridge University Press, 1982

Great Tower Street Tea Company, *Tea, Its Natural, Social and Commercial History*. London, 1889

Groom, Susanne, *At the King's Table: Royal Dining Through the Ages*. London, Merrell, in association with Historic Royal Palaces, 2013

Groundes-Peace, Zara, *Old Cookery Notebook*. Ed. Robin Howe. London, David and Charles, 1971

Gwynn, Mary, *Back in Time for Dinner*. London, Bantam Press, 2015

Hammond, Peter, *Food and Feast in Medieval England*. Stroud, Sutton Publishing, 1993; Stroud, Sutton Publishing, 2005

Harvey, Mark, Steve Quilley and Huw Beynon, *Exploring the Tomato: Transformations of Nature, Society and Economy*. Cheltenham, Edward Elgar, 2002

Heath, Francis George, *British Rural Life and Labour*. London, P.S. King & Son, 1911

Hickman, Peggy, *A Jane Austen Household Book, With Martha Lloyd's Recipes*. Newton Abbot, Readers Union, 1978

Hickman, Trevor, *The History of the Melton Mowbray Pork Pie*. Stroud, Sutton Publishing, 1997

Hopkins, Harry, *The Long Affray: The Poaching Wars 1760–1914*. London, Secker & Warburg, 1985

Hopley, Claire, *The History of Christmas Food and Feasts*. Barnsley, Pen & Sword, 2009

Hosking, Richard, ed., *Wild Food, Proceedings of the Oxford Symposium on Food and Cookery, 2004*. Totnes, Prospect Books, 2006

Houlihan, Marjory, *Tripe: A Most Excellent Dish*. Totnes, Prospect Books, 2011

Houston Bowden, Gregory, *British Gastronomy: The Rise of Great Restaurants*. London, Chatto & Windus, 1975

Hussain, Khadim, *Going for a Curry? A Social and Culinary History*. Middlesbrough, Ek Zuban Press, 2006

Jarosz, Ewa, 'Unequal Eating: The Context of Daily Meals' in Gershuny and Sullivan, eds, *What We Really Do All Day*

Jefferies, Richard, *Landscape with Figures: An Anthology of Richards Jefferies's Prose*. Ed. Richard Mabey. Harmondsworth, Penguin Books, 1983

Jeffreys, Henry, *Empire of Booze: British History Through the Bottom of a Glass*. London, Unbound, 2016

Johnson, Susanna, and Anne Tennant, *The Picnic Papers*. London, Hutchinson, 1983

Jones, Martin, *Feast: Why Humans Share Food*. Oxford, Oxford University Press, 2007

Jones, Owen, *Chavs: The Demonization of the Working Class*. London, Verso, 2011, 2012

Ker, John Bellenden, *A Supplement to the Two Volumes of the Second Edition of The Essay on the Archaeology of Our Popular Phrases, Terms, and Nursery Rhymes*. London, James Ridgeway, 1840

Kildea, Paul, *Chopin's Piano: A Journey through Romanticism*. London, Allen Lane, 2018

Kinealy, Christine, *The Great Irish Famine: Impact, Ideology and Rebellion*. Basingstoke, Palgrave Macmillan, 2002

Knight, Charles, *London*, Volume 1. London, 1843

Lane, Maggie, *Jane Austen and Food*. London, The Hambledon Press, 1995

Lang, Tim, *Feeding Britain: Our Food Problems and How to Fix Them*. London, Pelican, 2020

Lehmann, Gilly, 'Foreign or English? A Tale of Two Dishes: Olios and Fricasees' in White, ed. *The English Kitchen*

Lewis, Michael J., *The Real World of the Bayeux Tapestry*. Stroud, History Press, 2008

Manning, Roger B., *Hunters and Poachers: A Social and Cultural History of Unlawful Hunting in England, 1485–1640*. Oxford, Clarendon Press, 1993

Mansfield, Emma, *The Little Book of the Pasty*. Cornwall, Lovely Little Books, 2011

Marchant, John, Bryan Reuben and Joan P. Alcock, *Bread: A Slice of History*. Stroud, History Press, 2008

Mason, Laura, 'Everything Stops for Tea' in C. Anne Wilson, ed., *Luncheon, Nuncheon and Other Meals*

Mason, Laura, and Catherine Brown, *The Taste of Britain*. London, HarperPress, 2006. First published as *Traditional Foods of Britain*. Totnes, Prospect Books, 1999

McCance, R.A., and E.M. Widdowson, *Breads, White and Brown: Their Place in Thought and Social History*. London, Pitman Medical, 1956

McGee, Harold, *McGee on Food and Cooking: An Encyclopedia of Kitchen Science, History and Culture*. London, Hodder & Stoughton, 2004

McKenna, Maryn, *Plucked! The Truth about Chicken*. London, Little, Brown, 2017

McNeill, F. Marian, *The Scots Kitchen: Its Lore and Recipes*. London, Blackie and Sons, 1929; London, Panther Books, 1974

Mennell, Stephen, *All Manners of Food: Eating and Taste in England and France from the Middle Ages to the Present*. Illinois, University of Illinois Press, 1996

Morgan, Marjorie, *Manners, Morals and Class in England, 1774–1858*. Basingstoke, Macmillan, 1994

Morton, Timothy, ed., *Radical Food: The Culture and Politics of Eating and Drinking, 1790–1820*. London, Routledge, 2000

— *Shelley and the Revolution in Taste: The Body and the Natural World.* Cambridge, Cambridge University Press, 1994

Murcott, Anne, ed., *The Sociology of Food and Eating: Essays on the Sociological Significance of Food.* Aldershot, Gower, c.1983

Nicol, Donald M., *Byzantium and Venice: A Study in Diplomatic and Cultural Relations.* Cambridge, Cambridge University Press, 1988

O'Connor, Kaori, *The English Breakfast: The Biography of a National Meal with Recipes.* London, Kegan Paul, 2006

Palmer, Arnold, *Moveable Feasts: Changes in English Eating-Habits.* With an introduction by David Pocock. Oxford, Oxford University Press, 1984

Panayi, Panikos, *Fish and Chips: A History.* London, Reaktion Books, 2014

Pettigrew, Jane, *A Social History of Tea.* London, National Trust, 2001

Picton, Pierre, *A Gourmet's Guide to Fish and Chips.* London, New English Library, 1966

Pollan, Michael, *Cooked: A Natural History of Transformation.* London, Allen Lane, 2013

Poole, Steven, *You Aren't What You Eat: Fed Up with Gastroculture.* London, Union Books, 2012

Priestland, Gerald, *Frying Tonight: The Saga of Fish and Chips.* London, Gentry Books, 1972

Quinzio, Jeri, *Of Sugar and Snow: A History of Ice Cream Making.* Berkeley and London, University of California Press, c.2009

Rantzen, Esther, *Make Do and Send: Nostalgic Letters on Fifteen Years of Rationing in Britain.* London, Gibson Square, 1988

Renwick, Chris, *Bread for All: The Origins of the Welfare State.* London, Allen Lane, 2017

Repplier, Agnes, *To Think of Tea!* London, Jonathan Cape, 1933

Rogers, Ben, *Beef and Liberty: Roast Beef, John Bull and the English Nation.* London, Vintage, 2004

Rossi-Wilcox, Susan, *Dinner for Dickens: The Culinary History of Mrs Charles Dickens's Menu Books including a transcript of* What Shall We have For Dinner? *by 'Lady Maria Clutterbuck'.* Totnes, Prospect Books, 2005

Roud, Steve, *The English Year: A Month-by-month Guide to the Nation's Customs and Festivals, from May Day to Mischief Night.* London, Penguin Books, 2006

Savage, Mike, *et al.*, *Social Class in the 21st Century.* London, Pelican, 2015

Schaffer, Bruce, B. Nigel Wolstenholme and Anthony W. Whiley, *The Avocado: Botany, Production and Uses.* Wallingford and Boston, CABI, 2013

Serventi, Silvano, and Françoise Sabban, *Pasta: The Story of a Universal Food.* Tr. Antony Shugaar. New York and Chichester, Columbia University Press, 2002

Shore, Elliott, 'The Development of the Restaurant' in Paul Freedman, ed., *Food: The History of Taste*

Simon, André, ed., *A Concise Encyclopaedia of Gastronomy: Section 1: Sauces.* London, The Wine and Food Society, 1939

Smith, Page, and Charles Daniel, *The Chicken Book.* San Francisco, North Point Press, 1982

Smith, Andrew F., *The Tomato in America: Early History, Culture, and Cookery.* Columbia, SC, University of South Carolina Press, c.1994

— *The Turkey: An American Story*. Chicago and Urbana, University of Illinois Press, 2006

Smith, Drew, *The Oyster: A Gastronomic History (With Recipes)*. New York, Abrams, 2015

Soutar Morris, Helen, *Portrait of a Chef: The Life of Alexis Soyer, Sometime Chef to the Reform Club*. Cambridge, Cambridge University Press, 1938

Spang, Rebecca, *The Invention of the Restaurant: Paris and Modern Gastronomic Culture*. Cambridge, MA, Harvard University Press, 2001

Spencer, Colin, *Vegetarianism: A History*. London, Grub Street, 2016

Standage, Tom, *An Edible History of Humanity*. London, Atlantic Books, 2009

Steel, Carolyn, *Sitopia: How Food Can Save the World*. London, Chatto & Windus, 2020

Stewart, Amy, *The Drunken Botanist: The Plants that Create the World's Great Drinks*. London, Timber Press, 2013

Strong, Roy, *Feast: A History of Grand Eating*. London, Jonathan Cape, 2002

Stuart, Tristram, *The Bloodless Revolution: Radical Vegetarians and the Discovery of India*. London, HarperCollins, 2006

Tannahill, Reay, *Food in History*. Harmondsworth, Penguin, 1973, 1988

Thomas, Keith, *Man and the Natural World: Changing Attitudes in England 1500–1800*. London, Allen Lane, 1983

Thompson, E.P., *The Making of the English Working Class*. London, Victor Gollancz, 1963

Toussaint-Samat, Maguelonne, *A History of Food*. Tr. Anthea Bell. Chichester, John Wiley & Sons, 1992, 2nd edn 2009

Trentmann, Frank, *Empire of Things: How We Became a World of Consumers, from the Fifteenth Century to the Twenty-first*. London, Allen Lane, 2016

Trevelyan, G.M., *Illustrated English Social History*, Volume III. London, Penguin, 1964

Trevelyan, George Otto, *The Life and Letters of Lord Macaulay*, Volume II. London, Longman, Green and Co, 1878

Ukers, William, *All About Tea*. 2 volumes. New York, Tea & Coffee Trade Journal Co., 1935

Visser, Margaret, *Much Depends on Dinner: Since Eve Ate Apples*. New York, Grove Press, 1986, 2008

— *The Rituals of Dinner: The Origins, Evolution, Eccentricities, and Meaning of Table Manners*. London, Viking, 1992; London, Penguin, 1993

Walton, John K., *Fish and Chips and the British Working Class, 1879–1940*. London, Leicester University Press, 1994

White, Eileen, ed., *The English Kitchen: Historical Essays*. Totnes, Prospect Books, 2007

— 'First Things First: The Great British Breakfast' in C. Anne Wilson, ed., *Luncheon, Nuncheon and Other Meals*

— 'Warm, Comforting Food: Soups, Broths and Pottages' in White, ed., *The English Kitchen*

Wilson, Bee, *Consider the Fork: A History of Invention in the Kitchen*. London, Particular Books, 2012

— *The Sandwich: A Global History*. London, Reaktion Books, 2010

— *The Way We Eat Now: Strategies for Eating in a World of Change*. London, Fourth Estate, 2019

Wilson, C. Anne, ed., *Luncheon, Nuncheon and Other Meals: Eating with the Victorians*. Stroud, Sutton Publishing, 1994

— 'Supper, The Ultimate Meal' in C. Anne Wilson, ed., *Luncheon, Nuncheon and Other Meals*

Wolfman, Peri, *Forks, Knives and Spoons*. London, Thames & Hudson, 1994

Wood, Roy C., *The Sociology of the Meal*. Edinburgh, Edinburgh University Press, 1995

Woodham-Smith, Cecil, *The Great Hunger: Ireland, 1845–9*. London, Hamish Hamilton, 1962

Zuckerman, Larry, *The Potato: From the Andes in the sixteenth century to fish and chips, the story of how a vegetable changed history*. London, Macmillan, 1999

Zweiniger-Bargielowska, Ina, *Austerity in Britain: Rationing, Controls and Consumption 1939–1955*. Oxford, Oxford University Press, 2000

Newspaper and Journal Articles and Online Sources

Addison, Joseph, *Tatler*, no. 148, 21 March 1709

Baraniuk, Chris, 'Brits are eating venison faster than Scotland can produce it'. *Quartz*, 11 September 2016. https://qz.com/778790/brits-are-eating-venison-faster-than-scotland-can-produce-it/

Barcelona, Ainhoa, 'The Queen's favourite food revealed by former chef Darren McGrady – and it may surprise you'. *Hello!*, 3 May 2020. https://www.hellomagazine.com/cuisine/2019061174040/the-queen-favourite-food-darren-mcgrady-recipes/

Blackledge, Richard, 'Jack Monroe: "Cooking from tins is a reality for many – I'm tired of the snobbery around food"'. *inews*, 29 May 2019. https://inews.co.uk/inews-lifestyle/food-and-drink/jack-monroe-cans-food-banks-67870

Brennan, Siofra, 'People reveal what they think makes them middle class in a hilarious online debate (including eating lots of avocados and having no family members with tattoos)'. *Daily Mail*, 13 April 2013. https://www.dailymail.co.uk/femail/article-3536156/People-reveal-makes-middle-class.html

British Museum, 'The Bread and Butter Manufactory or the Humors of Bagnigge Wells' in 'Prints'. https://www.britishmuseum.org/collection/object/P_2010-7081-3809

Burrell, Paul, interviewed by Emine Saner and Lucy Clouting, 'What's wrong with licking your plate?' *Guardian*, 13 October 2006. https://www.theguardian.com/uk/2006/oct/13/britishidentity.lifeandhealth

Burrells Antique Desks, www.burrellsantiquedesks.com

Carpenter, Louise, 'Food and class: does what we eat reflect Britain's social divide?' *Guardian*, 13 March 2011. https://www.theguardian.com/lifeandstyle/2011/mar/13/food-class-social-divide-diet

Carrington, Damian, 'Giving up beef will reduce carbon footprint more than cars, says expert'. *Guardian*, 21 July 2014. https://www.theguardian.com/environment/2014/jul/21/giving-up-beef-reduce-carbon-footprint-more-than-cars Original study:https://link.springer.com/article/10.1007%2Fs10584-014-1169-1

Caster, Yvette, '20 signs you're too middle class for words'. *Metro*, 9 April 2015. https://metro.co.uk/2015/04/09/20-signs-youre-too-middle-class-for-words-5133183/

Chan, Eugene Y., and Natalina Zlatevska, 'Jerkies, Tacos, and Burgers: Subjective Socioeconomic Status and Meat Preference'. *Appetite*, Volume 132, 1 January 2019. https://doi.org/10.1016/j.appet.2018.08.027

Churchill, Winston, 'Fifty Years Hence'. *The Strand Magazine*, December 1931

crodriguez2014, 'A Timeline of Cadbury Adverts'. *Chocolate Class: Multimedia Essays on Chocolate, Culture and the Politics of Food*, 14 March 2014. https://chocolateclass.wordpress.com/2014/03/14/a-timeline-of-cadbury-adverts/

Curly, Rebecca, 'To Av and to Hold: Middle-class millennials now proposing with avocados in bizarre new trend'. *The Sun*, 21 February 2018. https://www.thesun.co.uk/news/5631426/middle-class-millennials-now-proposing-with-avocados-in-bizarre-new-trend/

Daily Telegraph, Obituary, Alice Thomas Ellis. 10 March 2005. https://www.telegraph.co.uk/news/obituaries/1485280/Alice-Thomas-Ellis.html

Daniels, Jeff, 'Avocado sales could more than double this year, helped by demand from China's middle class'. CNBC, 10 January 2018. https://www.cnbc.com/2018/01/10/chinas-middle-class-is-boosting-demand-for-avocados.html

Day, Chris, 'The Great War British Bake Off'. National Archives, 21 September 2015. http://blog.nationalarchives.gov.uk/blog/great-war-british-bake/

Day, Ivan, *Historic Food*. https://www.historicfood.com/portal.htm

— 'A Jubilee Ox Roast'. *Food History Jottings*, 9 August 2012. http://foodhistorjottings.blogspot.com/2012/08/a-jubilee-ox-roast.html

Debrett's, 'Table Rules'. https://www.debretts.com/expertise/etiquette/table-manners/table-rules/

Delgado, Martin, 'Sainsbury, M&S... and the great ad-vocado war'. *Mail on Sunday*, 25 May 2009. http://www.dailymail.co.uk/femail/food/article-1186938/Avocado-wars-M-S-Sainsburys-battle-introduced-fruit-first.html

De Quincey, Thomas, 'Dinner, Real and Reputed'. *Blackwood's Magazine*, December 1839

Diaz-Arnesto, Laura, 'Byzantine women – The Princess Theophano and Introducing the fork into Europe'. *Byzantine Blog*, 9 November 2010. https://mybyzantine.wordpress.com/2010/11/09/byzantine-women—the-princess-theophano-and-introducing-the-fork-into-europe/

Dickens, Charles (conducted by), 'The London Tavern'. *Household Words*, Volume IV, p.74, 18 October 1851. https://www.djo.org.uk/household-words/volume-iv/page-73.html

The Economist, 'The British at Table'. Volume 408, No. 8846, 2013

Ellson, Andrew, 'Anti-competitive Google must be brought to heel'. *The Times*, 26 December 2019. https://www.thetimes.co.uk/article/anti-competitive-google-must-be-brought-to-heel-lhz88xxhj

French, Phoebe, 'London now home to fifth of England's Gin Distilleries'. *The Drinks Business*, 13 November 2017. https://www.thedrinksbusiness.com/2017/11/london-now-home-to-fifth-of-englands-gin-distilleries/

Google Books, Ngram viewer, 'luncheon'. https://books.google.
com/ngrams/graph?content=luncheon&year_start=1800&year_
end=2000&corpus=15&smoothing=3

Gretton, Lel, 'Table cloths in the Middle Ages'. *Old and Interesting*, 26 February
2010. http://www.oldandinteresting.com/medieval-tablecloths.aspx

The Grocer, Hot Beverages Report 2016, 'Class divide: what your tea says about
your social standing'. 28 September 2016

Guardian, 'Tea with Grayson Perry. Or is it dinner, or supper?' 3 August 2012.
https://www.theguardian.com/lifeandstyle/2012/aug/03/tea-with-grayson-
perry-supper-dinner

Gyford, Phil, *The Diary of Samuel Pepys: Daily entries from the 17th century
London diary.* https://www.pepysdiary.com

Harding, Nick, 'Modern poachers and the wildlife police who are trying to rein
them in'. *Independent*, 16 November 2015. https://www.independent.co.uk/
news/uk/crime/modern-poachers-and-the-wildlife-police-who-are-trying-to-
rein-them-in-a6736946.html

Henley, Jon, and Eleanor Ainge Roy, 'Are female leaders more successful at
managing the coronavirus crisis?' *Guardian*, 25 April 2020. https://www.
theguardian.com/world/2020/apr/25/why-do-female-leaders-seem-to-be-more-
successful-at-managing-the-coronavirus-crisis

HMRC, 'Excepted items: Confectionery: The bounds of confectionery, sweets,
chocolates, chocolate biscuits, cakes and biscuits: The borderline between
cakes and biscuits'. *Internal manual, VAT Food.* 13 March 2016. Updated 7
August 2018. https://www.gov.uk/hmrc-internal-manuals/vat-food/vfood6260

Holehouse, Matthew, 'Poor going hungry because they can't cook, says Tory
peer'. *Daily Telegraph*, 8 December 2014. https://www.telegraph.co.uk/news/
politics/11279839/Poor-going-hungry-because-they-cant-cook-says-Tory-peer.
html

Holley, Peter, 'These chickens live in luxury'. *Washington Post*, 4 March 2018.
https://www.washingtonpost.com/news/business/wp/2018/03/02/feature/the-
silicon-valley-elites-latest-status-symbol-chickens/

Hubbell, Andrew, 'How Wordsworth Invented Picknicking and Saved British
Culture', *Romanticism*, Volume 12.1, 2006

— 'I picnic lonely as a cloud…' *Times Higher Education*, 7 March 2003. https://
www.timeshighereducation.com/features/i-picnic-lonely-as-a-cloud/175225.
article

Hughes, Glyn, 'Quartern Loaf'. *The Foods of England Project*, 2 September,
2018. http://www.foodsofengland.co.uk/quarternloaf.htm

Hupkens, Christianne, *et al.*, 'Social class differences in food consumption: The
explanatory value of permissiveness and health and cost considerations'.
European Journal of Public Health, Volume 10, Issue 2, June 2000, pp.108–
13. https://doi.org/10.1093/eurpub/10.2.108

Johnson, Samuel, 'Review of Jonas Hanway's *Essay on Tea*'. *The Literary
Magazine*, 1757

Kraft Foods, Frequently Asked Questions. http://kraftfoods.custhelp.com/app/
answers/detail/a_id/588

The Literary Gazette: A Weekly Journal of Literature, Science, and Fine Arts, 'Review of "Essays, Moral, Philosophical, and Stomachical, on the important Science of Good Living." By Launcelot Sturgeon"'. 16 February 1822

London Society: An Illustrated Magazine of Light and Amusing Literature, 1870

Luty, Jennifer, 'Eating out frequency in the United Kingdom (UK) 2016'. *Statista*, March 2017. https://www.statista.com/statistics/419297/eating-out-frequency-in-the-united-kingdom-uk/

Maffey, Dr Georgina, *et al.*, 'Farming for Venison: investigating the barriers to deer farming in Scotland'. February 2015. http://deerfarmdemoproject. scottish-venison.info/wp-content/uploads/2015/04/Venison-Farming-Final-Report.pdf

Mars, Valerie, 'Ordering Dinner: Victorian Celebratory Domestic Dining in London'. PhD thesis, University of Leicester, May 1997

McDonnell, Adam, 'It's scone as in "gone" not scone as in "bone"'. YouGov, 31 October 2016. https://yougov.co.uk/topics/politics/articles-reports/2016/10/31/its-scone-gone-not-scone-bone

Moore, Charles, 'We selfish gits must wear the name with pride'. *Spectator*, 12 October 2019. https://www.spectator.co.uk/2019/10/we-selfish-gits-must-wear-the-name-with-pride/

Morrissy-Swan, Tomé, 'The best chef's knives'. *Daily Telegraph*, 8 January 2020. https://www.telegraph.co.uk/recommended/home/best-chefs-knives/

Naylor, Tony, 'The end of small plates: why the dinner-ruining dishes may finally be over'. *Guardian*, 14 March 2019. https://www.theguardian.com/food/2019/mar/14/the-end-of-small-plates-why-the-dinner-ruining-dishes-may-finally-be-over

Norton, Rictor, 'The Macaroni Club: Homosexual Scandals in 1772'. *Homosexuality in Eighteenth-Century England: A Sourcebook*, 19 December 2004, updated 11 June 2005, updated 13 June 2017. http://rictornorton.co.uk/eighteen/macaroni.htm.

Orwell, George, 'A Nice Cup of Tea'. *Evening Standard*, 12 January 1946

Pechey, Rachel, *et al.*, 'Why Don't Poor Men Eat Fruit: Socioeconomic differences in motivations for fruit consumption'. *Appetite*, 84, 2015. https://doi.org/10.1016/j.appet.2014.10.022

Pepys, Samuel, https://www.pepysdiary.com/diary/1666/07/25/

Pic Nic, Number 1, 8 January 1803

Pimlott, J.A.R., 'Christmas under the Puritans'. *History Today*, Volume 10, Issue 12, December 1960

Reid, Rebecca, 'Avocado hand: the most middle class injury ever?' *Metro*, 10 May 2017. https://metro.co.uk/2017/05/10/avocado-hand-the-most-middle-class-injury-ever-6627979/

Robertson, Debora, 'Pardon, toilet and sitting room: We really are all middle-class now'. *Daily Telegraph*, 5 August 2017. https://www.telegraph.co.uk/women/life/pardon-toilet-sitting-room-really-middle-class-now/

Ross, Deborah, 'Lord, forgive them'. *Independent*, 29 June 1998. https://www.independent.co.uk/arts-entertainment/lord-forgive-them-1168282.html

Shahbandeh, M. 'Avocado production worldwide from 2000 to 2018'. *Statista*, 2 March 2020. https://www.statista.com/statistics/577455/world-avocado-production/

Smith, Lewis, 'Tale of Two Cities shows north south divide on obesity'. *The Times*, 2 March 2004. https://www.thetimes.co.uk/article/tale-of-two-cities-shows-north-south-divide-on-obesity-s8d9j0bl695

Smith, Oli, '"Dinner parties fuel stabbings". Government blames middle class for knife crime chaos'. *Express*, 27 May 2018. https://www.express.co.uk/news/uk/965728/Knife-crime-middle-class-stabbings-cocaine-users

Socialist Health Association, 'Food Health and Income: Changes in the Nation's Diet. Historical Comparisons'. 27 March 1936. https://www.sochealth.co.uk/national-health-service/public-health-and-wellbeing/food-policy/food-health-and-income/food-health-and-income-changes-in-the-nations-diet-historical-comparisons/

Tatler, 'The Great British Country Supper'. 11 September 2012. https://www.tatler.com/article/the-great-british-country-supper

Thackeray, writing as M.A. Titchmarsh, 'Memorials of Gourmandising, Paris, May 1841'. *Fraser's Magazine for Town and Country*, Volume 23, January–June 1841

Tripe Marketing Board, *Tripe Adviser*. https://tripemarketingboard.co.uk/tripe-adviser/

UK Tea and Infusions Association, 'FAQs about tea'. https://www.tea.co.uk/tea-faqs

The Vegan Society, 'Statistics'. https://www.vegansociety.com/news/media/statistics

Warner, Anthony, aka The Angry Chef. https://angry-chef.com

Warner, Jessica, 'Gin in Regency England'. *History Today*, Volume 61, Issue 3, March 2011

White, Marco Pierre, 'If the smug organic mob get their way, millions of families will never again be able to afford roast chicken for Sunday lunch'. *Daily Mail*, 9 September 2012. https://www.dailymail.co.uk/news/article-2200477/If-smug-organic-mob-way-millions-families-able-afford-roast-chicken-Sunday-lunch.html

Wilkes, David, 'Don't tell Hyacinth but the doily is dead'. *Daily Mail*, 17 May 2007. https://www.dailymail.co.uk/news/article-455636/Dont-tell-Hyacinth-doily-dead.html

Williams, Zoe, 'Will coronavirus spell an end to the great Chinese buffet?' *Guardian*, 2 May 2020. https://www.theguardian.com/world/2020/may/02/will-coronavirus-spell-an-end-to-the-great-chinese-buffet

Wilson, Bee, 'Mmmm, chicken nuggets', Review of *The London Restaurant* by Brenda Assael. *London Review of Books*, 15 August 2019. https://www.lrb.co.uk/the-paper/v41/n16/bee-wilson/mmmm-chick

Endnotes

Introduction

1. Rebecca Reid, 'Avocado hand: the most middle class injury ever?', *Metro*, 10 May 2017.
2. Jack Goody, *Cooking, Cuisine and Class*, p.157.
3. Quoted in Stephen Mennell, *All Manners of Food*, p.30.
4. Frank Trentmann, *Empire of Things*, p.xx.
5. Quoted in Norbert Elias, *The Civilizing Process*, p.59.
6. See Tim Lang, *Feeding Britain: Our Food Problems and How to Fix Them*.
7. Auguste Escoffier, *A Guide to Modern Cookery*, p.vii.
8. Jean-Anthelme Brillat-Savarin, *Physiologie du goût*, p.13.
9. Mike Savage, *Social Class in the 21st Century*, p.51.
10. Pierre Bourdieu, *Distinction*, pp.177–96.
11. Ibid., p.180.
12. Abhijit Banerjee and Esther Duflo, *Poor Economics*, p.37.
13. George Orwell, *The Road to Wigan Pier*, Chapter VI, pp.88–9.
14. Ina Zweiniger-Bargielowska, *Austerity in Britain*, p.44.
15. George Mikes, *How to Be an Alien*, p.12.

Part One
Breakfast

1. Quoted in George Dodd, *The Food of London*, p.100–end Chapter 2.
2. Nicholas Breton, *Fantasticks*, (unnumbered pages).
3. Eileen White in *Luncheon, Nuncheon and Other Meals*, ed. C. Anne Wilson, p.2.
4. Samuel Pepys, *The Diaries of Samuel Pepys*, 27 July 1663, p.297.
5. Ibid., 2 May 1660, p.38.
6. William Austen-Leigh and Richard Arthur Austen-Leigh, *Jane Austen, Her Life and Letters: A Family Record*, p.196.
7. Jane Austen, *Mansfield Park*, Chapter XXIX, p.270.
8. John Burnett, *Plenty and Want*, p.181.
9. Ibid., p.162.
10. Mennell, *All Manners of Food*, p.228.
11. Matthew Holehouse, 'Poor going hungry because they can't cook, says Tory peer', *Daily Telegraph*, 8 December 2014.
12. Charlotte Brontë, *Jane Eyre*, Volume I, Chapter VII, p.63.
13. Quoted in F. Marian McNeill, *The Scots Kitchen*, p.88.
14. Ibid., pp.88–90.
15. George Borrow, *Wild Wales*, Volume III, Chapter LXXIII, p.36.
16. Benjamin Disraeli, *Sybil, or The Two Nations*, Book VI, Chapter IX, p.330.
17. Ibid., Book V, Chapter VII, p.276.

18. Ibid., Book III, Chapter III, p.136.
19. Anthony Trollope, *The Warden*, Chapter VIII, p.67.
20. Ibid.
21. Jilly Cooper, *Class*, p.266.
22. Sir Kenelm Digby, *The Closet of Sir Kenelm Digby Opened*, p.157.
23. Kaori O'Connor, *The English Breakfast*, p.41.
24. Agnes Jekyll, *Kitchen Essays*, p.83.
25. 'Wyvern', *Culinary Jottings for Madras*, p.171.

The Sandwich

1. Jane Austen, *Pride and Prejudice*, Volume II, Chapter XVI, p.235.
2. Maria Rundell, *A New System of Domestic Cookery*, p.i.
3. N.A.M. Rodger, quoted in Bee Wilson, *Sandwich: A Global History*, p.21.
4. Wilson, *Sandwich*, p.18.
5. Burrells Antique Desks, https://www.burrellsantiquedesks.com/history-of-the-english-desk
6. Charles Dickens, *The Pickwick Papers*, Chapter LV, p.735.
7. Burnett, *Plenty and Want*, p.178.
8. J.E. Panton, *From Kitchen to Garrett*, p.43.
9. *Guardian*, 'Tea with Grayson Perry. Or is it dinner, or supper?', 3 August 2012.
10. Cooper, *Class*, p.256.
11. David Pocock in Palmer, *Moveable Feasts*, p.xxi.
12. Google Books, Ngram viewer, https://books.google.com/ngrams/graph?content=luncheon&year_start=1800&year_end=2000&corpus=15&smoothing=3
13. John Bellenden Ker, *A Supplement to the Two Volumes of the Second Edition of The Essay on the Archaeology of Our Popular Phrases, Terms, and Nursery Rhymes*, p.129.
14. George Otto Trevelyan, *The Life and Letters of Lord Macaulay*, Volume II, p.332
15. Ker, *A Supplement*, p.129.
16. David Pocock in Palmer, *Moveable Feasts*, p.xxiv.
17. *London Society: An Illustrated Magazine of Light and Amusing Literature*, 1870, Volume XVII.
18. John Burnett, *England Eats Out*, p.42.
19. Mrs C.F. Leyel, *The Gentle Art of Cookery*, pp.335–8.
20. Ministry of Information, *Rationing of Food in Great Britain*.
21. Wilson, *Sandwich*, p.4.

Etiquette

1. Elias, *The Civilizing Process*.
2. Frederick J. Furnivall, ed., *Early English Meals and Manners*.
3. Hannah Woolley, *The Gentlewoman's Companion or a Guide to the Female Sex*, p.67.
4. Ibid., p.110.
5. Fanny Burney, *Evelina*, Letter XX, p.92.
6. Cited in Roy Strong, *Feast*, p.249.

7. Charles William Day, *Hints on Etiquette and the Usages of Society, With a Glance at Bad Habits*, p.1.

8. Quoted in Mennell, *All Manners of Food*, p.75.

9. A Member of the Aristocracy, *Manners and Tone of Good Society*, p.102.

10. Lady Troubridge, *Etiquette and Entertaining*, p.105.

11. Paul Burrell interviewed by Emine Saner and Lucy Clouting, 'What's wrong with licking your plate?' *Guardian*, 13 October 2006.

Tea

1. Pepys, *Diaries*, 25 September 1660, p.81.

2. William H. Ukers, *All About Tea*, Volume I, pp.60–63.

3. Ibid., p.68.

4. Samuel Johnson, review of Jonas Hanway's *Essay on Tea* in *The Literary Magazine*, 1757.

5. Ukers, *All About Tea*, Volume I, p.94.

6. Quoted in Great Tower Street Tea Company, *Tea, Its Natural, Social and Commercial History*.

7. Simon Paulli, *A Treatise on Tobacco, Tea, Coffee, and Chocolate*, tr. Dr James, p.129.

8. Parson James Woodforde, *The Diary of a Country Parson*, pp.91, 92.

9. François de La Rochefoucauld, *A Frenchman in England*, p.23.

10. Jane Pettigrew, *A Social History of Tea*, p.40.

11. Colley Cibber, *The Lady's Last Stake; or, the Wife's Resentment*, Act I.

12. William Cobbett, *Cottage Economy*, section 32.

13. Burnett, *Plenty and Want*, p.162.

14. Ukers, Volume 1, pp.142–3.

15. Trentmann, *Empire of Things*, p.168.

16. George Orwell, 'A Nice Cup of Tea', *Evening Standard*, 12 January 1946.

17. Evelyn Waugh, 'Open Letter to the Honble Mrs Peter Rodd (Nancy Mitford) on a Very Serious Subject', *Essays, Articles and Reviews*, pp.298–99.

18. Cooper, *Class*, p.266.

19. UK Tea and Infusions Association, https://www.tea.co.uk/tea-faqs

20. Hot Beverages Report 2016, 'Class divide: what your tea says about your social standing', *The Grocer*, 28 September 2016.

Afternoon Tea

1. Henry James, *The Portrait of a Lady*, Chapter I, p.59.

2. Burney, *Evelina*, p.355.

3. Austen, *Mansfield Park*, Chapter XXXIV, p.328.

4. Steventon to Godmersham, 18 December 1798, *Jane Austen's Letters*, ed. R.W. Chapman, p.37.

5. Ukers, *All About Tea*, Volume I, p.405.

6. Pettigrew, *A Social History of Tea*, p.202.

7. Mrs Isabella Beeton, *Mrs Beeton's Book of Household Management*, p.1242. Cited by Laura Mason, 'Everything Stops for Tea', in *Luncheon, Nuncheon and Other Meals*, p.73.

8. Flora Thompson, *Lark Rise to Candleford*, p.197.

9. Jekyll, *Kitchen Essays*, p.124.
10. Pettigrew, *A Social History of Tea*, p.164.
11. Constance Spry and Rosemary Hume, *The Constance Spry Cookery Book*, p.1052.

High Tea

1. Dorothy Hartley, *Food in England*, p.16.
2. Charles Dickens, *Bleak House*, Chapter XIX, p.315.
3. Mrs Gaskell, *Mary Barton*, Chapter II, p.16.
4. Arabella Boxer, *Arabella Boxer's Book of English Food*, p.209.
5. McNeill, *The Scots Kitchen*, p.95.
6. Ibid.
7. Cooper, *Class*, p.256.
8. Bee Wilson, *The Way We Eat Now*, p.10.
9. Peter Brears, *Traditional Food in Yorkshire*, p.190.

The Dinner Party

1. Oli Smith, '"Dinner parties fuel stabbings". Government blames middle class for knife crime chaos', *Daily Express*, 27 May 2018.
2. Andrew Ellson, *The Times*, 26 December 2019.
3. Strong, *Feast*, p.269.
4. Brillat-Savarin, *Physiologie du goût*, p.14.
5. John Trusler, *The Honours of the Table*, pp.1–5.
6. Charles Dickens, *Our Mutual Friend*, Book I, Chapter II, p.21.
7. G.V., *Dinners and Dinner Parties, or the Absurdities of Artificial Life*, p.38.
8. Ibid., p.45.
9. Ibid., p.41.
10. Thomas Walker, *Aristology, or The Art of Dining*, p.8.
11. William Makepeace Thackeray, *The Book of Snobs*, Chapter XX, p.85.
12. Launcelot Sturgeon, *Essays, Moral, Philosophical and Stomachical, on the Importance Science of Good-Living*, Essay XVIII 'On the Qualifications of Cooks', p.193.
13. Thomas Creevey, *The Creevey Papers*, p.108.
14. Disraeli, *Sybil*, Book IV, Chapter III, p.184.
15. Panton, *From Kitchen to Garrett*, p.33.
16. Walker, *Aristology, Or the Art of Dining*, p.14.
17. E.M. Forster, *A Room with a View*, Chapter VI, p.142.
18. Mollie Moran, *Aprons and Silver Spoons*, p.343.
19. Judith Listowel, *The Modern Hostess*, p.13.
20. Strong, *Feast*, p.311.
21. Nigella Lawson, *How to Eat*, p.330.
22. *Guardian*, 'Tea with Grayson Perry. Or is it dinner, or supper?', 3 August 2012.

Supper

1. Society of Antiquaries, *Household Ordinances*, 1790, p.151.
2. William Shakespeare, *Love's Labour's Lost*, Act I, Scene I.

3. Henri Misson, *M. Misson's Memoirs and Observations in His Travels over England*, p.313.
4. Jane Austen, *Emma*, Volume III, Chapter II, p.323.
5. Creevey, *The Creevey Papers*, p.93.
6. Quoted in McNeill, *The Scots Kitchen*, p.84.
7. Margaret Dods, *The Cook and Housewife's Manual*, p.75.
8. Austen, *Emma*, Volume I, Chapter III, p.25.
9. Thomas De Quincey, 'Dinner, Real and Reputed', *Blackwood's Magazine*, December 1839.
10. Rundell, *A New System of Domestic Cookery*, p.322.
11. C. Anne Wilson, 'Supper, The Ultimate Meal', in *Luncheon, Nuncheon*, p.148.
12. William Ellis, *The Country Housewife's Family Companion*, p.122.
13. William Kitchiner, *Apicius Redivivus; or, The Cook's Oracle*, p.110.
14. George Ewart Evans, *Ask the Fellows Who Cut the Hay*, p.98.
15. Henry Mayhew, *London Labour and the London Poor*, Volume I, p.166.
16. Orwell, *The Road to Wigan Pier*, Chapter I, p.12.
17. Lieutenant Colonel Newnham-Davis, *The Gourmet's Guide to London*, p.4.
18. Jekyll, *Kitchen Essays*, p.29.
19. 4 September 1926, quoted in Mennell, *All Manners of Food*, p.240.
20. Pocock in Palmer, *Moveable Feasts*, p.xxix.
21. Listowel, *The Modern Hostess*, p.18.
22. Jonathan Gershuny and Oriel Sullivan, *What We Really Do All Day*, p.184.

Part Two
Carving

1. Beeton, *Mrs Beeton's Book of Household Management*, entry 1005, p.506.
2. Genesis 1:26, King James Bible.
3. Andrew F. Smith, *The Turkey*, p.23.
4. Anonymous, *The Boke of Kervynge*, n.p.
5. *The Forme of Cury*: cockatrice: recipe XX.VIII.XV (175); hedgehog: recipe XX.VIII.XVI (176).
6. Lord Chesterfield, *Letters to His Son*, p.64.
7. Kitchiner, *Apicius Redivivus*, p.411.
8. Hannah Glasse, *The Art of Cookery Made Plain and Easy*, p.5.
9. Ibid., p.9.
10. Elizabeth Raffald, *The Experienced English Housekeeper*, p.34.
11. Rundell, *A New System of Domestic Cookery*, p.94.
12. Austen, *Emma*, Volume I, Chapter I, p.16.
13. Eliza Acton, *Modern Cookery for Private Families*, p.194.
14. Jane Austen, letter to Cassandra, 24 January 1813, *Jane Austen's Letters*, p.293.
15. Dods, *The Cook and Housewife's Manual*, p.44.
16. Ibid., p.53.
17. Ivan Day, 'A Jubilee Ox Roast', *Food History Jottings*, 9 August 2012.
18. Ibid.
19. Helen Soutar Morris, *Portrait of a Chef*, p.95.
20. Anne Walbank Buckland, *Our Viands*, p.70.

The Roast Beef of Old England

1. William Shakespeare, *Henry V*, Act III, Scene VII.
2. Pepys, *Diaries*, 6 January 1660, p.4.
3. Fynes Moryson, *An Itinerary: containing his ten yeeres travell*, Volume IV, p.168.
4. John Simpson, *A Complete System of Cookery*, 1806, quoted in Elizabeth David, *Spices, Salts and Aromatics in the English Kitchen*, p.172.
5. Roger B. Manning, *Hunters and Poachers*, p.109.
6. G.M. Trevelyan, *Illustrated English Social History*, Volume III, p.150.
7. Ben Rogers, *Beef and Liberty*, p.176.
8. *Tatler*, no. 148, 21 March 1709.
9. Writing as M.A. Titchmarsh, 'Memorials of Gourmandising, Paris, May 1841', *Fraser's Magazine for Town and Country*, Volume 23, January–June 1841.
10. Misson, *M. Misson's Memoirs and Observations*, pp.146–7.
11. Acton, *Modern Cookery for Private Families*, p.184.
12. Quoted in Burnett, *Plenty and Want*, p.161.
13. Ibid., pp.158–61.
14. Damian Carrington, 'Giving up beef will reduce carbon footprint more than cars, says expert', *Guardian*, 21 July 2014.
15. Burnett, *Plenty and Want*, p.340.

Roast Chicken

1. Margaret Visser, *Much Depends on Dinner*, p.128.
2. Quoted in Ulisse Aldrovandi, *Aldrovandi on Chickens*, p.311.
3. Digby, *The Closet of Sir Kenelm Digby Opened*, p.226.
4. Thomas Muffet, *Health's Improvement*, p.80.
5. Keith Thomas, *Man and the Natural World*, p.186.
6. Jason Bernert, 'These chickens live in luxury', *Washington Post*, 4 March 2018.
7. Aldrovandi, *Aldrovandi on Chickens*, Volume II, Book XIV.
8. Bonington Moubray, *A Practical Treatise on Breeding, Rearing, and Fattening All Kinds of Domestic Poultry*, p.4.
9. Burnett, *Plenty and Want*, p.172.
10. Maryn McKenna, *Plucked! The Truth About Chicken*, pp.68–73.
11. Eugene Y. Chan and Natalina Zlatevska, 'Jerkies, Tacos, and Burgers: Subjective Socioeconomic Status and Meat Preference', *Appetite*, Volume 132, 1 January 2019, pp.257–66.
12. Marco Pierre White, 'If the smug organic mob get their way, millions of families will never again be able to afford roast chicken for Sunday lunch', *Mailonline*, 9 September 2012.
13. Bruce Feirstein, *Real Men Don't Eat Quiche*, 1982, p.74
14. Hugh Fearnley-Whittinstall, *The River Cottage Meat Book*, Hodder, London, 2004, p.129.
15. Winston Churchill, 'Fifty Years Hence', *The Strand Magazine*, December 1931.

ENDNOTES

Mashed Potato

1. Cooper, *Class*, p.263.
2. Lawson, *How to Eat*, pp.77–8.
3. William Shakespeare, *The Merry Wives of Windsor*, Act V, Scene V.
4. Quoted in Andrew Dalby and Maureen Dalby, *The Shakespeare Cookbook*, p.22.
5. J.E. Austen-Leigh, *A Memoir of Jane Austen, and Other Family Recollections*, 1871, p.32.
6. Ellis, *The Country Housewife's Family Companion*, p.295.
7. Quoted in Larry Zuckerman, *The Potato*, p.132.
8. Tom Standage, *An Edible History of Humanity*, p.125.
9. Cobbett, *Cottage Economy*, p.44.
10. Quoted in Zuckerman, *The Potato*, p.204.
11. Quoted in ibid. p.112.
12. Christine Kinealy, *The Great Irish Famine*, pp.111–14.
13. George Bernard Shaw, *Man and Superman*, Act IV.
14. Quoted in Zuckerman, *The Potato*, p.194.
15. Cobbett, *Cottage Economy*, p.43.
16. Sir Frederick Morton Eden, *The State of the Poor*, Volume I, p.14.
17. Acton, *Modern Cookery for Private Families*, p.310.
18. Ibid., p.314.
19. Letter to E. de la Rue, 24 March 1847, quoted in Susan Rossi-Wilcox, *Dinner for Dickens: The Culinary History of Mrs Charles Dickens' Menu Books*, p.278.
20. Mayhew, *London Labour and the London Poor*, Volume I, p.29.
21. Chris Day, 'The Great War British Bake Off', National Archives, 21 September 2015.
22. HC Deb. 10 November 1947 vol. 444 col.156.

The Cornish Pasty

1. Dr Caroline Jackson MEP, quoted in Emma Mansfield, *The Little Book of the Pasty*, n.p.
2. Andrew George MP, quoted in ibid.
3. Quoted in ibid.
4. Francis George Heath, *British Rural Life and Labour*, p.286.
5. Ibid.
6. Edith Martin, *Cornish Recipes Ancient and Modern*, n.p.

Peas

1. Fernand Braudel, *Civilization and Capitalism 15th–18th Century: Volume I: The Structures of Everyday Life*, p.136.
2. Hartley, *Food in England*, p.390.
3. Ellis, *The Country Housewife's Family Companion*, p.292.
4. Austen, letter to Cassandra, 1 December 1798, *Jane Austen's Letters*, p.34.
5. Charles Knight, *London*, Volume 1, p.131.
6. Beeton, *Mrs Beeton's Book of Household Management*, p.75.
7. Quoted in Evelyne Bloch-Dano, *Vegetables: A Biography*, p.64.

8. Thackeray, *The Book of Snobs*, p.4.
9. Jane Grigson, *Vegetable Book*, p.366.

The Gravy Wars

1. Alexandre Dumas, *Dumas on Food: Selections from Le Grand Dictionnaire de Cuisine*, p.75.
2. William Verral, *A Complete System of Cookery*, p.26.
3. Ibid., p.36.
4. Ibid., p.36.
5. Ibid., p.29.
6. 'Advertisement' for *A New System of Domestic Cookery* by Maria Rundell, 1806.
7. E.S. Dallas, *Kettner's Book of the Table*, p.413.
8. Beeton, *Mrs Beeton's Book of Household Management*, entry 356, p.190.
9. Louis Eustache Ude, *The French Cook*, first published 1813; this quote taken from the 10th edition, 1829, p.xli.
10. Geoffrey Chaucer, 'The General Prologue', *The Canterbury Tales*, p.7.
11. Alan Davidson, *The Oxford Companion to Food*, p.350.
12. Harold McGee, *On Food and Cooking*, p.619.
13. 'A.W.', *A Booke of Cookerie* , p.4.
14. Chatillon-Plessis, quoted in Mennell, *All Manners of Food*, p.309.
15. Charles Dickens, *Martin Chuzzlewit*, Chapter IX, p.135.
16. John Ayto, *The Diner's Dictionary: Word Origins of Food and Drink*, p.153.
17. Nigel Slater, *Eating for England*, pp.154–6.

Jelly

1. Quoted in Peter Brears, *Jellies and Their Moulds*, p.55.
2. Woolley, *The Gentlewoman's Companion*, p.155.
3. Dods, *The Cook and Housewife's Manual*, p.53.
4. Austen, *Mansfield Park*, Chapter XXIX, p.271.
5. Quoted in Dallas, *Kettner's Book of the Table*, p.216.
6. Kraft Foods, Frequently Asked Questions. 'Q: What is the source of gelatin used in JELL-O gelatin?'
7. Dallas, *Kettner's Book of the Table*, pp.258–9.
8. Ibid., p.47.
9. Charles Dickens, *Dombey and Son*, Chapter XXXI, p.492.
10. Quoted in Brears, *Jellies and Their Moulds*, p.177.
11. Rowntree's, *A Jelly for all Seasons*.

Christmas Pudding

1. J.A.R. Pimlott, 'Christmas under the Puritans', *History Today*, Volume 10, Issue 12, December 1960.
2. Thompson, *Lark Rise to Candleford*, pp.236–8.
3. Washington Irving, *Bracebridge Hall*, 'The Wedding', p.272.
4. Charles Dickens, *Great Expectations*, 1861, Chapter XIX, p.147.

5. Washington Irving, 'Christmas' in *The Sketch-Book of Geoffrey Crayon, Gent.*, p.16.
6. Charles Dickens, *A Christmas Carol*, Stave III, p.81.
7. Colm Tóibín, 'Christmas Pudding', *The New Yorker*, 22 November 2010.

Part Three
Turkey

1. Darina Allen, *Forgotten Skills of Cooking*, 2009, p.270.
2. William Rabisha, *The Whole Body of Cookery Dissected*, p.180.
3. Digby, *The Closet of Sir Kenelm Digby Opened*, pp.211–2.
4. Glasse, *The Art of Cookery Made Plain and Easy*, p.73.
5. Austen, *Mansfield Park*, Chapter XXII, p.204.
6. Buckland, *Our Viands*, p.69.
7. Jane Carlyle, letter to Jeannie Welsh, 28 December 1843, *The Carlyle Letters Online*.
8. Hartley, *Food in England*, p.198.
9. Jilly Cooper, *How to Survive Christmas*, p.100.
10. Gervase Markham, *The English Housewife*, p.96.
11. Charles Dickens, letter to Messrs Bradbury and Evans, 2 January 1840, quoted in Rossi-Wilcox, *Dinner for Dickens*, p.263.

Old Spice

1. *The Forme of Cury*, recipe XXI (21).
2. Ibid., recipe XX.VIII.IX (169).
3. Pepys, *Diaries*, 16 November 1665, p.555.
4. Tobias Smollett, *The Expedition of Humphry Clinker*, p.119.
5. John Keats, 'The Eve of St Agnes', *Complete Poems*, p.323.

Curry

1. Davidson, *The Oxford Companion to Food*, p.235.
2. Kitchiner, *Apicius Redivivus*, p.2.
3. Ibid., recipe 574.
4. Arthur Conan Doyle, 'The Adventure of the Naval Treaty', *The Complete Sherlock Holmes*, p.465.
5. Sandford Arnot, *Indian Cookery*, p.iv.
6. 'Wyvern', *Culinary Jottings for Madras*, p.1.
7. Ibid., p.15.
8. Ibid., p.16.
9. Flora Annie Steel, *The Complete Indian Housekeeper and Cook*, 1888, quoted in David Burnett and Helen Saberi, *The Road to Vindaloo*, p.160.
10. Madhur Jaffrey, *An Invitation to Indian Cooking*, p.12.
11. Lizzie Collingham, *Curry*, p.218.
12. Khadim Hussain, *Going for a Curry?*, p.9.

French Food

1. William of Malmesbury, *Deeds of the Kings of England/Gesta Regum Anglorum*.

2. Thomas Tusser, *Five Hundred Points of Good Husbandry*.
3. Hartley, *Food in England*, p.25.
4. Henry Jeffreys, *Empire of Booze*, p.12.
5. Pepys, *Diaries*, 12 May 1667, pp.770–1.
6. Rabisha, *The Whole Body of Cookery Dissected*, 'To the Reader'.
7. Hannah Woolley, *The Queen-Like Closet*, title page.
8. Eliza Smith, *The Compleat Housewife*, Preface.
9. François Massialot, *The Court and Country Cook*, n.p.
10. James Boswell, *The Life of Samuel Johnson*, pp. 245–6.
11. Woodforde, *The Diary of a Country Parson*, 8 June 1781, p.119.
12. Mennell, *All Manners of Food*, p.130.
13. Austen, *Pride and Prejudice*, Volume III, Chapter XII, p.360.
14. Jonathan Swift, *Directions to Servants*, p.22.
15. Mennell, *All Manners of Food*, p.208.
16. Beeton, *Mrs Beeton's Book of Household Management*, entries 1315, 367, 1216.
17. Mennell, *All Manners of Food*, p.221.
18. Leyel, *The Gentle Art of Cookery*, p.181.
19. P.G. Wodehouse, *Right Ho, Jeeves*, Chapter 11, p.89.
20. P.G. Wodehouse, *The Code of the Woosters*, Chapter 1, p.9.
21. Ainhoa Barcelona, 'The Queen's favourite food revealed by former chef Darren McGrady – and it may surprise you', *Hello!*, 3 May 2020.

Stews

1. Dickens, *Great Expectations*, Volume I, Chapter IV, p.25.
2. 'W.M', *The Compleat Cook*, pp.92–3.
3. Digby, *The Closet of Sir Kenelm Digby Opened*, p.165.
4. McGee, *On Food and Cooking*, p.162.
5. Pepys, *Diaries*, 12 May 1667, p.771.
6. Gilly Lehmann, 'Foreign or English? A Tale of Two Dishes: Olios and Fricasees', in Eileen White, ed., *The English Kitchen*, pp.57–75.
7. Glasse, *The Art of Cookery Made Plain and Easy*, pp.55–60.
8. Austen, *Pride and Prejudice*, Volume I, Chapter VIII, p.37.
9. Massialot, *The Court and Country Cook*, Preface.
10. Austen, letter to Cassandra, 17 November 1798, *Jane Austen's Letters*, p.28.
11. *The Literary Gazette*, 16 February 1822.
12. Sturgeon, *Essays*, Essay XIX 'On the Health and the Morals of Cooks', p.213.
13. Quoted from *Household Words*, 1851, in Kate Colquhoun, *Taste*, p.286.
14. Acton, *Modern Cookery for Private Families*, p.174.
15. Jerome K. Jerome, *Three Men in a Boat*, Chapter 14, p.135.
16. Jekyll, *Kitchen Essays*, p.122.
17. Jane Grigson, *The Mushroom Feast*, p.190.
18. Wodehouse, *The Code of the Woosters*, Chapter 1, p.14.
19. Elizabeth David, *French Country Cooking*, p.6.
20. Quoted in Davidson, *The Oxford Companion to Food*, p.143.
21. Ayto, *The Diner's Dictionary*, p.62.

Parmentier Potatoes

1. Standage, *An Edible History of Humanity*, pp.117–37.

Macaroni

1. *The Forme of Cury*: macrows, recipe XX.IIII.XII (92); loseyns, recipe XX.II.IX (49); loseyns in fyssh day, recipe XX.VI.VIII (128); hares in papdele, recipe XXIIII (24).
2. Rictor Norton, 'The Macaroni Club', *Homosexuality in Eighteenth-Century England: A Sourcebook*, 19 December 2004.
3. William Verral, *A Complete System of Cookery*, p.119.
4. Glasse, *The Art of Cookery Made Plain and Easy*, pp.69, 100, 155.
5. Raffald, *The Experienced English Housekeeper*, p.7.
6. B. Serafino Buonaiuti, *Italian Scenery; representing the Manners, Customs, and Amusements of the Different States of Italy*, p.5.
7. Davidson, *The Oxford Companion to Food*, p.581.
8. Quoted in Silvano Serventi and Françoise Sabban, *Pasta*, p.xi.
9. Ibid., p.xv.
10. Elizabeth David, *Italian Food*, pp.85, 80.

Ice Cream

1. Jeri Quinzio, *Of Sugar and Snow*, pp.14–15.
2. Mary Eales, *Mrs Mary Eales's Receipts*, p.92.
3. Ivan Day, *Ice Cream*, p.18.
4. Austen, letter to Cassandra, 30 June 1808, *Jane Austen's Letters*, p.209.
5. Frederick Nutt, *The Complete Confectioner*, p.125.
6. Quoted in Day, *Ice Cream*, p.21.
7. Mrs A.B. Marshall, *The Book of Ices*, and *Fancy Ices*.
8. Mayhew, *London Labour and the London Poor*, Volume I, p.206.
9. S. Beaty-Pownall, quoted by Day, *Ice Cream*, p.43.
10. Nancy Mitford, *Pigeon Pie*, Chapter 3, p.340.
11. Paul Kildea, *Chopin's Piano*, p.191.
12. Orwell, *The Road to Wigan Pier*, Chapter VI, p.88.
13. Allen, *Forgotten Skills of Cooking*, p.208.

Gingerbread

1. Geoffrey Chaucer, *The Prologue and Tale of Sir Thopas*, *The Canterbury Tales*, lines 161–5.
2. *Two Fifteenth-century Cookbooks*, ed. Thomas Austin.
3. Mennell, *All Manners of Food*, p.25.

Part Four
Where We Sit

1. *Debrett's Handbook: British Style, Correct Form, Modern Manners*, p.370.
2. *Walter of Henley's Husbandry, together with an anonymous Husbandry, Seneschaucie, and Robert Grosseteste's Rules*, p.137.
3. *Sir Gawain and the Green Knight*, Fit 2, line 1005.
4. Cooper, *Class*, p.255.

5. William Langland, *Piers Plowman*, Passus X, 96–102.
6. Trusler, *The Honours of the Table*, p.5.
7. Austen, *Pride and Prejudice*, Volume III, Chapter IX, p.333.
8. Ibid., Volume III, Chapter XII, p.358.
9. Henry Cockburn, *Memorials of His Time*, 1856, p.34.
10. Sturgeon, *Essays*, Essay III 'On the Theory and Practice of Dinatory Tactics', p.49.
11. La Rochefoucauld, *A Frenchman in England*, p.28.
12. Colquhoun, *Taste*, p.88.
13. Panton, *From Kitchen to Garrett*, p.43.
14. *Daily Telegraph*, Obituary, Alice Thomas Ellis, 10 March 2005.
15. Bourdieu, *Distinction*, p.183.
16. Owen Jones, *Chavs*, p.114, quoting *Jamie's School Dinners*, Channel 4, 2005.
17. Martin Jones, *Feast: Why Humans Share Food*, p.282.
18. Gershuny and Sullivan, *What We Really Do All Day*, pp.185–7.
19. Jennifer Luty, 'Eating out frequency in the United Kingdom (UK) 2016', *Statista*, March 2017.

The Restaurant

1. Celia Fiennes, *Through England on a Side Saddle*.
2. Charles Dickens, 'Refreshments for Travellers', *The Uncommercial Traveller*.
3. Boswell, *The Life of Samuel Johnson*, p.305.
4. *Household Words*, Volume IV, p.74, 18 October 1851.
5. Elliott Shore, 'Dining Out: The Development of the Restaurant' in *Food: The History of Taste*, ed. Paul Freedman, p.303.
6. John Farley, *The London Art of Cookery*, p.iv.
7. *Household Words*, Volume IV, p.74, 18 October 1851.
8. Quoted in Rebecca L. Spang, *The Invention of the Restaurant*, p.152.
9. Gregory Houston Bowden, *British Gastronomy*, p.63.
10. Elizabeth David, 'A Gourmet in Edwardian London', *An Omelette and a Glass of Wine*, p.197.
11. HC Deb. 28 November 1946 vol. 430 col. 1800.
12. *The Good Food Guide 1951–1952*, ed. Raymond Postgate, p.18.

Small Plates

1. Jane Austen, *The Watsons*, p.310.
2. Kitchiner, *Apicius Redivivus*, p.44.
3. Sturgeon, *Essays*, Essay V, 'The Fatal Consequences of Pride Considered in its Effects upon Dinners', p.70.
4. Jane Carlyle, letter to Jeannie Welsh, 'Holy Thursday' 1849, *I Too Am Here: Selections from the Letters of Jane Welsh Carlyle*, p.229.
5. Anthony Trollope, *Miss Mackenzie*, p.106.
6. Beeton, *Mrs Beeton's Book of Household Management*, p.955.
7. Davidson, *The Oxford Companion to Food*, p.281.
8. Jekyll, *Kitchen Essays*, p.41.
9. Boxer, *Arabella Boxer's Book of English Food*, p.81.
10. *Debrett's Handbook*, p.372.

11. Lawson, *How to Eat*, p.330.
12. Tony Naylor, 'The end of small plates: why the dinner-ruining dishes may finally be over', *Guardian*, 14 March 2019.
13. Zoe Williams, 'Will coronavirus spell an end to the great Chinese buffet?', *Guardian*, 2 May 2020.

Fish Knives

1. Tomé Morrissy-Swan, 'The best chef's knives', *Daily Telegraph*, 8 January 2020.
2. Quoted in Visser, *The Rituals of Dinner*, p.187, and *Mrs Groundes-Peace's Old Cookery Notebook*, ed. Robin Howe, p.50.
3. Woolley, *The Gentlewoman's Companion*, p.113.
4. Peri Wolfman, *Forks, Knives and Spoons*, p.87.
5. A Member of the Aristocracy, *Manners and Tone of Good Society*, p.99.
6. *Debrett's Handbook*, p.349.
7. Deborah Ross, 'Lord, forgive them', *Independent*, 29 June 1998.
8. Debora Robertson, 'Pardon, toilet and sitting room: We really are all middle-class now', *Daily Telegraph*, 5 August 2017.

Forks

1. Adam Mars-Jones, *Kid Gloves*, p.217–18.
2. Laura Diaz-Arnesto, 'Byzantine women – The Princess Theophano and Introducing the fork into Europe', *Byzantine Blog*, 9 November 2010; Donald M. Nicol, *Byzantium and Venice*, p.47.
3. Thomas Coryat, *Coryat's Crudities*, p.235.
4. John Fletcher, *The Queen of Corinth*, Act IV, Scene I.
5. Ben Jonson, *The Devil Is an Ass*, Act V, Scene IV.
6. Ivan Day in Peter Brown, ed., *British Cutlery: An Illustrated History of Its Design, Evolution and Use*, p.36.
7. Pepys, *Diaries*, 30 December 1664, p.456.
8. Trusler, *The Honours of the Table*, p.11.
9. Mrs Gaskell, *Cranford*, Chapter IV, p.64.
10. Mrs Humphrey, *Manners for Men*, p.74.
11. Ibid., p.69.
12. Chris Renwick, *Bread for All*, p.89.
13. Gerald Priestland, *Frying Tonight*, p.17.
14. *Debrett's*, Table Rules, 20 June 2016.

Doilies, Napkins and Tablecloths

1. Bourdieu, *Distinction*, p.196.
2. Alan S.C. Ross, 'Linguistic class-indicators in present-day English', *Neuphilologische Mitteilungen*, Volume 55 (1954), pp.113–49.
3. *Sir Gawain and the Green Knight*, Fit II, lines 884–6.
4. Peter Hammond, *Food and Feast in Medieval England*, p.102.
5. Lel Gretton, 'Table cloths in the Middle Ages'. *Old and Interesting*, 26 February 2010.

6. David Mitchell, 'Napery, 1600–1800' in Philippa Glanville and Hilary Young, eds, *Elegant Eating*, p.52.
7. Pepys, *Diaries*, 22 January 1669, p.980.
8. Austen, *Emma*, Volume II, Chapter VIII, p.216.
9. Pocock in Palmer, *Moveable Feasts*, p.xxvii.
10. Kate Fox, *Watching the English*, pp.105–10.
11. David Wilkes, 'Don't tell Hyacinth but the doily is dead', *Daily Mail*, 17 May 2007.

Food in Tins

1. Advertisement in England for *The Art of Preserving*, 1811, p.1.
2. J.C. Drummond, *Historic Tinned Food*, p.13.
3. Bee Wilson, *Consider the Fork*, p.292.
4. 'Wyvern', *Culinary Jottings for Madras*, p.26.
5. Quoted in Mennell, *All Manners of Food*, p.189.
6. 27 February 1926, quoted in Mennell, *All Manners of Food*, p.243.
7. Arnold White, *Efficiency and Empire*, p.104.
8. Orwell, *The Road to Wigan Pier*, Chapter VI, p.91.
9. John Carey, *The Intellectuals and the Masses*, p.21.
10. Burnett, *Plenty and Want*, p.135.
11. Ambrose Heath, *Good Dishes from Tinned Food*, p.7.
12. Houston Bowden, *British Gastronomy*, p.63.
13. Nickie Charles and Marion Kerr, *Women, Food and Families*, p.171.
14. Fox, *Watching the English*, p.429.
15. Richard Blackledge, 'Jack Monroe: "Cooking from tins is a reality for many – I'm tired of the snobbery around food"', *inews*, 29 May 2019.

Part Five
The Venison Pasty

1. Josceline Dimbleby, quoted in Susanna Johnston and Anne Tennant, eds, *The Picnic Papers*, p.60.
2. Moryson, *An Itinerary*, Volume IV, p.172.
3. Pepys, *Diaries*, 18 July 1660, p.64.
4. Woolley, *The Queen-Like Closet*, recipe 276.
5. Quoted in Hartley, *Food in England*, pp.166–7.
6. Georgina Maffey et al., 'Farming for Venison: investigating the barriers to deer farming in Scotland', The Deer Farm and Park Demonstration Project, February 2015.
7. Chris Baraniuk, 'Brits are eating venison faster than Scotland can produce it', *Quartz*, 11 September 2016.
8. Pepys, *Diaries*, 6 January 1660, p.4.
9. Markham, *The English Housewife*, Chapter II, recipe 112.
10. Robert May, *The Accomplisht Cook*, p.121.
11. Alice B. Toklas, 'Guigot de la Clinique', *The Alice B. Toklas Cook Book*, p.33.

Tripe

1. Quoted in Marjory Houlihan, *Tripe*, p.9.

2. *Fish Trades Gazette*, 7 August 1909, 'The Fish Frier and His Trade (How to Establish and Carry on an Up-to-Date Business)' by William Loftas from Sheffield, aka 'Chatchip', quoted in Priestland, *Frying Tonight*, p.64.

3. *Ninety Nine homely & delicious ways of preparing and serving U.C.P. Tripe & Cowheels*.

4. Pepys, *Diaries*, 24 October 1662, p.229.

5. Charles Dickens, *The Chimes*, p.120.

6. Charles Elmé Francatelli, *A Plain Cookery Book for the Working Classes*, recipe 82, p.51.

7. Orwell, *The Road to Wigan Pier*, Chapter I, p.6.

8. Tripe Marketing Board, Tripe Adviser.

Oysters

1. Dickens, *The Pickwick Papers*, Chapter XXII, p.294.

2. Mayhew, *London Labour and the London Poor*, Volume I, p.75.

3. Ibid., p.64.

4. Recipes taken from May, *The Accomplisht Cook*.

5. Drew Smith, *Oyster*, p.90.

Fruit

1. J.C. Drummond and Anne Wilbraham, *The Englishman's Food*, p.379.

2. Thomas Elyot, *The Castel of Helth*, p.19.

3. Anonymous, *The Boke of Kervynge*, n.p.

4. William Shakespeare, *The Winter's Tale*, Act IV, Scene II.

5. Anonymous, *A Proper New Booke of Cookery*, n.p.

6. Thomas Dekker, *The Honest Whore, Part II*, Act I, Scene I.

7. Ellis, *The Country Housewife's Family Companion*, p.285.

8. Austen, *Pride and Prejudice*, Volume III, Chapter III, p.281.

9. Alexis Soyer, *The Modern Housewife or Ménagère*, Letter No. XVI.

10. Rachel Pechey *et al.*, 'Why don't poor men eat fruit? Socioeconomic differences in motivations for fruit consumption', *Appetite*, Volume 84, 1 January 2015, pp.271–9.

Saloop

1. John Evelyn, *Sylva; or, a Discourse of Forest Trees*, p.32.

2. Charles Dickens, *The Old Curiosity Shop*, Chapter 58, p.430.

3. Brillat-Savarin, *Physiologie du goût*, p.112.

4. Eden, *The State of the Poor*, Volume I, p.528.

5. Rundell, *A New System of Domestic Cookery*, p.284.

6. Anne Pratt, *Flowering Plants and Ferns of Great Britain*, p.206, quoted without acknowledgement in Hartley, *Food in England*, p.576.

7. Charles Lamb, 'The Praise of Chimney-Sweepers', *Elia*, pp.250–62.

8. Mayhew, *London Labour and the London Poor*, Volume I, p.160.

9. Hartley, *Food in England*, p.576.

10. Amy Stewart, *The Drunken Botanist*, pp.191–2, 235.

Metheglin and Mead

1. *The Book of Taliesin: Poems of Warfare and Praise in an Enchanted Britain*, p.43.
2. Geoffrey Chaucer, *The Knight's Tale*, line 2279.
3. Charles Butler, *The Feminine Monarchie*, Preface.
4. Digby, *The Closet of Sir Kenelm Digby Opened*, p.95.
5. Pepys, 25 July 1666, https://www.pepysdiary.com/diary/1666/07/25/
6. Smollett, *The Expedition of Humphry Clinker*, p.326.
7. Austen, letter to Cassandra, 8 September 1816, *Jane Austen's Letters*, p.466.
8. Thompson, *Lark Rise to Candleford*, p.117.
9. G.R. Gayre, *Wassail! In Mazers of Mead*, p.98.
10. Fox, *Watching the English*, p.377.

Gin

1. Daniel Defoe, *A Brief Case of the Distillers and of the Distilling Trade in England*, p.18.
2. Ibid., p.32.
3. Richard Barnett, *The Dedalus Book of Gin*, p.45.
4. William Hogarth, *A Dissertation on Mr Hogarth's Six Prints*, p.10.
5. Lord John Hervey, quoted in Barnett, *The Dedalus Book of Gin*, p.76.
6. Barnett, *The Dedalus Book of Gin*, p.61.
7. Hogarth, *A Dissertation on Mr Hogarth's Six Prints*, p.9.
8. Ibid., p.28.
9. Daniel Defoe (as Andrew Moreton, Esq.), *Second Thoughts are Best*, p.4.
10. William Hogarth's advertisement for his prints, *London Evening Post*, 14–16 February 1751.
11. Jessica Warner, 'Gin in Regency England', *History Today*, Volume 61, Issue 3, March 2011.
12. Charles Dickens, *Sketches by 'Boz'*, p.218.
13. George Eliot, *Essays and Leaves from a Notebook*, p.291.
14. William Makepeace Thackeray, *Vanity Fair*, Chapter XXXIV, p.400.
15. John Rack, *The French Wine and Liquor Manufacturer*, pp.82–104.
16. Charles Dickens, *American Notes*, pp.69–70.
17. *Cassell's Dictionary of Cookery*, p.253.
18. Ibid., p.xciii.
19. Quoted by Kingsley Amis, *Everyday Drinking*, p.143.
20. Amis, *Everyday Drinking*, p.116.
21. Phoebe French, 'London now home to fifth of England's Gin Distilleries', *The Drinks Business*, 13 November 2017.

Bread and Butter

1. Giles Coren, *How to Eat Out*, p.xx.
2. Ukers, *All About Tea*, Volume II, pp.388–96.
3. Ibid.
4. William B. Boulton, 'London's Tea Gardens' in *The Amusements of Old London*, p.67.
5. British Museum, 'The Bread and Butter Manufactory or the Humors of Bagnigge Wells' in 'Prints'.

6. Charlotte Brontë, *Shirley*, Volume I, Chapter VII, p.114.
7. Day, *Hints on Etiquette and the Usages of Society*, p.20.
8. McNeill, *The Scots Kitchen*, p.94.
9. George Orwell, *Down and Out in Paris and London*, Chapter XXV, p.143.

Part Six
Almond Milk

1. *The Forme of Cury*, recipe XX.III.IX (69).
2. Frederick J. Furnivall, ed., *Early English Meals and Manners*, pp.37–41, 50.
3. *The Good Huswife's Handmaide for the Kitchin*, 1594, recipe 197.
4. *A Noble Boke off Cookry*, p.111.
5. *Two Fifteenth-century Cookbooks*, pp.85, 34, 20.
6. *A Noble Boke off Cookry*, p.47.
7. *Le Ménagier de Paris (The Goodman of Paris)*, c.1392.
8. Statutes 2 and 3 of Edward VI, 1549.
9. Glasse, *The Art of Cookery*, Chapter IX.
10. John Partridge, *The Treasurie of Commodious Conceits*, 1573, quoted in Dalby and Dalby, *The Shakespeare Cookbook*, p.40.
11. Andrew Marvell, 'To his Worthy Friend Doctor Witty Upon his Translation of The Popular Errors', 1650.
12. McGee, *On Food and Cooking*, p.505.
13. Glasse, *The Art of Cookery Made Plain and Easy*, p.85.
14. Austen, *Pride and Prejudice*, Volume I, Chapter XI, p.59.

Vegetables and Vegetarians

1. Orwell, *The Road to Wigan Pier*, Chapter XI, p.162.
2. David Gentilcore, *Food and Health in Early Modern Europe*, p.58.
3. Tristram Stuart, *The Bloodless Revolution*, p.xx.
4. See Timothy Morton, *Shelley and The Revolution in Taste*.
5. Colin Spencer, *Vegetarianism*, p.236.
6. Percy Bysshe Shelley, *Queen Mab*, Canto VIII.
7. Advertisement for *Observations Concerning the Diet of the Common People* by William Buchan, 1797.
8. William Buchan, *Observations Concerning the Diet of the Common People*, p.8.
9. Ibid., p.44.
10. Jane Austen, *Northanger Abbey*, Volume II, Chapter VII, p.182.
11. John Evelyn, *Acetaria: A Discourse of Sallets*, 1699, p.23.
12. Rundell, *A New System of Domestic Cookery*, p.168.
13. Acton, *Modern Cookery for Private Families*, p.326.
14. Ibid., p.340.
15. Ibid.
16. Anna Kingsford, *The Perfect Way in Diet*, p.61.
17. R.E. O'Callaghan, *The Best Diet for a Working Man*, n.p.
18. George Bernard Shaw to Symon Gould, 31 August 1948. Cited by Janet Barkas, *The Vegetable Passion: A History of the Vegetarian State of Mind*, p.97.
19. Spencer, *Vegetarianism*, p.276.
20. The Vegan Society, 'Statistics'.

Rationing

1. Burnett, *Plenty and Want*, pp.322–32.
2. Zweiniger-Bargielowska, *Austerity in Britain*, p.73.
3. Esther Rantzen, *Make, Do and Send*, p.183.
4. Ibid., p.104.
5. Burnett, *Plenty and Want*, p.327.
6. David Cannadine, *Class in Britain*, p.147.
7. HC Deb. 10 November 1947 vol. 444 col.156.
8. Zweiniger-Bargielowska, *Austerity in Britain*, p.87.

Bread

1. Markham, *The English Housewife*, Chapter IX, pp.209–11.
2. Glyn Hughes, 'Quartern Loaf', *The Foods of England Project*, 2 September, 2018.
3. Ellis, *The Country Housewife's Family Companion*, p.263.
4. J.H., an Advocate for Public Welfare, *A Letter on Occasion of the Public Enquiry Concerning the Most Fit and Proper Bread to be Assized for General Use*, 1773, quoted in R.A. McCance and E.M. Widdowson, *Breads, White and Brown*, p.41.
5. Anonymous, *An Essay on Modern Luxuries, Tea, Sugar, White Bread and Butter, etc.*, 1777.
6. *The Gentleman's Magazine*, 1776, quoted in Drummond and Wilbraham, *The Englishman's Food*, p.174.
7. Wilson, *The Way We Eat Now*, p.121.
8. David Davies, *The Case of Labourers in Husbandry Stated and Considered in Three Parts*, quoted in McCance and Widdowson, *Breads, White and Brown*, p.38.
9. Burnett, *Plenty and Want*, p.17.
10. Brontë, *Shirley*, Volume III, Chapter III, p.465.
11. Ellis, *The Country Housewife's Family Companion*, p.53.
12. Ibid., p.67.
13. Mayhew, *London Labour and the London Poor*, Volume I, p.187.
14. Austen, *Northanger Abbey*, Volume II, Chapter XV, p.253.
15. Eliza Acton, *The English Bread Book for Domestic Use*, 1857, p.23.
16. H.A. Page, *Thomas de Quincey: His Life and Writings*, quoted in McCance and Widdowson, *Breads, White and Brown*, p.38, p.48.
17. Mayhew, *London Labour and the London Poor*, p.187.
18. Sir Walter Scott, *Waverley*, Chapter XII, p.100.
19. Peter Kropotkin, *The Conquest of Bread*, p.54.
20. Drummond and Wilbraham, *The Englishman's Food*, p.447; Socialist Health Association, 'Food Health and Income: Changes in the Nation's Diet. Historical Comparisons', 27 March 1936.
21. Drummond and Wilbraham, *The Englishman's Food*, p.438.
22. Orwell, *The Road to Wigan Pier*, Chapter V, p.88.
23. Fox, *Watching the English*, p.431.

Brussels Sprouts and Brassica Cousins

1. McGee, *On Food and Cooking*, p.322.
2. Dallas, *Kettner's Book of the Table*, p.98.
3. 'The British at Table', *The Economist*, Volume 408, Number 8846, 2013.
4. Pellegrino Artusi, *Science in the Kitchen and the Art of Eating Well*, p.312.
5. A.A. Gill, *Table Talk*, 2007, p.63.
6. Samuel Taylor Coleridge, letter to Eliza, 23 July 1832. Cited by Jane Grigson, *Vegetable Book*, p.13.
7. Richard Jefferies, *Landscape with Figures*, pp.31–2.
8. Glasse, *The Art of Cookery Made Plain and Easy*, p.57.
9. *The Goodman of Paris*, tr. Eileen Power, quoted in Maggie Black, *The Medieval Cookbook*, p.80.
10. 'The British at Table', *The Economist*, Volume 408, Number 8846, 2013.

The Avocado

1. Rebecca Reid, 'Avocado hand: the most middle class injury ever?', *Metro*, 10 May 2017.
2. Siofra Brennan, 'People reveal what they think makes them middle class in a hilarious online debate (including eating lots of avocados and having no family members with tattoos)', *Daily Mail*, 13 April 2013.
3. Rebecca Curly, 'To Av and to Hold: Middle-class millennials now proposing with avocados in bizarre new trend', *The Sun*, 21 February 2018.
4. Jeff Daniels, 'Avocado sales could more than double this year, helped by demand from China's middle class', *CNBC*, 10 January 2018.
5. Bruce Schaffer, B. Nigel Wolstenholme, Anthony W. Whiley, eds, *The Avocado, Botany, Production and Uses*, p.15.
6. William Dampier, *A New Voyage Around the World*, Chapter VII, p.179.
7. David, *Spices, Salts and Aromatics in the English Kitchen*, p.96.
8. Martin Delgado, 'Sainsbury, M&S... and the great ad-vocado war', *Mail on Sunday*, 25 May 2009.
9. Lawson, *How to Eat*, pp.357, 322.
10. Schaffer *et al.*, *The Avocado*, p.20.
11. M. Shahbandeh, 'Avocado production worldwide from 2000 to 2018', *Statista*, 2 March 2020.

The Tomato

1. Quoted in Mark Harvey, Stephen Quilley and Huw Beynon, *Exploring the Tomato*, pp.26–30.
2. Andrew F. Smith, *The Tomato in America: Early History, Culture, and Cookery*, p.15.
3. Ibid., p.17.
4. Gervase Markham, *The English Housewife*, p.62.
5. John Hill and Mr Hale, *Eden, or a compleat body of gardening*, p.47.
6. Claudia Roden, *The Book of Jewish Food*, p.286.
7. McGee, *On Food and Cooking*, pp.806, 329.
8. Thompson, *Lark Rise to Candleford*, p.121.
9. 'Wyvern', *Culinary Jottings for Madras*, p.207.
10. Fox, *Watching the English*, p.429.

Chocolate

1. Bernal Diaz del Castillo, *The Conquest of New Spain*, p.226.
2. Sophie D. Coe and Michael D. Coe, *The True History of Chocolate*, p.161.
3. 25 October 1671, quoted in ibid., p.151.
4. Pepys, *Diaries*, 24 April 1661, p.133.
5. D. de Chélus, *The Natural History of Chocolate*, p.40.
6. Brillat-Savarin, *Physiologie du goût*, p.107.
7. Roald Dahl, *Charlie and the Chocolate Factory*, p.50.

Part Seven
The Pork Pie

1. May, *The Accomplished Cook*, p.221.
2. Ibid., p.256.
3. Dickens, *Great Expectations*, Volume I, Chapter II, p.16.
4. Trevor Hickman, *The History of the Melton Mowbray Pork Pie*, p.14.

Cheddar and Stilton

1. Davidson, *The Oxford Companion to Food*, p.158.
2. *Larousse Gastronomique*, p.1019.
3. Val Cheke, *The Story of Cheese-making in Britain*, p.102.
4. Daniel Defoe, *A Tour Through the Whole Island of Great Britain*, Letter VII.
5. From 'Bajazet to Gloriana', a reworking of a poem attributed to Aphra Behn, in *State Poems*, 1697.
6. Defoe, *A Tour Through the Whole Island of Great Britain*, Letter VII.
7. Alexander Pope, *Imitations of Horace*, Book II, Satire VI, p.388.
8. Langland, *Piers Plowman*, Passus VI, lines 4361–8.
9. Eden, *The State of the Poor*, Volume I, p.496.
10. Hartley, *Food in England*, p.484.

Rabbit

1. Hartley, *Food in England*, pp.174–6.
2. Cited in Manning, *Hunters and Poachers*, p.128.
3. William Cobbett, *Rural Rides*, 1830, pp.396–401.
4. Lady Saba Holland, *A Memoir of the Reverend Sydney Smith*, p.166.
5. HC Deb. 29 April 1874 vol. 218 col. 1387.
6. Glasse, *The Art of Cookery Made Plain and Easy*, p.51.
7. Rundell, *A New System of Domestic Cookery*, p.96.
8. Nick Harding, 'Modern poachers and the wildlife police who are trying to rein them in', *Independent*, 16 November 2015.

Fish and Chips

1. Glasse, *The Art of Cookery Made Plain and Easy*, p.99.
2. Mayhew, *London Labour and the London Poor*, Volume I, p.165.
3. Roden, *The Book of Jewish Food*, p.100.
4. Priestland, *Frying Tonight*, pp.66–7.
5. Figures from National Federation of Fish Friers.

6. Quoted in John K. Walton, *Fish and Chips and the British Working Class, 1870–1940*, p.151.
7. Quoted in ibid., p.139.
8. Quoted in Priestland, *Frying Tonight*, p.75.
9. Orwell, *The Road to Wigan Pier*, Chapter V, p.83.
10. Louise Carpenter, 'Food and class: does what we eat reflect Britain's social divide?', *Guardian*, 13 March 2011.
11. Lewis Smith, 'Tale of Two Cities shows north south divide on obesity', *The Times*, 2 March 2004.

Picnics

1. Pepys, *Diaries*, 5 June 1661, p.139.
2. Ibid., 21 July 1667, p.810.
3. Ellis, *The Country Housewife's Family Companion*, p.99.
4. Brears, *Traditional Food in Yorkshire*, p.32.
5. Heath, *British Rural Life and Labour*, p.66.
6. D.H. Lawrence, *Sons and Lovers*, 1913.
7. *Pic Nic*, Number 1, 8 January 1803.
8. Quoted in Johnston and Tennant, *The Picnic Papers*, p.9.
9. Dorothy Wordsworth, letter to Mrs Clarkson, 3 August 1808, *Letters of William and Dorothy Wordsworth: The Middle Years, Volume 1, 1806–June 1811*, p.239.
10. Andrew Hubbell, 'How Wordsworth invented picknicking and saved British Culture', *Romanticism*, Volume 12, Number 1, 2006, p.46.
11. Austen, *Emma*, Chapter XLII, p.347.
12. Beeton, *Mrs Beeton's Book of Household Management*, entries 2149–52, p.960.
13. Dickens, *The Pickwick Papers*, Volume II, Chapter XIX, p.252.
14. Kenneth Grahame, *The Wind in the Willows*, Chapter I, p.7.
15. Hubbell, 'How Wordsworth invented picknicking and saved British Culture', p.49.
16. Roden, *Picnics and other Outdoor Feasts*, p.xiii.
17. Charles Moore, 'We selfish gits must wear the name with pride', *Spectator*, 12 October 2019.
18. Yvette Caster, '20 signs you're too middle class for words', *Metro*, 9 April 2015.

Foraging

1. Felipe Fernández-Armesto, *Food: A History*, p.95.
2. Dodd, *The Food of London*, p.320.
3. Drummond and Wilbraham, *The Englishman's Food*, p.174.
4. McNeill, *The Scots Kitchen*, p.27.
5. Markham, *The English Housewife*, p.8.
6. Nicholas Culpeper, *The English Physitian*, p.385.
7. Maguelonne Toussaint-Samat, *A History of Food*, p.622.
8. Richard Mabey, *Food for Free*, p.118.
9. Hartley, *Food in England*, p.396.
10. Evelyn, *Sylva*, p.145.
11. Evelyn, *Acetaria*, p.32.

12. William Hone, *The Everyday Book*, 1826, p.438.
13. Francatelli, *A Plain Cookery Book for the Working Classes*, p.26.
14. Florence White, *Good Things in England*, 1932, pp.337–60.
15. Mabey, *Food for Free*, p.216.
16. Ibid., p.129.
17. Arthur G. Miller, Hook Norton School, letter 14 December 1945, quoted in Rantzen, *Make, Do and Send*, p.46.
18. David Lloyd George, Foreword to Vicomte de Mauduit, *They Can't Ration These*.
19. Richard Mabey, *Food for Free*, p.6.
20. Hugh Fearnley-Whittingstall, *A Cook on the Wild Side*, 1997, p.4.
21. Vicomte de Mauduit, *They Can't Ration These*, p.7.

Cake

1. Adam McDonnell, 'It's scone as in "gone" not scone as in "bone"', YouGov, 31 October 2016.
2. Hartley, *Food in England*, p.516.
3. Steve Roud, *The English Year*, p.75.
4. Robert Herrick, 'To Dianeme, A Ceremonie in Glocester', *Hesperides*, 1648.
5. Anonymous, *Mother Bunch's Closet Newly Broke Open*, 1685, quoted in Roud, *The English Year*, pp.105–8.
6. Dods, *The Cook and Housewife's Manual*, p.451.
7. Thackeray, *Vanity Fair*, Chapter V, p.54.
8. *John Evelyn, Cook: The Manuscript Receipt Book of John Evelyn*, p.48.
9. Digby, *The Closet of Sir Kenelm Digby Opened*, pp.215–219.
10. Raffald, *The Experienced English Housekeeper*, p.134.
11. HMRC, 'Excepted items: Confectionery: The bounds of confectionery, sweets, chocolates, chocolate biscuits, cakes and biscuits: The borderline between cakes and biscuits', *Internal manual, VAT Food*. 13 March 2016. Updated 7 August 2018.
12. Charles and Kerr, *Women, Food and Families*, p.77.
13. David, *English Bread and Yeast Cookery*, p.484.
14. White, *Good Things in England*, 1932, p.9.
15. Christianne Hupkens *et al.*, 'Social class differences in food consumption: The explanatory value of permissiveness and health and cost considerations', *European Journal of Public Health*, Volume 10, Issue 2, June 2000, pp.108–13.
16. McNeill, *The Scots Kitchen*, p.240.

Conclusion

1. Charles Elmé Francatelli, *The Modern Cook*, 1846, pp.533–5.
2. Ibid., p.291.
3. Ibid., pp.291–2.
4. P.G. Wodehouse, *Jeeves and the Feudal Spirit*, p.101.
5. Jon Henley and Eleanor Ainge Roy, 'Are female leaders more successful at managing the coronavirus crisis?', *Guardian*, 25 April 2020.

Acknowledgements

Thanks to: Dave Atkinson for his family memoirs, Nellie's Diary; Isabel Blake for her story about brown bread ice cream; Margaret Bluman for advice and encouragement; Rosie Boycott for her advice and insights; Isabelle de Cat for design advice; Sarah Christie for her point about Vanitas paintings; Henry Eliot for his family's gravy wars; Grant Fitzner for Australian wisdom about *steak frites*, for constant support (and a lot of printing out); Laura Freeman for allowing me to quote from her wonderful book, *The Reading Cure*; Diana Gerald for her reminiscences on tins; Georgina Laycock for advice and encouragement; Claire McElwee for her breakfast of scallops and farls; Tom Penn for asking me the question about why food changed, which set this all off; Louisa Price for her and her husband's thoughts on small plates eating; Stuart Proffitt for wise words about the title; Katharina Schmoll for many wise thoughts and contrasts with how they do things in those foreign countries, Germany and Academia; Katie Snape for sharing her memory of northern tea; Phoebe Taplin for many insights; the Milton Keynes Uber driver who'd only had a Wispa for lunch (and who promised me he'd go to cookery classes); James Urquhart for 'The Godzilla'; Justin Vogler for builder's tea (and another story he'd rather not be identified with); my mum, Jill Vogler, for shaping my food and class antennae (even without either of us being aware of it); Emma Whiting for advice and encouragement; my colleagues at Penguin Press who have been so supportive.

Huge gratitude to everybody who helped me test recipes: Margaret Bluman, Sarah Christie, Bella Cutts, Isabelle de Cat, Ayen Doctors, Simone Doctors, Matt Hutchinson, John Kingman, Eleanor Kingman, Eleanor Koss, Harriet Martin, Ruth Segal, Phoebe Taplin, James and Jane Urquhart, Miranda Vogler-Koss, Surfy's Meat Curing for saltpetre and advice about salting the spiced beef – more here: https://www.homecuring.co.uk

Heartfelt thanks to my editor, James Nightingale, and the team at Atlantic Books, particularly Kate Straker. And to Carmen Balit for the cover design and Dan Mogford for the illustrations. To Tamsin Shelton for her skilful and super-helpful copy-edits. To my agent Julian Alexander, particularly for his advice on how to shape what was, for years, a baggy monster in my mind. And to Jay Rayner and Regula Ysewijn for their generous endorsements.

Index

INDEX